P9-AEX-491

HIKING
TRAILS

OF SOUTH AFRICA

HIKING TRAILS

OF SOUTH AFRICA

Willie & Sandra Olivier

First published in 2003 by Struik Publishers
(a division of New Holland Publishing
(South Africa) (Pty) Ltd)

New Holland Publishing is a member of the
Johnnic Publishing Group

Garfield House
86–88 Edgware Road
W2 2EA London
United Kingdom
www.newhollandpublishers.com

Cornelis Struik House
80 McKenzie Street
Cape Town
8001
South Africa
www.struik.co.za

14 Aquatic Drive
Frenchs Forest
NSW 2086
Australia

218 Lake Road
Northcote, Auckland
New Zealand

Copyright © 2003 in published edition: Struik Publishers
Copyright © 2003 in text, maps and the illustration on p. 24: Willie and Sandra Olivier
Copyright © 2003 in photographs: see picture credits below

Publishing managers: Annlerie van Rooyen and Dominique le Roux
Managing editor: Lesley Hay-Whitton
Design director: Janice Evans
Concept designer: Robin Cox
Cover designer: Alison Day
Designer: Illana Fridkin
Editor and project manager: Monique Whitaker
Research assistant: Nicky Steenkamp
Proofreader and Indexer: Inge du Plessis
Cartographer: John Hall
Illustrator: Dr Jack

Reproduction by Hirt & Carter Cape (Pty) Ltd
Printed and bound by Paarl Print, Oosterland Street, Paarl, South Africa

1 3 5 7 9 10 8 6 4 2

ISBN 1 86872 787 4

All rights reserved. No part of this publication may be reproduced, stored in a retrieval system or transmitted,
in any form or by any means, electronic, mechanical, photocopying or otherwise, without the prior written
permission of the publishers and copyright holders.

Whilst every effort has been made to ensure the accuracy of the information provided, some information will become
outdated during this edition's lifespan. Readers are advised to check information regarding trail facilities, etc. with the
relevant trail authority, especially when making reservations for overnight hiking trails. The publishers would appreciate
information relating to new, upgraded or defunct trails for incorporation into subsequent editions.
Please write to: *The Editor, Hiking Trails of South Africa*
Struik Publishers
P O Box 1144
Cape Town 8000

Picture credits
Shaen Adey: SA; Karl Beath: KB; Tony Camacho: TC; Colour Library: CLB; Nigel Dennis: NJD; Gerhard Dreyer: GD; Hein von Hörsten: HvH; Lanz
von Hörsten: LvH; Walter Knirr: WK; Peter Pickford: PP; Roger de la Harpe: RDLH; Mark Skinner: MS; Struik Image Library: SIL; Keith Young: KY
Copyright © 2003 in photographs: Willie and Sandra Olivier, with the exception of:
Front cover: (main) KB, (top right) SA/SIL, (bottom right) MS/SIL; **back cover:** (left and centre) HvH/SIL, (right) LvH/SIL; **page 65:** (top) HvH/SIL, (bottom)
KY/SIL; **66:** (centre) LvH/SIL; **67:** (top) HvH/SIL; **70:** (top) HvH/SIL; **71:** (bottom) LvH/SIL; **121:** (bottom) GD/SIL; **122:** (bottom) HvH/SIL; **123:** (top) SA/SIL;
124: (top) SA/SIL; **125:** (bottom) WK/SIL; **126:** (top) SA/SIL, (bottom) PP/SIL; **128:** (centre) RDLH/SIL; **161:** (bottom) SA/SIL; **162:** CLB/SIL; **163:** (bottom)
SA/SIL; **166:** (top) TC/SIL, (centre) KY/SIL; **217:** (bottom) WK/SIL; **218:** (top left and right) ND/SIL, (bottom) LvH/SIL; **222–3:** SA/SIL; **224:** (both) LvH.

AUTHORS' ACKNOWLEDGEMENTS
The publication of this book would not have been possible without the interest and
support of the various trail authorities and owners who supplied us with the necessary
information. To all of you, a big thank you! We also wish to thank Struik's staff, especially
Annlerie van Rooyen, who commissioned us, Lesley Hay-Whitton, Janice Evans, Illana Fridkin,
Robin Cox, and John Hall. Thank you also to Nicky Steenkamp who had the enormous
task of updating the trails database, as well as Sandra Adomeit who initially assisted her.
Finally, we'd like to thank Monique Whitaker, who proved to be a thorough, patient and
considerate editor who was always willing to accommodate changes.

Log on to our photographic website **www.imagesofafrica.co.za** for an African experience

CONTENTS

WINDHOEK ✈

Walvis
Bay

KALAHARI

NAMIBIA

BOTSWANA

Namib Desert

ATLANTIC
OCEAN

N10   N14

Upington   LANGEBERGE

R64

N7   N14

R27

Springbok   S O U T H   A F R I C A

Northern Cape   N10

Britstown
De Aar   N10

R53   N12

Calvinia   N1

R27   GREAT KAROO

Clanwilliam   Beaufort
West   N1   N9

CEDARBERG   Sutherland   N1

St Helena
Bay   N12

Saldanha Bay   SWARTBERG

Western Cape   Oudtshoorn   KOUGA MTNS

HEX RIVER MTNS   Worcester

Paarl   N1   Robertson   LITTLE KAROO

CAPE TOWN   N15   George   Knysna

Stellenbosch   Swellendam   Mossel Bay   N2

N2

Cape
Point   Cape
Infanta

Cape Agulhas

KEY TO MAPS

Motorway
National road   N1
Main road tarred   R 44
Main road untarred
Minor road tarred
Minor road untarred
Scenic route
Mountain pass
Border crossing   ✦ Bray
International boundary
Provincial boundary
River with lake or dam   Sout
Seasonal river
National Park, Nature Reserve   Karoo NP
International airport   ✈
Airport   ✈
Toll road   T
City   DURBAN
Major town   ⊙ Evaton
Town   ○ Upington
Small town   ◉ Springbok
Large village   ◎ Hermanus
Village   ○ Cedarberg
Hiking route number   ⑨
(see regional maps)

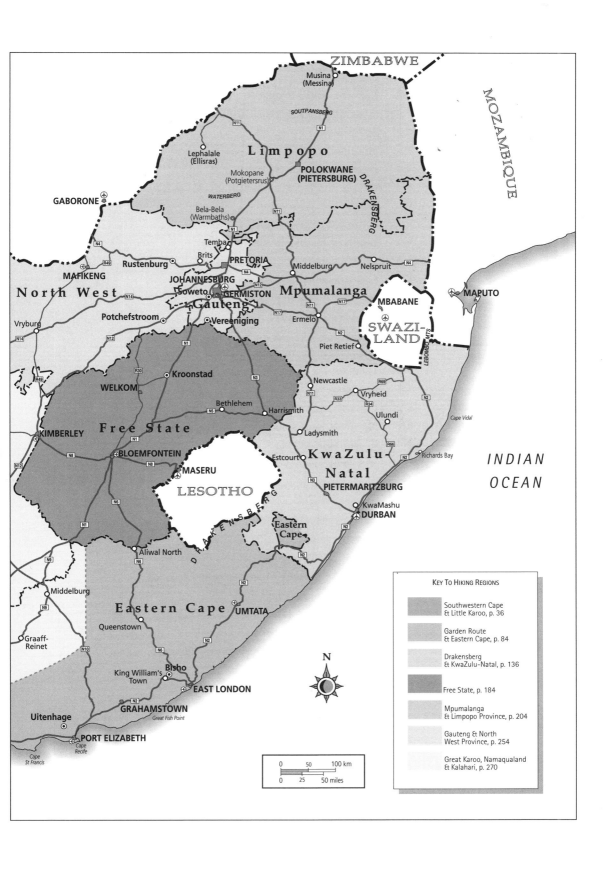

ZIMBABWE

MOZAMBIQUE

Musina
(Messina)

SOUTPANSBERG

Limpopo

N11

N1

Lephalale
(Ellisras)

Mokopane
(Potgietersrus)

**POLOKWANE
(PIETERSBURG)**

GABORONE

WATERBERG

DRAKENSBERG

Bela-Bela
(Warmbaths)

N11

N1

N4

R49

N4

Temba

Brits

MAFIKENG

Rustenburg

PRETORIA

Middelburg

Nelspruit

N4

JOHANNESBURG

N4

MBABANE

MAPUTO

North West

Soweto

GERMISTON

N12

Mpumalanga

N17

**SWAZI-
LAND**

N14

Gauteng

Potchefstroom

Vereeniging

N17

N12

Ermelo

LEBOMBO MTS

Vryburg

N14

N12

Piet Retief

N2

N8

N1

R30

Kroonstad

N3

Newcastle

R69

Vryheid

N2

N8

WELKOM

Bethlehem

N11

R33

N5

Harrismith

R34

Ulundi

KIMBERLEY

Free State

N1

Ladysmith

R66

N12

N8

BLOEMFONTEIN

Estcourt

**KwaZulu-
Natal**

Richards Bay

Cape Vidal

N6

MASERU

LESOTHO

N3

PIETERMARITZBURG

*INDIAN
OCEAN*

N1

DRAKENSBERG

N2

KwaMashu

DURBAN

N9

Middelburg

Aliwal North

N6

**Eastern
Cape**

N2

N2

N10

N2

N9

Eastern Cape

UMTATA

Graaff-
Reinet

Queenstown

N2

N

N6

King William's
Town

Bisho

N10

EAST LONDON

Uitenhage

N2

GRAHAMSTOWN

Great Fish Point

Cape
St Francis

PORT ELIZABETH

Cape
Recife

0   50   100 km

0   25   50 miles

KEY TO HIKING REGIONS

Southwestern Cape
& Little Karoo, p. 36

Garden Route
& Eastern Cape, p. 84

Drakensberg
& KwaZulu-Natal, p. 136

Free State, p. 184

Mpumalanga
& Limpopo Province, p. 204

Gauteng & North
West Province, p. 254

Great Karoo, Namaqualand
& Kalahari, p. 270

SOUTHWESTERN CAPE & LITTLE KAROO

GARDEN ROUTE & EASTERN CAPE

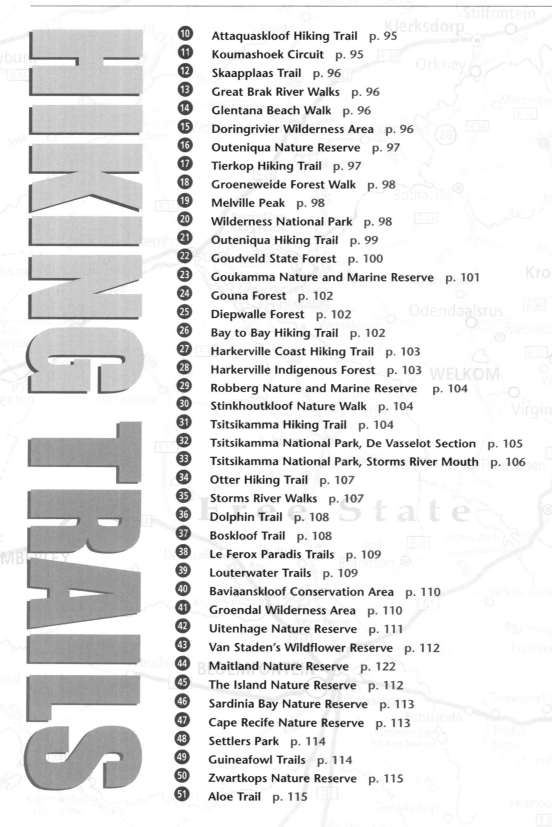

DRAKENSBERG & KWAZULU-NATAL

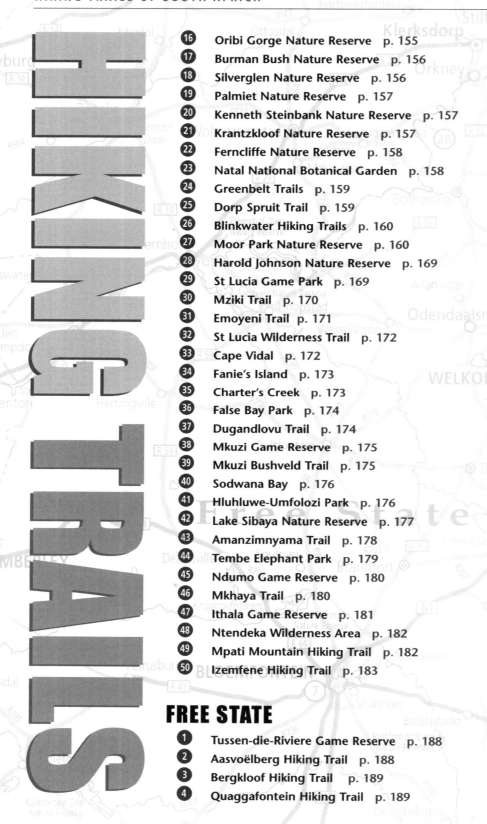

FREE STATE

MPUMALANGA & LIMPOPO PROVINCE

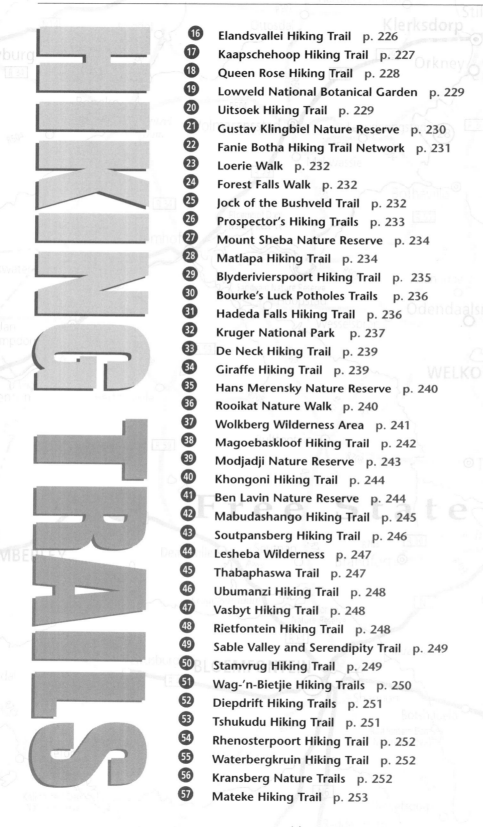

GAUTENG & NORTH WEST PROVINCE

GREAT KAROO, NAMAQUALAND & KALAHARI

INTRODUCTION

Get the most out of this guide by taking time to familiarise yourself with the headings and terminology used, and study the information on planning and preparation for your hike, to maximise your enjoyment of the trail and avoid common hiking injuries.

USING THE BOOK

Given the number of walks and overnight trails in South Africa, it is not possible to include every one, and so only those of one hour and over are listed in this guide. However, a few exceptional walks of under an hour have been included, where these are one of the primary attractions for walkers in the area.

The walks and trails in this book have been grouped into broad geographic, rather than political, areas. Not only are these areas commonly used in promoting tourism, but in many instances the fauna, flora, climate and geological features are essentially similar in geographical regions. In some instances, however, the geographical regions overlap with political regions.

For each region a brief overview of the flora, fauna, geology, climate and other relevant aspects is given. By reading this section you will enhance your appreciation and enjoyment of each area's natural highlights.

As a general rule all day walks have been listed under the name of the attraction, conservation area (nature reserve, national park or botanical garden) or city/town where they are located. This will enable readers easily to locate walks and trails in a particular area.

However, where a hike, particularly an overnight hiking trail, is well known by its own name it is listed under that name, rather than that of the nature reserve or park in which it is located. Cross-references are provided to other walks within the same conservation area.

The information provided should assist you in choosing a walk or overnight trail to suit your interest, level of fitness, and the time you have available. Each trail or group of trails has its own entry, with a shaded box at the start that provides information about the hike(s) under the following headings:

Trails For entries with just one walk or trail, the distance in kilometres, time required (hours or number of days) and the trail design are given. Where there are several walk or trail options, the number of walks in a specific reserve or park, city or town, the distance and duration

of the shortest and longest walks and the trail designs are provided at the start of the entry. In these instances, the distance, duration and trail design of each individual trail is provided at the end of that trail's description.

The term **open-ended** denotes a trail that has different starting and ending points. The starting point of a **circular** trail is the same as its ending point. A **network** denotes several different trail options, which are often interlinked, while **network from basecamp** denotes a trail design that, usually, forms a figure eight. Trails like this can typically be done with only a daypack. **Out-and-return** describes a trail that follows the same outward and return route (i.e. you hike to the end of the trail and then turn around and retrace your steps).

Permits If an address is provided, advance booking is essential. In many cases (e.g. wildflower gardens, national botanical gardens, nature reserves and national parks) payment for an entry permit or overnight accommodation entitles you to do the walks without a further permit. In some cases a self-issue permit system is in place, with charges only during peak seasons. When booking you should enquire about the minimum number of hikers and, in the case of groups, the maximum number.

Maps Information is provided on the type of map (sketch map, trail pamphlet with map, etc.) available.

Facilities/Activities All facilities and amenities, as well as recreational activities, available are briefly described under this heading.

Pertinent information Here you will find important information applicable to the walk or trail. In each regional description there is also a section on important information relating to that region.

The main body of each entry provides a brief description of the type of walk or trail, and also things such as the flora, fauna and landscape along the route, followed by a description of the trail itself.

All trees mentioned in the text follow the names of the National List of Indigenous Trees. For any other flora the scientific name is provided in brackets so as to avoid confusion, since there are no standardised common names for most non-tree species.

Trail terminology

With the proliferation of walks and trails in South Africa, trail terminology has unfortunately gone out of the window. In addition, low-budget travellers are referred to as backpackers, confusing the terminology even further.

Hiking trail is a continuous well-defined route through a natural or human-made environment on which the user carries equipment and food in a backpack. Specific overnight stops are provided at the end of each day's hike.

Backpacking trails are not along designated footpaths and you are free to blaze your own trail. No overnight facilities are provided and sleeping is in the open, in caves or in a tent carried by the backpacker. In some instances basic shelters are available.

Wilderness trails are conducted by a trails officer, in natural and wild areas such as national parks and game reserves. Although game-viewing forms part of the expedition, the primary aim of these trails is to give trailists an understanding of and appreciation for nature.

Interpretative trails are usually no more than a few kilometres long, and emphasise education and the interpretation of the environment. A trail pamphlet is supplied to guide you, and at intervals along the route numbered markers indicate features that are explained in the brochure.

Day walks are ideal for those who want to stretch their legs without having to don a heavy backpack. They range in duration from 30 minutes to a full day.

BEFORE YOU GO

Planning

Without proper planning a walk or overnight trail could easily end in disaster, so do spend time on planning your trip. After all, half the fun is in the planning and preparation!

If you are not a seasoned hiker, one of the best ways to familiarise yourself with this very rewarding activity is to join a hiking club. This will enable you to learn from those with years of experience and to join club outings. An internet search for hiking clubs in South Africa will be useful if you are thinking of joining a club.

The monthly South African magazine *Getaway* regularly features articles on hiking trails and provides updates on equipment and new developments. There are also a number of books with detailed descriptions of day walks and overnight hikes.

Most walks, and just about every hiking and backpacking trail, involves physical exertion, and it stands to reason that, the fitter you are, the more enjoyable you will find your walk or hike. Regular physical exercise is, therefore, essential, and if you intend doing a difficult trail you would be well advised to increase your exercise levels for some time before you attempt it.

When planning a walk or hike, keep the following important points in mind:

- Choose a walk or trail to suit your fitness level. Begin with a few day walks, and then progress to an easy weekend trail, before attempting something too demanding. Always bear the weakest member of the party in mind and ensure that everyone is fit.
- Taking the climate into consideration is of vital importance and will determine what clothing and equipment you need to take. Far too many day outings on Table Mountain and in the Drakensberg have turned into disaster because of rapid weather changes, inexperience, and inadequate preparation.
- Obtain the necessary maps and make sure you know how to use them. This is especially important when backpacking in wilderness areas. Here, 1:50,000 topographical maps of the Surveyor-General's office will be useful. Ensure that you know how to read and navigate with maps.
- One of the golden rules is never to set off alone, especially on long day walks and hiking trails. On hiking trails, the minimum number of people you should consider walking with is three, but four is safer.
- Check your equipment beforehand and ensure that it is serviceable, especially your boots.
- Before setting off, check the weather forecast and, if necessary, call off your walk or hike.
- Always inform someone of your intended route and expected time of return. In backpacking areas where there is a mountain register it should be completed correctly and in detail.

Food

Whether on a day walk or a long hiking trail, it is important to replace the energy your body has used by eating healthily. On day walks, snacks like peanuts and raisins, energy bars, dried fruit and snacks with a high nutritional value will suffice. It is important, though, to eat at regular intervals to ensure you keep your energy levels up.

Fortunately for overnight hikers, the days of lugging tins of bully beef and the rather unpalatable old-style soya protein meals up the mountain are long gone. A wide range of new, instant, dehydrated soya protein meals, vegetables, mashed potatoes, instant soups and desserts are available. And with a bit of imagination, and a few fresh ingredients and herbs, the taste of soya protein meals can be even further improved.

If you are prepared to pay quite a bit more for food, specialist outdoor stores usually carry a range of lightweight meals. They are not only very palatable, but are also extremely light and often require little cooking. On the downside, you might find the portions too small if you have a healthy appetite.

Kilojoule intake varies from person to person, but men on average burn up 17 to 21,000 kJ (4 to 5,000 cal) and women 13 to 17,000 kJ (3 to 4,000 cal) a day. About 4,185 kJ (1,000 cal) a day should be added for a trail averaging 15 km a day, or when hiking in cold weather. Also, you need about two and a half times as many kilojoules to gain 300 m in altitude as you would if you were walking on level terrain.

The following points are a rough guide to the average person's daily nutritional requirements:

- Two servings of milk or milk products; one serving is 250 ml milk, 60 ml milk powder (dry), 45 g cheese.
- Two servings of protein-rich food; one serving is 80 to 250 ml nuts, 60 ml peanut butter.
- Four servings of fruit and vegetables; one serving is a piece of fruit, 125 ml cooked dehydrated vegetables.
- Four or more servings of carbohydrates; one serving is one slice of bread, 125 ml cooked cereal, 125 ml cooked pasta or rice.

Also remember the following:

- When planning your menu, cater for a maximum of 1 kg of food per person per day, bearing in mind that in cold weather you will have a bigger appetite.
- When hiking in very arid areas, take a few fresh items – vegetables like cucumber, tomatoes and carrots. They are worth the extra weight, which is mainly water.
- Each person should have a supply of snacks, like glucose sweets, nuts, dried fruit, biltong and energy bars.
- Decant the contents of glass bottles into plastic containers. If carrying the foil bag from a box of wine, ensure that it won't be pierced by a sharp object!
- Always carry an extra day's emergency rations of high-energy food, such as chocolate, nuts and raisins, glucose sweets and energy bars. Don't be tempted to tuck into the rations before completing the trail!
- Pack utensils and food so that they are easily accessible for tea and lunch stops.

THREE-DAY SAMPLE MENU

This menu, which caters for three hikers, can be adapted to your group's tastes and the conditions of the particular trail you are hiking. Always consider the facilities at the overnight stops when planning a menu. If wood is available, you can vacuum-pack fresh meat for a braai on the first night.

	Breakfast		Lunch		Supper	
DAY 1	muesli	300 g	6 slices rye bread	375 g	dehydrated beans	90 g
	3 rusks	60 g	6 cheese wedges	100 g	bacon (vacuum-pack)	150 g
	1 orange	300 g	1 small salami	200 g	2 carrots	125 g
	3 sheets crispbread	95 g	1 packet dried figs	125 g	dehydrated onion	25 g
			peanuts and raisins	150 g	tomato	25 g
			3 apples	500 g	1 cube chicken stock	10 g
			1 isotonic drink	80g	rice	150 g
	If starting from basecamp,				1 packet instant	
	replace this meal with usual				pudding	100 g
	breakfast fare.					

	Breakfast		**Lunch**		**Supper**	
DAY 2	oats	150 g	6 sheets crispbread	190 g	3 cups instant soup	35 g
	3 rusks	60 g	3 hard-boiled eggs	190 g	instant mashed potato	112 g
	1 grapefruit	300 g	1 tin sardines	106 g	1 tin tuna	185 g
	3 slices rye bread	188 g	cucumber	150 g	1 small green pepper	100 g
			1 fruit roll	80 g	dehydrated onion	25 g
			1 isotonic drink	80 g	dehydrated peas	50 g
					1 chicken stock cube	10 g
					instant custard powder	100 g
DAY 3	muesli	300 g	6 sheets crispbread	190 g	3 cups instant soup	35 g
	3 rusks	60 g	6 cheese wedges	100 g	pasta	250 g
	stewed fruit	200 g	1 tomato	200 g	instant pasta sauce	50 g
			1 small tin pâté	100 g	parmesan cheese	120 g
			1 packet dried dates	125 g	1 chocolate slab	200 g
			peanuts and raisins	150 g		
			3 naartjies	500 g	*Black olives or smoked mussels*	
			1 isotonic drink	80 g	*can be added to sauce*	
MISCELLANEOUS						
	peanut butter	250 g	18 tea bags	54 g	sugar	500 g
	jam	300 g	hot chocolate	100 g	6 coffee bags	75 g
	milk powder (4 sachets)	400 g	3 packets biscuits	600 g	salt, pepper, herbs	25 g

Weights given are average and will vary according to the product brand.

Equipment

First-time hikers are confronted by a wide range of scientifically designed, lightweight equipment and deciding what to buy can be a daunting task. The following are some guidelines on buying equipment. Since designs and features are changing continuously, only the general features and principles are discussed.

Golden rules when buying equipment

- Before buying equipment, spend some time talking to fellow backpackers, browse through manufacturers' catalogues, and consult the literature on equipment.
- Carefully consider your personal requirements. It would serve little purpose, for instance, to buy a lightweight sleeping bag suitable for caravanning if you're planning to hike in the Drakensberg in winter.
- Shop assistants in specialist backpacking stores are an invaluable source of information.
- Don't be tempted to buy specialist equipment from supermarkets. It might be cheaper, but in most cases the staff simply do not have the expertise to advise you.

- Always buy equipment with a reputable brand name. This does not, however, mean that you must buy the most expensive equipment in the store.
- Think of comfort and functionality, not fashion. Personal requirements and taste should ultimately dictate what you buy.
- Decide what price you are prepared to pay. Be realistic, but never compromise on quality for a lower price.

Footwear

Few things can spoil a hike as much as blistered and aching feet, and on any trail comfort begins at ground level, with your feet. Trailing footwear can be divided into four broad categories:

- Lightweight boots or hiking shoes for day walks over easy terrain.
- Medium-weight boots for hiking and backpacking along well-defined trails.
- Mountaineering boots for hiking and backpacking in rugged mountainous terrain and snow.
- Specialist rock-climbing boots.

World-wide there has been a trend towards light- and medium-weight footwear, and in South Africa the use of Alpine-type mountaineering boots – once the norm – has to a large extent become restricted to winter backpacking trips in the Drakensberg.

This trend was brought about partly by the lower quality and poorer performance of leather boots, due to the soaring cost of leather, and partly because of environmental considerations.

Taking general trail conditions in South Africa into consideration, lightweight footwear is suitable for most day walks and rambles, while medium-weight boots are suitable for most hiking and backpacking trails.

When buying boots the most important considerations are size, comfort and protection. To ensure a good fit you should wear your hiking socks when fitting boots. Before tying up the laces, push your foot as far forward as possible, until your toes rub against the toe cap. If you can still squeeze a finger down the inside of your heel, you have the right fit. The extra room is necessary to allow your feet to expand and to prevent your toes from rubbing against the toe of the boot when you are walking downhill. Do the laces up firmly, but not too tightly, and ensure that the boots don't constrict the broad part of your feet and that there is sufficient room for your toes to move freely. Walk around the shop and check that your heels are held firmly in the back of the boots. If they lift more than about 6 mm you should try a smaller size.

Always try boots on both your feet. In most people, one foot is slightly bigger than the other and although a boot might fit one foot perfectly, you could find that a boot of the same size is either too big or too small on the other foot.

Once you have the right pair of boots it is important to give them a chance to adjust to the shape of your feet before embarking on your first trip – be it a day walk, or an overnight hike. The time it will take to break in your boots will depend on the material (leather or fabric) and the flexibility of the sole. Begin by wearing the boots around the house and on walks over easy terrain, until you are satisfied that they have been properly worn in.

Good-quality boots are expensive and should, therefore, be cared for properly. One of the most common mistakes is to dry wet boots in front of a fire. This causes shrinkage, which can in turn cause the sole to separate from the uppers. Wet boots should be aired as much as possible and then worn until they are dry.

In the course of your travels your boots may be subjected to a great deal of hard wear, rain and sunshine. After every trip, brush the uppers lightly to remove any mud, grime, or dust, especially in the seams, and ensure that they are dry. Stuff them with newspaper and store in a dry place. If you opted for leather boots, you should apply polish after every trip and treat them occasionally with Dubbin. This will revitalise the leather and help it to retain its unique qualities – breathability, suppleness, strength, and durability – and will also waterproof the boots without affecting their breathability. And, contrary to popular belief, Dubbin does not cause stitch-rot.

Packs

After footwear, your pack is the piece of equipment most crucial to your enjoyment of an outing. Comfort is once again of the utmost importance.

Day packs range in capacity from 18 to 42 litres, with an average of around 35 litres. Well-padded back and shoulder straps are important features, and a waist strap is useful on larger volume packs.

Backpacks In South Africa most packs are internal frame packs, although external frame packs are still very popular in Europe and the United States.

As with footwear it is important to select the correct length of pack or frame. This is not as simple as it sounds. For example, if you are tall this does not mean a long-frame backpack will necessarily be the right fit. What is important is that the size of the frame/pack is correctly related to your torso size. Most good-quality internal frame packs have a self-adjusting system, enabling people of different heights to use the same pack.

One of the most important features of a backpack is a well-padded hip belt, which helps to transfer up to 70 per cent of the weight from your shoulders to your hips. Load the pack with a few heavy items and fasten the hip belt so that its top edge is just above your hip bone. Adjust the shoulder straps until the pack fits snugly against your back, ensuring that the top harness point is not more than 5 cm below your high prominent neck bone. Ask a shop assistant or friend to help you gauge this position correctly. Because the sizes of packs and frames vary, you might have to try several times before finding the correct fit.

Check that the back of the pack is well padded, and that there is sufficient room between the pack and your back for air ventilation. Remember the old adage: 'If it's a large pack, fill it up. If it's a small pack, it won't fit in.' Considering general weather and other conditions in South Africa, packs with a capacity of 50 to 55 litres and 60 litres are sufficient for women and men respectively, for a weekend trail. For longer trails (e.g. five-day hikes) women will need a pack with a capacity of 55 to 60 litres and men 60 to 75 litres.

Ensure that the fabric is strong, waterproof and abrasion resistant. Backpacks are manufactured from a variety of fabrics, with guarantees ranging from five years to a lifetime, if you're investing in a good-quality pack.

Ask yourself these questions when buying a backpack:
- Are the hip belt and shoulder straps well padded?
- Are the shoulder straps easily adjustable?
- Does the hip belt have a quick release buckle?
- How many side pockets are there?
- Is there a sack extension (an extension of the backpack's inner fabric enabling you to use the space under the pack's top flap)?
- Are the zips covered with flaps in order to make them more waterproof?

Sleeping bag

When choosing a sleeping bag, your most important choice will be between down and artificial fibre. Once again, there are several factors to consider: weight, warmth, size when packed up, design, and price. Your final choice will be determined by how well these suit the intended use of the bag.

Down sleeping bags have the advantage of being light, compact and warm. However, they lose their insulating properties when wet, require special care during washing, and are expensive. In recent years the quality of artificial-fibre sleeping bags has improved tremendously, and they are proving to be viable options to down. They are warm, retain their insulating properties when wet, are easy to wash, and their price is competitive. In addition, the disadvantage of years gone by, bulk, is no longer a factor, and they compare favourably with down sleeping bags in this respect.

Two basic styles of sleeping bag are available: rectangular and cowl top, or mummy-shaped. If you are likely to spend extended periods in cold weather climates a cowl top makes good sense, as the body-contoured shape provides the best warmth-to-weight ratio.

The bag should have a well-shaped cowl and draw cords, so it can cover your head in cold weather, leaving just a breathing hole open, to reduced heat loss. Some cowl top bags have short zips, but the First Ascent range has 'foot friendly zips' (a South African registered design), so you can use it as a duvet, or zip two bags together.

Rectangular bags are the most popular sleeping bags in South Africa. They usually come with a full zip, which offers the advantage that you can control the temperature inside the bag. On warm evenings the bag can be unzipped to reduce the temperature and in cold weather two bags can be zipped together for extra warmth. And, at home, the bag can be used as a duvet.

Ensure that the bag you buy has a draught tube (a thin down-filled baffle sewn along the inside of the zip and the face area of the cowl) to prevent heat loss.

Caring for your sleeping bag
- Keep your bag dry. If it does get wet, dry it out in the open as soon as possible. Gently squeeze out excess water, but do not wring the bag. Take care not to damage the draught tube when zipping up or unzipping the bag.
- Never expose your bag to excessive heat, such as direct sunlight or a fire. In down sleeping bags this could cause the down to harden.
- Store your bag loosely – preferably by hanging it up when not in use. If down bags are compressed for extended periods, the natural resilience of the filling will be strained.
- Keep your sleeping bag as clean as possible, both inside and outside. The use of a sleeping bag inner sheet and a sleeping bag cover will not only keep your bag clean, but will also give added warmth; although you'll add about 1 kg in weight.
- Down sleeping bags should always be hand-washed. Fill a bath tub with lukewarm water (40 °C) and add special down soap. Gently wash the bag, avoiding harsh twisting or wringing. Drain the tub, and rinse in fresh water, repeating the process until all the soap is removed. Gently squeeze as much water as possible out of the bag before lifting it out; supporting it from underneath. Dry the bag carefully in a warm place, away from direct heat. Gently massage down lumps into individual plumules.

Closed-cell ground pad

On trails where there are no overnight huts with bunks and mattresses, a closed-cell ground pad (a thin, 6 to 10 mm, high-density foam mattress with excellent insulating properties) is essential to prevent the cold from creeping up from the ground. First time out, you might find the ground pad a bit hard, but remember: it's a lot more comfortable than just sleeping on a ground sheet! In terms of comfort, weight and size (rolled up) it is far superior to open foam and airbeds. High-quality closed-cell ground-pads with a thickness of 9 mm are suitable for temperatures as low as -10 °C.

When investing in a ground pad, don't compromise on quality. Cheap products are available, but their durability and the density of the foam are far inferior to a good-quality closed-cell ground pad.

For backpackers prepared to increase the weight of their packs for comfort, a self-inflating mattress is an option. These ingenious mattresses are ideal for backpacking – they are lighter than airbeds, more compact and you just unroll them. Their disadvantages are that they are heavier than ground pads, more expensive, and tend to puncture easily.

Ground sheet

When sleeping out in the open, a ground sheet is useful to keep the area around your sleeping bag clean. The choice here is between a light plastic ground sheet or a sportsman's blanket, which is lined with aluminium foil on the one side and weighs about 310 g. In cold conditions it can be wrapped around you to preserve heat and it can also be used as a makeshift shelter.

The emergency blanket is a very light (70 g) sheet of aluminium foil, one side of which is highly reflective. It takes up hardly any space, is relatively inexpensive, but does not stand up to rough handling and should, therefore, be used only in emergencies for extra insulation, or as an emergency shelter against rain or sun.

Rain gear

Selecting rain gear is bound to be difficult, unless you're prepared to delve deep into your pocket to buy a high-quality product made from outer fabrics such as K-Tech® or Goretex®, which are waterproof and breathable.

Casual rain jackets are usually either water-repellent or waterproof. Water-repellent garments have the advantage of breathability and perform satisfactorily in light rain. However, when adverse weather conditions set in for prolonged periods, they are totally inadequate.

Waterproof garments made from PVC-coated nylon, on the other hand, provide a sealed shell that is unable to breathe. Warm, humid air released by the body is unable to escape through the waterproof material and water vapour is formed inside the shell. This results in an excessive heat build-up and condensation and you end up being soaked inside the garment.

The answer to these problems is garments made from K-Tech® and Goretex®, which are 100 per cent waterproof, but breathable, and virtually impenetrable to wind. These fabrics are expensive, but in inclement weather you will regret not having invested in a high-quality garment.

Backpacking stove

A backpacking stove (a lightweight, portable stove that uses gas – a butane/propane mixture – methylated spirits, benzene or alcohol as a source of fuel) is not only convenient for a quick mug of tea along the trail, but also if you find firewood stocks depleted at overnight huts along a trail. In addition, because of the danger of open fires, the negative environmental impact of burning wood, and the cost of providing it, firewood is no longer supplied on many trails.

In years gone by, mountaineers relied heavily on their often temperamental benzene stoves, but nowadays gas seems to be the most popular choice. Other options include methylated spirit (alcohol) and pressurised multi-fuel stoves.

Lightweight gas stoves are clean burning and reasonably efficient when shielded from the wind. Some models have a wider base and an improved burning ring – a great step up from the rather unstable early models, with their high centre of gravity. In windy conditions, at high altitudes and in cold weather, however, cannister gas stoves perform poorly. Empty gas canisters have, unfortunately, become a major source of pollution.

Methylated spirit stoves, commonly known as storm cookers, are easy to operate and reasonably efficient. They perform well in windy conditions, and their wide base makes them stable. A kit consisting of two pots, a frying pan, potgrip, wind shield, burner, and (with some models) a kettle, packs into a compact unit. On the negative side, they have a low fuel to heat ratio, requiring you to carry a large supply of fuel on long trips. This not only takes up space, but also adds to the weight of your pack. In addition, you'll have to invest in some lightweight metal bottles to decant the meths into. Another negative factor is that this stove will blacken the pots during cooking.

Pressurised multi-fuel stoves are quite expensive, but in terms of performance are far superior to any other stoves, especially at high altitudes and low temperatures. Some models use any type of fuel, from paraffin to aviation fuel.

Tent

On some trails you might have to be self-sufficient, right down to accommodation, and you should never rely on finding caves, or basic shelters, unoccupied.

Mercifully, lighter fabrics have long replaced the trusty old canvas tents of early mountaineers. Not only were they bulky and heavy, but if you happened to touch the inside of the tent accidentally during rain, water would seep through and you would later get a shower of water caused by condensation.

This problem was largely solved by the invention of the double-skinned tent, consisting of an inner tent and a flysheet. The inner tent is made of either an absorbent cotton or a breathable nylon fabric, and is suspended from the tent poles in such a way that it does not touch the flysheet or outer tent. Vapour passes through the breathable fabric of the inner tent and condenses when it comes into contact with the cold flysheet. At the same time, the air trapped between the inner tent and the flysheet acts as an effective insulator.

Features to look for in a quality backpacking tent are a waterproof, sewn-in groundsheet with fairly high side-walls, mosquito-netting at the doors and a bell on either side. A bell is a triangular extension of the flysheet at either end of an A-framed tent, designed to cover the entrances. It reduces wind resistance and creates more space, which can be used for storing equipment.

Tents come in a variety of styles, from the conventional A-frame, to a bewildering selection of dome-shaped models. The advantages of dome tents are that they are easy to erect, more spacious, and their streamlined shapes can withstand high winds.

Clothing

Keeping a cool head in hot temperatures is important, so a wide-rimmed hat is preferable to a peak cap. Ensure that your hat provides adequate shade for your face and neck. If you are trailing in an area where cold temperatures can be expected, bear in mind that about 30 per cent of the body's heat is lost from the head. Pack a balaclava or a woollen cap that can be pulled over your ears.

In summer, short-sleeved shirts or blouses are more suitable than T-shirts, which provide little ventilation and tend to cling to one's body. Cotton shirts are more airy and have the added advantage of a collar that can be turned up to protect your neck against the sun.

In winter, it is advisable to pack a long-sleeved, woollen shirt for extra warmth. You'll also need a warm jersey, or a densely knitted, fleece-lined tracksuit top and trousers. Wool is, in all cases, preferable to other fabrics, on account of its excellent insulating qualities. For cold weather conditions you'll need to invest in something more substantial, like a Polartec® or down jacket.

Even in cold, wet conditions, shorts are preferable to trousers, which can cause discomfort and chafing once they are wet. Never wear jeans – they are heavy (even more so when wet) and take ages to dry.

Your normal underwear should do for a hike, although cotton garments are more comfortable. For cold-weather trailing, thermal underwear is highly recommended. On a hike of a few days you don't need to take a change of underwear for every day, as it's usually possible to wash or rinse underwear on the trail.

A general rule to prevent loss of body heat is to cover the body with three layers of clothing rather than a single, thick layer. This is because heat is prevented from escaping by the dry air trapped between the different layers of clothing.

When it comes to socks, there is no substitute for wool, and although a wool/fibre mixture is acceptable, you must ensure that the percentage of wool is larger than that of the artificial fibre. Avoid nylon socks, as they will overheat your feet and cause blisters. Many hikers prefer to wear two pairs of socks – a thin inner pair of either wool or cotton, and a thick woollen outer pair. This reduces the likelihood of blisters considerably, as the inner socks absorb the chafing that would normally occur on your skin.

Miscellaneous items

I use a Maglite® torch as they last forever, but Petzl® head-torches are also excellent and very popular for hiking. The well-organised hiker will, however, have little need for a torch, and a small torch is usually adequate for cooking and finding your way to the toilet at night. Not only do they take up little space, but are also light, as are the spare batteries.

A 2-litre waterbottle or two 1-litre bottles are essential on any trail. Plastic waterbottles are most commonly used, but have the disadvantage of giving water an unpleasant flavour when it is warm. Some plastic waterbottles have a felt covering, which helps to keep water cool as long as the felt is kept damp.

A plastic, dish-shaped bowl, or a plate with a rim, is preferable to a flat plate as porridge and saucy food tend to spill over the edge of the plate. Clip-together cutlery sets are useful, but a sharp knife from your kitchen drawer will also prove invaluable. Beware of aluminium mugs; although they retain heat for a long time, they can cause some nasty blistered lips when you are over-eager to begin drinking hot drinks.

Packing your backpack

Here are some hints to assist you when you are packing your backpack:

- Limit the weight of your pack as far as possible. Your pack should never exceed a third of your body weight. Ideally it should weigh 20 per cent of the body weight of women and children, and 25 per cent of the body weight of men. Don't end up stumbling along a trail, burdened by a heavy backpack filled with lightweight equipment.
- Before packing, line your backpack with a large garbage bag or a sac liner (a heavy-duty plastic bag manufactured specifically to line the inside of packs). This will keep the contents dry if you're caught in the rain during your hike. Although most good quality packs do stand up to their claim of being waterproof, water does still sometimes seep through seams and zips, while older packs can lose their waterproof coating.
- Pack systematically to ensure that unnecessary items are not included, and that essential items are not left out. There is nothing as frustrating as discovering that you have forgotten to pack something when you are already on a trail!
- Items you are likely to use often during the day should be easily accessible.
- The bulk of the weight in your pack should be in line with your centre of gravity. Heavy items should be packed in the top half of the pack, closest to your back, so that the lower half of the pack is left for lighter items.
- The kit list opposite is for a five-day trail. You do not need to follow it religiously – rather adapt it to suit the type of trail you are going on, its length, and your personal needs.

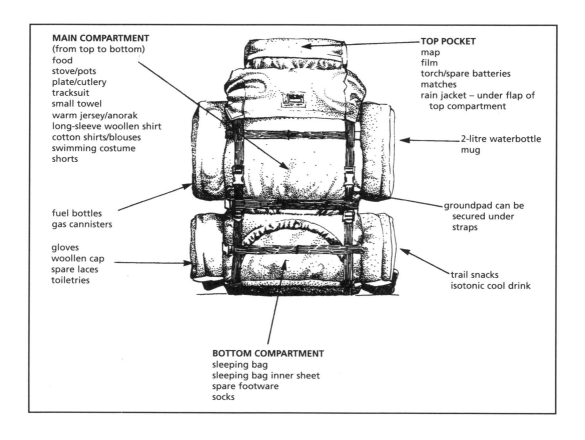

MAIN COMPARTMENT
(from top to bottom)
food
stove/pots
plate/cutlery
tracksuit
small towel
warm jersey/anorak
long-sleeve woollen shirt
cotton shirts/blouses
swimming costume
shorts

fuel bottles
gas cannisters

gloves
woollen cap
spare laces
toiletries

TOP POCKET
map
film
torch/spare batteries
matches
rain jacket – under flap of
    top compartment

2-litre waterbottle
mug

groundpad can be
    secured under
    straps

trail snacks
isotonic cool drink

BOTTOM COMPARTMENT
sleeping bag
sleeping bag inner sheet
spare footware
socks

KIT LIST

Item	Mass in grams	E = Essential O = Optional C = Check facilities	Item	Mass in grams	E = Essential O = Optional C = Check facilities
Backpack			detergent (biodegradable)	50	E
65 litre backpack	1,800	E	dishcloth	80	E
pack cover	25	O	trail snacks	500	E
			trail food (5 days)	5,000	E
Sleeping gear			emergency rations	500	E
sleeping bag	1,800	E	waterbottle 2 litre (full)	2,075	E
inner sheet	500	O			
pillow	100	O	**Toiletries**		
mattress/groundpad	400	C	tissues	10	O
ground sheet	720	C	toilet paper and trowel	250	E
mosquito net	250	O	towel (small)	250	E
tent, poles and pegs	3,000	C	biodegradable soap	50	E
			face cloth/sponge	35	O
Footwear			shaving kit	65	O
boots/walking shoes	1,800	E	toothbrush and -paste	45	E
spare bootlaces	50	E	comb	15	O
spare footwear	750	E	sunscreen cream	120	E
warm, thick socks (2 pairs)	400	E	lip balm	20	E
light, breathable socks (2 pairs)	200	E	foot powder	50	O
gaiters	150	O	insect repellent	50	E
			moisturiser, body lotion	150	O
Clothing					
woollen cap/balaclava	125	C	**Miscellaneous**		
sunhat	75	E	first aid kit (see p. 30)	300	E
cool hiking shirt/T-shirt x 2	400	E	emergency blanket	70	E
warm long-sleeved shirt	250	E	water purification tablets	50	C
jersey	700	E	litter bag	25	E
shorts x 2	300	E	torch, spare batteries/bulb	115	E
underwear x 3	150	E	pocket knife	100	O
thermal underwear	300	C	candle	60	O
sleepwear	300	C	camera and film	1,000	O
tracksuit	700	E	binoculars (compact)	400	O
gloves/mittens	100	C	map	50	E
waterproof raingear	600	E	compass	100	O
swimming costume	150	O	permit	7	E
			passport/driver's licence	40	C
Cooking and food			waterproofing bags	50	E
cutlery	50	E	survival bag	240	C
plate and mug	110	E	cord (5 m, thin nylon)	50	E
can opener	20	E	notebook and pencil	50	O
stove, pots, pot grip, fuel	2,000	E	whistle	10	E
matches (water proofed)	15	E	field guides	variable	O
pot-scourer	20	E	walking stick	variable	O

Hiking hints

Few things can be as frustrating as arriving at the end of a hard day's hike in the rain only to discover that your matches are soaked, or that the batteries of your torch have run down. As you gain more experience of the outdoors, you will learn how to avoid these annoying mishaps and turn a good trip into a memorable one. Here are a few basic common sense hints:

- To avoid the feeling of despair when you switch on your **torch** and nothing happens, turn one of the batteries the wrong way around when not in use to avoid them running down if the torch is accidentally switched on. And always remember to pack **spare batteries** and a **spare bulb**.
- **Waterproof matches** can be bought at speciality back-packing stores, but are expensive and sometimes even these matches do not work when wet. Take a **cigarette lighter**, some matches, and a small piece of striker from a match box in an empty film cannister; it's 100 per cent waterproof when closed properly.
- A **potgrip** will prevent you from getting your fingers burnt when you move pots, or even worse, seeing your meal end up on the ground. Also very useful, is a **long-handled spoon** for stirring food when cooking over an open fire.
- Avoid glass bottles – they are heavier than plastic and can break. Decant liquids into screw-top **plastic bottles** or **aluminium containers**. Some aluminium containers are available in different colours, to ensure that you do not confuse water and fuel bottles. Don't use aluminium containers for acidic liquids as the acids will corrode the aluminium.
- A **squeeze tube** is handy for honey, jam, peanut butter and condensed milk. It is filled from the lower end, which is then sealed with a sliding clamp. It is re-usable, but remember not to turn the screw top too tightly, or it may crack.
- If you will be crossing wide rivers during the course of your trail, take along a **survival bag** (a large red or orange heavy-duty plastic bag) to float equipment across. In emergencies it can also be used as a cover for your sleeping bag, although excessive heat build-up and condensation inside the survival bag can be a problem.
- Although each group should have a well-equipped first aid kit, each person should carry a few **plasters**.
- A very common complaint on trails is sore feet. You should take along an extra pair of **light footwear**

(running shoes or sandals), which will give your feet a much-needed rest after a hard day of hiking.
- A 5-m length of thin **nylon rope** can be useful for emergency situations, repairs, and as a washing line.
- Always remember to take **precautions against the sun** – wear a sunhat, use sunscreen, and so on.
- Remember to **pack food away** before going to sleep, or you might discover in the morning that mice or small predators have ruined, or made off with, some of your provisions.
- A **pocket knife** or **multi-tool** is useful on a trail. It is light and compact, and most models have all the gadgets needed: can opener, knife, tweezers and scissors. Attach it to your pack with a piece of string.

TRAIL ETHICS

In view of the increasing number of people using the great outdoors, it has become vitally important to adhere to trail ethics. By doing so you will help to conserve the natural environment for your own enjoyment, and for future generations.

Land

- Don't litter. Tissues tucked into sleeves or under watchstraps inevitably fall out and are one of the most common forms of trailside litter. Cigarette ends, sweet wrappers, toilet paper, and empty gas cannisters are also a nuisance and should never be left along a trail. Even orange peels, commonly regarded as biodegradable, should not be discarded, as they can take months to decompose.
- Carry a refuse bag and pick up litter along the way.
- Never bury litter. In most cases it will be uncovered by the elements or animals, such as baboons. This is not only unsightly, but broken glass and tins with sharp edges can injure fellow trailists and animals. Remember: Carry out what you carry in.
- Avoid shortcuts, as the trail gradient and the potential for erosion increases. It also demands greater exertion.
- Step over erosion bars, barriers of either logs or rock, not on them, and avoid dislodging stones.
- Avoid areas with little or no vegetation. They are extremely susceptible to erosion, and can take years to recover from damage.
- Likewise, avoid scree slopes. Hiking on them causes miniature rockfalls, which destroy vegetation that has established itself under difficult conditions.

- Never roll rocks down slopes or over cliffs. This may injure other people, cause fires or erosion, and it destroys vegetation.
- When camping in the wilds, you must make sure that the area is disturbed as little as possible. Set up your camp on level ground, not only for your own comfort, but also because sloping ground erodes easily once the vegetation on it is compacted.
- Keep your backpack as light as possible. This will not only lighten your burden and increase your enjoyment of the outdoors, but will also reduce erosion and compaction, as the lighter the total load, the less the compaction you will cause.

Water

Many of South Africa's streams and rivers are the habitat of rare and endangered aquatic life, which can easily be destroyed by carelessness. Keep the following in mind:

- Avoid camping closer than 60 m to any body of water, wherever possible.
- Do not use soap in streams or rivers – a good swim is normally sufficient to clean up – and don't brush your teeth directly in streams or rivers. Cooking and eating utensils should be washed away from the water.

Air

One of the main reasons people go trailing is to seek solitude. Noise pollution is as objectionable as littering, so bear these points in mind:

- Avoid shouting, yelling and whistling – it decreases your chances of seeing wildlife.
- If you smoke, take care, especially in dry grasslands. Never smoke while you are hiking. Stop, sit down and relax. Use a flat rock as an ashtray and remember to put the filter in your litter bag.
- Smoke from campfires causes air pollution. Where fires are permitted, keep them small.

Flora and fauna

- Don't pick flowers (they will only wilt) or uproot bulbs.
- Avoid shortcuts as they could destroy sensitive and endangered vegetation.
- Where fires are permitted, remember the following:
- Use existing fireplaces, rather than making new ones.
  - Choose a level spot where the fire will be well protected from the wind.
  - Don't make fires under trees, near vegetation or on the roots of trees; clear the area around the fireplace of all leaves and humus.

- Keep your fire small; that way it's more comfortable to cook over, more intimate, easier to control and you will conserve wood.
- Where the collection of firewood is permissible, use only fallen wood and do not break seemingly dead branches off trees; it is not only unsightly, but often the branches are merely dormant.
- Never leave your fire unattended, and always make sure you keep some water handy.
- Extinguish your fire properly before going to bed or breaking up camp. If the wood hasn't burn to ash, douse the coals thoroughly with water.
- Don't cut nearby vegetation to sleep on – rather carry a ground pad with you.
- Disturb animals and birds that you come across as little as possible, particularly those with young or in nests, as well as seemingly lost or injured animals or birds. Some animals hide their young during the day, and birds will often not associate with nestlings once they have been handled by humans. In most cases there is little one can do to help an injured animal or bird.
- Don't feed animals or birds. Some animals, especially baboons, soon learn to associate humans with food if they are fed, and can become aggressive scavengers. In addition, you might well pass on harmful bacteria to the animals.

General

- Where toilets are not provided, human waste should be disposed of by the 'cat method'. Select a flat, screened spot at least 60 m from the footpath and open water. Dig a hole no deeper than 20 to 25 cm to keep within the biological layer, where active decomposition takes place, and after use fill the hole with loose soil and trample lightly over it. Toilet paper should be burned, but take care not to set the veld alight.
- Don't sleep in caves with rock paintings, except where this is expressly permitted, and never tamper with or spray water over rock paintings. Archaeological sites should not be disturbed, nor should artefacts be removed. It is an offence under the Monuments Act.
- Your enjoyment and appreciation of the outdoors will be considerably enhanced if you read more about the area beforehand. There are numerous pocket-sized field guides on flora and fauna that can be taken along on walks and trails.

HIKING SAFETY

On any walk or trail, safety is always of the utmost importance. Most of the common fatal or serious injuries that occur whilst hiking can be avoided if you make sure that you observe a few common sense rules.

Bear the following points in mind – they will not only ensure pleasant hiking, but could also help you to avoid a disaster:

- The group should always be led by the most experienced person amongst you.
- Plan the day's hike carefully and make an early start if there's a long hike ahead, if the terrain is difficult or unfamiliar to you, or if the weather is hot or will be later in the day.
- Keep in mind that there's considerably fewer daylight hours in winter than in summer.
- Hike at a steady pace. Three kilometres an hour is a good average. For every 300 m gain in altitude an hour can be added to your total walking time. On steep sections it is advisable to shorten your stride, and carry on walking. Avoid long breaks, rather have short rest stops and use the opportunity to appreciate your surroundings. It is best to stop for a five-minute break every hour. In between, breaks should be limited to taking just a 'breather', except for tea and lunch breaks. During extended breaks your muscles cool down and it takes quite an effort to get going again.
- Keep the group together. A member lagging behind is an almost sure sign of trouble, exhaustion or exposure. Establish the cause of the problem, assist the person by spreading the weight of their pack among other members of the group and keep them company. In large groups it is advisable to appoint someone to bring up the rear; you'll always know who the last person is.
- Always carry a whistle. It can be used to attract attention should you get lost. Remember the morse code for the international SOS – three short, three long and three short whistles.

Energy and water

- Keep your energy levels up by eating snacks – peanuts and raisins, glucose sweets, chocolate (not in hot weather, as it melts) and dried fruit – between meals.
- Always carry a 2-litre waterbottle and fill it up wherever you can. Remember that smaller streams are often dry during the winter months in summer rainfall areas and during the summer in winter rainfall areas.

- Make sure that you keep your water intake up, especially in hot weather, to prevent dehydration, and always keep a reserve supply for emergencies. It is also worth carrying a rehydration solution along.
- Waterbottles should always be filled from safe, fast-running streams above any areas of human habitation. Water from any part of the river below an area of human habitation should be regarded as unsafe, and should not be drunk before it has been thoroughly boiled.
- Water that may be infested with bilharzia, cholera or other waterborne diseases should be boiled for at least five minutes. This method is preferable to using commercially available chemicals. Strain water through a handkerchief to remove debris before boiling it.

Inclement weather

- If you encounter bad weather, or if the route proves physically too demanding, do not hesitate to turn back if you have not reached the halfway mark of the day's hike by midday.
- Most of South Africa receives rain in the summer, and thunderstorms are common in the afternoon. Try to reach your destination before the storm sets in.
- Avoid the dangers of lightning by staying clear of prominent features such as trees, ridges, summits, shallow caves, and large boulders. Find an open slope; sit on a ground pad or a backpack (preferably on a clean, dry rock), with your knees drawn up, feet together and hands in your lap. If you are in a tent during an electric storm, sit in a crouching position and avoid touching the sides.
- Mist often occurs at high altitudes. If mist does set in, seek a suitable shelter and stay put until it lifts.
- If you are caught in a snowfall, seek shelter and move to a lower altitude at the earliest opportunity, to avoid being trapped if conditions deteriorate.

River crossings

Be aware of the dangers of flash floods and never cross a flooding river. Fortunately, most South African rivers soon return to their normal level after flooding. Either wait until the flood has subsided or make a detour.

- Never camp in riverbeds or valleys. Rainfall in the upper reaches of the river can cause unexpected flash floods with disastrous consequences.
- Some routes necessitate frequent river crossings. At times it might be possible to boulder-hop across, but

avoid long jumps with a heavy pack, which could result in a slip, and not only a soaking, but also injury.
- If you're not sure about a river's depth always probe it without your pack. Even if a river is shallow (i.e. knee-deep) you can lose your balance if there are rocks under the water, in which case you will need to discard your pack quickly, as there is a danger of being pinned down underwater by a heavy pack. Undo the pack's hip belt and loosen the shoulder straps, so that you can offload it quickly, if necessary.
- Float packs across deeper rivers – a survival bag is ideal for keeping your pack dry.
- Avoid crossing rivers near the mouth, unless there is a sand bar. If the mouth is open, cross further upstream, where the flow is slower and the river is often shallower. Avoid bends, where the flow is usually stronger and the river deeper.
- When crossing a strong-flowing river, start swimming at a point much higher up than the one you're aiming for. Swim diagonally across, with the flow, and not straight to the other side.

Veld fires
- In the event of a veld fire, try to find shelter in a kloof or ravine rather than going up a slope. Avoid waterfalls, to prevent being trapped below or above the falls by the fire, and make sure that you take care and time to minimise unnecessary risks.

First aid
Most emergency situations are either related to extremes of weather, a physical injury or disability. It is, therefore, essential for every hiker to understand the principles of preventative measures and first aid. It is strongly advisable to read some of the many authoritative publications available on this subject or to enrol for a first aid course. Unless you are medically trained, you can give only emergency first aid, which will, hopefully, prevent any deterioration in the condition of the patient until help arrives.

The three most serious physical problems you may encounter are: cessation of breathing, bleeding and shock. All these situations call for immediate action and the following general directions should be followed:

Take control The leader of the group must take control of the situation immediately. If the leader is injured, the next most experienced member must take control. Remain calm, assess the situation and direct the other members of the group to improvise equipment or a shelter.

Approach safely In the event of a serious fall on difficult terrain, care should be taken not to cause rockfalls or to endanger the lives of others. If the casualty cannot be reached safely or the necessary equipment is unavailable, help should be summoned without delay.

Apply emergency first aid procedures If the casualty can be reached, assess their condition and, if the injury appears to be related in any way to the spinal column, avoid any movement.

Check for breathing Lick your fingers and hold them in front of the injured person's nose, or mouth; put your hand on the chest, or stomach. If you cannot feel breathing, or movement, apply artificial respiration, first removing any obstruction to the air passages.

Check the pulse If the casualty does not have a pulse, begin cardiopulmonary resuscitation (CPR).

Check for serious bleeding Internal bleeding may be indicated if the person is pale, clammy and restless. This can be fatal and medical assistance must be sought immediately. Try to stop fast or heavy external bleeding by applying direct pressure, using a pad of folded cloth and if possible elevating the wound.

Treat for shock After any major injury, be on the lookout for signs of shock, which can cause paleness, clammy skin, a fast, weak heartbeat, quick breathing, dizziness or weakness.

After loosening tight clothing, lay the person down, with their feet higher than their head. Reassure and keep the patient comfortable and warm, covering them, without allowing them to get too hot. If possible, give them small sips of warm, sweet tea or sugar water.

Check for other injuries and give first aid treatment. Start with the neck and work your way down systematically, examining the body for bleeding, sensitivity, fractures, pain, or swelling.

Plan what to do Your plan of action depends on whether the casualty can carry on unassisted, if evacuation by the group is possible, or whether outside help is required.

Take the following into account: the nature of the injuries, the time of day, weather conditions, the terrain, the availability of shelter and water, the size and physical condition of the group, and the availability of outside help.

Execute the plan of action If the situation requires evacuation with outside help, at least two members of your group should be sent. They should preferably be stronger members of the group, and they must follow a predetermined route, from which they should not deviate at any point, if all possible. They should have the following information:

- Where, when and how the accident occurred.
- The number of casualties, as well as the nature and seriousness of the injuries.
- What first aid has been administered, what supplies are still available to those who have remained behind and the condition of the casualties.
- The distance between the casualties and the closest roads and the nature of the terrain.
- The number of people at the evacuation scene.
- What type of equipment might be necessary.

While waiting for help to arrive the remaining members of the group can make shelters and prepare hot meals and drinks for the casualty and themselves.

FIRST AID KIT

A well-equipped first aid kit should always accompany a hiking party, even on a day walk or short weekend outing. When putting together your kit, remember that space is limited and that it is always possible to improvise. Trailists suffering from chronic ailments, such as diabetes, asthma, allergies, or weak ankles or knees, should ensure that they have sufficient medicine or equipment to take care of themselves.

- ❏ antibiotics
- ❏ anti-diarrhoea pills
- ❏ anti-histamine: cream and tablets
- ❏ anti-inflammatory gel
- ❏ antiseptic: cream and solution
- ❏ bandages: wide crepe & narrow gauze
- ❏ cotton wool
- ❏ eardrops: antiseptic, analgesic
- ❏ eye bath
- ❏ eyedrops
- ❏ isotonic drink
- ❏ mosquito repellent
- ❏ nail scissors

- ❏ needle and thread
- ❏ painkillers
- ❏ plasters: zinc oxide and sealed individual plasters
- ❏ safety pins
- ❏ sulphacetimide eye ointment
- ❏ surgical gloves (for use when there is any bleeding, to avoid the transmission of any blood-borne diseases, such as HIV or hepatitis)
- ❏ thermometer
- ❏ throat lozenges
- ❏ tweezers
- ❏ wound dressing

Prevention and cure

About 90 per cent of all ailments on trails are foot and leg problems. The best solution is prevention and avoidance. Make early decisions and treat any ailments or wounds as soon as they occur. Common injuries and health hazards that trailists should be aware of are discussed briefly below. (For ease of reference they are listed alphabetically.)

Bilharzia: This disease, which is fairly common in the rural areas of the east coast and the northeast of South Africa, is caused by a snail-borne parasite that attacks the intestines, bladder and other organs of its hosts. Bilharzia is unlikely to occur in streams and rivers above 1,200 m in altitude, because of the unsuitability of fast-flowing water as a habitat for the snail hosts. (High-altitude rivers are typically fast-flowing, as they are usually at quite a steep gradient.) It is also less likely to be found in any body of water that is mixed with sea water. Water temperatures of 0 °C, for three or four nights, are sufficient to kill the snail hosts, while water temperatures of over 28 °C are poorly tolerated by the hosts.

Bilharzia is usually associated with human habitation; so avoid drinking, swimming or washing in water downstream from any human settlement, especially in rural areas. If bilharzia is suspected, boil the water for at least five minutes before use.

Bites and stings: With the majority of spider bites, as well as bee, scorpion and wasp stings, discomfort can be relieved by applying an anti-histamine lotion and taking anti-histamine medication. If the patient has an allergic reaction to a sting, arrange for evacuation. Thick-tailed Parabuthus scorpion stings and button spider bites could be dangerous, in which case urgent medical assistance is essential.

Blisters: Blisters are the most common cause of discomfort and should be treated before they form. If certain spots on your feet are prone to blisters, cover them with a dressing and a broad strip of plaster before putting on your boots. A potential blister can usually be detected when a tender 'hot spot' starts to develop. Cover the affected area immediately with a dressing and zinc oxide plaster. If a blister forms and you have not completed your trip, it is best to lance the blister with a sterilised needle. Gently press out the liquid, dab the blister with antiseptic and then cover it with a dressing and zinc oxide plaster. This should, ideally, be done once the day's backpacking is over. Check the affected spot regularly for infection. If you have completed your trip, it should preferably not be lanced, but rather left uncovered to heal by itself.

Bruises: Swelling from a bad bruise can be reduced by holding the affected area in cold running water, such as a stream, and keeping it elevated and still.

Burns: Besides blisters, sunburn (a first-degree burn) is probably the most common ailment suffered on trails. Prevention is better than cure, so wear a sunhat and apply sunscreen lotion frequently, especially on the nose and face. Turn up the collar of your shirt (one of the reasons why a button-up shirt is preferable to a T-shirt) to prevent sunburn to your neck.

Scalds and minor burns should be treated by holding the affected area in cold water until the pain subsides. Do not apply greasy ointments and do not lance burn blisters. If available, cover the burn lightly with a gauze dressing, held in place with a plaster; burns heal better if left exposed to the air.

Burns of a more serious nature should not be immersed in water. Instead, cover the area with a sterile dressing or clean cloth. If clothing sticks to the burn, leave it on. Treat for shock and give the patient plenty of water and isotonic drink. Help should be summoned as soon as possible.

Cramps: Muscular cramps are caused by a shortage of salt or water, or both, combined with physical exertion. Allow the patient to rest, keep the affected area warm and massage gently. Give the patient an isotonic drink and avoid further strenuous exercise until they recover fully.

Diarrhoea and vomiting: Diarrhoea and vomiting are natural body mechanisms to dispose of bacteria and should preferably not be treated with commercial medication, unless continuing the hike is unavoidable. For both complaints the patient should be rested and given frequent doses of isotonic drink mixed to half strength.

Stomach pains and billiousness, without diarrhoea and vomiting, could be serious if they are accompanied by a persistent fever. The patient should rest, keep warm and maintain a high fluid intake. Evacuation might be necessary.

Dislocation: The symptoms of dislocation are visible deformity and severe pain. It is important to get skilled help quickly, because the dislocated joint will soon begin to swell. Do not attempt to push it back into place unless you are medically trained, as this can damage blood vessels and nerves or cause fractures. Wrap the joint in wet cloths, immobilise with splints if necessary and get the injured person to a doctor as soon as you can.

Ear infections: Earaches can be treated with an oily, antiseptic, analgesic eardrop, such as Aurone®. Middle ear infections are far more serious and can affect balance. If you are more than 12 hours from help and the person has a temperature, a wide-spectrum oral antibiotic should be administered.

Foreign bodies, such as insects, in the ear can usually be floated out with warm water or oil. Heat a little oil in a teaspoon (test a drop on the back of your hand to ensure that it's not too hot), pour into the ear and leave for five minutes before letting it run out. Take care not to push the object, especially smooth, hard objects, deeper into the ear in an attempt to get it out.

Exhaustion: Prevent exhaustion by avoiding over-exertion, eating trail snacks between meals, and drinking water regularly. If exhaustion does set in, the patient should be allowed to rest at a comfortable temperature, and given food and water with a high glucose content.

Eye injuries and infections: Foreign bodies should only be removed if you are able to take them out easily. Any object that is partially embedded in the eyeball should not be removed; cover the eye with a dough-nut-shaped bandage held in place with another bandage and evacuate the patient.

In most cases, however, the natural watering of the eye will dislodge and wash away small objects. Bring the upper lid down over the lower eyelid for a second or two; the tears caused by this might wash the object away. If this does not work, let the person blink their eye in an eye bath (a small plastic container that can be held over the eye) and apply eyedrops into the inner corner of the eye. Carefully lift the eyelid by the lashes and let the drops run over the eyeball. Blinking during irrigation might help. You could also try lifting the object out with the corner of a piece of sterile gauze.

Eye infections should be treated with a sulphace-timide eye ointment and covered with a light bandage.

Fever: Normal human oral temperature is 37 °C. A temperature which drops below 35 °C should be regarded as serious, whereas up to 39 °C indicates a mild fever and over 40 °C a high fever. Rest, and a large fluid intake, are essential. Cool the patient down by removing any hot clothing or bedding and wipe them with a wet cloth. Fanning them and giving them aspirin will also help. If there is no obvious cause and the fever persists, evacuation should be considered. Check for malaria symptoms.

Heat exhaustion: This condition is caused either by exposure to a hot environment or overheating caused by physical exertion. Symptoms are nausea, dizziness,

thirst, profuse sweating and headaches. Lie the patient down in a cool, shady place with their feet higher than their head, loosen their clothing and cover them lightly. Give them frequent isotonic drinks.

Heatstroke or sunstroke: Heatstroke is more serious than heat exhaustion as it affects the nervous centre that controls body temperature. It can set in very rapidly, and occurs when the sweating process and other body temperature regulatory mechanisms fail.

Symptoms are an excessive high body temperature, red, dry skin, headaches, irrational behaviour, shivering, cramps, dilated pupils, and, finally, collapse and unconsciousness. Cool the patient down immediately by moving them into the shade, taking off any tight clothing, pouring water over them and wiping them down with wet cloths, and fanning. If the patient is conscious, give them fast-acting aspirin and lots of isotonic drink. Get medical help urgently.

Hypothermia: The lowering of the body's core temperature to the point where the heat loss exceeds the heat the body is able to generate, results in hypothermia. It is usually caused by a combination of very cold weather, inadequate food intake and unsuitable clothing, as well as over-exertion. One or more of the following symptoms may be present: weakness, slowing of pace, shivering, lack of co-ordination, irrationality, a blue skin colour, difficulty in speaking, decreased heart and respiratory rate, diluted pupils and unconsciousness.

Prevent further heat loss and keep the patient moving, while looking for a suitable shelter. If a suitable shelter is not found within a few minutes, erect the best possible shelter. Remove wet clothing and immediately replace with warm, dry clothes. The patient should then be zipped into a pre-warmed sleeping bag, or warmed up between two people, well covered with sleeping bags. If the patient is able to eat, warm food and drink (sugar/glucose water, chocolate and soup) should be taken. Do not give them alcohol, coffee or any other stimulants. Do not rub the victim to restore circulation, or put them near a fire; direct heat is dangerous.

Lung and throat infections: A sore throat without fever can be treated by gargling with salt water or an antiseptic solution, or by sucking throat lozenges. A sore throat with fever will require antibiotics, and the patient should be kept warm and rested.

Bronchitis (symptoms include a bad cough, phlegm, fever/chills, sore/tight chest and some shortness of breath) can be serious and the patient will need rest, warmth and a wide-spectrum antibiotic. If the fever persists, the patient should be evacuated.

Malaria: A bite by an infected Anopheles mosquito can transmit microscopic blood parasites, resulting in malaria. In areas where malaria is endemic there is always a risk of contracting the disease, while in areas where it is epidemic the risk is generally confined to the rainy months. However, it is advisable to take anti-malaria precautions when visiting any malaria area, even if you are only in transit. Consult your doctor to find out which prophylaxis should be taken.

Taking a few simple preventative measures can reduce the chances of being bitten. After sunset, wear long trousers, a long-sleeved shirt, and socks. Apply a mosquito repellent to areas of bare skin (remember to reapply the repellent every few hours, as it loses its effectiveness after a while) and burn mosquito coils indoors.

In its early stages malaria is easily cured, so it is essential to consult a doctor immediately should you develop any flu-like symptoms. These are: a general body ache, severe fever, headache, nausea, and diarrhoea. Inform your doctor that you visited a malaria area.

Nosebleeds: Change in altitude, increased activity and cold temperatures are the main causes of nosebleeds. Fortunately, most nosebleeds are minor and can be stopped by applying direct pressure firmly against the nostril or pinching the tip of the nose for 5 to 10 minutes. If bleeding persists, pack the nostril with gauze, or cotton wool, pinch for 10 more minutes, and leave the dressing in for two hours or so. Remove carefully. Do not blow your nose for at least four hours after a nosebleed.

Pain: Treat general pain with the painkillers in your first aid kit, taken with plenty of fluid. If the pain persists and there is no obvious cause, seek medical treatment.

Snakebite: Chances of being bitten by a snake are extremely remote and only about 16 of the 160-odd South African snake species are deadly. Once again, it is wise to take preventative measures. Keep your eyes open, especially when the path is overgrown. If you carry a stick, swish it in the grass in front of you. Considering that 75 per cent of all bites are below the knee, wear stout boots and gaiters when bundu-bashing. About 15 per cent of bites are inflicted on the hand and finger and, therefore, it is wise to look before placing your hand behind a rock. Similarly, look under and around a rock or log before sitting down on it. Do not overturn logs or rocks; step onto them, not over them.

Except in unusual circumstances, the life of a snakebite victim will seldom be in immediate danger. The venom of a puff-adder, which is responsible for most bites, is seldom life-threatening within 10 hours of the bite, while cobra bites usually take two to four hours to cause distress symptoms. Although mamba bites can seriously affect breathing within one or two hours, it is highly unlikely that the victim will die in five minutes, as is popularly believed. Boomslang venom is extremely poisonous, but bites from this back-fanged snake are extremely rare as it is not an aggressive snake. Berg adder bites are never fatal, with patients showing an improvement within three to four days of being bitten.

The main problem when hiking is that a serious snake bite, such as mamba and cobra bites, require 60 to 80 ml antivenom, while snakebite kits usually only contain 20 ml. In addition, the antivenom should be injected intravenously, as after 12 hours as little as 20 per cent of antivenom injected intra-muscularly may have reached the circulation system.

In the event of a snakebite, the following basic first aid treatment should be given:
- Immobilise the victim as any unnecessary movement will increase the heart rate and consequently the spread of the venom.
- Examine for fang marks and keep the bite area below the level of their heart.
- Reassure the victim and administer a painkiller (avoid aspirin, as it thins the blood) to them if necessary. Do not allow the intake of alcohol.
- If the snake cannot be identified, clean and disinfect the bite area and wait 10 to 15 minutes to see if symptoms develop. If there are no symptoms, keep the victim immobilised and under observation for two to three hours.
- A suction device can be used immediately after the bite, but care should be taken to ensure that you do not massage the bite area. If a suction device is not available, suction with the mouth can be applied through a thin film of plastic.
- For mamba and cobra bites on a limb, apply a crepe bandage or torn strips of cloth firmly (but not

too tightly) from just above the bite to the top of the limb. **Do not use a tourniquet** unless you are medically trained, as improper application could reduce the blood flow, causing harm to body tissue. Cold cloths applied to the bite will further slow down the action of the poison. Monitor the patient's breathing and heart rate and, if either or both cease, apply mouth-to-mouth ventilation and/or external chest compression.

- For adder and boomslang bites, do not use a tourniquet or bandage. Adder bites are cytotoxic, or tissue-damaging, and the reduced flow of blood from a tourniquet may intensify this tissue damage. Immobilise the victim and apply cold water or cold wet cloths to the bite.
- If attacked by a spitting snake (such as a cobra or rinkhals) immediately wash the eyes out with water for at least 10 minutes. Lift the eyelids up so that the water washes under them as well. If water is not available, improvise; use milk, soft drinks, cold tea, or in emergencies even urine, but do not wash the eyes out with diluted antivenom.
- Don't make an incision at the site of the bite, as this is likely to damage tissue.
- Don't try to kill the snake for identification; a second person could be bitten.
- If it is a serious snake bite, two members of the group should get help and alert the nearest doctor, or hospital, providing them with the identity of the snake if possible.

Sprains and strains: Sprains are caused by either tearing or stretching ligaments, or a separation of muscle tendon from the bone, and are most common in the ankle, knee, wrist and shoulder. The symptoms are extreme pain and severe swelling caused by fluid and blood accumulating in the tissue. Elevate the injured limb, and lightly apply cold water or wet cloths. An anti-inflammatory gel can also be used. This will reduce the swelling and minimise deep bleeding. Give the patient a painkiller and, if you are medically trained, bind the joint with a long crepe bandage. Keep the immobilised joint in a comfortable resting position. After 24 hours, change over to heat treatment: warm the sprained joint in the sun or at a fire, or soak it in hot water three or four times a day.

It is often difficult to differentiate between a sprain and a fracture and, if pain persists, splint the affected limb (improvise a splint) and obtain medical help. Signs of fractures include severe pain, a floppy foot or hand, or difficulty in moving fingers or toes.

Strains are caused by overextending or tearing muscle fibre and are usually less serious than sprains. Treat these as for sprains.

Tickbites: Do not attempt to remove a tick if it does not pull off easily. Rather, cover it with an oily substance, like Vaseline, as the lack of air will likely cause it to loosen its grip.

Disinfect the area of the tickbite well and, should any signs of infection or fever appear within 10 days, visit a doctor right away.

Exploring the outdoors on foot is a thoroughly enjoyable and rewarding pasttime, but requires thorough planning and is, unfortunately, not without hazards. By following the tried and tested advice and hints in this introductory section you will avoid many of the common mistakes inexperienced hikers are prone to making when they go hiking, and your enjoyment of the trail will be enhanced.

The Cedarberg wilderness contains spectacular rock formations of sandstone and shale, which were deposited between 500 and 345 million years ago.

SOUTHWESTERN CAPE & LITTLE KAROO

The hikes in these two regions make the most of the spectacular coastal and mountain scenery, and a floral diversity that is unrivalled worldwide. Whether you are a casual rambler or a serious hiker there is a huge range of options, from short easy strolls on the slopes of Table Mountain, to full-day coastal hikes, and even five-day trails through wild mountains. Adventure-seekers will love the adrenaline-pumping kloofing trips, with jumps over waterfalls, and backpackers can blaze their own trails in the Cedarberg and Groot Winterhoek wilderness areas.

The area covered in this section stretches from Africa's southwestern-most point, northwards, to the Cedarberg. The boundary of the southwestern Cape is formed by the Breede River to the east, and the Cape Folded Mountains to the north.

One of the region's greatest attractions is its fynbos. 'Fynbos' is the collective term for the area's richly varied, fine-leaved mountain vegetation – especially striking in spring when masses of ericas create a riot of colour on mountain slopes, while many protea species and bulbs flower in winter.

The southwestern Cape lies at the heart of the Cape Floral Kingdom, which stretches from the Cape Peninsula, northwards, in a 40- to 150-km-wide belt to Nieuwoudtville, and eastwards to Port Elizabeth, with isolated patches occurring as far east as Grahamstown. It contains at least 8,550 species of flowering plant (over 40 per cent of South Africa's plant species), with 1,400 bulb species, more than 500 *Erica* species, some 300 types of protea and a wealth of restios (reeds and rushes). In the Cape Peninsula there are 2,285 plant species, while Table Mountain alone has 1,470 species.

Some 5,800 species are endemic to the region, occurring nowhere else on earth. Sadly, though, more than a third of fynbos species are classified as vulnerable, critically rare or endangered, while 29 have already become extinct.

Although it covers only 0.04 per cent of the earth's land surface, the Cape Floral Kingdom is three times richer than its nearest 'competitor', with more than 1,300 species per 10,000 ha, compared to 420 species for its nearest rival in Central America.

Large trees are largely absent from fynbos, except in relic forest patches in protected kloofs, with tree species such as yellowwood, assegai, red alder, wild peach, hard pear and candlewood.

Along the West Coast, the coastal plains are transformed into a blaze of colour when strandveld flowers burst into bloom in August and September. Especially conspicuous are the yellow, orange, red and white flowers of the gousblom (*Arctotis* and *Gazania*) species, nemesias and vygies. During autumn and winter a variety of bulbs such as gladioli and lachenalia can be seen flowering.

The southwestern Cape's bird checklist includes 380 species, about 100 of which occur regularly in fynbos. Species to look out for are the fynbos specials: the Cape sugarbird, orange-breasted sunbird, Cape rockjumper, Victorin's warbler and Cape siskin.

Langebaan Lagoon is a wetland of international importance, supporting over 37,000 birds (mainly waders) in summer. The off-shore islands are important breeding habitats of African penguin, Cape gannet, Hartlaub's gull and crowned cormorant. Keep an eye out too for African oystercatcher.

Animals you are most likely to see are baboon, grey rhebok, klipspringer and rock dassie. Grysbok favour densely bushed areas at lower elevations, while steenbok inhabit open grassland. Also to be seen are common duiker, while discarded quills often betray the presence of porcupines.

The leopard is the most important predator found in this area, but because of its secretive and nocturnal habits it is seldom encountered. Other predators include black-backed jackal, caracal, Cape clawless otter, the small grey mongoose, and small- and large-spotted genets.

In many conservation areas, large mammals that used to occur in the region, such as bontebok, eland, and Cape mountain zebra, have been reintroduced.

Larger mammals are neither spectacular nor plentiful in this region, but numerous endemic reptiles and amphibians are found here. Many rivers are home to rare and endangered freshwater fish species; the Olifants River system, for example, has eight endemic fish species.

The cliffs of the southwestern Cape coastline are ideal vantage points to look out for the southern right whales that migrate here to calf. They usually make their appearance in June, and start migrating to the Antarctic in November. The coast between Hermanus and De Hoop Nature Reserve offers some of the world's best land-based whale-watching, and there are many other rewarding sites too, such as False Bay, Kleinmond, Witsand, Mossel Bay and Nature's Valley.

The southwestern Cape's spectacular scenery is another drawcard, with attractions such as Table Mountain and Cape Point. The Cape Folded Mountains with their contorted rock strata, deep kloofs, waterfalls and sheer, lichen-encrusted rock faces also provide great scenic beauty, and a dramatic backdrop for a coastline varying from picturesque rocky bays and coves, to long expanses of white sandy beach.

A long-standing favourite of outdoor enthusiasts is the Cedarberg range, with its open-air gallery of rock formations, sculpted by the elements. Delicate rock paintings in many caves and overhangs are a testimony to the Later Stone Age Bushmen who once lived here.

The southwestern Cape enjoys a Mediterranean climate, with cold, wet winters and hot, dry summers. In winter, the high mountain peaks are often covered in snow, causing temperatures to drop to below freezing point, although most of the region does not get this cold. In summer, temperatures are regularly in the high 20s, and often in the 30s. Dense banks of mist, accompanied by strong winds, are common in the high mountains, especially during winter, while the southeasterly wind can reach gale force during summer.

The Little Karoo stretches from Worcester in the west to Uniondale in the east, along a narrow valley, and is bounded to the north by the Witteberg and Swartberg ranges, and in the south by the Langeberg and Outeniqua mountains.

The vegetation of this semi-arid region is characterised by a diversity of hardy, small shrubs, Karoo scrub, bulbs and a great variety of succulents. A visit to the area is especially rewarding between August and October, during many of the plants' peak flowering period.

Bird species include a variety of larks and chats, Karoo korhaan, Layard's titbabbler, Karoo eremomela, Namaqua prinia and chat flycatcher. Among the raptors are the black and booted eagles, black harrier, peregrine falcon and rock kestrel.

Sadly, the vast game herds that once roamed the Little Karoo have long since been exterminated. Animals you may see during a hike include baboon, klipspringer, grey rhebok, steenbok, common duiker, rock dassie, and, if you are very fortunate, leopard. There are, however, many small mammals and other creatures, often overlooked but no less fascinating; for example, the aardwolf, honey badger, Cape clawless otter, small-spotted cat and the African leaf-toed gecko, which is restricted to the northern slopes of the Swartberg Mountains. The Little Karoo's Gamka Mountains are a sanctuary for an isolated population of Cape mountain zebra.

IMPORTANT INFORMATION

• The mountains of the southwestern Cape are notorious for sudden weather changes, especially during winter, when high winds, driving rain, mist and snow can cause life-threatening situations for those who are ill-equipped and poorly prepared.

• Summer weather can also be unpredictable. When the southeaster blows, Table Mountain can be enveloped in its characteristic 'tablecloth' of cloud within an hour or two, and it can snow in the Langeberg in December! So, before setting off, obtain a weather forecast, and, if necessary, cancel your hike.

• Fynbos offers no overhead cover, so wear a wide-brimmed hat and take precautions against the sun. Always carry water, as mountain streams may be dry in summer.

• Fires are a serious threat to fynbos during the dry summer months. Always carry a backpacking stove and take all possible precautions when smoking or making a fire, where it is permitted (see under *Flora and fauna*, p. 27).

• Beware of ticks. Try to remove them immediately, and check your body thoroughly at the end of the day's hike (see *Tickbites*, p. 34).

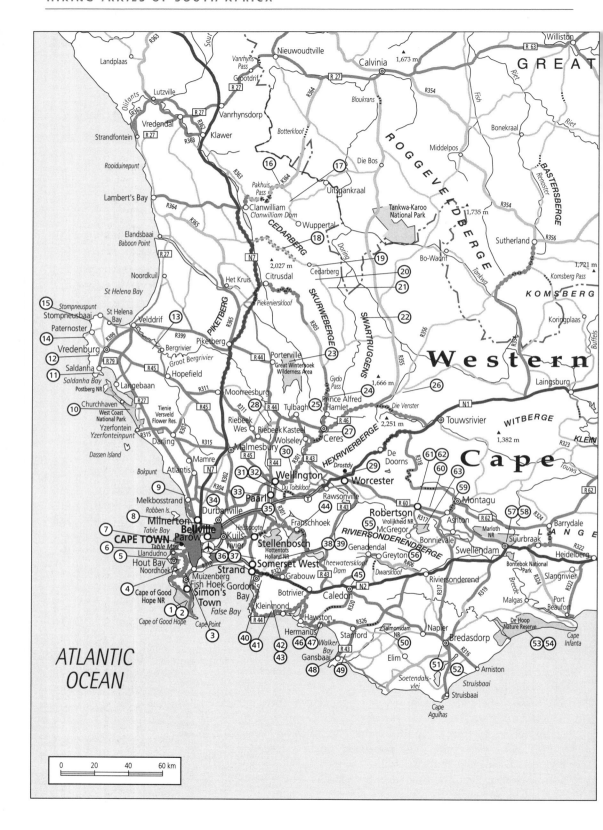

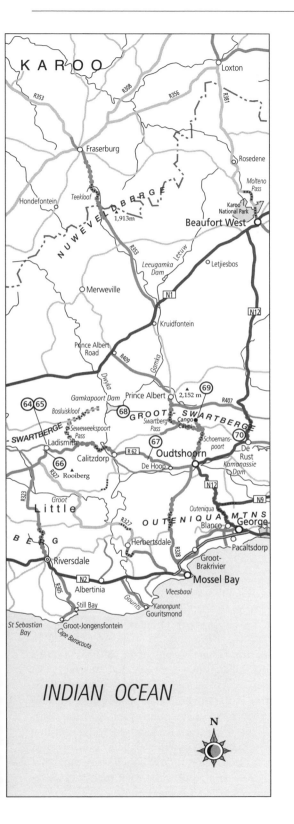

HIKING TRAILS

1 **Cape of Good Hope** p. 40
2 **Cape of Good Hope Hiking Trail** p. 41
3 **Silvermine** p. 41
4 **Elephant's Eye Cave** p. 42
5 **Hout Bay Walks** p. 42
6 **Kirstenbosch National Botanical Garden** p. 43
7 **Table Mountain** p. 43
8 **Tygerberg Nature Reserve** p. 45
9 **Koeberg Nature Reserve** p. 45
10 **West Coast National Park** p. 46
11 **SAS Saldanha Nature Trail** p. 47
12 **Oranjevlei Holiday Farm** p. 47
13 **Helderwater Trails** p. 47
14 **Tietiesbaai to Swartriet** p. 48
15 **Stompneusbaai to Paternoster** p. 48
16 **Sevilla Rock Art Trail** p. 48
17 **Biedouw** p. 49
18 **Cedarberg Wilderness Area** p. 49
19 **Sanddrif/Dwarsrivier** p. 50
20 **Kromrivier** p. 51
21 **Nuwerust** p. 51
22 **Kagga Kamma Private Game Reserve** p. 52
23 **Groot Winterhoek Wilderness Area** p. 52
24 **Long Acres Hiking Trail** p. 53
25 **Christie Prins Hiking Trails** p. 53
26 **Vaalkloof Hiking Trail** p. 53
27 **Ceres Mountain Fynbos Reserve** p. 54
28 **Silwerfontein Hiking Trail** p. 54
29 **Karoo Desert National Botanical Garden** p. 55
30 **Bains Kloof, Limietberg Nature Reserve** p. 55
31 **Du Toitskloof, Limietberg Nature Reserve** p. 56
32 **Limietberg Hiking Trail** p. 56
33 **Paarl Mountain Nature Reserve** p. 57
34 **Vineyard Trail** p. 57
35 **Jonkershoek Nature Reserve** p. 57
36 **Helderberg Nature Reserve** p. 58
37 **Helderberg Farm Trail** p. 58
38 **Boland Hiking Trail** p. 59
39 **Hottentots Holland Nature Reserve** p. 60
40 **Danie Miller Trail** p. 61
41 **Harold Porter National Botanical Garden** p. 61
42 **Kogelberg Nature Reserve** p. 61
43 **Highlands Hiking Trail** p. 62
44 **Mont Rochelle Nature Reserve** p. 63
45 **Caledon Wildflower Garden** p. 63
46 **Fernkloof Nature Reserve** p. 63
47 **Cliff Path** p. 64
48 **Duiwelsgat Hiking Trail** p. 64
49 **Heidehof Nature Trails** p. 64
50 **Salmonsdam Nature Reserve** p. 73
51 **Heuningberg Nature Reserve** p. 73
52 **De Mond Nature Reserve** p. 74
53 **De Hoop Nature Reserve** p. 74
54 **Whale Trail** p. 75
55 **Genadendal Hiking Trail** p. 76
56 **Boesmanskloof** p. 76
57 **Marloth Nature Reserve** p. 76
58 **Swellendam Hiking Trail** p. 77
59 **Montagu Mountain Nature Reserve** p. 78
60 **Pat Busch Nature Reserve** p. 78
61 **Dassiehoek Hiking Trail** p. 78
62 **Arangieskop Hiking Trail** p. 79
63 **Vrolijkheid Nature Reserve** p. 79
64 **Elandsberg Trail** p. 80
65 **Towersig Trail** p. 80
66 **Klapperbos Trail** p. 80
67 **Oukraal Hiking Trail** p. 81
68 **Gamkaskloof** p. 81
69 **Swartberg Hiking Trail** p. 82
70 **Mons Ruber Trail** p. 82

1. CAPE OF GOOD HOPE
Cape Peninsula National Park

See no. 2 (p. 41) for Cape of Good Hope Hiking Trail.

> **Trails:** 9 trails (the 2 not listed are under 1 hour); 30 min to 5 hours; circular; open-ended and out-and-return.
> **Permits:** Entrance fee. No permit required for walks.
> **Maps:** Pamphlet with sketch maps of walks at information kiosk.
> **Facilities/Activities:** Angling, snorkelling and scuba diving; braai and picnic sites; swimming at Bordjiesrif and Buffels Bay tidal pools; whale viewing sites; Visitors' Centre with information kiosk, restaurant, fast food outlet, curio shop; funicular railway at Cape Point car park.

Established in 1939, as the Cape of Good Hope Nature Reserve, the 7,765-ha reserve now forms one of the focal points of the Cape Peninsula National Park. The 250-m-high cliffs at Cape Point are amongst the highest sea cliffs in the world. From the viewpoint you can enjoy the dramatic vista, and wonder at what Sir Francis Drake described in 1666 as the 'fairest cape and the most stately thing we saw in the whole circumference of the globe'.

The vegetation here is dominated by a wealth of fynbos plants (1,200 species), especially attractive in winter and spring. Mammals to be seen include baboon, bontebok, grey rhebok, red hartebeest springbok, eland, and Cape mountain zebra. Among the approximately 250 bird species are the rare African oystercatcher and fynbos 'specials' such as the orange-breasted sunbird and Cape sugarbird. The Cape Point cliffs are an ideal spot for seeing seabirds.

1. Antoniesgat Trail winds along the False Bay coast, from the turning circle south of Buffels Bay to Antoniesgat, one of several caves eroded into the coastal cliffs by the pounding waves. Along the way, trailists will enjoy magnificent views of False Bay and the Hottentots Holland Mountains, the historic Cape Point lighthouse, and Vasco da Gama Peak. **3.5 km; 1 hour; out-and-return.**

2. Lighthouse Walks There are two walks: one to the old lighthouse that was operational between 1860 and 1919, and the Spine Walk, which leads to several outlook points with dramatic views over False Bay, Cape Point, and the Cape of Good Hope. The Spine Walk is not advisable for those with a fear of heights. Both routes start at the Cape Point car park. **60 min; out-and-return.**

3. Thomas T Tucker Trail is named after the American liberty ship that ran aground here on her maiden voyage, on the night of 28 November 1942. The outward route follows the coastline past the stern and midship sections of the wreck. A short way on are the remains of the coaster *Nolloth*, which ran onto the rocks at Duikerklip, on the night of 10 April 1965. From here you can either retrace your steps or return along the escarpment, which will add another 1.8 km to the distance. **5.2 km; 1.5 hours; out-and-return.**

4. Gifkommetjie/Platboom Trail meanders from the Gifkommetjie parking area to the coast and then south along the Atlantic shoreline. Beyond Bloubergstrand, the Cape of Good Hope and the old Cape Point lighthouse come into view. The Island, a reef just offshore of Platboom, is a well-known landmark and extensive kelp beds can be seen off Platboom, where the trail ends. **5 km; 1.5 hours; open-ended.**

5. Kanonkop The route gains height steadily to the old signal cannon after which Kanonkop was named. From this vantage point there are fine views of the Da Gama Monument, Buffels Bay, and Cape Point. Of interest on the return route, an easy descent, is an old kiln used to burn sea shells for lime. **4.8 km; 2 hours; circular.**

6. Phyllisia Circuit owes its name to the 452-tonne fishing trawler that ran aground at Hoek van Bobbejaan, just before midnight on 2 May 1968. Starting at the Gifkommetjie parking area, the outward leg of this circuit winds parallel to the coast, while the return leg meanders along the coastline itself. Close to Gifkommetjie there is an optional shortcut that you can take, which leads through a bushy area and reduces the total trail distance by 1.3 km. **7 km; 2.5 hours; circular.**

7. Sirkelsvlei From the car park at Olifantsbos, this route meanders through fynbos to the eastern shores of Sirkelsvlei. Game is often seen at this natural vlei fed by local seepage. On the return leg, the trail goes through a sandstone rock arch, past the Eye-of-the-Needle rock formation, and along the short Lumbago Alley rock passage. **9.5 km; 3 hours; circular.**

2. CAPE OF GOOD HOPE HIKING TRAIL
Cape Peninsula National Park

See no. 1 (p. 40) for walks.

> *Trail:* 33.8 km; 2 days; circular
> *Permits:* Cape Peninsula National Park, P O Box 37, Constantia 7848, tel: (021) 701 8692, fax: 701 8733.
> *Maps:* Pocket guide of trail with map.
> *Facilities/Activities:* Overnight hut with bunks, mattresses, two-plate gas stove, braai place, solar lighting, shower and toilet.
> *Pertinent information:* Start the first day's hike before 09:00 and collect the hut key from the Access Control Officer.

The first day's hike (23.3 km; 9 hours) starts from the entrance gate to Rooihoogte and then continues around the southern end of Sirkelsvlei, before passing through Blaaubergvlei, which is only open to hikers. From Hoek van Bobbejaan, the coastline is followed closely for 6.7 km to Pegram's Point. From here hikers can either take a shortcut, to reach the hut 19 km from their starting point, or take the longer option (4.5 km longer), which offers some of the best views of the Cape of Good Hope, Cape Point and False Bay along the entire trail.

The second day's hike (10.5 km; 5 hours) meanders along the escarpment above Antoniesgat and Rooikrans to the Homestead, and then ascends to the summit of Kanonkop. Continuing northwards, the trail skirts the base of Paulsberg, then heads along the edge of the escarpment to the Smitswinkel Bay view site, close to the end.

3. SILVERMINE
Cape Peninsula National Park

> *Trails:* 1.5 to 7 hours; network.
> *Permits:* Entrance fee. No permit required.
> *Maps:* Sketch map.
> *Facilities/Activities:* Picnic sites with water, litter bins and toilets.

Covering over 2,400 ha of some of the Cape Peninsula's most spectacular scenery, the Silvermine section of the park extends from the lower slopes of the Kalk Bay and Muizenberg mountains in the east to Noordhoek Peak in the west. The area is dissected by the Ou Kaapseweg.

The vegetation is dominated by fynbos, and among the nearly 900 plant species known to occur here are 15 endemics, including *Mimetes hirtus*. Patches of indigenous forest are found in the Spes Bona and Echo valleys, and along the Silvermine River. Animals to keep an eye out for include grey rhebok, Cape grysbok and baboon.

1. The Amphitheatre Walk, in the Kalk Bay Mountains, east of Ou Kaapseweg, passes through delightful patches of indigenous forests and magnificent mountain scenery. Starting at the Kalk Bay end of Boyes Drive, the route climbs to Weary Willy's and then ascends steadily up Echo Valley to a magnificent patch of indigenous forest. About an hour's walk beyond Weary Willy's, the trail emerges into the Amphitheatre, a small basin bounded by sandstone ridges. Continue across the plateau of Ridge Peak and turn right to descend along Spes Bona Valley with its small indigenous forest. On reaching the gravel road, turn right and make your way back to Boyes Drive. **5 km; 2 hours; circular.**

2. Kalk Bay Mountains This route features some of the most spectacular mountain scenery in the Silvermine area. From the Waterfall parking area, east of Ou Kaapseweg, the route meanders to Junction and Nellie's pools and traverses the twin summits of the Kalk Bay Mountains. It then skirts the head of Spes Bona Valley, and descends to the Amphitheatre. After this it returns to the start along Klein Tuinkloof. **7 km; 3 hours; circular.**

3. Noordhoek Peak, at 754 m the highest point in Silvermine, rewards trailists with spectacular views over Hout Bay and the Sentinel. From the Silvermine Reservoir parking area, west of Ou Kaapseweg, follow a gravel track to the fire lookout. The short detour is worth it for the superb views of Chapman's Peak Mountain. Return to the main track, turn left and continue up until a cairn indicates the turnoff to the summit of Noordhoek Peak, reached after a short climb. From here follow the Panorama Path for about 75 minutes to its junction with a gravel road, which you follow back to the car park. **7 km; 3 hours; circular.**

4. ELEPHANT'S EYE CAVE
SAFCOL (South African Forestry Company Limited) Tokai Plantation

Trail: 6 km; 3–4 hours; out-and-return.
Permits: Self-access permits at the gate of the Tokai Arboretum.
Maps: Sketch map of walk.
Facilities/Activities: Interpretative Centre, toilets, picnic sites, mountain bike trail, horse-riding.
Pertinent information: Don't take shortcuts, but follow the zigzags. Water must be carried.

Established in 1885, Tokai Arboretum is the country's oldest arboretum and amongst its attractions is an experimental stand of American redwoods, planted in 1902. The arboretum, and adjoining pine and eucalyptus plantations, support a variety of birds, especially raptors.

The starting point for this trail is the Interpretative Centre in the Tokai Arboretum. On leaving the arboretum, the route soon rises steadily along a series of zigzags through pine plantations, emerging into fynbos just below the fire lookout point. From here it is a short walk to Elephant's Eye Cave, which is named after the resemblance of the silhouette of Constantia Mountain to the back and head of an elephant, with the cave forming the eye. From the cave you simply backtrack along the outward route.

5. HOUT BAY WALKS
Hout Bay

Trails: Several options; 2 to 5 hours
Permits: Not required at time of writing, but South African National Parks may extend the Go Green Card to areas of the Cape Peninsula National Park where there is no access control at present.
Maps: None. See Shirley Brossy's Walking Guide for the Hout Bay to Simon's Town Mountains.
Facilities/Activities: None.

The tranquil harbour town of Hout Bay and the mountains surrounding it offer a choice of numerous different walks, ranging from a short historical ramble through the town to a full day's hike for the more energetic.

1. Chapman's Peak Nek to Blackburn Ravine Follow the Chapman's Peak route to Chapman's Peak Nek, but, instead of turning right, turn left and follow the contour path below Noordhoek Peak. The trail winds in and out of several ravines and there are expansive views over Hout Bay harbour and the Sentinel. Blackburn Ravine is reached about 40 minutes' walk beyond Chapman's Peak Nek. After a short descent, follow the gravel track to a parking area on Chapman's Peak Drive, close to East Fort. **2.5 hours; open-ended.**

2. Chapman's Peak Towering nearly 600 m above the Atlantic Ocean, with precipitous cliffs dropping down to the sea, Chapman's Peak does not present as daunting a challenge as you might think at first glance. Starting at the viewpoint just before Chapman's Peak Drive, you round the peak after which the drive is named. You will find that the first 30 minutes involve a fairly steep climb along a ravine to Chapman's Peak Nek. From here the path rises gently through stands of proteas, traversing the western slopes of Lower Chapman's Peak, before reaching the summit of Chapman's Peak. The 360 degree view from the top is simply breathtaking. **3.5 hours; out-and-return.**

3. Karbonkelberg and Suther Peak From the end of Bay View Road the trail follows the zigzag gravel road below Kaptein's Peak and Karbonkelberg to the remains of the World War II radar station on Karbonkelberg. As you gain height there are spectacular views of Hout Bay and the Sentinel below, Chapman's Peak at the far side of the bay, the white expanse of Noordhoek Beach, and the Table Mountain chain. A worthwhile 60-minute detour to Suther Peak will be rewarded with breathtaking views of Little Lion's Head and Sandy Bay. **3.5–4 hours; out-and-return.**

6. KIRSTENBOSCH NATIONAL BOTANICAL GARDEN
Cape Peninsula

See no. 7 (this page), Table Mountain.

Trails: 2 trails; 1.5 to 3 hours. Access to popular Table Mountain walks, such as Skeleton Gorge, is also through Kirstenbosch.
Permits: Entrance fee. No permit required.
Maps: Colour map of walks available at Visitors' Centre.
Facilities/Activities: Visitors' Centre with bookshop and toilets; self-service and á la carte restaurants; conservatory; guided walks for groups; Braille Trail and Fragrance Garden for the visually impaired; garden centre; summer concerts; educational centre for school groups.

Set against the backdrop of Castle Rock and Fernwood Buttress, Kirstenbosch ranks among the top botanical gardens in the world. It includes 492 ha of natural fynbos and indigenous forest and 36 ha of cultivated gardens, lawns, pathways, and water features. Nearly 6,000 plant species indigenous to South Africa have been established in the cultivated garden, while some 900 species occur naturally in this region.

1. Yellowwood Trail Except for small patches of fynbos, this trail passes through splendid indigenous forest on the lower slopes of Table Mountain. After a steady climb to the Contour Path the route continues to Skeleton Gorge from where it is a gentle descent along Smuts' Track to the Fragrance Garden, which is also the starting point. **3 km; 1.5 hours; circular.**

2. Silvertree Trail From the Rycroft Gate, the trail ascends to the Contour Path, which you follow past Nursery Ravine and Skeleton Gorge. Beyond Window Stream the path ascends steeply to skirt The Aloes and then descends along the historic Woodcutters' Path (dating back to the 1660s, the era of the Dutch East India Company) to Lubbert's Gift. The route then doubles back, following a path parallel to the Contour Path, but at a lower elevation. The final section makes its way through the protea garden with its abundance of silver trees, a member of the protea family. **7.7 km; 3 hours; circular**

7. TABLE MOUNTAIN
Cape Peninsula National Park

Trails: Network of paths; 3 to 20 km; 1 to 8 hours.
Permits: Not required at time of writing, but South African National Parks might extend the Go Green Card to areas of Table Mountain.
Maps: The map Approved Paths on Table Mountain, published by the Cape Town section of the Mountain Club of South Africa, is indispensable.
Facilities/Activities: Cableway; self-service restaurant, bistro and shop near Upper Cable Station; abseiling; mountain bike trails.
Pertinent information: The mountains of the Western Cape are notorious for rapid and unexpected weather changes. Dense banks of cloud often roll in to form the mountain's characteristic 'tablecloth', reducing visibility severely. Do not set off on unfamiliar paths and never descend the mountain by taking shortcuts.

One of the world's most famous natural landmarks, Table Mountain forms the focal point of the Cape Peninsula National Park, proclaimed in May 1998. Flanked by Lion's Head (669 m) and Devil's Peak (1,001 m), the mountain forms an imposing backdrop to the Mother City.

The Peninsula mountain chain has an incredibly rich diversity of fynbos flora, with some 1,470 species known to occur on Table Mountain alone. Among its floral splendours are the red disa (*Disa uniflora*), drip disa (*Disa longicornis*), silver tree (*Leucadendron argenteum*), proteas, ericas, and fields of watsonias. Patches of indigenous yellowwood, assegai and wild peach forest grow in the eastern valleys and sheltered ravines of the mountain.

Among the small mammals you may see are baboon, rock dassie, common duiker and grysbok. The mountain's birdlife includes the rock kestrel, Cape sugarbird, lesser double-collared and orange-breasted sunbirds, Cape rock thrush and ground woodpecker.

Since a description of every one of the walks on Table Mountain is impossible, only the most popular routes are described below.

Western Aspect

Overlooking Camps Bay, the western side of Table Mountain is dominated by a series of buttresses, known as the Twelve Apostles. Access to the ascents along the western aspect is along the well-known Pipe Track. **4.5 to 9 km; 3.5 hours; out-and-return.**

Kasteelspoort

The start of this popular ascent is reached by following the Pipe Track from Kloof Nek to the signposted turnoff. The path ascends diagonally under Barrier, Valken and Kasteels buttresses, and then climbs steadily up the left side of the ravine before crossing Kasteelspoort River to emerge on the top. From here it is an easy walk to the Woodhead Reservoir. Alternatively, take the path to the Upper Cable Station via the Valley of the Red Gods, Echo Valley, and Fountain Peak. **2.5 hours to top of Kasteelspoort; open-ended.**

Lion's Head

Lion's Head, to the northwest of Table Mountain, is separated from the main table by Kloof Nek and offers a relatively easy ascent with stunning all-round views from its 670-m-high summit.

The route starts about 600 m beyond Kloof Nek, on the Signal Hill road, and initially follows a jeep track before a footpath branches off to the right. The path winds almost around the mountain to the base of the summit cliffs where a ladder provides access to a higher contour path. The final section of the path

follows a narrow ridge with a second ladder, which brings you to the summit. The hike to the summit takes about 1.5 hours, with an altitude gain of nearly 400 m. **Approx. 4,5 km; 2.5 hours; out-and-return.**

The North Face

The North Face of Table Mountain forms an amphitheatre, with dramatic sheer cliffs rising up above the centre of Cape Town.

1. Platteklip Gorge, the oldest recorded route up Table Mountain, was ascended in 1503 by the Portuguese navigator Antonio de Saldanha. The gorge, which separates the western and central tables, provides the most direct ascent up the mountain. However, its steep gradient, stepped rock path, and exposure to the sun, make this an exhausting climb. The gorge is signposted along Table Mountain Road, about 1.5 km beyond the Lower Cable Station. From the top of Platteklip, it is a 15-minute walk to the Upper Cable Station, or a 45-minute walk to the 1,085-m-high Maclear's Beacon, the highest point on Table Mountain. **3 hours; open-ended.**

2. Venster–India is a quick way up or down the mountain, but requires some rock scrambling and should be attempted only by experienced hikers. Follow the path from the Lower Cable Station to the Upper Contour Path, then continue along a well-defined track that skirts Venster Buttress, before making your way diagonally across the upper slopes of India Ravine. Some rock scrambling is necessary to get up the buttress between India Ravine and Africa Ravine, and the path then winds below Arrow Face to Kloof Corner Ridge. From here the top is easily reached along Fountain Ledge, where caution should be exercised, as there are some sheer drops at one or two spots along here. **3–3.5 hours; open-ended.**

Devil's Peak

Devil's Peak lies to the northeast of Table Mountain, separated from it by a saddle.

1. Saddle Path From the parking area, which is about 2.5 km beyond the Lower Cable Station on Tafelberg Road, the path zigzags to the Upper Contour Path from where the Saddle Path ascends to Saddle Rock. The route then continues along a firebreak to the 1,001-m-high summit of Devil's Peak, where you will be rewarded with spectacular all-round views of Cape Town. The total altitude gain over the course of the hike is about 600 m. **4.5 hours; out-and-return.**

2. Devil's Peak Circuit A delightful alternative, this circuit winds from Newlands Forest to the Contour Path, continuing via King's Blockhouse to Mowbray Ridge. From here the Middle Traverse is followed around the northern and western slopes of Devil's Peak, to Saddle Rock and the firebreak, and up to the summit. The return route is via the Saddle and a steep descent down Newlands Ravine. **5–6 hours; circular.**

Eastern Aspect and Constantia Nek

1. Skeleton Gorge is a popular route to the Back Table, as the hike is in the shade of the densely wooded gorge. The path follows Smuts' Track to the Contour Path and then ascends steeply up the left of the ravine. Ladders assist trailists in a few steep, rocky sections. Above this section, the gorge opens out, to emerge on the Back Table. Here, you can either turn right to Maclear's Beacon (70 minutes one way), or left to return via Castle Rock and descend via Nursery Ravine. **3–4 hours; circular via Nursery Ravine.**

2. Constantia Nek to Woodhead Reservoir Also known as the Bridle Path, this is the longest, but easiest, route up Table Mountain. You start the hike at the picnic area opposite the Constantia Nek tea room and, after passing through a gate, turn left, to follow a footpath up the slopes of Constantia Corner and Bel Ombre. After a steady climb, the footpath joins the jeep track at a Z-bend. From here, the trail continues along the jeep track past the De Villiers, Alexandria, and Victoria reservoirs, to reach Woodhead Dam about 8 km from the beginning of the hike. **5 hours; out-and-return.**

8. TYGERBERG NATURE RESERVE
Bellville

Trails: 7.7 km; 6–8 hours; network.
Permits: Obtainable at entrance gate.
Maps: Basic map indicating trails

obtainable from Bellville Municipality, tel: (021) 918 2911.
Facilities/Activities: Picnic sites (no fires); environmental education centre, with book shop and herbarium; educational activities for children.

Set against the western slopes of Tygerberg, this 123-ha nature reserve is an island amidst the urban sprawl of the Cape and Tygerberg metropoles. It is one of the few nature reserves that provides protection to West Coast renosterveld, a vegetation type that has virtually been replaced by agriculture and urban development. Among the 115 bird species recorded are the red-breasted sparrowhawk, rock kestrel, Cape francolin and ground woodpecker.

Uitkyk Walk leads to a vantage point with views of Paarl Mountain, False Bay and Table Bay with Cape Town and Table Mountain beyond.

9. KOEBERG NATURE RESERVE
Melkbosstrand

Trails: 2 trails; 5.7 and 19.3 km; 2 and 6 hours, with shorter options.
Permits: Koeberg Visitor Centre, Private Bag X10, Kernkrag 7440, tel: (021) 553 2466, fax: 553 4171.
Maps: Pocket guide with maps available.
Facilities/Activities: Picnic site; birdhide; lookout point.

Set aside by Eskom to protect the fragile environment of the West Coast, the Koeberg Nature Reserve covers 3,000 ha of strandveld vegetation, dune fields, wetlands, and coastal scenery. It is home to herds of bontebok and springbok, Burchell's zebra, grysbok, steenbok, and common duiker, as well as a variety of smaller mammals such as caracal and genet. With a bird checklist of over 169 species, the reserve offers good birding possibilities. Points of interest along both trails are numbered and explained in the trail brochure.

1. Grysbok Trail traverses the section of the reserve to the southeast and south of the Koeberg nuclear power station. It alternates between dunes, the coastline, milkwood trees and typical strandveld vegetation, which is especially attractive in spring. A viewpoint just off the coast provides an ideal vantage point for southern right whales between May and November. **5.7 km; 2 hours with a 2.5-km option; circular.**

2. Dikkop Trail to the north of the power station winds through strandveld vegetation and restio fields, across dunes and along the beach. A shelter near the half-way mark provides much-appreciated protection against the sun and the wind. Good birding can be enjoyed at the evaporation dams. **19.3 km; 6 hours with 6.5-km and 16.3-km options; circular.**

10. WEST COAST NATIONAL PARK
Saldanha

Trails: 2 hiking trails; 24 and 30 km; 2 days; circular. Day walk; 10 km; 4 hours; circular.
Permits: Geelbek Goldfields Environmental Centre, P O Box 25, Langebaan 7357, tel: (022) 772 2798, fax: 772 2720.
Maps: Sketch maps.
Facilities/Activities: Geelbek: Goldfields environmental education centre, comprising Geelbek homestead and birdhides. Postberg: overnight campsite with braai grids, wood and toilets (no showers); picnic sites.
Pertinent information: Postberg is only open in August and September, and trails in this section must be completed before 16:00, when the gate closes. It is advisable to apply insect repellent to discourage stinging flies, especially during spring and early summer. Ticks are common, so you should always wear long trousers.

The West Coast National Park covers nearly 28,000 ha, incorporating Langebaan Lagoon and the adjoining land to the east, most of the peninsula to the west of the lagoon, 16 Mile Beach and four islands. The lagoon is a wetland of international importance, supporting upwards of 37,000 birds in summer, of which 92 per cent are waders, mainly Palaearctic species. Among the 250 species on the park's bird checklist are flamingo, African marsh harrier, chestnut-banded plover, Cape francolin, and Cape long-billed lark. The vegetation is typical strandveld, characterised by dense low shrubs, succulents, grasses and reeds. Game includes eland, kudu, steenbok, grysbok, and common duiker.

Geelbek
Geelbek, at the southern end of the lagoon, is the site of a beautiful Cape Dutch manor house built in 1860.

Strandveld Educational Trail On this self-guided interpretative route, trailists are introduced to the many fascinating facets of the West Coast – strandveld, dunes and the coast. The first day's route covers 14 km (5 hours), while the second day's hike covers 16 km (5–6 hours), including a pleasant stretch of coastal walking along 16 Mile Beach. Since hikers return to the Geelbek homestead at the end of each day's hike, only a daypack is required. Hikers must report at Geelbek on a Monday or Friday evening. The trail fee is inclusive of all meals. **30 km; 2 days; circular from basecamp.**

Postberg Section
Situated on the peninsula to the west of Langebaan Lagoon, this 1,800-ha section of the park is renowned for its annual spring flower display in August and September. During these months the veld is transformed into a blaze of colour by fields of daisies, geophytes and succulents. Adding to its allure are granite outcrops, the rocky coastline and herds of game.

1. Postberg Hiking Trail The first day's hike (13 km; 6 hours) skirts Konstabelkop and winds along the slopes below Postberg and Lookout, from where there are splendid views over the lagoon. The trail then heads southwest to the overnight stop at Plankiesbaai. On the second day's hike (11 km; 3.5 hours) the rocky coastline gives way to the sandy expanses of 16 Mile Beach, which you follow to the wreck of the *Pantelis A. Lemos*. From here the trail doubles back to the starting point. **24 km; 2 days; circular.**

2. Steenbok Day Walk follows the same route as the Postberg Hiking Trail for 2 km and then deviates to the left, heading for the Vingerklippe – spectacular granite monoliths pointing skywards like fingers. Still further on, the route links up with the overnight trail, which you follow to Plankiesbaai, and then Kreeftebaai. At Tzaarsbank the trail curves back to the start. **10 km; 4 hours; circular**.

11. SAS SALDANHA NATURE TRAIL
Saldanha

> *Trails: 38.6 km; 4 trails; 1 to 5 hours.*
> *Permits: SAS Saldanha, Private Bag X4, Saldanha 7395, tel: (022) 702 3523, fax: 702 3629.*
> *Maps: Colour trail pamphlet indicating walks.*
> *Facilities/Activities: Water and toilets at start of trail.*
> *Pertinent information: Precautions against ticks are advisable. Parking for this trail is only allowed at the North Gate area.*

The rocky headland embracing the northern side of Saldanha Bay has a long military history and has served as a naval training base since 1948. The entire military area of 1,800 ha has been set aside as a nature reserve, and among the game to be seen are springbok, red hartebeest, grey rhebok and ostrich. The trail network takes trailists past World War II military sites, numerous archaeological sites, and many geological features. Hiking is especially rewarding during the spring flower season.

1. Blue Route, the shortest of the four circuits, winds around Malgaskop, the site of the gun batteries of the coastal artillery and the spotlights that lit the bay during World War II. **4 km; 1.5 hours; circular**.

2. Green Route meanders around Malgaskop and Baviaansberg, which can be ascended along a footpath. From the summit there are stunning views of the entrance to Saldanha Bay. The trail then skirts a salt pan as it continues to Long Point before looping back to the start. **9.6 km; 3 hours; circular**.

3. Yellow Route follows the same course as the Red Route, except that it does not go along North Bay and around Môresonkop. **11 km; 4 hours; circular**.

4. Red Route Starting at the Bomsgat, the trail follows the coastline of North Bay and then meanders between Malgaskop and Baviaansberg. It then skirts a salt pan before reaching Long Point. The return leg leads over the summit of Môresonkop back to the end at West Gate. **14 km; 5 hours; circular**.

12. ORANJEVLEI HOLIDAY FARM
Saldanha

> *Trail: 1 trail; 12 km; 4–6 hours.*
> *Permits: Oranjevlei Holiday Farm, P O Box 11, Saldanha 7395, tel. and fax: (022) 714 2261, email: oranje@mweb.co.za*
> *Maps: Rough sketch map.*
> *Facilities/Activities: Guestrooms; tennis; swimming; parasailing; horse-riding; mountain biking.*

Situated on a hill, the historic farm Oranjevlei has a commanding view of Saldanha Bay and its surroundings. The trail leads from the farm complex through wheat lands and then follows a 10-km (4-hour) circular route through natural fynbos vegetation where springbok, common duiker and grysbok can be seen.

13. HELDERWATER TRAILS
Hopefield

> *Trails: 2 trails; 10 and 20 km; 3 and 6 hours.*
> *Permits: Langrietvlei, P O Box 121, Hopefield 7355, tel. and fax: (022) 783 0856.*

Maps: Sketch maps.
Facilities/Activities: Self-catering chalets; braai area on river; canoeing; swimming; water-skiing.
Pertinent information: Middle October to middle May is generally the best time, as the wetlands are difficult to negotiate outside of these months. The summer months can be hot.

Situated along the Lower Berg River, the farm Langrietvlei dates back to 1715. With its tidal, seasonal and permanent pans, river frontage and fynbos vegetation, it offers trailists a diverse hiking experience and excellent birding opportunities.

1. Helderwater Trail mainly follows the Berg River, offering good birding and the chance to see wild pigs in the reeds during the early mornings and late afternoons. Braai facilities are provided at the 9-km mark where a rowing boat can be dropped off for those wishing to explore the river. **10 km; 3 hours; circular.**

2. Langrietvlei Trail meanders along the Berg River and past a tidal pan, which attracts a rich diversity of waterbirds. In the vlei areas, trailists might chance upon wild horses; the descendants of horses used by the British military during the South African War (1899–1902). Up to 2,000 flamingos can be seen at Pink Pan, which normally holds water until January, while the seasonal pans usually begin to dry up from mid-October. **20 km; 6 hours; circular.**

14. TIETIESBAAI TO SWARTRIET
Paternoster

Trails: 17 km; 6 hours; open-ended.
Permits: Saldanha Bay Municipality, Private Bag X12, Vredenburg 7380, tel: (022) 701 7000, fax: 715 1518.
Maps: Sketch map.
Facilities/Activities: Campsite with ablutions in Cape Columbine Nature Reserve.
Pertinent information: Carry water.

Featuring rocky beaches, coastal fynbos, and dunes, this coastal hike is especially worthwhile during the spring flower season. Among the seabirds to look out for are the African black oystercatcher, sanderling, kelp gull, tern, and white-breasted, Cape, bank and crowned cormorants. The rich marine life of the rocky pools and gullies are well worth exploring. The trail ends in the Cape Columbine Nature Reserve.

15. STOMPNEUSBAAI TO PATERNOSTER
Stompneusbaai

Trail: 30 km; 10 hours; open-ended.
Permits: Saldanha Bay Municipality, Private Bag X12, Vredenburg 7380, tel: (022) 701 7000, fax: 715 1518.
Maps: Sketch map.
Facilities/Activities: None.
Pertinent information: An early start is essential. Trailists must carry their own water.

This rather long walk follows the coast from Stompneusbaai past Golden Mile, Britannia Bay and Cape St Martin before skirting the Groot Paternoster Nature Reserve. The landscape along the trail alternates between the rocky coastline, sheltered bays and sweeping white beaches. In spring, the sand plain fynbos adds a blaze of colour to the landscape.

16. SEVILLA ROCK ART TRAIL
Clanwilliam

Trail: 6 km; 4 hours; circular
Permits: Mr H Strauss, P O Box 209, Clanwilliam 8135, tel. and fax: (027) 482 1824.
Maps: Trail pamphlet with descriptions of nine rock art sites; map of marked plants.
Facilities/Activities: Fully equipped self-catering cottages sleeping from five to 10 persons; restaurant serving local dishes for groups.

The outward leg of the trail winds above and below rocky ledges and high cliffs overlooking the bed of the Brandewyn River. There are 10 fascinating rock art sites along the course of the trail, and among the paintings to be seen are quaggas (an extinct species, resembling a zebra), a group of dancing women, yellow elephants, and numerous handprints. From the last rock art site the trail traverses Rooigang and then crosses the Brandewyn River to reach the cottages at Sevilla. A short detour to Milden's Pool, where you can swim, is especially worthwhile on a hot day. The return leg offers a choice of following the road back to Traveller's Rest, or taking the longer, but very rewarding, Sevilla Olive Tree Walk. A map for plants marked along the trail is available.

17. BIEDOUW
Biedouw Valley

Trail: 9.5 km; 3 hours; circular.
Permits: Mr B Lubbe, Mertenhof,
P O Box 220, Clanwilliam 8135,
tel. and fax: (027) 482 2845.
Maps: Sketch map with plant list.
Facilities/Activities: Self-catering cottage for up to 12 people.

Laid out in the Biedouw Valley east of the Cedarberg, this delightful walk allows trailists to discover the fascinating plantlife of the area. Some 51 plant species along the trail have been numbered and a key list, giving the plants' names, is available. Other highlights along the trail include potholes and a waterfall on the Biedouw River, as well as two rock art sites. Especially rewarding in spring.

18. CEDARBERG WILDERNESS AREA
Citrusdal, Clanwilliam

Trails: Over 250 km; 2 to several days; network.
Permits: The Manager, Cedarberg

Wilderness Area, Private Bag X6, Clanwilliam 8135, tel: (027) 482 2812, fax: 482 2406. The wilderness area has been divided into three blocks, and there is a limit of 50 people in each block. Groups are limited to a minimum of three and a maximum of 12. Access to the Maltese Cross and the Wolfberg Cracks is through Dwarsrivier. Permit obtainable from Messrs Nieuwoudt, tel. and fax: (027) 482 2825.
Maps: The 1:50,000 map of the Cedarberg Wilderness Area, published by Cape Nature Conservation (CNC), is indispensable.
Facilities/Activities: The Algeria campsite has ablution blocks and two fully equipped cottages, accommodating five and 10 people respectively. Electricity, bed linen and kitchenware are provided. Basic accommodation without electricity, bed linen or kitchenware is available at Uitkyk (10 people), Waenhuis (six people), and Prik-se-Werf, Peerboom and Sas-se-Werf (five people each). Kliphuis, 20 km east of Clanwilliam, has 10 campsites with ablution blocks. Book through CNC at above address. In the wilderness area there are basic mountain huts, without any facilities, at Boontjieskloof, Middelberg, Crystal Pool, Sneeukop, Sleepad, and Sneeuberg. When not in use by CNC staff, the huts can be used on a first-come-first-served basis.
Pertinent information: Fires are not allowed in the wilderness area. A close-cell ground pad, good sleeping bag and warm clothing are essential, especially between May and September, when snow can occur.

Extending from the Middelberg Pass at Citrusdal, northwards, to beyond the Pakhuis Pass, the Cedarberg Wilderness Area covers 71,000 ha of spectacular mountainscapes. Over countless aeons the combined forces of nature have eroded the sandstone rock into fascinating natural sculptures. Well-known features include the 15-m-high Wolfberg Arch, the Wolfberg Cracks, a narrow cleft reaching 30 m into the bowels of the Wolfberg, and the Maltese Cross, which stands 20 m high.

The vegetation is characterised by fynbos, with relic forest patches in sheltered kloofs. Endemic to the Cedarberg, the Clanwilliam cedar (*Widdringtonia cedarbergensis*) grows amongst the rocks and crags at altitudes of over 1,000 m above sea level. Following a devastating fire in 1989, a cedar reserve was set aside as part of a cedar restoration programme, initiated by Cape Nature Conservation, to ensure the survival of the cedar.

Another Cedarberg endemic, the beautiful snow protea (*Protea cryophila*), grows only above the snowline. It occurs in very few places, among them Sneeuberg and Tafelberg. The northern Cedarberg is the habitat of yet another endemic member of the protea family, the rocket pincushion (*Leucospermum reflexum*).

Mammals include baboon, rock dassie, spectacled dormouse (or namtap), grey rhebok, grysbok and common duiker. The Cedarberg is an important refuge for leopard, and in 1988 a leopard conservation area was established in conjunction with private landowners. Tracks are often seen in the footpaths, but owing to their nocturnal habits leopards are seldom encountered.

Among the 200-odd bird species to be seen are the Cape rockjumper, Cape sugarbird, orange-breasted sunbird, protea canary, Victorin's warbler, Cape siskin and black eagle.

1. Block A covers the northern Cedarberg and includes Pakhuis, the Krakadouw range and Skerpioenberg. Although not as popular as the central and southern zones, the rugged scenery of the Krakadouws makes this an extremely worthwhile area to explore. From Kliphuis a footpath descends along Amon se Kloof to the Jan Dissels River Valley, where a cave near a South African War (1899–1902) blockhouse serves as an overnight stop. From here a footpath ascends along Krakadouw Poort to Heuningvlei. The third day's hike is an easy stroll along a jeep track, back to Pakhuis Pass. **40 km; 3 days; circular.**

2. Block B extends from Skerpioensberg, southwards, to the Wolfberg. A popular two-day hike is the Crystal Pool circuit. From Algeria a footpath ascends steadily along Helsekloof, past a beautiful waterfall, to Middelberg. Continuing from here, you come to the well-known landmark of Cathedral Rocks, with their crenellated spires, before crossing the Grootlandsvlakte. After following Wildehoutdrif the path ascends steeply up Groot Hartseer before reaching Crystal Pool. On the second day the route ascends along Engelsmanskloof to the jeep track, which is followed to Sleepad Hut. After descending to Grootlandsvlakte, you backtrack along the outward route. Other well-known destinations in Block B include Welbedacht Cave, Tafelberg, Wolfberg Arch via Gabriël's Pass, and Wolfberg Cracks (see below). **26 km; 2 days; circular.**

3. Block C covers the western and southern part of the wilderness area, as well as the southwestern end. The most direct access to the Maltese Cross is through Dwarsrivier Farm (see below). The 2,027-m-high Sneeuberg, the highest point in the Cedarberg, forms an impressive backdrop, and, as the name 'Snow Mountain' suggests, is often covered in snow during winter. Also of interest is Duiwelsgat, a remote valley passed when hiking from Sneeuberg Hut to Cedarberg Pass via Noordpoort. **12 km; 5 hours; open-ended.**

19. SANDDRIF/DWARSRIVIER
Cedarberg, Citrusdal

Trails: 4 trails; 35 min to 3 hours.
Permits: Nieuwoudt Bros,
P O Box 84, Clanwilliam 8135,
tel. and fax: (027) 482 2825,
email: sandrif@mweb.co.za
Maps: Included on 1:50,000 Cedarberg
topographical map.
Facilities/Activities: Self-catering chalets
and campsite at Sanddrif; mountain bike
trails; observatory; wine-tasting.

Overlooked by the Wolfberg to the east and Sneeuberg to the west, the Dwarsrivier Valley is a great attraction for outdoor enthusiasts keen to explore the Cedarberg's best-known landmarks, such as the Wolfberg Cracks and Arch, and the Maltese Cross.

1. Wolfberg Cracks and Arch Sanddrif is an ideal base for a hike to the Wolfberg Cracks, which dominate the skyline north of the farm and the Wolfberg Arch. From the start it is a steep climb to the spectacular third crack, which ranges in height and width from a tight squeeze to several metres. Of special interest are two enormous rock arches, spanning 29 m and 20 m respectively. A short way on, you have to clamber to a higher level and then squeeze underneath a huge boulder. On emerging from the Cracks, it is an easy walk of about 90 minutes to the Wolfberg Arch. To return, either backtrack or descend along Gabriël's Pass and follow the jeep track back. **13 km; 7 hours; out-and-return, or 16 km; 7–8 hours; circular.**

2. Maltese Cross From the parking area, about 7 km from Dwarsrivier, a footpath and cairns point the way to the well-known Maltese Cross. The path ascends steadily, and you will reach the formation after a 90-minute walk. **7 km; 3.5–4 hours; out-and-return.**

20. KROMRIVIER
Cedarberg, Citrusdal

Trails: 6 trails; 90 min to 8 hours.
Permits: Cedarberg Tourist Park,
P O Box 284, Clanwilliam 8135,
tel. and fax: (027) 482 2807,
email: namapip@netactive.co.za
Maps: Included on 1:50,000 Cedarberg topographical map.
Facilities/Activities: Self-catering cottages; campsites; mountain biking; rock climbing; 4x4 route; horse-riding.

Kromrivier Farm and the Cedarberg Tourist Park are long-standing favourites with many outdoor enthusiasts. Adjoining the Cedarberg Wilderness Area and Breekkrans, a property of the Mountain Club of South Africa, Kromrivier is also conveniently close to the Stadsaal Caves.

1. Disa Pool is a fairly easy ascent along the Kromrivier, passing Kromrivier Cave and a waterfall before reaching Disa Pool, where clumps of *Disa tripetaloides* can be seen flowering in profusion between December and February. **3–4 hours; out-and-return.**

2. Maltese Cross The outward leg traverses the slopes below Dwarsrivierberg and Sugarloaf Peak, and then

curves around the northern slopes of The Pup to reach the Maltese Cross, which lies a short way further on. The return leg heads over Kokspoort and then ascends along the Kromrivier, passing Disa Pool and the Kromrivier Cave on the way. **7–8 hours; circular.**

The four other options include an easy ramble from the top of Kromrivier Pass to the Stadsaal Caves and **Truitjieskraal** (3 hours), **Witkleigat** (2–3 hours), and **Apollo Cave and Lunar Tunnel** (7–8 hours).

21. NUWERUST
Cedarberg, Citrusdal

Trail: 3 trails; 2 to 7 hours.
Permits: Nuwerust Restcamp,
Post Office Cedarberg 8136,
tel. and fax: (027) 482 2813.
Maps: Brochure of walks with map.
Facilities/Activities: Self-catering cottages.

Nuwerust, in the southeastern Cedarberg, nestles amidst beautiful surroundings dominated by the deep, narrow kloof of the Brandkraals River and sheer orange sandstone cliffs. Situated on the western edge of the Little Karoo, the vegetation is typically renosterveld, with a variety of geophytes, succulents and scrub, as well as fynbos. Game include grey rhebok, grysbok, klipspringer and the elusive leopard.

1. Waterfall Route ascends gently along the lower slopes of Klipbokkop to a waterfall in the Klipbokkop River and then loops back. Along the way there are fine views of the Brandkraals River valley. **6 km; 2 hours; circular.**

2. Rooiberg Trail begins with a steep ascent to the Rooiberg Plateau, north of the Brandkraals River. From the plateau there are spectacular views of the Swartruggens to the east, and the Breekkrans Mountains to the west. The trail then winds down to the deep kloof of the Brandkraals River, which you follow for 3 km to the restcamp. **12 km; 4.5 hours; circular.**

3. Klipbokkop Trail gains over 700 m in altitude to the peak, Klipbokkop, after which the mountain is named (*klipbok* is a colloquial Afrikaans name for the klipspringer). The final ascent involves some rock scrambling, but the stunning views make the climb worthwhile. The first and last sections of the trail follow the Waterfall Route. **15 km; 7 hours; circular.**

22. KAGGA KAMMA PRIVATE GAME RESERVE
Northeast of Ceres

> *Trails:* 2 self-guided trails; 1 and 2 hours. Guided walks can be arranged.
> *Permits:* Kagga Kamma Private Game Reserve, L'Ideal Estate, Paarl 7646, tel: (021) 872 4343, fax: 872 4524, email: info@kaggakamma.co.za
> *Map:* Not available.
> *Facilities/Activities:* Luxury huts and 'caves'; restaurant; swimming pool; Bushmen cultural tours; sundowner, night- and game-drives.

Situated high up in the Swartruggens range, separating the Karoo from the Koue Bokkeveld, Kagga Kamma lies amidst rugged, but spectacular, scenery. Weirdly shaped sandstone formations, rock arches and crags form an awesome backdrop to a landscape of valleys, mountains and canyons. Other highlights include rock painting sites dating back as far as 6,000 years. There is now a community of Khomani Bushmen on the farm, resettled here in 1990. The black eagle, rock kestrel, double-banded courser, southern black korhaan and gymnogene are among the nearly 245 bird species recorded in this area to date. Game to be seen include springbok, gemsbok, bontebok, eland and grey rhebok.

Self-guided Trails The two self-guided trails in Kagga Kamma Private Game Reserve meander amongst a number of spectacular rock formations, and to several, fascinating rock painting sites. Alternatively, an interpretative walk, which is guided either by an expert on rock paintings or by Bushmen trackers, can be arranged.

23. GROOT WINTERHOEK WILDERNESS AREA
Porterville

> *Trails:* 90 km; 2 or more days; network.
> *Permits:* The Manager, Cape Nature Conservation, West Coast Region, P O Box 26, Porterville 6810, tel: (022) 931 2900, fax: 931 2913. Sneeugat: Mr Franz Zeeman, tel: (023) 230 0729. De Hoek: Mr Flip Langenhoven, tel: (023) 240 0339.
> *Maps:* Reserve pamphlet with trails indicated.
> *Facilities/Activities:* Basic overnight huts (no facilities) at Groot Winterhoek and De Tronk; basic shelters at Perdevlei.
> *Pertinent information:* No fires allowed except at overnight huts at De Tronk. After heavy rains, the Groot Kliphuis River and other streams can be difficult to cross. Only six people per day admitted on the Die Hel to De Hoek route, which is closed during harvest season (1 December to 30 April).

Proclaimed in 1985, the Groot Winterhoek Wilderness Area covers 19,200 ha of wild countryside and rugged mountains, dominated by the 2,077-m-high Groot Winterhoek peak. Among the profusion of fynbos plants are many proteas, including some exceptionally large waboom (*Protea nitida*), bearded protea (*Protea magnifica*) and *Protea recondita*. There is also a rich diversity of ericas, which are especially attractive in summer. Unlikely to escape attention in January and February is the abundance of red disas (*Disa uniflora*) gracing the stream and riverbanks. Other highlights include inviting mountain pools and interesting rock formations.

1. De Tronk One of the highlights of Groot Winterhoek is the deep gorge carved by the Vier-en-Twintig Riviere, which plunges over a waterfall into a magnificent pool at Die Hel. From the parking area to the overnight stop at De Tronk (13 km; 3 hours) you will follow the course of the Groot Kliphuis River. The hike to Die Hel is 10 km out-and-return. A few rock paintings can be seen in an overhang on the way into Die Hel. **36 km; 2 days; out-and-return.**

2. Perdevlei–De Tronk Circuit A longer circuit leads from the parking area to Groot Kliphuis (16 km; 5 hours), and then to Perdevlei (7 km; 2 hours). From Perdevlei it is a 12-km; 4-hour hike to De Tronk, and a 10-km; 3-hour walk to Die Hel and back. The 13-km return leg along the Kliphuis River to the parking area takes about 4 hours. **58 km; 3 or 4 days; circular**.

Other options include a demanding two-day kloofing trip from Die Hel to De Hoek, and a 14-km out-and-return hike from the farm Rooiland to the Sneeugat River. For both these hikes permission must be obtained from the landowners (see 'Permits', above).

24. LONG ACRES HIKING TRAIL
Prince Alfred Hamlet

Trails: 3 trails; 2.5 hours to 2 days.
Permits: Long Acres, P O Box 182,
Prince Alfred Hamlet 6840,
tel: (023) 313 3367, fax: 313 3684,
email: longacres@lando.co.za
Maps: Sketch map.
Facilities/Activities: Guesthouse; campsites.

The network of trails on Long Acres Farm, north of Prince Alfred Hamlet, passes spectacular rock formations, natural pools and along a deep cleft. Another highlight is a waterfall and, from the top of Gydoberg, Table Mountain can be seen on a clear day.

Three options are available:

1. Route One is a pleasant, easy walk from the guesthouse past fascinating rock formations. **7 km; 2.5 hours; circular.**

2. Route Two passes through fields of proteas, ascending gradually to a waterfall in a kloof. **12 km; 4 hours; out-and-return.**

3. Route Three ascends gradually from the waterfall to the overnight camp. On the second day it leads

through an impressive rock cleft and climbs to two viewpoints on the edge of Gydoberg before descending the mountain slopes. **24 km; 2 days; circular.**

25. CHRISTIE PRINS HIKING TRAILS
Prince Alfred Hamlet

Trails: 2 trails; 2 to 4 hours.
Permits: F D Conradie Primary School,
P O Box 31, Prince Alfred Hamlet 6840,
tel: (023) 313 3407, fax: 313 3054,
email: admin@fdconradie.wcape.school.za
Maps: Sketch map.
Facilities/Activities: None.

The trail, through fynbos on the eastern slopes of Skurweberg, offers great views of this mountain, and also Witsenberg to the southwest. Black eagles can sometimes be seen, as well as Cape sugarbirds and sunbirds. Klipspringer and baboon are also found here.

1. Short loop is an easy ramble with several stream crossings and viewpoints overlooking a waterfall. **5 km; 2 hours; circular.**

2. Long loop initially follows the short loop route, before ascending steeply for about 1 km and continuing through mountain fynbos to a swimming pool. It then descends steeply to the old Gydo Pass, taking a gravel road back to the start. **3–4 hours; circular.**

26. VAALKLOOF HIKING TRAIL
Northwest of Ceres

Trail: 21.5 km; 2 or 3 days; circular.
Permits: Vaalkloof Nature Reserve, P O Box
744, Ceres 6835, tel: (023) 316 1690,
email: info@naturereserve.co.za
Maps: Trail indicated on photocopy of
1:50,000 topographical map.
Facilities/Activities: Overnight huts with
mattresses, shower, toilet, firewood and
braai utensils; mountain bike trails; 40-km

4x4 trail; guided tours to rock paintings.
Pertinent information: *Although essentially a two-day trail, the hike can be extended to three days by using Fountain Hut, 8 km from the start, as the first overnight stop.*

This trail traverses the rugged landscape of the Ceres-Karoo in the transition zone between the Fynbos and Karoo biomes. As a result, the vegetation ranges from mountain fynbos and renosterveld, to a rich diversity of Karoo succulents. Covering 5,520 ha, Vaalkloof is the largest Natural Heritage Site in the Western Cape. Game to be seen includes gemsbok, springbok, eland, grey rhebok, klipspringer and steenbok. Also to be seen are the tent tortoise and several other reptile species.

The first day's hike (13 km; 7 hours) ascends to the plateau of the Bontberg and then continues to Kerneelskloof, where there is a freshwater spring. The route meanders past interesting rock formations, along narrow passages and down wooden ladders, to Suicide Kloof and the overnight hut at the foot of Kerneelskloof. The second day's hike (8 km; 4 hours) ascends the mountain along Tierkloof, with its sheer cliffs, rewarding trailists with beautiful views. The route descends along Vaalkloof back to the start.

27. CERES MOUNTAIN FYNBOS RESERVE
Ceres

Trail: 3 hours; circular.
Permits: Witzenberg Municipality, P O Box 44, Ceres 6835, tel: (023) 316 1882, fax: 312 2070.
Maps: Rough sketch map.
Facilities/Activities: Pine Forest Resort at start. Restaurant/tea room at toll house.

Toll House Walk offers an easy ramble through part of the 6,800-ha Ceres Mountain Fynbos Reserve. From the Pine Forest Holiday Resort the trail winds down the Skurweberge's fynbos-covered slopes to the historic tollhouse, alongside Michell's Pass. Part of the route follows the original wagon route, in use

from 1765 until the completion of Michell's Pass in 1848. Along the railway line section of the return route there are lovely views of the Dwars River.

28. SILWERFONTEIN HIKING TRAIL
Gouda

Trail: 15 km; 7-hours or 2-day hike; circular
Permits: Silwerfontein Guest Farm, P O Box 235, Tulbagh 6820, tel: (023) 232 0531, email: bernd@silwerfontein.co.za
Maps: Sketch map.
Facilities/Activities: Self-contained guest cottage (sleeps two); converted double-decker bus (sleeps 10) with shower, toilet and boma, with braai facilities, at start; Ontong overnight cave (no facilities); swimming; windsurfing; angling; mountain biking.
Pertinent information: Open fires are strictly prohibited.

Situated in the mountains above Voëlvlei Dam, the 1,000-ha Silwerfontein Farm has been declared a Natural Heritage Site and has 35 species of the *Protea* family (10 per cent of the total number of *Proteaceae* species in South Africa). Among these are seven red data species, including the only remaining population of 27 plants of *Sorocephalus imbricatus*. Silwerfontein, a member of the 200-km² Voëlvlei Nature Conservancy, is also a sanctuary to 10 per cent of the world's geometric tortoise population. Among the 203 bird species recorded here are blue crane and African fish eagle. Animals you might chance upon include gemsbok, grey rhebok, klipspringer, grysbok, and leopard.

The first day of the Silwerfontein Hiking Trail (6 km; 4 hours) leads through eucalyptus and pine plantations, before climbing up through the fynbos on the slopes of the Voëlvlei Mountains to a saddle. The trail then ascends to the cave below the 815-m-high Ontongskop; a total gain of nearly 700 m in altitude from the start. The second day's hike (9 km; 3 hours) makes its way to Beacon Peak (634 m) and on to Corner Peak (622 m), then follows a kloof to a contour path that takes you back to the start of the trail. On both days trailists can enjoy great views over Voëlvlei Dam and the surrounding winelands.

29. KAROO DESERT NATIONAL BOTANICAL GARDEN
Worcester

Trails: 7 km; 3 hours; network.
Permits: Entrance fee. No permit required.
Maps: Brochure of garden available.
Facilities/Activities: Book shop; toilets; guided walks (on request); plant sales.

Set against the Brandwag Mountains near Worcester, the Karoo Desert National Botanical Garden is the only true succulent garden in the southern hemisphere and on the African continent. The garden covers 144 ha of natural vegetation (protected as a flora reserve), and 11 ha are under cultivation. It lies at the heart of the succulent Karoo biome and, as well as the 400 plant species that occur here naturally, some 6,000 species, including 300 rare and endangered species, have been established. The cultivated section features group plantings of related species and gardens reflecting the flora from different regions, such as the Richtersveld, the Worcester-Robertson Karoo, Knersvlakte and Namibia. The succulents are most impressive between April and October, while *vygies* provide a blaze of colour from mid-July to mid-October.

Several short trails traverse the lower reaches of the garden, including the 450-m-long **Karoo Adventure Trail**, which displays some typical Karoo vegetation, the **Braille Trail** of just under 1 km, and the **Shale Trail**, which meanders for 1.7 km among the shale koppies. Longer trails, ranging from 4 to 7 km, traverse the natural northern section of the garden.

30. BAINS KLOOF, LIMIETBERG NATURE RESERVE
Wellington

See no. 31 (p. 56) for walks and no. 33 (p. 56) for hiking trail.

Trails: 4 trails; 2 to 6 hours.
Permits: Southwest Regional Office, Cape Nature Conservation,

*Private Bag X7, Bellville 7535,
tel: (021) 945 4570, fax: 945 3456,
email: swinfo@cncjnk.wcape.gov.za
Maps: Trail pamphlet with basic maps.
Facilities/Activities: Campsite and picnic site at Tweede Tol.*

The Limietberg Nature Reserve stretches over 117,000 ha of mountain slopes, cliff faces and wild river valleys, from the Jonkershoek Mountain in the south, to the Groot-Drakenstein Mountains in the east, and Voëlvlei Mountains in the north. The vegetation is predominantly mountain fynbos, with a profusion of ericas, proteas and restios. Animals to be seen include klipspringer, grey rhebok, baboon, and dassie, and there are also leopard in the reserve.

1. Murasie Trail Starting at Eerste Tol, this trail follows a jeep track past a memorial to a student and three would-be rescuers who drowned in 1895 during an outing of the Huguenot College in Wellington. They died during an attempt to get a marooned student across the flooding river. The trail ends at the ruins of Hugo's Rest, a house seemingly surrounded by ill fortune. Hugo died before the house was completed and in 1949 it was burnt down by a veld fire. After a hiking couple was brutally murdered in the house by an escaped convict in 1978, the ruins were demolished. Also of interest is Die Witrivier se Grip, a furrow built by farmers in 1856 to divert water from the Wit River to the Berg River Valley. This trail is an easy walk, ideal for large groups, with some good swimming pools along the way. **6 km; 2 hours; out-and-return.**

2. Bobbejaans River Trail winds from the Eerste Tol parking area down to Wit River. You cross the river, then ascend briefly and take an easy walk along a contour above the Bobbejaans River. After about 3.5 km you turn off to rock pools in the river. The final 750 m of the trail ascends steeply to the three-tiered Bobbejaans River waterfall. **9 km; 3 hours; out-and-return.**

3. Happy Valley Trail follows the same route as the Murasie Trail to Hugo's Rest. From here, it follows the course of the Wit River, with its natural pools, to Junction Pool, one of the best pools for swimming in the Boland Mountains. **9 km; 4 hours; out-and-return.**

4. Rockhopper Trail provides a moderate to difficult adventure, where trailists find their own way down the boulder-strewn bed of the Wit River. Starting from Eerste Tol, the trail involves rock-hopping, swimming and walking, and ends at Tweede Tol. Noteworthy among the riverine vegetation is the Breede River yellowwood. **8 km; 6 hours; open-ended.**

31. DU TOITSKLOOF, LIMIETBERG NATURE RESERVE
Paarl

See no. 30 (p. 55) for walks and no. 32 (this page) for overnight trail.

> **Trails:** *4 trails; 2.5 to 3 hours.*
> **Permits:** *Southwest Regional Office,*
> *Cape Nature Conservation,*
> *Private Bag X7, Bellville 7535,*
> *tel: (021) 945 4570, fax: 945 3456,*
> *email: swinfo@cncjnk.wcape.gov.za*
> **Maps:** *Trails pamphlet with basic maps.*
> **Facilities/Activities:** *Fenced parking area*
> *700 m east of the Worcester exit of the*
> *Huguenot Tunnel.*

1. Donkerkloof offers a delightful walk, with several stream crossings and dense indigenous forest, to a small waterfall. The walk is especially rewarding in mid-summer when there is a profusion of flowering red disas (*Disa uniflora*). The stony terrain necessitates good walking shoes. The trail starts at the well-known hairpin-bend on the Paarl side of the old Du Toitskloof Pass. **6 km; 2.5 hours; out-and-return.**

2. Krom River From the parking area near the Worcester exit of the Huguenot tunnel backtrack for 700 m and turn right. After crossing the Molenaars River, the trail heads upstream for about 10 minutes and then ascends along the right-hand slopes of the Krom River. Just before reaching the first waterfall the path passes through a magnificent patch of indigenous forest. Extreme caution must be exercised when climbing to the second waterfall with its magnificent pool. **7 km; 2.5 hours; out-and-return.**

3. Elands River This hike starts immediately to the south of the Worcester exit of the Huguenot Tunnel. After an initial steep climb, the trail levels off to follow the Elands River, with an occasional climb away from the river. The trail then descends to Fisherman's Cave, where an inviting pool awaits the weary hiker. From here, the path continues for another 500 m along the river course, ending at sheer cliffs. **8 km; 3 hours; out-and-return.**

4. Mias Poort Walk begins with a long and steep ascent (about 2 hours) to the ridge of Huguenot Kop. An easy walk along the ridge is followed by another steep climb to the cross, erected in February 1945 by the Italian prisoners of war who built the Du Toitskloof Pass. The unsurpassed views are, however, ample compensation for all the exertion in getting to the 1,318-m-high summit of Huguenot Kop. The trail head is on the Paarl side of the old Du Toitskloof Pass. **8 km; 3 hours; out-and-return.**

32. LIMIETBERG HIKING TRAIL
Limietberg Nature Reserve, Paarl

See no. 30 (p. 55) and no. 31 (this page) for walks.

> **Trails:** *36 km; 2 days; open-ended.*
> **Permits:** *The Booking Office, Cape Nature*
> *Conservation, Private Bag X7, Bellville 7535,*
> *tel: (021) 945 4570, fax: 945 3456.*
> **Maps:** *Trail indicated on photocopy of*
> *1:50,000 topographical maps 3319 CC*
> *Franschhoek and 3319 CA Bainskloof.*
> **Facilities/Activities:** *Happy Valley: wooden*
> *hut with bunks, mattresses, water and toilets.*
> *Tweede Tol: campsite at the end of the trail.*
> **Pertinent information:** *Fires are not*
> *permitted along the trail. Open-ended*
> *route necessitates two vehicles.*

This popular weekend trail traces its way along the Hawequas and Limiet mountains, which link the Dutoitskloof and Bainskloof passes. From the Limietberg Nature Reserve Centre the first day's leg (19 km; 6 hours) winds steadily uphill to Suurvlakte, before descending gradually to the Wit River. Junction Pool, a long-standing favourite with Cape hikers, invites the weary hiker for a refreshing dip. The remaining 4.5 km follows the Wit River along Paradise Kloof to Limietberg Hut, in Happy Valley. The nearby pool is especially appreciated on a hot day. The second day's hike (17 km; 6 hours) steadily ascends the slopes of the Limietberg, and then goes steeply up the 1,049-m-high Pic Blanc, the highest point along the trail. Along this trail there are panoramic views over the Berg River Valley and Table Mountain, Simonsberg and the Franschhoek Mountains to the south, and Voëlvlei Dam and the Swartland to the north. The final 4 km descends along Wolfkloof.

33. PAARL MOUNTAIN NATURE RESERVE
Paarl

> **Trails:** *1 to 5 hours; network.*
> **Permits:** *Entrance fee. No permit required.*
> **Maps:** *Information brochure and map of reserve.*
> **Facilities/Activities:** *Picnic sites, fireplaces and toilets.*
> **Pertinent information:** *Precautions against ticks are advisable.*

Dominating the landscape to the west of the Berg River is the huge, shiny granite outcrop to which the historic town of Paarl (which means 'pearl') owes its name. Covering an area of 50 km², the mountain has a length of 12 km and a maximum width of up to 5 km. The upper elevations fall within the 1,990-ha Paarl Mountain Nature Reserve, which also incorporates the small Meulwater Wildflower Reserve.

1. Klipkershout Trail in the southern part of the reserve winds through fynbos with a profusion of proteas. Wild olive trees and the klipkershout, or rock candlewood (*Maytenus oleoides*), to which the trail owes its name, are conspicuous among granite outcrops. **4.5 km; 1.5 hours; circular.**

2. Bretagne Rock is the highlight of the reserve for most visitors and offers an easy walk up to its summit. There is a chain to assist you with the final ascent

to the top, from where there are wonderful 360-degree views of the Berg River Valley, Table Mountain and False Bay. There are also several other footpaths and a number of gravel roads that traverse the reserve.

34. VINEYARD TRAIL
Stellenbosch/Kuilsriver

> **Trails:** *4 trails; 4 to 8 hours; network.*
> **Permits:** *Stellenbosch Tourism and Information Bureau, P O Box 368, Stellenbosch 7599, tel: (021) 883 3584, fax: 883 8017, email: eikestad@iafrica.com*
> **Maps:** *Sketch map.*
> **Facilities/Activities:** *None.*

The Vineyard Trail network winds through a patchwork of vineyards, orchards and cultivated lands in the Stellenbosch winelands. The trail surroundings are especially attractive in autumn, when the vegetation turns shades of yellow, orange and burgundy.

Starting on the slopes of the Papegaaiberg, in Stellenbosch, the four options initially follow the same route. The trail ascends steeply, gaining some 200 m in altitude, and then continues to Protea Heights where the **Red Route** (12 km; 4 hours) loops back to the start. Some 2 km on, the **Green Route** (16 km; 5 hours) branches off to follow the Devon Valley Road back to the start. The route now traverses undulating hills and ridges, ascending steadily to the 476-m-high summit of Bottelaryberg, where hikers are rewarded with extensive views. A short way beyond Ribbokkop, where the trail passes through renosterveld, the **Blue Route** (24 km; 8 hours) splits off to return to the start. The **Yellow Route** (24 km; 8 hours) continues for another 10 km to Kuils River.

35. JONKERSHOEK NATURE RESERVE
Stellenbosch

> **Trails:** *4 trails; 2 to 7 hours.*
> **Permits:** *The Manager, Jonkershoek Nature Reserve, Private Bag X1, Uniedal 7612,*

tel: (021) 889 1566, fax: 889 1567.
Maps: *Reserve pamphlet indicating walks.*
Facilities/Activities: *None.*
Pertinent information: *The Jonkershoek Mountains are notorious for sudden weather changes.*

Situated about 9 km from Stellenbosch, the Jonkershoek Valley ranks amongst the most beautiful in South Africa. Enclosed by the spectacular Jonkershoek Twins peaks, the three Ridge Peaks, Guardian Peak, Pic-Sans-Nom, and the Stellenbosch Mountain, the upper Jonkershoek Valley lies within the 8,900-ha Jonkershoek Nature Reserve. The reserve's vegetation is dominated by a rich diversity of fynbos, while riverine forest is typically found in protected kloofs.

1. Swartboskloof–Sosyskloof This easy scenic route ascends along the western slopes of Swartboskloof for about 2 km, passing through a patch of beautiful indigenous forest. It then traverses along a contour to Sosyskloof before winding back to the start. **5.3 km; 2 hours; circular, or 6.9 km; 2.5 hours; circular if longer route to lookout is taken.**

2. Tweede Waterval Walk is an easy ramble along the Eerste River past Eerste Waterval (First Waterfall), followed by a steep climb along a gorge to the foot of Tweede Waterval (Second Waterfall). The dangerous ascent to this waterfall is closed. **6.4 km; 2 hours; out-and-return.**

3. Panorama Circuit From the bridge on the hairpin bend of the Circular Drive, there is a steep climb to a contour path just below Third Ridge and Banghoek peaks. Following the contour path, you reach Bergriviernek, from where there are amazing views of Assegaaiboskloof. The path then winds across the Dwarsberg Plateau, with its marshy areas and streams surrounded by disas, to Kurktrekker, at the head of Swartboskloof. There is a short detour to the summit of Guardian Peak (1,227 m) here, with stunning views of the Cape Peninsula, from Table Mountain to Cape Point, Robben Island, False Bay, Cape Hangklip and the peaks of the Hottentots Holland range. From Kurktrekker the path descends along Swartboskloof past Second and First waterfalls to the starting point. **17 km; 6 hours; circular.**

4. Swartboskloof Route ascends the steep Swartboskloof, gaining over 900 m in altitude over the first 4.5 km, but the panoramic views are ample reward. The route then traverses fairly level terrain to the top of Kurktrekkernek where there is a steep 2.5-km descent to the Waterfall Route. **18 km; 6 hours; circular.**

36. HELDERBERG NATURE RESERVE
Somerset West

Trails: *35 min to 3 hours; network.*
Permits: *Entrance fee. No permit required.*
Maps: *Available in reserve.*
Facilities/Activities: *Information centre, museum, picnic area (no fires), restaurant.*

The Helderberg provides an impressive backdrop to the 245-ha Helderberg Nature Reserve on its lower southern slopes, which are covered in fynbos. It is a very popular birding destination, counting specials, such as the Cape sugarbird, orange-breasted sunbird, Victorin's warbler and protea canary, among its 140 bird species. There is also small game, including grysbok, common duiker and steenbok, which trailists may chance upon.

The reserve is traversed by a network of interlinking footpaths, providing options ranging from a short 35-minute amble in the cultivated section, to longer hikes higher up the mountain slopes. A highlight of the reserve is Disa Gorge, just below the cliffs, with its remnant indigenous forest of red alder and yellowwood trees. Disas can be seen in bloom here in December and January.

37. HELDERBERG FARM TRAIL
Helderberg

Trails: *Up to 6 hours or overnight trail; network.*
Permits: *Entrance fee. No permit required for day walks. For overnight trail, book with Helderberg Farm Trail,*

P O Box 507, Somerset West 7129,
tel. and fax: (021) 855 4308.
Maps: Sketch map.
Facilities/Activities: Huts with beds,
water and toilets at start and on trail;
tea garden; picnic sites.
Pertinent information: Carry water.
No swimming allowed in streams and
pools. Fires are not permitted.

Hugging the western foothills of the Helderberg, the historic Helderberg Farm dates back over three centuries to 1692. The vegetation is typical mountain fynbos, interspersed with patches of rock candlewood, wild peach, wild olive and blossom trees. Close on 100 bird species have been recorded here, and baboon, grysbok and common duiker are among the animals to be seen.

The trail network consists of a number of interlinked colour-coded loops that can either be done individually as day walks, or together as a two-day hiking trail. Highlights include Granny's Forest, with its mixture of indigenous and exotic trees and 17 fern species, and a viewpoint with spectacular views over False Bay to the south, the Stellenbosch winelands to the north, and the Cape Peninsula to the west.

38. BOLAND HIKING TRAIL
Hottentots Holland Nature Reserve

See no. 39 (p. 60) for walks.

Trails: Several options; 2 to 3 days; network.
Permits: The Booking Office,
Cape Nature Conservation,
Private Bag X7, Bellville 7535,
tel: (021) 945 4570, fax: 945 3456.
Maps: Detailed colour trail map.
Facilities/Activities: Information
centre; showers, toilet and parking
at Nuweberg.
Pertinent information: All hiking routes
are closed in June and July owing to
adverse weather conditions.

This network of trails passes through deep valleys, across amber-coloured streams and through the fynbos of the mountain slopes in the Hottentots Holland Nature Reserve. Some 1,300 plant species have been recorded in the 42,000-ha reserve, which is situated at the very heart of the Cape Floral Kingdom. Masses of ericas (there are over 150 species) blanket the slopes during spring and summer, while the proteas can be seen at their best between July and September. Among the conspicuous members of the protea family are the striking silver mimetes (*Mimetes argenteus*) and Stokoe's protea. Birds to keep an eye out for while hiking include the Cape rockjumper, ground woodpecker and black eagle. You might also spot one of the typical fynbos species such as the Victorin's warbler, orange-breasted sunbird, Cape siskin and protea canary.

1. Sphinx Route The first day's hike (11 km; 4 hours) follows the same route as Stokoe's Pass Route for 4 km, and then continues along an easy gradient past the Sphinx, a rock outcrop after which it is named. Further along, the trail follows Palmietpad, which skirts the headwaters of the Palmiet River. The second day's hike (7 km; 2 hours) is a short and relatively easy descent along a jeep track that takes you back to Nuweberg. **18 km; 2 days; circular.**

2. Stokoe's Pass Route Starting at Nuweberg, the first day's hike (17 km; 7 hours) ascends steadily through pine plantations before emerging into the fynbos. Beyond the Keerom River there is a long, but gradual, climb along Stokoe's Pass, which owes its name to Stokoe's proteas. Restricted to the extent of the Hottentots Holland and Kogelberg ranges, this beautiful protea was named after its discoverer, amateur botanist Thomas Stokoe. Beyond the pass the trail levels off, and the last 5 km is an easy descent. The second day's hike (7 km; 2 hours) is an untaxing walk along a jeep track that leads back to Nuweberg. **24 km; 2 days; circular.**

3. Boesmanskloof/Orchard Route From Nuweberg the trail ascends along a jeep track for about 3.5 km before branching off. The crossing of Boegoekloof is followed by a steady climb up Noordekloof to Pofaddernek. From here it is a torturous descent to Boesmanskloof Hut, reached 17 km (7 hours) from the start. The second day's hike is a relatively easy

14-km (5-hour) traverse back to Nuweberg, from where there are wonderful views over the Theewaterskloof Dam, and the apple and pear orchards in the Vyeboom Valley. The only long climb is the one that has to be negotiated after you cross the Riviersonderend. **31 km; 2 days; circular.**

4. Nuweberg Route is a three-day circuit. The first day's hike (11 km; 4 hours) follows the Sphinx Route to Landdroskop. On the second day, hikers follow the Sneeukop Road for just over 3 km and then join up with the Boesmanskloof Trail, reaching the huts 17 km (7 hours) after setting off from Landdroskop. The third day's hike (14 km; 5 hours) makes its way back to Nuweberg along the Orchard Route (see above). **42 km; 3 days; circular.**

Other options include a 29- or 35-km (two-day) open-ended hike from Nuweberg to Landdroskop, and on to Jonkershoek, or a two- or three-day open-ended hike that ends at the Jan Joubertgat Bridge on the Franschhoek Pass. Another option is the 20.5-km Boegoekloof circuit from Nuweberg, which is closed between April and September.

39. HOTTENTOTS HOLLAND NATURE RESERVE
Grabouw

See no. 38 (p. 59) for hiking trails.

Trails: 7 trails; 2 to 8 hours.
Permits: The Booking Office, Cape Nature Conservation, Private Bag X7, Bellville 7535, tel: (021) 945 4570, fax: 945 3456.
Maps: Reserve pamphlet with walks indicated.
Facilities/Activities: Information centre, showers, toilet and parking at Nuweberg.
Pertinent information: Kloofing routes are open from November to April, depending on water levels and weather conditions. Extension of this opening period is under consideration.

There are a number of different starting points for trails in the reserve:

Nuweberg

1. Palmiet Blind Trail, close to Nuweberg, follows an easy and safe route in the environs of the Palmiet River. The route is lined with tree trunks that serve as tapping guides, with guide rails at difficult spots. A change in the gravel surface of the trail indicates points of special interest, marked by interpretative labels in Braille and print. The trail is suitable for visually impaired and disabled people, but not for wheelchairs. **6 km; 2 hours; circular.**

2. Riviersonderend Kloofing Trail The route follows the deep gorge of the Riviersonderend, alternating between rock-hopping and swimming. Two waterfalls (the second one is 7 m high) have to be negotiated along the way. Junction Pool is an ideal lunch stop. **15 km; 6 hours; circular.**

3. Suicide Kloof is definitely not for the faint-hearted, and, although great fun, is very difficult. The route initially follows a deep gorge, which requires several daring jumps over waterfalls (the highest is a 14-m jump), before joining Riviersonderend Kloof at Junction Pool. **17 km; 6 hours; circular.**

4. Boegoekloof Trail From Nuweberg, follow the outward route of the Boesmanskloof Trail, past Eensbedrogenpoel, to Boegoekloof, named for the abundance of buchu growing here. Follow the path to the left, up the kloof to Dwarsberg Pool, not the one that descends to Red Hat Crossing. From here, backtrack to Nuweberg. **24 km; 8 hours; out-and-return.**

5. Groenlandberg Trail ascends, along a jeep track, to a radio mast on the Groenlandberg, south of Nuweberg. There are expansive views over the orchards of the Elgin Valley to the south, and the Theewaterskloof Dam to the north. Among the diversity of *Proteaceae* growing on Groenlandberg are *Mimetes capitatus*, Stokoe's protea (*Protea stokoei*), and blue sugarbush. **22 km; 7 hours; out-and-return.**

Sir Lowry's Pass
The walk starts from the parking area on the Grabouw side of Sir Lowry's Pass.

1. Gantouw Pass is an easy ramble to the very first route across the Hottentots Holland Mountains, originally used by herds of migrating eland. The Khoikhoi name 'Gantouw' translates as 'Eland's' Pass. By 1820 some 2,800 wagons were using the pass annually, and the deep ruts cut into the rock by the wagon wheels can still be seen. Nearby, on Kanonkop, are two signalling cannons, used during the days of the Dutch East India Company to warn of an impending Khoikhoi attack or to signal the arrival of ships. **5 km; 2 hours; out-and-return.**

Houwhoek

1. Houwhoek Trail is a moderate route through fynbos on Houwhoek Mountains' slopes. On the way there are great views over the old pass, the wheat fields of Botrivier and further afield. **8 km; 3 hours; circular.**

40. DANIE MILLER TRAIL
Gordon's Bay

Trail: 4 km; 1.5 hours; out-and-return.
Permits: Not required.
Maps: None.
Facilities/Activities: None.

Starting in Aurora Drive, the trail climbs the slopes of the Hottentots Holland Mountains to the landmark anchor, from where there are great views of Gordon's Bay, and across False Bay to the Cape Peninsula.

41. HAROLD PORTER NATIONAL BOTANICAL GARDEN
Betty's Bay

Trail: 4 trails; 1 to 3 hours.
Permits: Entrance fee. No permit required.
Maps: Map of botanical garden available.
Facilities/Activities: Picnic sites, restaurant.

Set between sea and mountains, the Harold Porter National Botanical Garden lies in the heart of the Cape Floral Kingdom. The garden covers 200 ha of mountain fynbos and forested kloofs, with streams,

two waterfalls and natural rock pools. There is also a small area under cultivation, with collections of various plant families, and ponds and lawns. One of eight national botanical gardens, Harold Porter focuses on the flora of the Western Cape winter rainfall region.

1. Zigzag Walk As the name suggests, this trail zigzags up the mountain slopes, gaining some 200 m in altitude, to Bobbejaankop, from where there are spectacular views of the coast and the rugged mountains. A side branch of the trail leads to Disa Pool, beneath a magnificent waterfall. Red disas cling to the moist cliffs and can be seen flowering in January. **2–3 hours; out-and-return.**

2. Leopard's Gorge features deep pools, waterfalls, and a lovely patch of forest, with assegai, red alder, yellowwood, wild olive and candlewood trees. The ascent of the gorge to the first waterfall is steep, but well worth it. **3 km; 2 hours; out-and-return.**

42. KOGELBERG NATURE RESERVE
Kleinmond

See no. 43 (p. 62) for hiking trail.

Trails: 7 trails; 1 to 8 hours.
Permits: The Booking Office,
Cape Nature Conservation,
Private Bag X7, Bellville 7535,
tel: (021) 945 4570, fax: 945 3456.
Maps: Reserve pamphlet with walks indicated.
Facilities/Activities: Overnight accommodation at Oudebosch, with bunks, mattresses, fridge, two-plate cooker, bath and toilet; whitewater kayaking (1 June to 30 September); mountain biking from Oudebosch office to Stokoe's Bridge and back; swimming; angling at Rooisand (permit required).

Situated in the heart of the Cape Floral Kingdom, an estimated 1,600 plant species (nearly 20 per cent of all fynbos species) occur in the Kogelberg Nature Reserve. The reserve is a sanctuary for some of the finest examples of fynbos and pristine riverine vegetation.

Among the 150 endemic plant species here is the endangered marsh rose (*Orothamnus zeyheri*), while six of the country's 13 *Mimetes* species also occur here. To date, some 176 *Erica* species have been recorded here; more than a quarter of the total number of South African *Erica* species.

The reserve consists of an area of 18,000 ha that forms the core of the Kogelberg Biosphere Reserve, and several smaller fragments. The first official biosphere reserve to be proclaimed in South Africa, its core area is bordered by buffer and transition zones.

There are several starting points for the walks:

Oudebosch

1. Oudebosch–Harold Porter initially follows the same route as the Kogelberg Trail, but crosses into the Harold Porter National Botanical Garden. From the watershed the trail follows a contour path along the western slopes of Leopard's Kloof, before descending along the ZigZag Trail to the cultivated section of the garden. **6 km; 3 hours; open-ended.**

2. Palmiet River Trail ascends the valley of the Palmiet River, along a jeep track, for about 4.5 km, and then follows a footpath along the Palmiet River to Stokoe's Bridge. From the bridge you can double back along the river or follow a parallel jeep track, and then descend along the same route as the return leg of the Kogelberg Trail. **18 km; 8 hours; circular.**

3. Kogelberg Trail begins at the reserve office and follows the slopes above the Oudebos River, past Oudebosch, to Platbos, a patch of relic indigenous forest. From Platbos the route follows the one remaining spoor of a rehabilitated jeep track to Louwsbos, and then continues on a fresh jeep track along the course of the Louws River. The descent follows the outward section of the Palmiet River Trail, on the eastern slopes of Dwarsberg. **24 km; 8 hours; circular.**

Highlands

The starting point, on the eastern boundary of the reserve, is reached via Highlands Road and the SAFCOL Highlands Plantation.

1. Perdeberg Trail From the western boundary of the SAFCOL Highlands Plantation (the area has been rehabilitated to fynbos, in light of the fact that

SAFCOL plantations are being phased out in the Western Cape), the trail initially meanders along a jeep track across the plateau of the Palmiet Mountains. It then follows a footpath along the upper slopes of the Perdeberg, with a short detour to the summit of Perdeberg (654 m) from where there are expansive views over the coast and the scenic Palmiet Valley to the north. The trail then doubles back to rejoin the jeep track. **16 km; 5 hours; out-and-return.**

Kleinmond

1. Three Sisters Walk From the starting point, just beyond Jean's Hill above Kleinmond, the path winds in a clockwise direction along the lower slopes of the Three Sisters before ascending steeply to their 634-m-high summit. From here there are far-reaching views over Kleinmond, Cape Hangklip to the west, and Danger Point to the east. The route then follows a path along the edge of sheer cliffs, and, after skirting around the 479-m-high Sandown Peak, it makes its way along the edge of Perdeberg to Jean's Hill, where it descends steeply to the end. **8 km; 4 hours; circular.**

43. HIGHLANDS HIKING TRAIL
Kogelberg Nature Reserve

See no. 42 (p. 61) for walks.

Trail: *37 km; 2 days; circular.*
Permits: *The Booking Office, Cape Nature Conservation, Private Bag X7, Bellville 7535, tel: (021) 945 4570, fax: 945 3456.*
Maps: *A map and trail description.*
Facilities/Activities: *Overnight hut in Kleinmond Caravan Park, with bunk beds, fireplace and communal ablutions.*
Pertinent information: *Make sure you pack a swimming costume for the Botrivier Lagoon crossing.*

The trail begins on the farm Iona, on the Highlands Road, from where it makes its way through orchards, pine plantations and fynbos, before descending steeply to the Botrivier Lagoon. Depending on the time of year, the crossing can either be ankle deep or waist deep. The trail then follows the sandy coastline to the overnight hut in Kleinmond, reached 21 km (6–7 hours) from the start. On the second day (16 km; 8 hours), the trail skirts the Three Sisters and then ascends steeply up the slopes of the Perdeberg. The last 9 km follows a jeep track back to the start.

44. MONT ROCHELLE NATURE RESERVE
Franschhoek

> **Trails:** *3 trails; 5 and 6 hours.*
> **Permits:** *Mont Rochelle Nature Reserve,*
> *P O Box 61, Franschhoek 7690,*
> *tel. and fax: (021) 876 4792.*
> **Maps:** *Sketch maps.*
> **Facilities/Activities:** *None.*

Situated to the east of historic Franschhoek, Mont Rochelle Nature Reserve covers 1,728 ha of spectacular mountain peaks and wild kloofs, and has a rich diversity of fynbos. The reserve forms part of the Theewaterskloof Conservancy, and game that, historically, occurred in the area is being reintroduced.

1. Cats' Pass Trail Starting just outside Franschhoek, the first 2.5 km of the trail steeply ascends the original Cats' Pass. Built in 1819, it was the first pass over the Franschhoek Mountains, and some 400 m in altitude is gained to the intersection with the modern pass, at the summit of this new pass. There are some lovely views of the patchwork of farms in the Franschhoek Valley. From the summit of the Franschhoek Pass the 8-km descent follows Cats' Pass and then the alternative built by Major Holloway. Historic reminders along the way include Muller's Bridge, Jan Joubertgat Bridge (1825), the Cats' Toll House, and the old outspan, where travellers and oxen used to rest. **10.5 km; 5 hours; open-ended.**

2. Dutoitskop An ascent of Dutoitskop from the reserve office (near the hairpin bend at the summit of the Franschhoek Pass) involves a steady climb along a ridge to the 1,418-m-high Dutoitskop, gaining over 700 m in altitude. From the summit of Dutoitskop there are great views of the Wemmershoek Mountains and Dam to the north, and the Franschhoek Valley to the west. **12 km; 5 hours; out-and-return.**

3. Perdekop From the reserve office (near the hairpin bend at the summit of the Franschhoek Pass) the trail steadily ascends a kloof, to the watershed and the Wemmershoek viewpoint. You follow the watershed to the 1,575-m-high Perdekop, in the northeastern corner of the reserve, but the great views are ample reward for the climb. **15 km; 6 hours; out-and-return.**

45. CALEDON WILDFLOWER GARDEN
Caledon

> **Trail:** *10 km; 3.5–4.5 hours; circular.*
> **Permits:** *Entrance fee. No permit required.*
> **Maps:** *Sketch map.*
> **Facilities/Activities:** *Tea room; public toilets; picnic sites.*

The Caledon Nature Reserve and Wildflower Garden, set against the slopes of Swartberg, was laid out on land granted to the municipality by Queen Victoria, in 1899, for the establishment of a park. The cultivated section of the garden consists of 56 ha of flower beds, lawns, ponds, pathways, and picnic sites, while the natural indigenous vegetation in the remaining 158 ha has been left undisturbed.

From the start, just beyond the tea room, the trail ascends steeply to the crest of the Swartberg. Along this section trailists are rewarded with extensive views of the Overberg. The trail then winds back along Vensterkloof, past Die Venster (The Window), a rock arch overlooking the garden.

46. FERNKLOOF NATURE RESERVE
Hermanus

> **Trails:** *Network; over 50 km;*
> *45 minutes to full day.*
> **Permits:** *Entrance fee. No permit required.*

Maps: Information pamphlet with detailed map of trails.
Facilities/Activities: Visitors' Centre; herbarium; nursery; picnic sites.

Fernkloof Nature Reserve, with deep ravines, streams and cascades, lies at the western end of the Kleinriviers Mountains and covers 1,446 ha. Among the reserve's more than 1,050 plant species are several Kleinriviers Mountains endemics. The flowers are at their best in September and October, but many of the over 40 protea species bloom during winter.

The various trails offer breathtaking views across Walker Bay to the south, and the Hemel-en-Aarde Valley and Kleinmond to the west. An ascent of the 842-m-high Aasvoëlkop, the highest point in Fernkloof Nature Reserve, is well worth the effort for the fine views. Other highlights include the ravine of Fernkloof, Boekenhoutbos with its fine specimens of Cape beech trees, and Cave Falls, named after the waterfall that cascades through the roof of the cave.

47. CLIFF PATH
Hermanus

Trail: 12 km; 4 hours; open-ended.
Permits: Not required.
Maps: Trail pamphlet with map available from Hermanus Tourism Bureau.
Facilities/Activities: Water points; toilets.

This unique coastal trail, lying in a nature reserve, traverses the coves and sandy beaches from the new harbour to the mouth of the Klein River in the east. A variety of vegetation types, ranging from coastal scrub and dune fynbos, to patches of forest, are encountered along the walk, which has over 100 benches set at various scenic vantage points. Hermanus offers some of the best land-based whale-watching in the world, and the Cliff Path is especially popular between June and November. During these months large numbers of tourists flock to the town to view the numerous southern right whales that visit the coast to calf. Of historic interest along the trail is the Old Harbour, with its small museum.

48. DUIWELSGAT HIKING TRAIL
Gansbaai

Trail: 7 km; 3 hours; open-ended.
Permits: Not required.
Maps: Sketch map.
Facilities/Activities: None.

This scenic trail links several historic sites along the coast of Gansbaai. From the municipal campsite the trail goes through Stanford's Cove, used as a harbour to ship farm produce to the Cape in the 1840s. Further along the coast the trail takes you past De Kelders, a cave containing a freshwater swimming pool, created by water seepage, and then Die Stal (The Stable). Horses from the *Birkenhead*, which struck the Danger Point reef in 1852, were said to have swum ashore here. A short way on is Duiwelsgat, the deep hole in the rocks after which the trail is named. The trail ends at Klipgat, a cave that was inhabited by Stone Age people. There are excellent whale-watching opportunities from the cliffs between June and November.

49. HEIDEHOF NATURE TRAILS
Gansbaai

Trails: 3 trails; 1 to 6 km; circular.
Permits: Heidehof Farm, P O Box 654, Gansbaai 7220, tel: (028) 388 0073, fax: 388 0592, email: franays@telkomsa.net
Facilities/Activities: Picnic sites.
Pertinent information: Guided walks are conducted for groups of three to 10 people.

Located about 20 km southeast of Gansbaai, Heidehof Farm covers 180 ha of pristine limestone fynbos vegetation and 20 ha of cultivated fynbos. Among the flora are no fewer than 32 erica species, endemic proteas, six buchu species, and a profusion of reeds and rushes, as well as Heidehof's enormous white milkwoods. Noteworthy birds include the ground woodpecker and Cape rock thrush, and the Cape sugarbird and sunbird are likely to be ticked.

LEFT: *The famous Mr Smith Rock greets hikers just below Kanonkop in the Cape of Good Hope Nature Reserve.*
BELOW: *Hiking at Cape Point you'll encounter sheer cliffs, which are amongst the highest coastal cliffs in the world.*

THIS PAGE: *Hikes through the Cedarberg wilderness take in famous landmarks like Tafelberg and The Spout (above), and pass many of the cedar trees (left) that are endemic to the area. The overnight shelters (below) along the way may be basic, but they're set in spectacular surroundings.*

RIGHT: *The Wolfberg Arch is over 15 m high and 18 m wide, and is one of the great highlights of the Cedarberg.*
BELOW: *This view of the Dwarsrivier Valley and the 20-m-high Maltese Cross makes the demanding hike to the summit of Sneeuberg, the highest peak in the Cedarberg, very worthwhile.*

ABOVE: *De Hoop Nature Reserve offers numerous hikes and walks, as well as a chance to explore the spectacular coastline at Koppie Alleen, an excellent vantage point for whale-watching.*
RIGHT: *Footpaths in the Harold Porter National Botanical Garden, just an hour or so from Cape Town, meander through cultivated areas, as well as natural fynbos and forested kloofs with mountain streams.*

THIS PAGE: The Boland Hiking Trail passes many natural pools (left), which are perfect for a refreshing swim. This hike makes its way through the heart of the Cape Floral Kingdom – look out for the striking red disa (Disa uniflora, above) en route.

THIS PAGE: *It's important for hikers to take precautions against the sun, as there are few trees and little else in the way of overhead cover on the Boland Hiking Trail, which crosses over the Riviersonderend River (below).*

TOP and LEFT: *Hikers on the Swartberg trail, in the southwestern Cape, can enjoy incredible views of the Little Karoo (top), and may come across animals like this stately kudu (left).*

ABOVE: *Goedgeloof Hut is one of two you'll stay in along the Swellendam Hiking Trail, also in the southwestern Cape.*

NEXT PAGE: *The difficult sections of the Harkerville coast hike, on the Garden Route, have chain handholds to assist hikers.*

Guided walks are conducted by the owners, who will share their intimate knowledge with trailists. There is a choice of three trails. The 1-km trail traverses the flatter areas, while the 3-km trail covers the more easily accessible areas of the limestone hills. The 6-km trail traverses the upper reaches of the limestone hills.

50. SALMONSDAM NATURE RESERVE
Stanford

> **Trails:** *3 trails; 45 min to 5 hours.*
> **Permits:** *Entrance fee. No permit required.*
> **Maps:** *Reserve pamphlet with walks indicated.*
> **Facilities/Activities:** *Mountain drive; camping area; basic huts with beds, mattresses, gas stove, fridge, and hot-water ablution facilities – visitors must supply own bedding, cooking and eating utensils.*
> **Pertinent information:** *Fires are only allowed in designated fireplaces.*

Situated right at the foot of the Perdeberg Mountains, about 20 km east of Stanford, the 834-ha Salmonsdam Nature Reserve consists of a central basin with a vlei area, enclosed by a semi-circle of mountains. The vegetation is typical mountain fynbos, with patches of indigenous forest in the kloofs.

Game to be seen in the reserve includes bontebok, grey rhebok, common duiker, klipspringer and baboon. The reserve is also home to over 120 species of bird, amongst which are the Cape rock thrush, mountain chat, Cape rockjumper and Cape sugarbird, as well as several sunbird species.

1. Waterfall Trail is especially rewarding after rain. The trail leads through fynbos to the scenic Zigzag Falls in Watervalkloof, with its indigenous forest of Cape beech and spoonwood trees. The return leg follows an old jeep track. **2 km; 45 min; circular.**

2. Ravine Trail follows the western slopes of Keeromskloof, and then passes through magnificent indigenous forest before crossing the river. Leopard and Elandskrans caves are passed on the return leg, which

traverses the eastern slopes above the kloof. Arch Rock is a familiar landmark. **3 km; 1 hour; circular.**

3. Mountain Trail ascends from the foot of Perdeberg to Ravenshill, from where there are expansive views of Caledon, Bredasdorp and Walker Bay. Landmarks along the return leg, which partly follows Keeromskloof, include the Balancing Rock and Uitsig Rock. **4 km; 1.5 hours; circular.**

51. HEUNINGBERG NATURE RESERVE
Bredasdorp

> **Trails:** *2 trails; 3.5 to 4 hours.*
> **Permits:** *Entrance fee. No permit required.*
> **Maps:** *A pamphlet of the reserve and trails is available.*
> **Facilities/Activities:** *Resting shelters; toilets.*

The nucleus of this reserve on the slopes of Heuningberg, southeast of Bredasdorp, was initially established as a wildflower garden, which was subsequently incorporated into an 800-ha nature reserve. Among the more than 300 plant species growing here are several endemics, including such rarities as the trident pincushion (*Leucospermum heterophyllum*), and the Bredasdorp lily (*Cyrtanthus gutherieae*), which flowers in March and April.

1. Eps Joubert (White) Trail winds through the southern section of the reserve, ascending the slopes of Drinkwaterkloof to the watershed. The trail then meanders above Uitvlugkloof before linking up with the Yellow Route at the 7-km mark. Lot's Wife is a conspicuous rock formation close to the beacon (366 m) on Heuningberg. **10 km; 3.5 hours; circular.**

2. Yellow Route contours around the western and northern slopes of Heuningberg to the Pulpit Rock. From here it is a steady ascent to the plateau, where the route links up with the Eps Joubert Trail, followed by an easy descent. **12 km; 4 hours; circular.**

Both trails offer wonderful views over Bredasdorp and the Ruggens to the north, the Heuningberg range to the west, Struisbaai and the Soetanys Mountains to the south, and Waenhuiskrans and De Hoop Nature Reserve to the east.

52. DE MOND NATURE RESERVE
Bredasdorp

Trail: *7 km; 2 hours; circular.*
Permits: *Entrance fee. No permit required.*
Maps: *Reserve pamphlet with walk indicated.*
Facilities/Activities: *Picnic sites (no fires permitted); freshwater and marine angling (permits required).*
Pertinent information: *Trailists must keep to demarcated path to avoid damage to sensitive vegetation. The reserve is an important breeding habitat for rare bird species; birds should not be disturbed.*

Centred on the Heuningnes River mouth, De Mond Reserve covers 954 ha of shifting and stabilised sand dunes, tidal flats, salt marshes and fynbos vegetation.

The reserve is a very important breeding habitat for South Africa's most endangered coastal bird, the Damara tern. The Caspian tern and rare African black oystercatcher are also found in this reserve.

Sterna Trail Starting at the reserve office, the trail passes through riverine vegetation, as well as dune forest and stabilised dunes, before following the sandy coastline for just over 2 km. After heavy winter storms the wreck of the *Maggie* is visible to the south of the river mouth. The final section of the trail makes its way across tidal flats and skirts the salt marshes.

53. DE HOOP NATURE RESERVE
East of Bredasdorp

See no. 54 (p. 75) for hiking trail.

Trails: *6 trails; 2 to 4 hours.*
Permits: *Entrance fee. No permits required.*
Maps: *Sketch map.*

Facilities/Activities: *Cottages equipped with a stove and fridge, but visitors must provide own bedding, cooking and eating utensils, and food; campsites; picnic site and mountain bike trail. Potberg Environmental Education Centre caters for groups of students.*
Pertinent information: *Water must be carried on all day walks. Trailists can take along snorkelling gear for the Coastal Trail.*

Covering 36,000 ha, De Hoop Nature Reserve is a mosaic of wetland, coastal fynbos, shifting sand dunes, coastal plains and limestone hills. De Hoop Vlei, a wetland of international importance, forms part of the western boundary, while Potberg dominates the scenery in the north.

Of the reserve's more than 1,500 plant species, 50 are endemic to the Bredasdorp, Agulhas and Infanta area, while 12 species are endemic to Potberg. Among these are a small ground protea (*Protea denticulata*) and *Aspalathus potbergensis*.

Mammals to be seen include bontebok, Cape mountain zebra, eland, grey rhebok, grysbok and baboon. There are over 250 species of bird here, including 12 waterfowl species, 13 species of migrant waders, the African fish eagle, secretary bird and African black oystercatcher.

The coast off De Hoop has the highest density of southern right whales along the whole South African coast, and between June and November up to 50 whales can be seen at a time, some as close as 500 m offshore.

Potberg
The 611- m-high Potberg, which lies in the north of the reserve, is of special importance from a conservation point of view. It is not only home to numerous endemic plant species, but its cliffs provide nesting sites for the largest Cape vulture colony in the Western Cape. Although there is no public access to the colony, these magnificent birds are often seen soaring overhead from the Klipspringer Trail.

1. Klipspringer Trail winds along the lower slopes of Potberg, past pools in the Potberg River, and

Black Eagle Cave. Cape vulture are often seen at close range in the mornings as they take off from their roosting and nesting sites in Vulture Kloof. **5 km; 2 hours; circular.**

2. Potberg Trail leads to the summit of Potberg, with panoramic views over the reserve, the Breede River and Witsand. About 400 m in altitude is gained during the course of this trail. **8 km; 3.5 hours; out-and-return.**

De Hoop

Situated on the eastern edge of the vlei, the historic De Hoop homestead is the focal point of the reserve. The Vlei Trail network consists of a 15-km loop, with two shorter options, and offers magnificent views over De Hoop Vlei. The vlei attracts huge numbers of birds, up to 30,000 at one time. Among the species found here are flamingo, waterfowl, waders and African fish eagle.

1. Coot Trail 5 km; 2 hours; circular.

2. Heron Trail 8 km; 3 hours; circular.

3. Grebe Trail 15 km; 4 hours; circular.

De Hoop Coast

De Hoop Nature Reserve is bounded to the south by a spectacular, 45-km-long stretch of coastline, ranging from white sandy beaches, to rocky coves, and sandstone and limestone cliffs, which have been fashioned into fascinating shapes by the wind and waves.

1. Coastal Trail From Klipkoppie in the west to Koppie Alleen in the east, the coastline is characterised by a sweeping sandy beach, backed by shifting sand dunes, reaching up to 90 m above sea level. East of Koppie Alleen, the rocky coast contains small coves and fascinating weathered rock formations, which give way to the kilometre-long expanse of white beach at Potbergstrand. Along the course of the hike there is ample opportunity to explore the marine life in the rock pools. Klipkoppie and Koppie Alleen are excellent whale-watching points. **Klipkoppie to Koppie Alleen: 6.5 m; 2 hours; open-ended. Koppie Alleen eastwards: 9 km; 3 hours; out-and-return.**

54. WHALE TRAIL
De Hoop Nature Reserve

See no. 53 (p. 74) for walks.

> *Trail:* 56.7 km; 5 days; circular.
> *Permits:* De Hoop Nature Reserve, Private Bag X16, Bredasdorp 7280, tel: (028) 542 1126, fax: 542 1247, email: dehoopinfo@sdm.dorea.co.za – minimum of six and maximum of 12 people.
> *Maps:* Trail map.
> *Facilities/Activities:* Cottages with beds, mattresses, kitchen, living room, hot showers, toilets, fireplace, and solar-powered electricity.
> *Pertinent information:* Pack snorkelling gear. Hikers are transported from Koppie Alleen back to Potberg by shuttle bus.

The Whale Trail offers trailists an opportunity to explore the diverse landscapes and major habitats of De Hoop Nature Reserve.

The first day's hike (14.7 km; 8 hours) is the most demanding. The trail climbs to the summit of Potberg and then winds along the slopes above Groenkloof, descending to the Cupidoskraal overnight hut.

On day two (14 km; 8 hours) the trail ascends to the crest of Potberg, gaining some 300 m in altitude. Further along, the trail traverses limestone hills, where you are likely to see many Bredasdorp protea (*Protea obtusifolia*) before descending to Noetzie, a delightful bay along the coast.

Day three's hike (8 km; 6 hours) stretches between Noetzie and Hamerkop, and since only a short distance is covered there is ample time to explore the coastline. Stilgat, a natural tidal pool, offers trailists rewarding snorkelling opportunities, and there are also several whale-watching points.

The fourth day's hike to Vaalkrans (11 km; 7 hours) starts with a long stretch along the beach. Beyond Lekkerwater the coast becomes quite rocky. Highlights of this section include rock pools and calcrete formations, eroded into fascinating shapes.

The final day's hike (9 km; 6 hours) makes its way along the rocky coast past Potberg Beach, a white sandy cove. It then continues along the rocky shore past Whalewatch Point to Koppie Alleen, where the trail ends. Along the way there are once again ample opportunities for snorkelling.

55. GENADENDAL HIKING TRAIL
Genadendal

Trail: 25.3 km; 2 days; circular.
Permits: The Manager, Vrolijkheid Nature Reserve, Private Bag X614, Robertson 6705, tel: (023) 625 1645, fax: 625 1674, email: vrolijkheid@cnc.org.za – groups limited to 14 people; maximum 24 hikers per day.
Maps: Trail pamphlet with map.
Facilities/Activities: Overnight facilities are available at the Moravian Mission Church in Genadendal and also at the overnight stop on the farm Die Hoek.
Pertinent information: Hikers need to carry water, especially on the second day of the hike. Fires are only permitted at Die Hoek.

The trail starts and ends in the historic settlement of Genadendal, which dates back well over 200 years. In 1783, Moravian missionaries established a mission station at the foot of the Riviersonderend Mountains that would later develop into the town of Genadendal. From Genadendal the route traverses the 69,500-ha Riviersonderend Conservation Area, which is surrounded by the towns of Riviersonderend, Villiersdorp, McGregor and Greyton, as well as private land.

The first day's trail (14.3 km; 8 hours) starts with a steep ascent up the eastern slopes of Perdekop, and about 500 m is gained in altitude to Wonderklippe, an ideal rest stop. The trail then continues to Klein Koffiegat and Groot Koffiegat, where there are cool mountain pools, ideal for swimming in on a hot day. From here the trail gradually descends to the overnight hut at Die Hoek. The initial gentle ascent of the second day's hike (11 km; 7 hours) is followed by a long, steady climb to a nek between Arendkop and Uitkykkop, where the weirdly shaped sandstone formations you will see are particularly striking. From here the trail descends along the southern slopes of Uitkykkop.

56. BOESMANSKLOOF
Greyton and McGregor

Trail: 14 km; 1 day; open-ended.
Permits: The Manager, Vrolijkheid Nature Reserve, Private Bag X614, Robertson 6705, tel: (023) 625 1645, fax: 625 1674, email: vrolijkheid@cnc.org.za – there is a limit of 50 hikers per day.
Maps: Trail pamphlet with map.
Facilities/Activities: Private accommodation at Greyton and McGregor, and at Die Galg, where the trail ends.
Pertinent information: Trailists need to make arrangements to drop off a vehicle at the end of the trail. Alternatively, the trail can be done as an out-and-return route.

Covering some 69,000 ha of state and private land, the Riviersonderend Conservation Area is managed as a mountain catchment area. This is an area of mountain peaks, steep cliffs, rugged kloofs and mountain fynbos. Over 50 species of restios are also found here. Of special conservation interest are two endemic *Erica* species: *E. galgebergensis* and *E. parvulisepala*.

This traverse of the Riviersonderend Mountains follows what was once the only direct link between the historic villages of McGregor and Greyton, and can be hiked in either direction. From Greyton the trail gains over 400 m in altitude along a jeep track to a viewpoint below Perdekop. It then descends to Boesmanskloof, where there are a series of pools at Oakes Falls, wonderful for swimming in on a hot summer's day. The trail ends at Die Galg (The Gallows), about 14 km from McGregor.

57. MARLOTH NATURE RESERVE
Swellendam

See no. 58 (p. 77) for hiking trail.

Trails: 3 trails; 1 to 9 hours.
Permits: Entrance fee. No permit required for hike.

Maps: Pamphlet of walks.
Facilities/Activities: Picnic site
at Hermitagekloof.

The Marloth Nature Reserve was named in honour of the renowned amateur botanist Dr Rudolf Marloth, who demarcated an area of 190 ha for a nature reserve in 1928. In 1981 the reserve was enlarged to 11,000 ha. The Langeberg range forms an impressive backdrop to the reserve, which protects a rich diversity of fynbos. Isolated patches of remnant indigenous forest occur on the southern slopes of the mountain.

1. Koloniesbos is a delightful patch of forest consisting of yellowwood, stinkwood, candlewood, Cape beech, red alder, and Cape gardenia. The name Koloniesbos dates back to the 1740s, when the district was known as *De Colonie in de Verre Afgeleegene Contreije* (the colony in the remote regions). This is an easy walk through a delightful forest. **3 km; 1 hour; circular.**

2. Die Plaat After a short uphill walk, the trail follows a contour through fynbos above Duiwelsbos and Koloniesbos, two remnant patches of indigenous forest. At Die Plaat you can either take a shortcut back to the main service road or continue to Doktersbos. **5.5 km; 2 hours; semi-circular.**

3. Tienuurkop to Twaalfuurkop This is a strenuous walk, but it has stunning views. The route gains over 700 m in altitude to Tienuurkop, then winds behind Elfuurkop to the nek between the two peaks. A short detour to the summit of Twaalfuurkop affords great views of the wheat fields of the Overberg and Swellendam far below. The return leg descends Langeberg's southern slopes. **8.5 km; 8–9 hours; semi-circular.**

58. SWELLENDAM HIKING TRAIL
Marloth Nature Reserve

See no 57 (p. 76) for walks.

Trails: 76.8 km (in total); 6 days,
with shorter options; circular.
Permits: The Manager, Marloth Nature

Reserve, P O Box 28, Swellendam 6740,
tel: (028) 514 1410, fax: 514 1488.
Maps: Colour trail map.
Facilities/Activities: Huts at the overnight
stops, with bunk beds, mattresses, basic
toilets and water.
Pertinent information: Fires are only
permitted at Wolfkloof Hut; a back-
packing stove is essential. Hikers are
not permitted on the farm close to
Goedgeloof Hut, or allowed to swim
in the farm dams.

This imposing trail traverses the 11,000-ha Marloth Nature Reserve in the Langeberg range above Swellendam. One of the most outstanding features is the reserve's floral wealth, which changes with the seasons. The trail leads to isolated valleys tucked away in the mountains, across streams and through remnant patches of indigenous forest. Along the way there are panoramic views of the patchwork wheat farms of the Overberg to the south, and the arid plains of the Little Karoo to the north.

The first day's hike (11.8 km; 5 hours) involves a steady ascent to Klipkraal, with an altitude gain of some 800 m. The trail then descends to the overnight hut, which lies at the head of the remote Boskloof.

Day two (10 km; 4 hours) begins with a climb along the Drosterspas to the watershed, with sweeping views of the Little Karoo. A steep descent through fields of yellow conebushes (*Leucadendron*) brings you to the stone huts at Goedgeloof.

The third day's hike (10 km; 4 hours) also starts with a steep ascent, but from Warmwaternek the trail levels out. This section passes above the appropriately named Protea Valley, with its profusion of the plants. Among them are the king protea (*Protea cynaroides*), peach protea (*P. grandiceps*), brown-bearded sugarbush (*P. speciosa*) and the broad-leaved sugarbush.

From Proteavallei Hut there are several options: a shortcut to Wolfkloof via Kruispad (6.2 km), the longer but more spectacular Vensterbank route to Wolfkloof (12.5 km), or the day-long trail to Nooitgedacht (13 km; 6 hours) and on to Wolfkloof (21.3 km; 9 hours) the following day.

On the last day (10.7 km; 4 hours), a steep climb out of Wolfkloof is followed by an easy hike, and the trail then descends into Hermitage Kloof. Before the end, though, there is a final climb out of the kloof.

Kruispad, close to Proteavallei Hut, and the Vensterbank route provide trailists with short cuts back to the forest station.

59. MONTAGU MOUNTAIN NATURE RESERVE
Montagu

> **Trails:** 2 trails; 4 and 5 hours.
> **Permits:** Montagu Tourism Bureau, P O Box 24, Montagu 6720, tel. and fax: (023) 614 2471.
> **Maps:** Sketch map.
> **Facilities/Activities:** Klipspringer Hut (1.3 km from Old Mill starting point), with bunks, mattresses, braai facilities, shower and flush toilet. Dassie Cabin is a 4-bed stone rondavel.

The northern slopes of the Langeberg, west of Montagu, are protected by the 1,200-ha Montagu Mountain Nature Reserve. The vegetation ranges from dry mountain fynbos and succulents on the lower slopes, to more mesic fynbos higher up.

Laid out in a figure eight, the trails can either be hiked as two day-trails or as an overnight trail.

1. Cogmanskloof Trail ascends steadily uphill for the first 2 km and then traverses the slopes above Droogekloof to Cogmanskloof, with its sheer cliffs. Along the way, trailists enjoy expansive views of the lichen-covered cliffs of the Droogekloof and the surrounding mountains. The return leg is a gentle ascent up the slopes above the valley in which Montagu lies. John Montagu, after whom the town is named, was a colonial secretary of the Cape in the 19th century. **12 km; 4 hours; circular.**

2. Bloupunt Trail winds up Rietkloof and then ascends to the summit of Bloupunt. From the 1,266-m-high summit there are spectacular views, with the towns of Montagu, McGregor, Robertson, Ashton and Bonnievale clearly visible. From here the trail traverses De Drie Bergen (The Three Mountains) and then descends along Donkerkloof, with its three small waterfalls. **15.6 km; 5 hours; circular.**

60. PAT BUSCH NATURE RESERVE
Robertson

> **Trails:** Network; 40 km; 30 min to 5 hours.
> **Permits:** Walks only accessible to guests. Book in advance with W D Busch, P O Box 579, Robertson 6705, tel. and fax: (023) 626 2033, email: patbusch@intekom.co.za
> **Maps:** Rough sketch map.
> **Facilities/Activities:** Fully equipped self-catering cottages and houses; trout and bass angling; mountain biking; 4x4 trail; swimming and canoeing in the dam.

Situated on two wine-producing farms, Bergplaas and Berg en Dal, the 2,000-ha Pat Busch Nature Reserve has been set aside to protect the flora and fauna of the Langeberg foothills. The vegetation is mainly mountain fynbos, with a profusion of proteas and ericas, but a variety of indigenous trees grow in the valleys and along the riverbanks. With a bird checklist of some 150 species, birding can be rewarding. Animals to be seen include gemsbok, grey rhebok, grysbok, steenbok, Cape clawless otter and caracal.

A network of trails runs through valleys and beside two streams, with delightful rock pools, in the undulating foothills of the range. By combining several shorter trails, trailists can follow a 12-km, 5-hour circular route, with longer options to the summit of Tafelberg (742 m) and Olifantskop, further afield in the Langeberg.

61. DASSIEHOEK HIKING TRAIL
Dassiehoek Nature Reserve, Robertson

> **Trail:** 38 km; 2 days; circular.
> **Permits:** Mrs Becker, P O Box 24, Montagu 6720, tel: (023) 614 1112, fax: 614 1841.

Maps: Sketch map.
Facilities/Activities: Hut with bunks, mattresses, hot water, braai facilities; picnic areas at Silwerstrand Holiday Resort. Dassiehoek: overnight hut, with beds, mattresses, hot-water showers, and fireplace.
Pertinent information: Precautions advisable against ticks. Water must be carried on the first day.

Laid out on the lower southern slopes of the Langeberg range, the trail initially winds through Karoo scrub, which gives way to mountain fynbos at higher altitudes. The first day's route (23 km; 10 hours) ascends steadily, gaining some 500 m in altitude over the course of the first 10 km. It then levels off as it winds in and out of several shady kloofs. Over the last 5 km the trail descends steeply to the Dassiehoek overnight hut. The second day's hike (15 km; 5 hours) makes its way over Droëberg and then drops down into a valley with a delightful pool.

62. ARANGIESKOP HIKING TRAIL
Dassiehoek Nature Reserve, Robertson

Trail: 21 km; 2 days; circular.
Permits: Mrs Becker, P O Box 24, Montagu 6720, tel (023) 614 1112, fax 614 1841.
Maps: Sketch map.
Facilities/Activities: Dassiehoek: overnight hut with beds, mattresses, hot-water showers and fireplace. Arangieskop: hut with beds, mattresses, lounge, hot shower, toilets and fireplace.
Pertinent information: This trail is extremely physically demanding and should only be attempted by fit hikers.

The scenery of Dassiehoek Nature Reserve, north of Robertson, is strikingly beautiful. With its sheer cliff faces, deep gorges and high mountain peaks it makes the perfect setting for this magnificent trail.

Traversing the north of the reserve, the first day's hike (9.5 km; 6.5 hours) involves a gruelling ascent of over 1,100 m to the overnight hut, which overlooks the Koo Valley to the north. From here there are breathtaking views of the wild mountain valleys and the mosaic of farms in the Breede River Valley, which make an ample reward for the day's difficult hike.

The second day's hike (11.7 km; 6 hours) begins with a climb to the 1,850-m-high Arangieskop, where hikers are again rewarded with great views. Over the course of the next 2.5 km the trail loses some 650 m in altitude as it makes its way down into a ravine with an inviting swimming hole and enormous red alder trees. Lower down the river, the trail leaves the ravine and, after a fairly level traverse, ascends briefly, before gradually descending to Dassiehoek.

63. VROLIJKHEID NATURE RESERVE
Robertson

Trails: 2 trails; 1 and 7–8 hours.
Permit: Entrance fee. Self-issue permit for walks at reserve entrance.
Maps: Pamphlet with walks indicated.
Facilities/Activities: Birdhides; toilets.
Pertinent information: From November to March extremely high temperatures are common and hiking should commence before 09:00.

The vegetation of the Vrolijkheid Nature Reserve, situated 15 km south of Robertson in the Elandsberg Mountains, is characterised by a mixture of succulents, dwarf shrubs and patches of renosterveld. The landscape is especially attractive between August and October, when a rich diversity of plants (over 160 species) can be seen in full bloom. Unlikely to escape attention in spring are huge sheets of gousblomme (*Gazania krebsiana*).

Mammals found in this area include springbok, klipspringer, grysbok, grey rhebok, and the caracal (*rooikat* in Afrikaans), after which the Rooikat Trail has been named. Among the 175 bird species are black and African fish eagles, jackal buzzard and pale chanting goshawk. A reptile of special interest is the Robertson dwarf chameleon.

1. Heron Trail traverses easy terrain across the plains to two dams, each with its own birdhide. These are ideal for those wanting to observe some of the reserve's waterbirds. Among these are grey and black-headed herons, African rail, red-chested flufftail, African spoonbill, South African shelduck, and several kingfisher species. **3 km; 1 hour; out-and-return.**

2. Rooikat Trail follows an undulating course along river valleys and ridges, gaining 435 m in altitude to Witkrantz, the highest peak in the reserve. The trail then leads over Kranskop and Klein Spitzkop before winding down to the plains. Along the way are beautiful views of the Riviersonderend Mountains to the south, and the Langeberg range to the north. Although caracal do live in the reserve, they are shy animals and are seldom encountered. **19 km; 7–8 hours; circular.**

64. ELANDSBERG TRAIL
Ladismith

> *Trail:* 12.6 km; 6 hours; circular.
> *Permits:* Not required.
> *Maps:* Rough sketch map.
> *Facilities/Activities:* None.

This trail ascends the slopes of the Elandsberg, which dominates the skyline above Ladismith. The first 1.5 km follows a firebreak at the foot of the mountain and then climbs steeply to near Stanley de Witt's Light. It then winds along the slopes of Toringberg (2,126 m) before descending steeply back to the start. The total altitude gain is 792 m, so the trail should only be attempted by fit hikers.

65. TOWERSIG TRAIL
Ladismith

> *Trails:* 2 to 12 km; network.
> *Permits:* Not required.
> *Maps:* Rough sketch map.
> *Facilities/Activities:* None.

The lower slopes of the Elandsberg, just north of Ladismith, provide the setting for this trail network, which consists of three interlinked loops of 2, 7 and 12 km respectively. Along the course of the various routes you will be rewarded with wonderful scenic views of the Little Karoo and Toringberg, which rises over 1,500 m above Ladismith. The vegetation of the trail's surroundings is characterised by mountain fynbos, and amongst the noteworthy species that you might chance upon while you are hiking is the particularly striking Ladismith protea.

66. KLAPPERBOS TRAIL
Ladismith-Klein Karoo Nature Reserve

> *Trail:* 12.6 km; 5 hours; circular.
> *Permits:* Arrange admission to the hike with the Ladismith Municipality, who will provide you with the key for the gate, tel: (028) 551 1023.
> *Maps:* Rough sketch map.
> *Facilities/Activities:* None.

Situated 4 km southwest of Ladismith, the Ladismith-Klein Karoo Nature Reserve covers some 2,800 ha of land, including hills, plains and valleys. The vegetation here is characterised by Karooveld, which consists of a rich variety of succulents, Karoo scrub and low bushes, including Karoo num-num, yellow pomegranate and blue kuni-bush. The klapperbos (*Nymania capensis*), to which the trail owes its name, is especially conspicuous between August and December, when it bears striking pink seed pods. Animals found here include herds of eland and springbok, common duiker, and steenbok.

The Klapperbos Trail winds through the eland camp, where you might spot some of these antelope. About 1.5 km after setting off on the hike you will come to the highest point of the trail (733 m), where there are lovely views of the vineyards and apricot and peach orchards of the Ladismith district. The path then continues along the slopes of Ladismith Hill and then makes a wide loop back to the start.

67. OUKRAAL HIKING TRAIL
Gamka Mountain Nature Reserve, Calitzdorp

> *Trail: 19.7 km; 2 days.*
> *Permits: The Manager,*
> *Gamka Mountain Nature Reserve,*
> *Private Bag X21, Oudtshoorn 6620,*
> *tel. and fax: (044) 213 3367.*
> *Maps: Pamphlet with trail map.*
> *Facilities/Activities: Tierkloof: information*
> *centre, picnic sites, toilets; basecamp with*
> *beds, mattresses, gas fridge and stove,*
> *fireplace, and ablutions. Oukraal: basic*
> *stone shelter, toilet.*
> *Pertinent information: Only one group*
> *allowed on overnight trail.*

Situated at the eastern end of the Gamka-Rooiberg range, this reserve covers 9,428 ha. The north of the mountain is characterised by deep ravines and steep slopes, rising to Bakenkop (1,100 m), the highest point in the reserve. The vegetation is dominated by mountain fynbos, with spekboomveld and mountain renosterveld occurring on the lower slopes. Animals found in the reserve include Cape mountain zebra, eland, red hartebeest, grey rhebok, klipspringer, common duiker and grysbok. Leopard are also found here. Among the many bird species to be seen are the martial eagle, gymnogene, peregrine falcon, pied barbet, Cape rock thrush and orange-breasted sunbird.

The first day's hike (10.6 km; 6 hours) ascends through riverine vegetation up Tierkloof for about 5 km, to an overhang. A short way further on, the trail splits off to the right, continuing its ascent to Oukraal, with a total altitude gain of some 700 m. From Oukraal there are spectacular views over the Little Karoo, the Outeniqua Mountains to the south, and the Swartberg to the northwest. The second day's hike (9.1 km; 3 hours) loops down the mountain slopes before rejoining the outward leg of the trail.

Short Trails
From the information centre there are also four easy walks, ranging from 700 m (20 min), to the

Pied Barbet Trail of 4.1 km (2 hours). Some of the plants and trees along the trails have been marked, and can be identified by referring to the list on the permit. The many bird species occurring in the Gamka Mountain Nature Reserve are also listed on the permit.

68. GAMKASKLOOF
Swartberg Nature Reserve

> *Trail: 6 km; 3 hours; circular.*
> *Permits: The Manager, Swartberg Nature*
> *Reserve, Private Bag X658, Oudtshoorn 6620,*
> *tel: (044) 279 1739, fax: 272 8110,*
> *email: sberg.cnc.karoo@pixie.co.za*
> *Map: Interpretative pamphlet with map.*
> *Facilities/Activities: Two restored houses*
> *(self-catering); bush camp and campsite,*
> *with cold shower and braai facilities;*
> *angling in the Gamka River.*

Also known as Die Hel, Gamkaskloof lies at the western end of the Swartberg Nature Reserve. The first farmers settled in the fertile valley in 1830 and for over a century, until 1963, when it was linked by a road to the Swartberg Pass, it was one of the most remote settlements in South Africa. Hardship forced the people to leave in the 1970s and, after the last farmer left in 1991, the area came under the control of Cape Nature Conservation. Among the numerous places of historic interest are an old Norwegian mill, threshing floors, the Middelplaas school, which was built in 1923, and old dwellings.

Grootkloof Interpretative Trail winds up Grootkloof for about 1.5 km and then traverses the surrounding mountain slopes, passing through Kleinkloof to Lemoenkloof, down which the trail descends. Along the trail there are 26 points of interest that are interpreted in the trail brochure. Many of them relate to particular plants of the area and the way in which they were used by the original inhabitants of Gamkaskloof. The trail brochure also provides a wealth of additional information on topics like the local geology and animals (such as baboon and porcupine), and on some of the old buildings and other structures found in the area.

69. SWARTBERG HIKING TRAIL
Swartberg Nature Reserve

Trails: 99 km; 2 to 5 days; network.
Permits: The Manager,
Swartberg Nature Reserve,
Private Bag X658, Oudtshoorn 6620,
tel: (044) 279 1739, fax: 272 8110,
email: sberg.cnc.karoo@pixie.co.za
Maps: Reserve pamphlet with
trails indicated.
Facilities/Activities: Overnight huts
with bunks, mattresses, cooking shelters.
Pertinent information: Always make sure
you are well prepared for sudden weather
changes; snow has been recorded
in December. The Crest Route between
Ou Tol and Bothashoek should under
no circumstances be hiked in inclement
weather, as visibility is poor in heavy
mist and the exposed ridge can be
lashed by strong winds.

This 121,000-ha nature reserve provides protection to the eastern Swartberg range, and stretches from the Gamka River in the west, to the Uniondale/Willowmore road in the east. Part of the Cape Folded Mountains, the range is characterised by spectacular folded and contorted rock formations, while the vegetation is dominated by mountain fynbos.

The animals here are typical fynbos species, including grey rhebok, klipspringer, common duiker, grysbok, steenbok, kudu and baboon. Among the 150 bird species found here are the black, martial and booted eagles, Cape rockjumper, Victorin's warbler, and Cape sugarbirds and sunbirds.

Laid out in a figure eight, with trail heads at De Hoek and Ou Tol, the trail network has options ranging from two to five days. The trails wind past contorted rock formations and deep kloofs. There are spectacular views of the Little Karoo, with its patchwork of farmlands, and of the vast Great Karoo plains stretching northwards.

From De Hoek, the trail (12.1 km; 6 hours) ascends steadily above the slopes of Grootkloof, and gains some 1,000 m in altitude before descending past the spectacular Plooiberg to Gouekrans Hut, where trailists spend the night.

The second day's hike (12.8 km; 5 hours) begins with a steady ascent before levelling off, and then drops down to Bothashoek Hut.

From Bothashoek, there are several options: returning to De Hoek (8.7 km) via the jeep track to Ou Tol (13.3 km), or taking the route that links up with the Swartberg Pass at Malvadraai and then walking back up the Swartberg Pass.

Ou Tol also offers a number of different options: two trails of 9.2 km and 9.4 km, or a hike to Bothashoek along the spectacular Crest Route with its expansive views.

70. MONS RUBER TRAIL
De Rust

Trails: 3.3 km; 1.5 hours; circular.
Permits: Mons Ruber Estate,
P O Box 1585, Oudtshoorn 6620,
tel. and fax: (044) 251 6550.
Maps: Trail brochure with map.
Facilities/Activities: Wine-tasting; toilets.

This trail on a wine estate, which lies some 7 km west of De Rust, winds through a site that forms part of the South African Natural Heritage Programme. It takes its name from the spectacular Red Hills (*Mons Ruber* in Latin), which dominate the surrounding landscape. These formations date back some 180 million years, when conglomerate was deposited in a huge basin. Subsequent erosion over countless aeons has exposed the orange-coloured Enon conglomerate hills.

Along the route the trail passes through Klein Karoo Gonna-Renosterbosveld, Spekboomveld, dry forest, wagon trees and fynbos. A checklist of the 80-odd bird species that have been recorded in the area is available. Species you may chance upon during the hike include the black and booted eagles, Karoo lark, Cape rock thrush, Karoo eremomela and long-billed pipit.

Adventure awaits hikers along the rocky shores of the Harkerville Coast Hiking Trail, on the Garden Route.

GARDEN ROUTE & EASTERN CAPE

For those keen to explore this fascinating region on foot, there are numerous options, ranging from short walks and easy coastal rambles to overnight trails in the Garden Route and the Drakensberg in the northeastern corner of the Eastern Cape. The Garden Route's mosaic of indigenous forests, lakes, lagoons and long expanses of desolate beach set against a backdrop of towering mountains, which stretch from Heidelberg, eastwards, to the verdant Tsitsikamma forests, make it a glorious area for walkers and trailists to explore.

One of the focal points of the Garden Route is the magnificent indigenous forest, with its ancient forest monarchs festooned with old man's beard, lush glades of ferns, moss-covered tree trunks and tranquil streams. Covering 60,000 ha, just 0.25 per cent of South Africa's land surface, the forest occurs discontinuously along the narrow coastal strip between Mossel Bay and Humansdorp, and constitutes the largest area of natural forest in South Africa. It is composed of about 87 different indigenous tree species, including real and Outeniqua yellowwoods, stinkwood, assegai, red alder, ironwood, white pear and Cape beech. In addition, there are also 55 woody shrub, 52 fern and 47 vine species, as well as a rich variety of geophytes, epiphytes, grasses and forbs.

The indigenous forests of Knysna and Tsitsikamma are the habitat of some 40 typical forest bird species. Among these are the crowned eagle, African sparrowhawk, Knysna lourie, Narina trogon, Cape, chorister and starred robins, terrestrial bulbul, and the olive thrush. Other species to look out for include the red-billed woodhoopoe, tambourine dove, crowned hornbill and Knysna woodpecker.

Large animals are poorly represented in the indigenous forests. The Knysna forests and the adjoining fynbos areas were once home to a large population of elephants, but sadly their numbers have decreased to just three, or even fewer, and chances of seeing them are extremely remote. Among the animal species you may chance upon are bushbuck, blue duiker and vervet monkey, while tell-tale signs of bushpig, porcupine, caracal and leopard may also be encountered. You are unlikely to see the animals themselves, though, as they are typically shy and nocturnal.

Another feature of the Garden Route is the string of lakes stretching between Wilderness and Sedgefield. Aptly named South Africa's 'Lake District', the five lakes are the habitat of 72 waterbird species and, at times, support up to 24,000 birds a month. Species to look for include the great-crested and black-necked grebe, yellow-billed duck, southern pochard, red-chested flufftail, and marsh harrier.

The coastal plains of the Garden Route are bounded by the lofty mountain peaks of the Langeberg, Outeniqua and Tsitsikamma ranges. Here, at the eastern limit of its distribution, the mountain fynbos is considerably poorer than that of the southwestern Cape, but between May and November the mountain slopes are transformed into a blaze of colour when several erica species are in bloom. Also to be seen is a variety of proteas, reeds, rushes and bulbs, while remnant patches of indigenous forest occur in sheltered kloofs. The usual fynbos mammals and birds occur (see p. 36).

The Garden Route offers a wide range of trails through indigenous forest, fynbos-covered mountains, and along the coast, which varies from long sandy beaches to rocky shores backed by steep cliffs. Options range from short day walks to extended overnight hikes.

East of the Tsitsikamma Mountains lie the Grootwinterhoek range and the Amatola Mountains. Steeped in the history of the Eastern Cape frontier wars, the Amatola Mountains are also renowned for their many splendid cascades, natural pools, stunning views and patches of indigenous forests.

Two animal species that occur in the Eastern Cape forests, but not further west, are the tree dassie and the samango monkey. Also found here is the giant *Michrochaetus* earthworm, the largest earthworm in the world (reaching lengths of up to 7 m), and the

Pirie Forest, northwest of King William's Town, is the best-known habitat of the endangered giant golden mole. In the forest canopy, look out for flocks of noisy Cape parrots, a species that reaches the western limit of its distribution in the Alexandria forests northeast of Port Elizabeth. Alexandria Forest is a distinct coastal forest type, named after the area in which it is predominantly found, around the town of Alexandria northeast of Port Elizabeth.

The Wild Coast is one of the most breathtaking stretches of coastline in the world. It extends from just northeast of East London, to the Mtamvuna River, the boundary between the Eastern Cape and KwaZulu-Natal provinces. The heart of the Wild Coast, however, extends from the Kei River to the Mtamvuna River. The coastline boasts small sandy coves fringed by wild banana trees, tranquil estuaries with mangrove communities, grassy headlands, and fascinating natural features. Well-known formations include the Mzamba petrified trees and other fossils, just south of the Mtamvuna River, Hole in the Wall, and Cathedral Rock, and at Waterfall Bluff two waterfalls cascade directly into the sea.

Numerous ships foundered along this stretch of coast with its strong currents and huge waves; among them the HMS *Grosvenor*, which reputedly had the gem-covered Peacock Throne of India, worth over $10 million, on board when it ran aground on the night of 2 August 1782. Other famous shipwrecks include those of the *Santo Alberto* (1593), *São João* (1552) and the *São Bento* (1554).

In the remote northeastern corner of the Eastern Cape, the southern extremity of the Drakensberg is found. It is characterised by spectacular sandstone outcrops, rugged valleys, clear mountain streams and high mountain peaks, which are often covered in snow during the winter months. Rock paintings on the walls of caves and overhangs are reminders of the early Bushmen people who lived here for centuries, possibly thousands of years, until the arrival of white settlers in the 19th century.

This area does not support large herds of game, but it does have a rich diversity of birds. Among the exciting species that you may see while you are hiking are the Cape vulture, bearded vulture and crowned crane. Noteworthy Drakensberg grassland species that you should look out for include the orange-breasted rockjumper, yellow-breasted pipit and Drakensberg siskin.

The Garden Route and the Eastern Cape lie in an all-year rainfall area. In the west, the rainfall is distributed fairly evenly throughout the year, but in the interior and further east the highest rainfall is recorded between October and March.

Temperatures along the coast are typically moderate during the summer months, but between May and September daily minimum temperatures drop to below 12 °C. In the interior, however, the mountains in the northeast of the Eastern Cape are often covered in snow, and during mid-winter daily minimum temperatures of below 5 °C are not uncommon.

IMPORTANT INFORMATION

• Weather conditions in the mountains are often extremely unpredictable, so you should always be prepared for sudden weather changes during your hike. Mist is quite common high up in the mountains, while snow can be expected on the high peaks in winter, especially in the Eastern Cape Drakensberg, which is also known for violent thunderstorms during the summer months.

• Trails in the mountains and in the forests can become very slippery after heavy rains, so it is essential to hike in boots that have a good grip.

• After heavy rains, rivers in mountainous areas can come down in flood and may be difficult to cross. Either wait until the river can be negotiated safely, or turn back to the overnight hut.

• It is advisable to use a good insect repellent and to take precautions against ticks. Try to remove any ticks that you find on yourself right away, if possible, and make sure that you check your body thoroughly when you return from your hike.

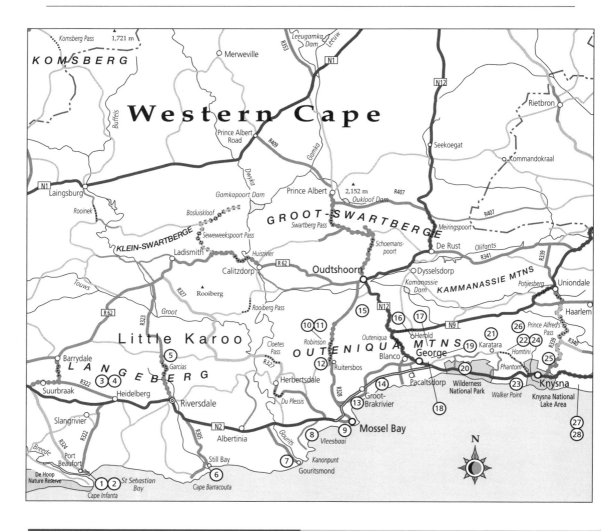

HIKING TRAILS

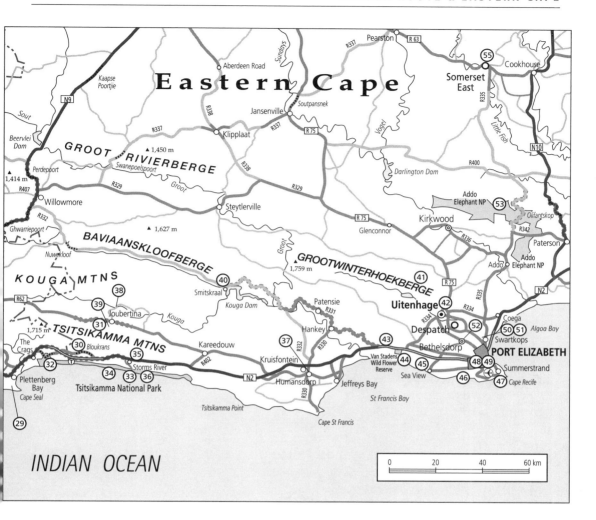

Continued on pp. 88–89

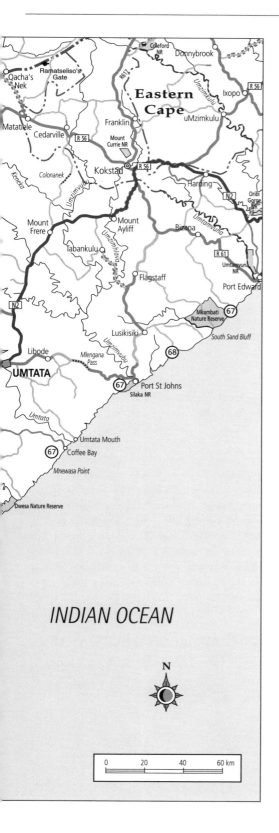

1. WITSAND WALKS
Witsand

> *Trails: Several walks; 5 to 20 km;*
> *1 to 6 hours; open-ended and out-and-return.*
> *Permits: Not required. Information from*
> *Witsand Association for Commerce and*
> *Tourism, tel: (028) 537 1010.*
> *Maps: None.*
> *Facilities/Activities: None.*

Situated on the eastern bank of the Breede River just before it enters the sea, the popular coastal resort of Witsand and historic Port Beaufort, a short way upstream, offer a variety of walks. St Sebastian Bay lies at the eastern end of the stretch of coast where the majority of southern right whale cow and calf pairs congregate between June and November. In 2001 up to 37 sightings were made in the bay, also known as the Whale Nursery of South Africa.

1. Infanta Walk starts at Kontiki on the western bank of the river and follows its sandy shore until it gives way to rocks at Kabeljoubank. Beyond Infanta the route winds up Infanta Hill, an excellent vantage point for whale-watching. **5 km; 2 hours; out-and-return.**

2. Breede River Mouth Walk meanders along the sandspit on the river's eastern bank. At lowtide the walk follows the river's edge and the sea, but at high tide the route is across soft sand and dunes. **6 km; 2 hours; out-and-return.**

3. Moodies Well Walk follows the sandy eastern sweep of St Sebastian Bay for 4 km, to a well dug by a Scotsman in the 19th century to store water on camping and fishing trips. The walk should be done at lowtide. **8 km; 3 hours; out-and-return.**

4. Puntjie Walk follows the coastline fromWitsand past Moodies Well, Voëlklip and Kleinfontein Beach, to Puntjie, at the mouth of the Duivenhoks River. The quaint settlement with its thatched *kapstyl* houses is a national monument. The hike can be done with a guide (call Pietie:

(082) 738 2101) during spring lowtide in summer. Trailists are collected by vehicle from the end. **15–20 km; 6 hours; open-ended.**

Other walks at Witsand include the **River View Walk**, which passes along the River View Drive, **Skuitbaai Walk** (3 km; 1 hour) and **Westfield Walk** (5 or 8 km; 2–2.5 hours).

2. OSTRICH TRAILS
Witsand

> *Trails: 12 to 22 km; 5–7 hours; circular.*
> *Permits: Ostrich Trails, P O Box 269,*
> *Heidelberg 6665, tel. and*
> *fax: (028) 537 1942,*
> *email: ostrichtrails@telkomsa.net*
> *Maps: Basic colour map.*
> *Facilities/Activities: Self-catering*
> *accommodation; mountain biking;*
> *farm and game drives.*
> *Pertinent information: The water in*
> *the Slang River is not drinkable.*

This network of trails makes its way amongst wheat fields, sheep paddocks, milkwood trees and fynbos. From the cliffs above the Slang River there are spectacular views of the river's tight turns and horseshoe bends. The return leg leads past the ostrich breeding camp. The historic Slang River homestead was built in 1796 by Jacob van Reenen, and Lady Ann Barnard and her party stayed in the house for two days whilst exploring the southern Cape in 1798.

3. BOOSMANSBOS WILDERNESS AREA
Heidelberg

See no. 4 (p. 91) for walks.

> *Trails: 27 km; 2 days or longer; circular.*
> *Permits: The Manager,*
> *Grootvadersbosch Nature Reserve,*
> *P O Box 109, Heidelberg 6665,*

tel: (028) 722 2412, fax: 722 2838,
email: grootvadersbosch@cnc.co.za
Maps: Trail pamphlet with sketch map.
Facilities/Activities: Campsite with hot-water ablutions at start; basic mountain shelters without facilities at Helderfontein and Klein Witbooisrivier.
Pertinent information: No fires permitted in wilderness area. The total number of people allowed in wilderness area per day is 12.

The Grootvadersbosch Nature Reserve in the Langeberg range is characterised by imposing mountain peaks, high krantzes and deep ravines. The vegetation is dominated by mountain fynbos and in spring the southern slopes are blanketed in magnificent pink ericas, while cone bushes create a yellow sea on the northern slopes. Outeniqua and real yellowwoods, stinkwood, Cape holly and candlewood are among the 35 common trees in the Grootvadersbosch, the largest indigenous forest west of Mossel Bay.

The first day's hike (14 km; 5 hours) steadily ascends the eastern slopes of Dwarsberg, winding in and out of Bobbejaanskloof and Vaalrivierkloof until reaching a nek. From here, the trail follows a fairly easy traverse in an easterly direction to reach the stone huts at Helderfontein.

Not to be missed is a visit to the nearby Boosmansbos, the lovely patch of forest to which the wilderness area owes its name. Another worthwhile excursion from Helderfontein is an ascent of the 1,638-m-high Grootberg, the highest peak in the area. From the summit there are uninterrupted 360 degree views as far as Cradock Peak in the east, the Riviersonderend Mountains in the west, Towerkop in the north and the patchwork of wheatfields of Heidelberg to the south and Riversdale to the southwest. The round trip takes about 4 hours.

The second day's hike (13 km; 4 hours) is an easy downhill walk along Barend Koen se Pad for about 7 or 8 km until a footpath deviates off to the right. The path descends steeply into the deep gorge carved by the Duivenhoks River, an ideal resting stop, and then climbs out of the valley to join a forestry road, which takes you back to the start.

4. GROOTVADERSBOSCH NATURE RESERVE
Heidelberg

See no. 3 (p. 90) for wilderness area.

Trails: 2 trails; 10 and 15 km; 3 and 5 hours, with shorter options; circular.
Permits: Entrance fee. No permit required for walks.
Maps: Pamphlet of walks with sketch map.
Facilities/Activities: Campsites with ablutions; canopy-level birdhide; mountain bike trail.

Situated about 22 km northwest of Heidelberg, the Grootvadersbosch forest lies at the foot of the Langeberg. Covering 250 ha, it is the largest indigenous forest west of Mossel Bay, and consists of dry and moist Knysna forest types. Among the common species found here are the Outeniqua and real yellowwoods, stinkwood, wild peach, assegai, Cape peach, and ironwood.

Among the nearly 200 bird species that have been recorded here to date are the Knysna lourie, crowned eagle, the elusive Narina trogon, the blue-mantled flycatcher, olive bush shrike and Knysna woodpecker. Amongst the other species spotted here are the black-rumped buttonquail, striped flufftail and Layard's titbabbler.

1. Bushbuck Trail is appropriately named after the bushbuck, which was first described from a specimen collected at Grootvadersbosch over two centuries ago in 1780. You may also spot baboon, as well as the Cape grysbok, which favours the forest margins and fynbos. **10 km; 3 hours; circular, with shorter options.**

2. Grysbok Trail After initially winding along the ecotone, or transitional zone, between the indigenous forest and fynbos, the Grysbok Trail traverses the beautiful fynbos-covered lower southern slopes of the Langeberg range. The Sunbird Loop offers a shorter 3-km option, if you prefer a quicker hike. The fynbos vegetation here is especially attractive between early August and end October. **15 km; 5 hours; circular.**

5. RIVERSDALE HIKING TRAILS
Riversdale

Trails: 1 day walk; 13.8 km; 8 hours; out-and-return. 2 hiking trails; 24.6 and 25.5 km; 2 to 5 days; open-ended and circular.
Permits: Riversdale Tourist Camp, P O Box 29, Riversdale 6670, tel: (028) 713 2418, fax: 713 3146.
Maps: Trails indicated on copy of 1:50,000 topographical map.
Facilities/Activities: Two huts with bunk beds, mattresses, water and firewood.
Pertinent information: The Rooiwaterspruit Hiking Trail can be hiked from either the Korentevette River Dam or the Toll House. Strong mountain winds are often experienced between May and August. Do not ascend Sleeping Beauty in misty weather. Beware of bees in the yellowwood forest on the Sleeping Beauty and Rooiwaterspruit trails.

The Langeberg range to the north of Riversdale is renowned for its profusion of fynbos plants, including rarities such as Riversdale heath (*Erica blenna*), and two cone bushes endemic to the Riverdale Mountains: *Leucospermum mundii* and *Leucospermum winterii*. Among the proteas are the king protea (*Protea cynaroides*), peach protea (*Protea grandiceps*), as well as broad-leaved, blue and greenhead sugarbushes.

The vegetation of the Langeberg's northern slopes is dry, with typical Karoo species, while patches of indigenous forests occur in the kloofs on the wetter southern slopes. Typical species that you may find here include yellowwood, stinkwood, red alder, hard pear, Cape beech, and candlewood.

1. Sleeping Beauty This day walk steadily ascends a kloof with numerous mountain streams to a yellowwood forest. The path then zigzags steeply to a nek behind Sleeping Beauty and over the last 1.5 km gains over 300 m in altitude. Named after its resemblance to the profile of a woman in a reclining position, the 1,341-m-high Sleeping Beauty towers over 1,000 m above the coastal plains. The spectacular views make the climb worthwhile. **13.8 km; 8 hours; out-and-return.**

2. Rooiwaterspruit Hiking Trail traverses the Langeberg range west of Garcia Pass. From the Toll House the first day's hike (15.6 km; 5 hours) ascends steeply for the first 5 km to Nekkie, where there is an optional 3-km out-and-return hike to the Sleeping Beauty. From here the trail descends along Oom Boet's Road to Stinkhoutbos and then winds down to the overnight hut along the Rooiwaterspruit with its inviting pools. The second day's route (9 km; 3 hours) is an easy hike, mainly through or alongside pine plantations to the Korentevette River Dam. This hike can be extended by using the Rooiwaterspruit huts as a base and doing a 14-km circuit to Stinkhoutbos. From here the trail descends below Aasvoëlkrans and then descends steeply to follow a contour back to the hut. **24.6 km; 2 days; open-ended.**

3. Kristalkloof Hiking Trail traverses the Langeberg range to the east of Garcia Pass. The steep 3-km ascent up Kristalkloof to Wildehondekloofnek is followed by a long descent to the overnight stop (reached 9 km; 3 hours from the start) along the Kruis River. On the second day's hike (16.5 km; 5 hours) the trail swings westwards and then follows an easy contour along the southern slopes of Kampscheberg. From the end of the trail it is a 4.5-km walk up Garcia Pass. **25.5 km; 2 days; circular.**

By combining the Rooiwaterspruit and Kristalkloof hiking trails and the Aasvoëlkrans circuit, a five-day hike can be undertaken.

6. STILBAAI WALKS
Stilbaai

Trails: 5 trails; 3 to 11 km; 1 to 4 hours; open-ended, circular and out-and-return.
Permits: Not required.
Maps: None.
Facilities/Activities: None.
Pertinent information: For more info contact Stilbaai Tourism Bureau, tel: (028) 754 2602.

Situated at the mouth of an estuary, Stilbaai is a coastal resort popular with both holiday-makers and anglers. The coastline and surrounding areas contain a wealth of archaeological treasures, including intertidal fish-trap complexes built by coastal Khoikhoi and Bushmen (possibly as far back as 2,000 years ago) and middens. Also, a distinctive variation of Middle Stone Age artefacts, characterised by symmetrical, leaf-shaped (stone) points, was first discovered at Stilbaai.

1. West Bank Route Amongst the highlights of this trail are views of the estuary, Khoikhoi and Bushman fish-traps and close-up views of the tame eels for which Stilbaai has become renowned. **3–6 km; 1–2 hours; open-ended.**

2. Pauline Bohnen Route in the eponymously named 150-ha nature reserve passes through coastal fynbos with expansive views of the ocean and the coast. Among the animals you might chance upon are bushbuck, grysbok and common duiker. **4–8 km; 1.5–3 hours; circular.**

3. Strandloper Route recalls the early Khoikhoi and Bushmen inhabitants of the area (known as *strandlopers* in Afrikaans, meaning 'beach walkers'). Starting from the Jagersbosch Community Hall in Stilbaai West, the trail winds along the rocky coastline past Morris Point and Kleinplaatjie before returning to the start. Attractions include views of the estuary, the fishing harbour, historic buildings, Khoikhoi and Bushman fish-traps and Stilbaai's famous tame eels. **8 km; 3 hours; circular.**

4. Lappies Beach Route is best hiked during lowtide. From Lappiesbaai Beach, the route follows the sandy coastline for about 4 km to the Preekstoel; a rock formation reminiscent of a pulpit. Look out for pansy shells washed up on the beach. **8 km; 3 hours; out-and-return.**

5. Noordkapper Route extends along the coastline from Morris Point to Jongensfontein. The first part of the walk is characterised by red sand dunes and except for sandy coves at Kleinplaatjie, Sandhoek and Koppiesbaai the coast is rocky. Highlights include ancient Khoikhoi and Bushman fish-traps and middens and the coastal cave at Jongensgat, while the variety of sea shells is a conchologist's delight. **11 km; 4 hours; open-ended.**

7. REIN'S NATURE RESERVE
Mossel Bay

Trails: *2 trails; 2.5 and 2.8 km; 2 hours; circular and out-and-return.*
Permits: *Not required by guests staying in the reserve. Rein's Nature Reserve, P O Box 298, Albertinia 6695, tel: (028) 745 3322, fax: 745 3324, email: info@reinsouthafrica.com*
Maps: *Trail brochure with map.*
Facilities/Activities: *Luxury accommodation in en suite rooms and executive lodges; fishermen's cottages with fully equipped kitchens; restaurant; fly-fishing; mountain biking; snorkelling; scenic tractor tour.*
Pertinent information: *Horse flies can be very irritating, so apply insect repellent. Plan to walk the Cormorant Trail at lowtide.*

Situated in a region known to the early Khoikhoi and Bushmen people as Gouriqua, Rein's Nature Reserve covers 3,550 ha of unspoilt coastal fynbos, fronting onto a magnificent stretch of coastline.

The fynbos flora consists of a rich variety of ericas and reeds, and is especially attractive between May and September. Several members of the protea family can be seen, including the real sugarbush, stinkleaf sugarbush, the Mossel Bay pincushion (*Leucospermum praecox*) and the hairless cone bush (*Leucadendron galpinii*). Conspicuous along the coast are white milkwoods that are stunted as a result of the strong coastal winds.

The reserve is home to bontebok, eland, Cape mountain zebra, bushbuck, common duiker and Cape grysbok, and caracal and porcupine are known to live here too. Also to be seen is the angulate tortoise. Typical fynbos birds include the Cape sugarbird, while African black oystercatcher, white-breasted cormorant and terns are among the coastal birds.

Southern right, humpback and Bryde's whales are often seen about 1 km offshore during the latter half of the year when they migrate to the South African coast to breed. Closer inshore, there are intertidal pools and gullies, which support a rich diversity of marine organisms.

The coastline is also of archaeological importance and there are several intertidal fish-traps. They date back some 2,000 years and were built by hunter-gatherers who roamed along the coast.

1. Cormorant Trail This self-guided interpretative trail focuses on various aspects of the coast. Aspects discussed in the informative trail-guide include waves and currents, the Khoikhoi and Bushmen fish-traps (see above), and coastal birds and animals in the intertidal pools. The boulder beach where the trail starts is unique and teems with marine life. It is the most extensive boulder beach along the South African coastline (about 3 km long, it extends from the beach, seawards, to beyond the lowtide mark). From an ecological point of view, it is unique because a host of marine creatures live underneath the round boulders (with a diameter of between 30 and 40 cm) rather than between or on top of them. Its cultural and historical importance lies in the use of the boulders to construct the fish-traps. **2.5 km; 2 hours; out-and-return.**

2. Protea Trail leads through coastal fynbos with a profusion of proteas and other fynbos species. There are eight marked points of interest along the route, which are described in detail in the trail-guide. Aspects covered range from termite mounds and fynbos vegetation to the importance of fire to fynbos. **2.8 km; 2 hours; circular.**

8. TRAIL OF THE OYSTERCATCHER
Mossel Bay

Trail: Guided; 55 km; 4 days; open-ended.
Permits: Trail of the Oystercatcher,
P O Box 1889, Mossel Bay 6500,
tel. and fax: (044) 699 1204,
email: info@oystercatchertrail.co.za
Maps: Colour map.
Facilities/Activities: Luxury guesthouses; innovative lunches and dinners (incorporating local traditional meals, fish braais, mussel soup and homemade bread for lunch); snorkelling; transfer from Rein's Nature Reserve to Mossel Bay.
Pertinent information: Trails are conducted

for groups of between 6 and 12 people from mid-April to the end of November. The minimum age for participants is 10 years.

This all-inclusive trail between Mossel Bay and Rein's Nature Reserve is conducted by a local guide and aims to create environmental awareness of the Garden Route. Along the way the guide will interpret the coastal environment and trailists will also have time to explore the fascinating rock pools along the coast.

Hikers meet the guide at the Mossel Bay Museum, and then visit the famous Post Office Tree and the Maritime Museum, which provides an insight into various aspects of the marine environment. After this the trail heads to the Khoisan Cave on Cape St Blaize, from where you continue westwards along the coastal cliffs, an ideal vantage point from which to spot southern right whales and dolphins. The first day (15 km) ends at Dana Bay.

The second day's hike (12 km) traverses mainly sandy beaches and along the way trailists can observe the African black oystercatcher. Also of interest are Khoikhoi and Bushmen shell middens and Stone Age implements. The day's hike to Boggomsbaai is short, so frequent swimming stops are made.

On day three (15 km) the beach is followed to the holiday resort of Vleesbaai. From here the trail continues along the rocky shores to Fransmanshoek, where trailists can snorkel in the rock pools and gullies. The trail then continues to Kanonpunt where a tractor ride up high sand dunes is a highlight of the afternoon. The final section of the day's hike follows the rocky coastline to the Gouritz River mouth, which is crossed by boat or a special tube.

Day four (13 km) follows the rugged coastline to Rein's Nature Reserve, with its ancient fish-traps (see above). The trail ends with a late afternoon drive on a thatched roof trailer and a candle-lit dinner.

9. ST BLAIZE TRAIL
Mossel Bay

Trails: 13.5 km; 5 hours; open-ended.
Permits: Not required.
Maps: Trail map available from Mossel Bay

Tourism Bureau, tel: (044) 691 2202,
fax: 690 3077, email: mbtb@mweb.co.za
Facilities/Activities: None.
Pertinent information: As there are high
cliffs children must be accompanied
by adults. Beware of high waves along
the coast. It is inadvisable to walk the trail
in strong winds.

The trail starts at the Cape St Blaize Cave immediately below the historic lighthouse, which came into operation in 1864. With a height of 8 m, a depth of 13 m and a width of 28 m, Cape St Blaize was inhabited as far back as the Middle Stone Age. From here the route moves westwards along the coastal cliffs, an ideal vantage point for whale and dolphin sightings and also a popular site for angling. The Cape gannet, black-backed gull and African black oystercatcher are among the birds you might tick along the way. The trail ends at Dana Bay.

10. ATTAQUASKLOOF HIKING TRAIL
Outeniqua Nature Reserve,
Robinson Pass

See no. 11 (this page) for walk.

Trail: 40 km; 3 days; circular.
Permits: The Manager,
Outeniqua Nature Reserve,
Private Bag X6517, George 6530,
tel: (044) 870 8323,
fax: 870 7138, email: outenr@mweb.co.za
Maps: Sketch map.
Facilities/Activities: Overnight hut with
bunks, mattresses, hot-water shower, toilet,
fireplace and wood.
Pertinent information: The trail has some
steep ascents and should not be attempted
by the unfit. Be prepared for mist.

On this trail hikers follow part of the historic Attaquaskloof Pass which was built after Isaac Schrijver pioneered a route across the Outeniqua Mountains in 1689. The trail leads through the pristine mountain fynbos vegetation and hikers are rewarded with expansive views over the coastal plains and the Outeniqua Mountains.

The first day's trail (19.2 km; 9 hours) climbs steadily along the southern slopes of Skurweberg to a saddle. The trail then loses altitude and joins the Attaquaskloof Pass, which first ascends and then winds down to the Perdekop Hut.

On the second day, hikers have an option of a short, 4.6-km circular route, to a magnificent pool in the upper reaches of the Kamma River. You can then spend the rest of the day relaxing, swimming or exploring the area.

Day three's hike (15.5 km; 7 hours) is fairly strenuous, as it includes three steep climbs. The first is a 400-m ascent up the Attaquas Mountains, the second is a 300-m ascent, and the third a 340-m climb from the Kouma River to the Robinson Pass. A natural rock pool near the halfway mark provides the perfect stopping point for a swim and lunch.

11. KOUMASHOEK CIRCUIT
Outeniqua Nature Reserve,
Robinson Pass

See no. 10 (this page) for hiking trail.

Trail: 16.5 km; 6 hours; circular.
Permits: The Manager,
Outeniqua Nature Reserve,
Private Bag X6517, George 6530,
tel: (044) 870 8323, fax: 870 7138,
email: outenr@mweb.co.za
Maps: Sketch map.
Facilities/Activities: None.
Pertinent information: A strenuous route:
for fit hikers only. Be prepared for mist.

The Koumashoek Circular Route passes through pristine fynbos vegetation and wild mountain scenery to the west of the Robinson Pass. The trail descends to the Koumashoek Valley and then ascends steeply up the mountain slopes to a ridge where the route follows a knife-edge. Further along, the outward route of the Attaquaskloof Hiking Trail is joined and the path then descends the southern slopes of Skurweberg. From the top of the Robinson Pass it is a 3-km walk down the pass.

12. SKAAPPLAAS TRAIL
Mossel Bay

Trail: 10 km; 5–6 hours; circular.
Permits: Skaapplaas, P O Box 724,
Hartenbos 6520, tel: (044) 631 0035.
Maps: Sketch map.
Facilities/Activities: Self-catering hut with boma, fireplace and water.
Pertinent information: The trail can either be done as a day walk or as an overnight trail, in which case it is advisable to carry a tent, if you prefer that to sleeping in a cave.

Situated in the foothills of the Robinson Pass, in the Ruitersbos area, Skaapplaas Trail makes its way along fynbos-covered ridges, with stunning views of the Mossel Bay area, and passes through fairy-tale indigenous forests of stinkwood, yellow-wood and tree ferns.

The route traverses private farmland and partly follows the course of the Kouma River, with its waterfalls and inviting pools. Also to be seen are rock paintings of antelope and human figures.

A cave along the trail serves as an overnight stop for those wishing to hike the trail at leisure.

13. GREAT BRAK RIVER WALKS
Great Brak River

Trails: 2 trails; 5 km; 1.5 hours; circular.
Permits: Not required.
Maps: None. For more information, contact the tourism office in Amy Searle Street, Great Brak River, tel: (044) 620 3338.
Facilities/Activities: Picnic sites with braai facilities, swimming pool and mini-golf at Pine Creek Caravan Park.

1. Wolwedans Trail Starting near the Pine Creek Caravan Park, this is a moderately easy walk to the Wolwedans Dam, which supplies water to PetroSA and the Greater Mossel Bay area. The trail returns along the Great Brak River, with its lush riverine vegetation. **5 km; 1.5 hours; circular.**

2. Great Brak River Village Walk combines a ramble through the town with walking along the beach, estuary and the Great Brak River. Attractions in the town include the biggest known pepper tree in South Africa, the Searle Memorial Church and Searle Family Graveyard, where the town's founders are buried, and the Watson Shoe Factory, to which the town owes its existence. **5 km; 1.5 hours; circular.**

14. GLENTANA BEACH WALK
Glentana

Trail: 6 km; 3 hours; out-and-return.
Permits: Not required.
Maps: None. For more information, contact the tourism office in Amy Searle Street, Great Brak River, tel: (044) 620 3338.
Facilities/Activities: Braai places, toilets and parking area at Glentana Beach.
Pertinent information: The walk can only be done at lowtide. The trail is not marked.

This easy walk from Glentana eastwards to Cape Windlass alternates between stretches of sandy beach and rocky outcrops. The trail passes the rusty remains of a floating dock, which ran aground here whilst being towed between England and Durban in 1902.

15. DORINGRIVIER WILDERNESS AREA
Outeniqua Nature Reserve, George

Trail: 14 km; 7 hours; circular.
Permits: The Manager, Outeniqua Nature Reserve, Private Bag X6517, George 6530,

tel: (044) 870 8323, fax: 870 7138,
email: outenr@mweb.co.za
Maps: Rough sketch map.
Facilities/Activities: None.

This trail traverses the Doringrivier Wilderness Area, which lies between the Outeniqua and Robinson passes on the northern slopes of the Outeniqua range. The first 6 km of the trail is a steady ascent, during which you gain about 420 m in altitude to a beacon (1,100 m) below Witberg. The route then swings in a southwesterly direction, descending steeply to the Doring River Valley. You follow a jeep track into the valley, where a pool in the Groot Doring River provides an ideal rest stop. The remainder of the trail is an easy descent back to the start. Along the trail there are scenic views of the Little Karoo and the Doring River Valley.

16. OUTENIQUA NATURE RESERVE
George

Trail: 4 trails; 4.7 to 19 km; 3 to 8 hours; open-ended and out-and-return.
Permits: Self-issue permits at start.
Maps: Sketch maps.
Facilities/Activities: None.

1. Pass to Pass Trail links the Outeniqua and the historic Montagu passes. An optional 2.6 km out-and-return detour to the summit of Losberg (851 m) will be rewarded with extensive views over George and the coastal plains. East of Losberg the trail drops down to the Keur River, with its delightful patch of indigenous forest, before ascending steeply to the end. This trail can be hiked in either direction. **4.7 km; 3 hours; open-ended.**

2. Cradock Pass Trail From Witfontein the route follows the George and Cradock peaks trails for about 1 hour and then branches off to cross Tierkloof. After that the trail ascends along a spur, following the old Cradock Pass. Built in 1812, this pass was the only way across the mountains until

the completion of the Montagu Pass in 1847. After crossing the railway line the trail climbs steeply up Cradock Kloof, and at one point the grooves cut by wagon wheels into the rock can still be seen. You gain nearly 800 m in altitude as you climb to the top of Cradock Pass, from where it is a 2-km downhill walk to the Montagu Pass. **12.4 km; 6 hours; open-ended.**

3. George Peak Trail From Witfontein the trail climbs steeply up the slopes, through fynbos, for about 2.5 hours to a nek where the George Peak and Cradock Peak paths split. From here it is a 30-minute climb to the 1,337-m-high summit of George Peak from where there are expansive vistas of George and the coastline stretching between Mossel Bay and Knysna. The trail gains over 1,000 m in altitude and is rated as strenuous. **17 km; 7 hours; out-and-return.**

4. Cradock Peak Trail follows the same route as the George Peak Trail for the first 2.5 hours. The trail then climbs steeply for about 1 hour to the summit of Cradock Peak, at 1,579 m, the highest point in the area. This is an extremely demanding trail, with an altitude gain of nearly 1,300 m, but the views are ample reward for the effort. **19 km; 8 hours; out-and-return.**

17. TIERKOP HIKING TRAIL
Outeniqua Nature Reserve, George

Trail: 30 km; 2 days; open-ended.
Permits: The Manager,
Outeniqua Nature Reserve,
Private Bag X6517, George 6530,
tel: (044) 870 8323,
fax: 870 7138, email: outenr@mweb.co.za
Maps: Sketch map.
Facilities/Activities: Overnight hut with bunk beds, mattresses, water and toilets.

On the first day's hike (17.5 km; 5 hours) the trail initially passes through pine plantations and then steadily gains about 420 m in altitude through the fynbos to Tonnelbos, a relic patch of indigenous forest. The route then loses height as it descends to George Dam in the Swart River before ascending steeply to Tierkop Hut.

The second day's route (12.5 km; 4 hours) is an easy descent through fynbos along a jeep track to the delightful Pepsi Pools and Waterfall. The final section of the trail follows the banks of the Garden Route Dam.

18. GROENEWEIDE FOREST WALK
Groenkop Forest, George

> *Trail:* 4.6 to 9.6 km; 1.5 to 3 hours; circular.
> *Permits:* Self-issue permits at start.
> *Maps:* Available at start.
> *Facilities/Activities:* Picnic sites.

The Groeneweide trails network traverses the 1,450-ha Groenkop indigenous forest with its numerous streams. Following forestry tracks and paths, the network offers three different hike options: the **Red Route** (9.6 km; 3 hours), the **Blue Route** (7.9 km; 2.5 hours) and the **Green Route** (4.6 km; 1.5 hours).

An enchanting pool in the Silver River is a highlight on the Red Route, which leads past a number of enormous Outeniqua yellowwoods. Other typical forest trees found here include the real yellowwood, white stinkwood, terblans, stinkwood and wild peach.

Animals to look out for include baboon, vervet monkey, blue duiker, bushpig, bushbuck and caracal, and leopard also live here. Among the many forest birds to keep an eye out for are the Knysna lourie, Narina trogon, olive thrush, chorister robin, crowned eagle and African sparrowhawk.

19. MELVILLE PEAK
Outeniqua Nature Reserve, George

> *Trails:* 25 km; 9 hours; out-and-return.
> *Permits:* The Manager, Outeniqua Nature Reserve, Private Bag X6517, George 6530, tel: (044) 870 8323, fax: 870 7138, email: outenr@mweb.co.za

> *Maps:* None.
> *Facilities/Activities:* None.
> *Pertinent information:* A demanding hike, which should only be attempted by fit and experienced hikers.

Starting at Saasveld, the Port Elizabeth Technikon's Faculty of Forestry, 10 km from George, this hike initially goes through the 1,450-ha Groenkop indigenous forest. The route then ascends steadily to the summit of the 1,300-m-high Melville Peak, one of the high peaks in the Outeniqua range.

20. WILDERNESS NATIONAL PARK
Wilderness

> *Trails:* 6 trails; 3 to 10 km; 1 to 4 hours.
> *Permits:* Entrance fee. Self-issue permits at start.
> *Maps:* Pamphlet with maps available.
> *Facilities/Activities:* Self-catering accommodation and camping at the Ebb and Flow North and South restcamps; picnic sites; birdhides; pedal boats and canoes for hire; angling (permits required).

Covering just over 2,600 ha, the Wilderness National Park provides protection to a string of four lakes, two estuaries and 28 km of coastline. The three western lakes (Island Lake, Langvlei and Rondevlei) are connected to the Touw River by the Serpentine, a narrow 5.5-km channel that passes through a marshy area. The park is surrounded by a National Lake Area of 10,000 ha, which does not form part of the park but is administered by the National Parks Board.

The wetlands are an important waterbird habitat, and are sometimes home to as many as 24,000 birds at a time. Waterbirds constitute over a third of the 240 bird species recorded to date, and among them are five kingfisher species, as well as red-knobbed coot, yellow-billed duck, darter, reed cormorant and dabchick. The lake system has one of the country's largest populations of African marsh harrier.

In the indigenous forests, trailists may well chance upon blue duiker, bushbuck, bushpig and vervet monkey, while the coastal scrub supports grysbok and a variety of rodents, such as the Cape dune molerat.

1. Bosbok Trail follows a loop through indigenous forest to the west of the Duiwe River. It has the same starting point as the Brown-hooded Kingfisher Trail. **3 km; 1.5 hours; circular.**

2. Half-collared Kingfisher Trail Starting at the water purification plant next to the railway bridge at Ebb and Flow North Restcamp, this trail follows the western bank of the Touw River upstream for about 1.9 km. From here you can either retrace your steps, with the option of taking the more demanding, but very rewarding, Bosduif Loop, or cross the river and follow the Giant Kingfisher Trail back. **3.8 km; 1–1.5 hours; out-and-return.**

3. Brown-hooded Kingfisher Trail passes through lush riverine bush along the Duiwe River, which is crossed several times (slippery rocks necessitate caution at river crossings). Just before the junction of the Duiwe and Klein Keurbooms rivers an optional short steep climb leads to a viewsite. A short way on, the trail branches off to follow the Klein Keurbooms River to a magnificent pool. The start is signposted on the Lakes Road, east of Ebb and Flow North Restcamp. **5 km; 2–3 hours; out-and-return.**

4. Cape Dune Molerat Trail traverses the area between Rondevlei and Swartvlei and offers excellent birding opportunities. Two interlinked options are available. **Route A** winds along the base of the dunes to the shores of Swartvlei, where a birdhide provides excellent birding opportunities. At the eastern end of the dune the trail climbs steeply to the dune crest, which provides excellent views over Swartvlei and the coastal plains. It then follows the dune crest before winding down the start. **6 km; 2 hours; circular.**

Route B splits off Route A after 1 km and then makes a wide loop, which winds partly along the banks of the Wolwe River. Birding in the reed beds along the river can be very rewarding, so remember to take binoculars. After 4 km the trail joins up with Route A, continuing to the shores of Swartvlei before returning along the dune crest. **8 km; 2.5 hours; circular.**

5. Giant Kingfisher Trail starts at the Ebb and Flow North Restcamp. The trail traverses the slopes above the Touw River before descending to the river, which it follows upstream. It then continues through indigenous forest and, further on, comes to a small waterfall and a series of rock pools. **7 km; 3–4 hours; out-and-return.**

6. Pied Kingfisher Trail Starting at the Ebb and Flow South Restcamp this route initially follows the edge of the Serpentine floodplain. Further along, it follows the boardwalk alongside Wilderness Lagoon to the Touw River mouth. From here you continue down the sandy coastline, eastwards, for about 2 km, before following a road back to the restcamp. **10 km; 3–4 hours; circular.**

21. OUTENIQUA HIKING TRAIL
Beervlei to Harkerville

Trail: 108 km; 7 days, with shorter options; open-ended.
Permits: Department of Water Affairs and Forestry, Private Bag X12, Knysna 6570, tel: (044) 382 5466.
Maps: Colour map and information pamphlet.
Facilities/Activities: Huts with bunk beds, mattresses, firewood and water.
Pertinent information: Be prepared for rain and mist. After rain the forest paths can be very slippery, necessitating footwear with a good grip.

The indigenous forests of the Knysna region constitute the largest natural forest area in the whole of South Africa, covering some 28,600 ha of state forest and 16,000 ha of private land. The forests are composed of some 142 woody tree and shrub species, among them real and Outeniqua yellowwood, stinkwood, ironwood, red alder, Cape beech, tree fuchsia, Cape holly and assegai. Along the stream banks there are a number of impressive fern, tree fern and colourful moss species to be seen.

On account of the dense vegetation and the high canopies birds are more often heard than seen. Among the 40 typical forest birds you may tick are the

Knysna lourie, Narina trogon, the chorister, Cape and starred robins, the olive thrush, and terrestrial bulbul.

The forests are the habitat of bushbuck, bushpig, blue duiker, vervet monkey and leopard, as well as a variety of seldom seen small mammals that are either elusive or nocturnal. On the second day of the trail, make sure that you keep an eye out for grey rhebok, klipspringer and baboon in the fynbos and mountainous areas.

This trail goes through majestic indigenous forest, aromatic pine plantations and fynbos-covered mountain slopes. Opened in November 1976, the original Outeniqua Hiking Trail was designed as an 8-day, 149-km hike between Witfontein, outside George, and Diepwalle. However, by the time many hikers had reached Tierkop Hut, after a murderous 22 km on the first day, their enthusiasm had gone. As a result, sections of the trail were re-routed, and the 4-day trail between Witfontein and Windmeulnek was eventually closed. Although the trail still has its fair share of ascents and descents, as well as fairly long distances on some days, it is a pleasant hike, with several shorter options.

From Beervlei day one's hike (16 km; 5.5 hours) traverses easy terrain through the Beervlei indigenous forest and then descends through pine plantations to the Hoëkraal River. The next 8 km to Windmeulnek Hut is a steady ascent through the pines of SAFCOL's Karatara Plantation.

The Windmeulnek/Platbos leg on day two (17 km; 5.5 km) is through fynbos, except for the last 3 km, which is through pine plantations. From Windmeulnek the trail makes its way down to the Karatara River and then steadily upwards along the slopes of Spitskop before reaching a pool in the Plaat River. After a gentle ascent up the slopes of the Kagiesberg, the trail makes its way down to Platbos.

On day three (15.5 km; 7 hours) the trail initially ascends through indigenous forest and pine plantations to the Homtini River, and from here it follows a gently undulating route through plantations and indigenous forest to Jubilee Creek. After you pass Jubilee Creek there is a steep climb that has to be negotiated before you reach Millwood Hut.

Just over half of the fourth day's hike (17 km; 5 hours) is either level or downhill, passing first through pine plantations and then indigenous forest. Continuing through magnificent indigenous forest, the trail gains over 300 m in altitude

as it climbs out of the kloof carved by the Knysna River. An easy downhill stretch rounds off the day's hike at Rondebossie Hut.

Day five's hike (13 km; 5 hours) moves back and forth through forest and pine plantation margins, to fynbos and the indigenous forest of Diepwalle. The day begins with a sustained climb to the beacon on Jonkersberg, followed by a long, gradual descent to the Gouna River. The final section is an easy 2.5-km climb to Diepwalle Hut.

The sixth day's hike (16 km; 5 hours) follows a trail with gentle descents and ascents at the four rivers you encounter along the way. Most of the hike to Fisantehoek is through indigenous forest interspersed with fynbos islands.

The final leg of the trail, on the seventh day (12 km; 4.5 hours), is a relatively easy hike through indigenous forest, with only one gentle incline close to the beginning of the trail. The remainder of the day's hike to Harkerville is either level or downhill.

22. GOUDVELD STATE FOREST
Knysna

Trails: 3 trails; 4 to 9 km; 1.5 to 3 hours; out-and-return and circular.
Permits: Self-issue permits at start.
Maps: Sketch map available.
Facilities/Activities: Picnic sites at Jubilee Creek, Millwood and Krisjan-se-Nek; Mining Museum, Bendigo mining village and tea room at Millwood.

Covering 5,150 ha, Goudveld is the largest tract of indigenous forest in the Knysna area and was once the scene of frantic gold mining. Prospectors and miners began flocking to the Knysna forests after the discovery of a gold nugget in the Karatara River in 1876.

Following the discovery of rich alluvial gold in 1885, and reef gold the following year, mining activity in the Knysna area reached fever pitch. By 1887 Millwood had a permanent population of 400 inhabitants (as well as about 600 diggers), six hotels, three newspapers and various shops. Most of the miners left for the Witwatersrand with the discovery of gold there in 1886, and by 1893

Millwood's population had decreased to 74. As the remaining inhabitants drifted off, the ramshackle tin and iron houses were reclaimed by the forest and all that remains from this era are the mine shafts, pieces of mining machinery, a cemetery, and the Matterolli House, one of only two surviving corrugated iron houses. It now serves as a tea room. The other one was dismantled and re-erected in Knysna where it now serves as a museum.

1. Jubilee Creek Walk From the Jubilee Creek picnic site, the route follows a section of the Outeniqua Hiking Trail through indigenous forest along a tranquil stream. Relics of the frantic search for gold in the 1880s include the remains of an old diggings pit and a water furrow. The trail ends at a pool and waterfall, where you swim. **4 km; 1.5 hours; out-and-return.**

2. Millwood Mining Walk passes through pine plantations and then ascends to Nols se Kop before swinging back to the old Bendigo Mine. The mine is being restored and among the displays are various pieces of mining machinery, including a portable steam engine, stamp battery, boiler and a crusher. Along the way there are also a few old mining adits. The trail starts and ends at the Millwood picnic site. **5.6 km; 2 hours; circular.**

3. Woodcutter Trail recalls the hectic gold mining days at Millwood when the indigenous forest was heavily exploited for mining timber. From the picnic site at Krisjan-se-Nek the trail passes through magnificent indigenous forest to Forest Creek and then makes a wide loop to Langrugpad, which is followed to Jubilee Creek. You will find the stream's inviting natural pools especially refreshing on a hot summer's day. The final section of the walk follows a gravel road. **9 km; 3 hours; circular.**

23. GOUKAMMA NATURE AND MARINE RESERVE
Sedgefield

Trails: 3 trails; 8 to 16 km; 2 to 5 hours; circular and open-ended.
Permits: Entry fee. No permit required.

Maps: Reserve pamphlet with trails indicated.
Facilities/Activities: Bushcamp on the shores of Groenvlei; picnic sites, swimming, sailing and canoeing on Keurboom's River; sea and freshwater angling (permits required).
Pertinent information: The Beach Walk is inaccessible during high spring tide and is best hiked at lowtide. Because of rip currents along the coast, swimming is dangerous.

The 2,500-ha Goukamma Nature and Marine Reserve protects a 14-km-long stretch of beach, the Goukamma River Estuary, vegetated dunes, coastal forest and Groenvlei Lake. Landlocked Groenvlei is the only freshwater lake in the string of lakes between Wilderness and Sedgefield, and as it is not fed by any rivers it is recharged only by rainwater seeping from the surrounding dunes. The marine reserve, next to the nature reserve, extends 1.8 km seawards.

The reserve's vegetation is characterised by coastal dune fynbos and coastal dune forest, with extensive stands of milkwood. Among the more than 220 bird species recorded to date are the African marsh harrier, African fish eagle, several waterfowl species, the giant and half-collared kingfisher, and the African finfoot. Also look out for African black oystercatchers along the coast.

Animals occurring in the reserve include bushbuck, grysbok, bushpig, water and grey mongoose, Cape clawless otter, caracal and porcupine.

1. Circular Route The outward leg of the trail follows the western bank of the Goukamma River for a short way and then follows a valley between the dunes. A distinctive feature here is the milkwood forest growing at the base of the dunes. After passing through this forest the trail ascends to the fynbos-covered ridge of the dune, from where there are wonderful views of the coast, the Goukamma River and its estuary. The trail then climbs gently along the ridge to a trigonometric beacon from where it descends steeply to the start. **8 km; 2–3 hours; circular.**

2. Beach Walk follows the unspoilt coastline between Rowwehoek and Platbank. Along the way trailists can explore the intertidal zone and look out for bottle-nosed and common dolphins. Between August and December there is the possibility of seeing southern right whales. You must arrange transport at Platbank or, alternatively, you can hike an out-and-return route half the distance. **14 km; 4 hours; open-ended.**

3. Goukamma to Groenvlei Trail follows the outward leg of the Circular Route to the information boards at the western end of the dune ridge. From here the trail makes its way up and over the dunes, and after passing through a milkwood forest reaches a table and benches on a dune ridge. A short way on, the trail swings to the northwest, passing through another milkwood forest above Groenvlei, before reaching the end. **16 km; 4–5 hours; open-ended.**

24. GOUNA FOREST
Knysna

Trails: 6.5 km; 2 hours; circular.
Permits: Self-issue permits at start.
Maps: Available at start.
Facilities/Activities: Picnic site at Grootdraai.

Terblans Walk owes its name to the Terblanz beech, known in Afrikaans as the Terblans. A member of the protea family, the Terblans occurs in the southern Cape only in the Gouna Forest and has a limited distribution elsewhere in South Africa.

Starting at Grootdraai picnic site, the route passes through a section of the 3,450-ha Gouna Forest, the second-largest tract of indigenous forest in the Knysna area. Along the course of the trail there are a number of large Outeniqua yellowwoods and magnificent groves of ferns. At Witplekbos, just beyond the halfway mark, there is a delightful swimming pool. Except at the Rooiels River crossing, where the descent is followed by a steep climb, the terrain is relatively flat.

25. DIEPWALLE FOREST
Knysna

Trails: 7 to 9 km; 2 to 3 hours; network.
Permits: Self-issue permits at start.

Maps: Available at start.
Facilities/Activities: Picnic sites at Ysterhoutrug, Big Tree and Velbroekdraai; cycle route to Garden of Eden.

The Diepwalle indigenous forest covers 3,200 ha and was once the last refuge of the famed Knysna elephants. Numbering between 400 and 500 in the 1800s, they were relentlessly hunted for their ivory following the Millwood gold rush, and by the early 1900s their numbers had declined to a mere 50.

By 1920 the population had decreased even further and for the next 50 years remained unchanged at between 11 and 13 animals. Only three elephants were found when a census was conducted in 1979 and a plan to resettle three young elephants from the Kruger National Park in 1994 was unsuccessful. Only one elephant, an old cow, was found during a search for the remaining elephants during the same year. Then, quite unexpectedly, a young bull was seen in the Gouna Forest in September 2000.

Elephant Walk This walk makes its way through indigenous forest dissected by numerous tranquil streams and rivers. The trail network passes through moist, medium moist, wet and very wet forest types. Trees in the moist forest type reach heights of 15–30 m and this type of forest is, therefore, also referred to as 'high forest'. Typical species include real and Outeniqua yellowwoods, stinkwood, white pear and ironwood. The wet forest type is confined to river valleys and ravines, and is characterised by red and white alder, tree fuchsia, stinkwood and Cape holly.

The trail network offers a choice of three different colour-coded routes: red (7 km; 2 hours), white (8 km; 2.5 hours) and black (9 km; 3 hours).

26. BAY TO BAY HIKING TRAIL
Nollshalte

Trail: 21.9 km; 2 days; circular.
Permits: The Manager, Millwood Nature Reserve, P O Box 48, Uniondale 6460, tel: (044) 874 2160, fax: 874 1567, email: george@cnc.org.za

Maps: Brochure with sketch map.
Facilities/Activities: Campsite with water and toilet, but no shower; covered picnic area.

Starting from Vergenoeg Apple Farm at Nollshalte, the trail ascends steadily, through fynbos, to the crest of the Outeniqua Mountains. An 8-km detour to the 1,453-m-high Spitskop is rewarded with spectacular views of the coast, from the Tsitsikamma coast to Plettenberg Bay, Knysna and Sedgefield.

The trail follows the crest and descends along a road to the overnight stop in the Millwood basin. The Millwood Nature Reserve is one of several small reserves proclaimed in the Knysna forests to protect the natural forests of the southern Cape. Of historic interest here are numerous relics of the gold rush era of the late 1800s. The day's hike covers 13.9 km, excluding the 8-km detour to Spitskop.

On day two (8 km; 4 hours) the trail backtracks to the crest, from where you follow the exit signboards back to the starting point.

27. HARKERVILLE COAST HIKING TRAIL
Harkerville Forest, Plettenberg Bay

See no. 28 (this page) for walks.

Trail: 27 km; 2 days; circular.
Permits: Department of Water Affairs and Forestry, Private Bag X12, Knysna 6570, tel: (044) 382 5466.
Maps: Colour map with information.
Facilities/Activities: Huts with bunk beds and mattresses, fireplaces, water and toilets.
Pertinent information: Chains have been anchored into rock faces to assist hikers at difficult places along the coast. Assistance might be necessary for those afraid of heights.

Part of the trail winds through the Sinclair Nature Reserve, with its indigenous forest, and along the rugged coastline. The first day's route (15 km; 7 hours) is an easy ramble through indigenous forest for about 11 km and then a steep descent to the

spectacular coast, with its sheer cliffs, small coves strewn with loose round rocks, gullies, and rocky headlands. Wooden ladders and a chain handhold assist hikers in difficult places. The 2.5-km coastal stretch is followed by a steep climb up to the coastal plateau and the Sinclair overnight hut.

The second day's hike (12 km; 6 hours) traverses the coastal plateau for about 2 km, then descends a forested kloof, and through fynbos, to the coastline. Once again there are many difficult sections, one of which has to be negotiated without a chain handhold. Further on, the trail passes through a rock arch and, after following the coastline for about 2 km, climbs steeply to the plateau. The trail ascends gradually through indigenous forest before levelling off.

28. HARKERVILLE INDIGENOUS FOREST
Plettenberg Bay

See no. 27 (this page) for hiking trail.

Trails: 2 trails; 9.4 and 9.5 km; 3 and 3.5 hours; circular.
Permits: Self-issue permits at start.
Maps: Obtainable at start.
Facilities/Activities: Picnic sites at Kranshoek Waterfall and Viewpoint.

1. Kranshoek Coastal Walk From the waterfall at the Kranshoek picnic site the trail descends steeply through indigenous forest down the gorge carved by the Kranshoek River. The route then follows the rugged coastline for about 3.5 km to the mouth of Crooks River. A steep climb up to the coastal plateau is followed by an easy walk along a gravel road back to the picnic site. **9.4 km; 3.5 hours; circular.**

2. Perdekop Nature Walk Starting at Harkerville Forest Station, the walk takes an easy route through cool, indigenous forest to Perdekop, with its lovely stand of hard pear trees. The pool below the waterfall in the Perdekop River is an ideal spot for a break or a swim. From here the route ascends steeply to Kleineiland Pad. The remainder of the walk is an easy ramble through indigenous forest. **9.5 km; 3 hours; circular.**

29. ROBBERG NATURE AND MARINE RESERVE
Plettenberg Bay

> **Trails:** 9 km; 3 hours, with shorter options; circular.
> **Permits:** Entrance fee. No permit required.
> **Maps:** Sketch map of trail.
> **Facilities/Activities:** Picnic sites; interpretation centre.
> **Pertinent information:** Parts of the trail to The Point traverse high cliffs and difficult, rocky terrain, which can be dangerous for inexperienced trailists. Freak waves and strong currents make swimming inadvisable. Do not climb the sand dune above Witsand, as it is unstable.

The 175-ha Robberg Nature and Marine Reserve protects the Robberg Peninsula, which is a 4-km-long promontory ranging in width from 250 m at The Gap to about 1 km in the vicinity of The Island. The vegetation alternates between coastal scrub and thickets, and amongst the animals you may chance upon are common duiker and Cape grysbok.

Highlights of the trail, which follows mainly the cliff edges, include the magnificent rock pools at The Point and the beautiful white beach at Percy's Bank. From the high cliffs there are also expansive views of the long sweep of white beach to Plettenberg Bay and the coastline to the west. There are two shorter options: a 2.1-km walk via The Gap and a 5-km walk via Witsand Island.

30. STINKHOUTKLOOF NATURE WALK
Bloukrans State Forest

> **Trail:** 8 km; 3 hours; circular.
> **Permits:** Self-issue permit at start.
> **Maps:** Available at start.
> **Facilities/Activities:** Picnic site at start; drinking water.

The trail initially goes through pine plantations before winding for a few hundred metres through the magnificent indigenous forest in the upper reaches of Stinkhoutkloof. It then returns to plantations for just over 1 km, passing through a small patch of fynbos before entering the indigenous forest once more. Several streams are crossed, and the tall tree ferns growing along the banks are unlikely to escape attention. Near the 5-km mark there is a lovely natural swimming pool. Continuing through forest, you reach the old Main Road, just beyond the 6-km mark, and follow it back to the Bloukrans Forest Station, which is also the start of the trail.

31. TSITSIKAMMA HIKING TRAIL
Nature's Valley/Storms River Bridge

> **Trail:** 60,8 km; 5 days; open-ended.
> **Permits:** SAFCOL Ecotourism,
> P O Box 1771, Silverton 0127,
> tel: (012) 481 3615, fax: 481 3622,
> email: ecotour@safcol.co.za
> **Maps:** A4 colour sketch map of trail.
> **Facilities/Activities:** Overnight huts with bunks, beds, cooking shelters, cold showers and toilets.

This delightful trail traverses the slopes of the Tsitsikamma Mountains, crossing amber-coloured streams and passing through small patches of forest, where leafy fern glades and colourful fungi create fairytale scenes. Most of the trail is, however, through mountain fynbos vegetation, with magnificent mountain scenery and far-reaching views.

The Tsitsikamma region supports a richer birdlife than the fynbos areas further west, and more than 217 species have been recorded in the area. This is mainly due to the more varied habitat created by the mix of fynbos and indigenous forest patches. Species to look out for include the Knysna and Victorin's warbler, Cape sugarbird, the malachite and orange-breasted sunbird, the Cape rock thrush, and greater honeyguide.

Day one's hike (16.6 km; 7 hours) passes mainly through the indigenous forests of Grootkloof and Platbos. Except for the climbs at Douwurmkop, soon after the beginning of the hike, and Staircase Falls, the terrain is easy. Staircase Falls, reached 4 hours from the start, is an ideal lunch stop. The remaining 5 km to Blaauwkrantz Hut is through pine plantations.

Day two (13.4 km; 4 hours) begins with a steep climb and then, save for the drop to the Bloukrans River, follows a gradual incline for most of the day. Most of the hike is through open fynbos, with small relic patches of forest at Buffelsbos and Benebos. Keurbos Hut is situated on the edge of a small patch of indigenous forest.

The gentle descent to the Lottering River on the third day's hike (13.4 km; 4 hours) is followed by a steady climb up the Rushes Pass. The trail then winds down to the Lottering River, from where you follow a gently undulating route through pine plantations to Heuningbos Hut.

Day four's hike (14.2 km; 7 hours) is mainly through fynbos, and involves two fairly steep climbs: up the Splendid Pass and to Nademaalnek. The Splendid Pass owes its name to the rare silver mimetes (*Mimetes splendidus*) which occurs here. If you make an early start, take your time, and enjoy the magnificent scenery, the day's hike will not be nearly as daunting as it appears. From Nademaalnek the trail descends Teebosrug, a ridge named after the abundance of wild bush tea (*Cyclopia subternata*) and then descends through indigenous forest to Sleepkloof Hut.

The final day's hike (3.2 km; 1 hour) is an easy walk through indigenous forest and rank fynbos to the Storms River Bridge, where the trail ends.

32. TSITSIKAMMA NATIONAL PARK
De Vasselot Section, Nature's Valley

See no. 33 (p. 106) for walks at Storms River Mouth and no. 34 (p. 107) for hiking trail.

Trails: 6 trails; 4.8 to 17.1 km; 2.5 to 7 hours; circular, open-ended.
Reservations: Entrance fee. No permit required for walks.
Maps: Colour trail map.
Facilities/Activities: De Vasselot campsite: self-catering forest cabins, campsites with ablutions; canoes for hire.

The De Vasselot section lies at the western end of the Tsitsikamma National Park and includes the coastal plateau (which rises some 300 m above sea level), forested slopes and a section of rugged coastline. Indigenous forests account for nearly two-thirds of the 2,560-ha section of the park, while fynbos covers the remainder.

Named after Comte Médéric de Vasselot de Regné, who was appointed in 1880 as Superintendent of Woods and Forests of the Cape Colony, the area was declared a forestry nature reserve in 1974. It became part of the Tsitsikamma National Park in 1987.

The network of interlinking trails runs through coastal scrub forest, high indigenous forest, and fynbos vegetation on the plateau.

1. Kalanderkloof Trail owes its name to the colloquial name for the Outeniqua yellowwood, which grows in great abundance here. Starting opposite the entrance to the De Vasselot campsite, the trail ascends steadily through indigenous forest before emerging into fynbos. From the viewpoint here, you can enjoy beautiful, expansive vistas, including the lagoon and the densely forested kloofs. The return leg is through indigenous forest, along the kloof. **4.8 km; 2.5 hours; circular.**

2. Groot River Trail follows the eastern banks of the Groot River to its mouth, and continues along the sandy beach, eastwards, to The Gully. From here the trail follows the last section of the Otter Trail in reverse, ascending The Point (the promontory above The Gully) from where there are magnificent views over the coastline. From the gate on the promontory retrace your tracks, cross the Groot River mouth, and follow the road back to your starting point at the De Vasselot campsite. **6 km; 2.5 hours; circular.**

3. Salt River Mouth From the shop at Nature's Valley the trail ascends through scrub forest to a viewpoint, and a short way further along joins a jeep track. You turn left here and follow the path to the Salt River. The return leg leads through scrub forest, and then along and above the rocks, past Pebble Beach, named after the pebbles of different hues and sizes washed up here. **9 km; 2.5 hours; circular.**

4. Salt River via Keurpad initially follows the outward leg of the Kalanderkloof Trail, but from the viewpoint the trail continues to the head of Kalanderkloof. After crossing the R102 the trail continues through fynbos, along the Keurpad Route, named after a grove of blossom trees, which are known in Afrikaans as *keurbome*. About 2 km after crossing the Salt River the trail links up with Rugpad, which leads through indigenous forest to the Salt River mouth, from where you can follow the coast back to Nature's Valley. **15.1 km; 6 hours; circular.**

5. Varinghoek via Keurpad starts at the picnic site on the Plettenberg Bay side of the Groot River Pass. The route is mainly through indigenous forest, except along Keurpad, which traverses the fynbos of the coastal plateau, and across two patches of fynbos along the Brak River Route. From the Salt River it is a steady climb back to the starting point. **16 km; 6 hours; circular.**

6. The Crags via Brak River Starting from the De Vasselot campsite, this route leads to Nature's Valley, from where you follow the Salt River Route across the Salt River. Further on, you make your way along the Brak River Route on a jeep track and a firebreak before joining a gravel road, which leads to the SANP (South African National Parks) ranger's house, where parking is available. **17.1 km; 7 hours; open-ended.**

33. TSITSIKAMMA NATIONAL PARK
Storms River Mouth

See no. 32 (p. 105) for walks in De Vasselot and no. 34 (p. 107) for hiking trail.

Trails: 3 trails; 3 to 6 km; 2.5 to 3 hours; out-and-return.
Permits: Entrance fee. No permits required.
Maps: Sketch maps.
Facilities/Activities: Self-catering accommodation; restaurant; underwater (scuba) trail; boat cruises up Storms River Gorge.

Stretching between Grootbank in the west and the Groot River near Humansdorp in the east, the 4,172-ha Tsitsikamma National Park is a kaleidoscope of sheer cliffs, secluded bays and deeply eroded gorges, as well as indigenous forests.

When the park was proclaimed in 1964 its offshore boundary extended about 300 m seawards, making it the first marine national park in South Africa. The marine boundary was subsequently extended to 5.5 km out to sea. The inland boundary more or less follows the 200-m contour line.

The vegetation of the coastal belt is typical, scrub-like, dry forest, lacking the luxuriant undergrowth of the high forests further inland. Species found here include white milkwood and wild camphor, while Outeniqua yellowwood, stinkwood, red alder, small-leaved saffron and Cape beech also occur. The flora of the coastal plateau is characterised by fynbos.

Some 40 of the 210 bird species recorded to date (such as the African black oystercatcher, turnstone, white-breasted cormorant, Caspian tern and kelp gull) are associated with the sea and shore. Among the forest species to look out for is the Knysna lourie, green-spotted dove, terrestrial bulbul, starred robin, blue-mantled flycatcher and olive bush shrike.

Mammals inhabiting the forest include the rare blue duiker, bushbuck, bushpig, vervet monkey, leopard and caracal, while the Cape clawless otter favours the area's perennial rivers and marshes.

1. Waterfall Trail follows the first 2.6 km of the Otter Trail to a magnificent waterfall that cascades over several steps into an inviting pool. **3 km; 3 hours; out-and-return.**

2. Mouth and Lookout Trail passes through indigenous forest to a cave (inhabited by Khoikhoi and Bushmen people in the distant past) above Storms River Mouth. Bounded by sheer cliffs, the mouth is crossed by means of a suspension bridge, and a steep climb to the plateau is rewarded with fine views over the restcamp and the rugged Tsitsikamma coastline. **4 km; 2.5 hours; out-and-return.**

3. Blue Duiker Trail makes its way through scrub to the Agulhas Lookout and then enters the indigenous dry forest, where you may chance upon a blue duiker. The trail crosses a small stream, with an enchanting cascade, and offers ample opportunity for birding. **6 km; 3 hours; out-and-return.**

34. OTTER HIKING TRAIL
Tsitsikamma National Park

See nos. 32 (p. 105) and 33 (p. 106) for walks.

> **Trail:** 41 km; 5 days; open-ended.
> **Permits:** Book well in advance. National
> Parks Board, P O Box 787, Pretoria, 0001
> tel: (012) 428 9111, fax: 343 0905,
> email: reservations@parks-sa.co.za
> **Maps:** Colour map and trail pamphlet.
> **Facilities/Activities:** Huts with bunks
> and mattresses, fireplaces, firewood,
> water and toilets.
> **Pertinent information:** Consult a tide table
> and plan to cross the Lottering River (day 3)
> and the Bloukrans River (day 4) at lowtide. A
> survival bag is useful to float your pack
> across if you must swim. Although firewood
> is usually supplied, it is not always available,
> making it advisable to carry a backpacking
> stove. Use water at the huts sparingly, as it
> comes from rainwater tanks filled by
> runoff from the hut roofs.

Twilight coastal forests, huge waves crashing against the rugged coastline, secluded bays and a coastal plateau covered with ericas and proteas – this is the beautiful scenery of the Otter Hiking Trail. The first official hiking trail to be opened in South Africa, in 1968, the route goes from the Storms River Restcamp to Nature's Valley, along what is undoubtedly one of the most spectacular stretches of coastline in South Africa.

The trail owes its name to the Cape clawless otter, which lives in the perennial rivers and marshes along the coast. Along the Tsitsikamma coast they also frequent the intertidal zone and the sea. Shy and noctural creatures, they are very seldom seen, but with some patience and luck you may see one in the late afternoon, usually where a river enters the sea.

The first day's hike (4.8 km; 2 hours) wends its way along the edge of the coastal forest and takes you over rocks to Waterfall River, with its beautiful waterfall that cascades into a huge natural pool. A short climb through indigenous forest, followed by a descent to a valley, brings you to the first overnight stop, which is at Ngubu's Huts.

At the very beginning of day two (7.9 km; 4 hours) the trail ascends steeply to the plateau. Beyond Skilderkrans the trail descends to a stream, before climbing once again, and then after a level stretch drops down to the Kleinbos River, with its narrow gorge, pools and waterfalls. From the Kleinbos River the trail returns to the plateau, only to lose height once again and, after a final steep climb, makes its way down to Scott's Huts on the banks of the Geelhout River.

Day three (7.7 km; 4 hours) follows quite an undulating course across forested slopes, stretches of the coast and the plateau. At lowtide the Lottering River-crossing is easy, but during high tide, or if a gully has been washed open after rains, you might be in for a swim. From here it is a 20-minute walk to Oakhurst Huts.

Although the fourth day (13.8 km; 6 hours) is the longest stretch of the trail, the gently rolling terrain is fairly undemanding. Alternating between the coastline and the indigenous forest, the trail leads you to the Bloukrans River after 10 km. Beyond the river the path climbs steeply to the coastal plateau, from where there are fine views over the coastline. The trail then descends steeply to Andre's Huts, which nestle in indigenous forest alongside the Klip River.

Day five (6.8 km; 3 hours) begins with a steep climb to the plateau and, except for a gentle descent and ascent at Helpmekaarkloof, this day involves just an easy ramble along the clifftops to The Point. From here you look down onto the Groot River estuary and the spectacular white sandy beach of Nature's Valley. After climbing down to the beach and crossing the estuary you have an easy walk to either Nature's Valley or the Groot River campsite.

35. STORMS RIVER WALKS
Storms River village and bridge

> **Trails:** 2 trails; 4.2 to 8 km; 1.5 to
> 2.5 hours. Shorter options available.
> **Permits:** Self-issue permits at start.

Maps: Available at start.
Facilities/Activities: Picnic sites at Ou Brug and Storms River Bridge.

1. Ratel Nature Walk has been laid out in the area surrounding the famous Tsitsikamma Big Tree and consists of three interlinked routes. The **Green Route** is a 1.2-km circular walk to the Big Tree. Towering an incredible 36.6 m above the forest floor, this enormous Outeniqua yellowwood has a circumference of 8.5 m at chest height and a crown spread of 32.5 m.

From the Big Tree, the **Yellow Route** (2.6 km) makes a wide loop, passing yet another enormous Outeniqua yellowwood along the way. The **Red Route** consists of a 1.6-km loop that branches off from the Yellow Route. There are also a number of huge hard pear trees that trailists will see during the course of the walk. **4.2 km; 1.5 hours, with shorter options; circular.**

2. Plaatbos Nature Walk makes its way through indigenous forests to the south of the N2. The trail network offers four options. The **Green** (5.09 km), **Red** (7.78 km) and **Yellow** (8.1 km) **routes** start and end at the Forestry Office in Storms River village, while the **Blue Route** (830 m) starts and ends at the Storms River Bridge picnic site. **8 km; 2.5 hours; circular.**

36. DOLPHIN TRAIL
Storms River

Trail: 20 km; 2 days; open-ended.
Permits: National Parks Board,
P O Box 787, Pretoria,
tel: (012) 428 9111, fax: 343 0905,
email: reservations@parks-sa.co.za
Maps: None available.
Facilities/Activities: Luxury overnight accommodation; gourmet dinners, breakfasts, picnic lunches and a forest tea.
Pertinent information: Since all luggage is carried by porters to the overnight stops, hikers need only carry a daypack and binoculars.

This luxury hike along the Tsitsikamma coast is a partnership between SANP and the private sector. Hikers are accompanied by trained field guides, who will introduce them to the wonders of nature and the marine environment.

From the Storms River Restcamp, guests are taken on a scenic drive in a four-wheel-drive vehicle along the old Storms River Pass to the Forest Ferns estate, where the trail starts. Here guests are shown the fernery and a video on the cultivation and export of the ferns. Accommodation is in luxury chalets built on the edge of the Sanddrift River.

The first day's hike leads through plantations and indigenous forests where a forest tea is served. The trail then descends to the rugged coastline, with its cliffs and natural tidal pools, which can be explored with snorkelling gear. Most of the day's hike is along the coast, but at the end there is a steep climb back to the plateau where accommodation is in the cottages of the Misty Mountain Dairy Farm.

The second day's hike, on the escarpment, leads through fynbos, and provides the ideal vantage point from which to see schools of dolphins and pods of whales. From Bakenrant the trail drops steeply down to the coast and crosses the Storms River by way of the suspension bridge. After a leisurely cruise in a motor launch along Storms River Gorge you hike the remaining 1.5 km from Storms River Mouth back to the restcamp, where accommodation is in log cabins. The hike concludes with a dinner in the Storms River Restcamp restaurant.

37. BOSKLOOF TRAIL
Humansdorp

Trail: 3 km; 1 hour; circular.
Permits: Not required.
Maps: Rough sketch map.
Facilities/Activities: None.

Starting from the entrance next to the gardens of Indaba House in Voortrekker Road, Humansdorp, the trail winds alongside a stream in Boskloof, ascending gently. At the head of the kloof the trail passes through a charming forest, an ideal resting place. The return leg follows the eastern bank of the stream.

Indigenous trees occurring along the trail include the broom cluster fig, Cape ash, red currant, candlewood, white pear, hard pear and Cape beech. Sections of the trail pass through scrub forest and fynbos, and krantz aloe, which are particularly conspicuous amongst the cliffs, can also be seen. Among the birds you may tick are the Cape robin, red-billed woodhoopoe, greater honeyguide and forest canary.

38. LE FEROX PARADIS TRAILS
Joubertinia

Trails: 6 km to tailor-made hikes of various distances; 4 hours to a full day; network.
Permits: Le Ferox Paradis, P O Box 218, Joubertinia 6410, tel: (042) 273 2079.
Maps: Sketch map.
Facilities/Activities: Fully equipped self-catering bungalow (sleeps 16); full-board accommodation in the farmhouse; camping.

The Le Ferox Paradis Private Nature Reserve forms part of a 2,000-ha farm, which is bounded to the north by the rugged Kouga Mountains and the Langkloof Valley to the south.

The vegetation ranges from indigenous forest in protected kloofs, and fynbos at higher elevations, to hardy Karoo scrub. Unlikely to escape attention is the bitter aloe (*Aloe ferox*) after which the nature reserve has been named. Also to be seen are rare elephant's foot plants (*Dioscorea elephantipes*), haworthias and cycads.

The Kouga River and its tributaries flow through the reserve, their wild kloofs adding to the allure of the reserve. Animals you may see include the common duiker, grey rhebok and grysbok, Aardwolf, civet and leopard are also found here, but are seldom seen. The reserve offers good birding opportunities, and among the species you may tick are black and fish eagles, blue crane and Knysna lourie.

Kloof Route follows the course of the Braam River upstream and features fascinating rock formations, inviting pools, rock paintings and indigenous forests. **6 km; 4–5 hours; circular.**

Trailists can also walk along the Kouga River, while the **Fynbos-Aloe Route** follows a circuit between the Kouga and Wabooms rivers. In the area south of the Wabooms River hikers can blaze their own trails, including a hike to the Tweerivier River.

39. LOUTERWATER TRAILS
Joubertinia

Trails: 4 trails; 4 to 10 km;
3 to 7 hours; circular.
Permits: Louterwater Estate,
P O Box 44, Louterwater 6435,
tel: (042) 272 1724, fax: 272 1493.
Maps: Sketch map.
Facilities/Activities: Self-catering wooden chalets with beds, mattresses, braai area and toilets; tractor tours.

Louterwater Estate, an apple and pear farm in the northern foothills of the Tsitsikamma Mountains, was the first farm in the Langkloof to open to the public. The basecamp for the hike is situated next to an inviting pool in the Louterwater River. In addition to enjoying the outdoors, visitors can also obtain an insight into the cultivation, harvesting and packing of the farm's fruit.

1. Bloukrans Bridge Route leads through fynbos along the northern slopes of the Tsitsikamma Mountains and then ascends to the crest of the range. From the summit there are far-reaching views of the Langkloof to the north and the Tsitsikamma forests and the 216-m-high Bloukrans River bridge to the south. **4 km; 3 hours; circular.**

2. Tsitsikammakloof Route meanders next to a river, through indigenous forest, where no fewer than 11 fern species and tall tree ferns can be seen. You pass natural pools along the way and there are a number of detours to waterfalls. The trail ascends steeply to emerge into fynbos where the king protea (*Protea cynaroides*) is conspicuous. **7 km; 5 hours; circular.**

3. Langkloof Route This route follows the contours of the Tsitsikamma Mountains, through fynbos, and offers lovely views of the Kouga and Baviaanskloof mountains to the north. Among the protea species to be seen are the white, broad-leaved, blue and real sugarbushes. Keep an eye out for grey rhebok, which can often be seen along the trail. On the return leg hikers can cool off in a farm dam, where a canoe is available. **10 km; 6 hours; circular.**

4. Peak Formosa For the more adventurous there is an off-the-beaten-track route to the 1,675-m-high Peak Formosa, the highest peak in the Langeberg range. This is a demanding hike that should only be attempted by fit and experienced hikers.

40. BAVIAANSKLOOF CONSERVATION AREA
Patensie

> *Trails:* Numerous footpaths throughout the conservation area.
> *Permits:* Officer-in-Charge, Baviaanskloof Conservation Area, P O Box 218, Patensie 6335, tel: (040) 635 2115, fax: 635 2535.
> *Maps:* The 1:50,000 topographical map, Baviaanskloof Wilderness Area, available from the reservation office, is indispensable.
> *Facilities/Activities:* Komdomo: camping sites with ablution facilities, picnic sites, canoeing, swimming; Geelhoutbos: self-catering chalets; Doodsklip and Rooihoek: basic camping sites, freshwater angling (permit required), swimming, mountain biking and 4x4 trails.
> *Pertinent information:* As the footpaths are not marked and the terrain is quite rugged, this area should only be explored by fit and experienced hikers. A map is essential.

Covering 200,000 ha of impressive peaks, deep ravines, valleys and plateaux, the greater Baviaanskloof Conservation Area is a remote and wild stretch of countryside. The core of the conservation area is the 120-km-long kloof, which is bounded in the north by the Baviaanskloof range, while the Grootwinterhoek range and the striking Cockscomb Peak and its southern slopes lie to the northeast. To the south lie the rugged Kouga Mountains.

The mountains in this region support a rich diversity of vegetation, ranging from mountain fynbos and patches of indigenous forest, to spekboomveld, Karoo shrubs and succulents, and valley-bushveld, characterised by the valley-bushveld euphorbia. Also to be seen are no fewer than 17 members of the protea family, the Willowmore cedar, which is endemic to the Kouga range, and the rare Karoo cycad.

Animals you may find here include kudu, grey rhebok, mountain reedbuck, bushbuck, leopard, caracal and baboon. In 1989, seven eland were released in the east of the conservation area and in the following year 14 Cape mountain zebra were reintroduced here.

Owing to the rich diversity of habitats and vegetation types, this conservation area is home to about 300 bird species. Noteworthy species include the peregrine and lanner falcon, African marsh harrier and striped flufftail. The conservation area is also an important breeding habitat for the blue crane. In the fynbos, keep an eye out for Cape sugarbird, orange-breasted sunbird, protea canary and Cape francolin.

This conservation area is traversed by numerous unmarked footpaths, and you can plan your own hike; the only limit to the length of the hike is the time available. Several paths ascend to the crest of the Baviaanskloof range, but be prepared for a steep climb.

In the Guerna area, south of Baviaanskloof, there are many different paths leading deep into the remote wilderness of the Kouga Mountains. Basic hiking shelters are available at Guerna, Riverside and Dieprivier.

41. GROENDAL WILDERNESS AREA
Uitenhage

> *Trails:* 4 trails; 14 to 38 km; 7 hours to 2 or more days; circular.
> *Permits:* The Officer-in-Charge, Groendal Wilderness Area, P O Box 445, Uitenhage 6230, tel: (041) 992 5418.
> *Maps:* Trail indicated on photocopy of 1:50,000 topographical map.
> *Facilities/Activities:* Showers and toilets at the office. Overnight accommodation in caves.

Covering 25,047 ha, the Groendal Wilderness Area lies at the eastern end of the Grootwinterhoek Mountains. Groendal Dam is at the centre of the wilderness area, and its surrounding landscape is characterised by a plateau dissected by deep ravines, set against a backdrop of rugged mountains. Strydomsbergpiek, the highest point in the wilderness area, rises to 1,180 m above sea level.

Vegetation at lower elevations is mainly valley-bushveld, dominated by the soetnoors (*Euphorbia coerulescens*), while porkbush, sneezewood, cat-thorn and honey-thorn also occur here. Fynbos and grasses are found at higher altitudes, and among the typical species are tall yellowbush, blue and large-leaved sugarbushes and the common pincushion. Deep ravines support indigenous forests of Outeniqua and real yellowwood, red alder and the Cape star-chestnut.

Bushbuck, blue duiker and samango monkey inhabit the forested areas, while the open mountain areas are home to grey rhebok, mountain reedbuck and baboon. Although leopard also occur here, they are seldom seen.

The birdlife is diverse, and among the species you may tick in the fynbos are Cape and red-necked francolins, grassbird, Cape sugarbird, and Cape siskin. In the valley-bushveld be on the lookout for Knysna woodpecker, white-browed robin, dusky flycatcher and southern tchagra. A variety of waterbirds are attracted to Groendal Dam and the rivers.

1. Blindekloof is a magnificent wild kloof with tranquil pools and waterfalls. The outward route follows a jeep track, eventually giving way to a footpath to the top of Blindekloof. From here the trail descends along the forested Blindekloof to Gemini Pools and past Perdekloof (the Kimcadle Falls are a little higher up in this kloof) to Skimmelkloof. After a short, steep climb out of Skimmelkloof you rejoin the jeep track and follow it back to the start. **14 km; 7 hours; circular.**

2. Emerald Pool Hemmed in by the steep cliffs of Upper Chase's Kloof, this popular weekend destination is situated below a series of small rapids and a 10-m-high waterfall cascading into a huge pool, aptly named Emerald Pool. Two nearby caves serve as overnight accommodation. The ascent of Strydomsberg Peak is an optional excursion from Emerald Pool, a steep climb with an altitude gain of over 550 m. **32 km; 2 days; circular.**

3. Upper Blindekloof route skirts the headwaters of Skelmkloof and Upper Skelmkloof. Ascending steadily, the trail gains some 750 m in altitude to Vermaakskop. Most of the route is through fynbos, but on the slopes above Groendal Dam the trail winds in and out of several kloofs, where the vegetation is typically valley-bushveld. Emerald Pool is a short detour off this circuit. **36 km; 2 days; circular.**

4. Dam Route takes a circular path around Groendal Dam, which was completed in 1932 to meet Uitenhage's demand for domestic and industrial water, and has a capacity of 11 million cubic metres. A highlight of the route is the Yellowwood Forest, nestling against the banks of a horseshoe bend in the Swartkops River. **38 km; 2 days; circular.**

42. UITENHAGE NATURE RESERVE
Uitenhage

Trails: 24 km (in total); 30 min to 3 hours; network.
Permits: Entrance fee. No permit required.
Maps: Map and pamphlet.
Facilities/Activities: Self-catering bungalows and camping sites at Springs Holiday Resort.

Situated 7 km north of Uitenhage, the reserve is centred on a natural spring that served as the town's first public water supply. The nature reserve provides protection to 900 ha of typical valley-bushveld vegetation, with elements of Karoo succulent veld and grassveld. Especially eye-catching between May and August are the aloes, which include the Uitenhage aloe (*Aloe africana*), bitter aloe (*Aloe ferox*), French aloe (*Aloe pluridens*) and coral aloe (*Aloe striata*). Also unlikely to escape attention are the candelabra trees (*Euphorbia*), porkbush and the Karoo cycad.

The network of trails leads from a densely wooded valley to the hills and ridges surrounding the resort. From these vantage points there are sweeping views of Uitenhage, and Algoa Bay to the east. In contrast to the valley-bushveld of the lower elevations, the vegetation of the hills and ridges is characterised by a variety of succulents and bulbs. Among these are aloes, crassula, vygies, haworthia and chinkerinchee.

43. VAN STADEN'S WILDFLOWER RESERVE
West of Port Elizabeth

Trails: 2 trails; 2.5 and 3 km; 1 to 1.5 hours.
Permits: Entry free. No permit required.
Maps: Rough sketch map.
Facilities/Activities: Information centre; picnic sites; toilets.

This 400-ha reserve consists of a cultivated section, where indigenous plants are propagated, and large tracts of natural vegetation. The reserve straddles the N2 and is bounded, to the west, by the impressive Van Staden's Gorge. The part of the reserve north of the N2, on the coastal plateau, contains mainly fynbos.

South of the N2, the coastal plateau gives way to slopes of Alexandria Forest (a type of coastal forest), representing the southwestern extension of the more tropical eastern forests. It is more drought-hardy than the coastal forests further east and is best developed in the Alexandria area, northeast of Port Elizabeth.

1. River Walk traverses natural fynbos and mass plantings of proteas, ericas and other species in the north of the reserve. It follows the edge of the Van Staden's Gorge, then swings back to the start. Cape sugarbird and six sunbird species are among the more than 100 bird species recorded here. **2.5 km; 1 hour; circular.**

2. Forest Walk, south of the N2, provides the opportunity to explore a fine tract of Alexandria Forest. Among the trees to be seen are yellowwood, bastard saffron, cabbage tree, white elder and black ironwood. The walk also offers excellent opportunities for ticking forest birds, such as the tambourine dove, Knysna lourie and forest canary. **3 km; 1 hour; circular.**

44. MAITLAND NATURE RESERVE
Port Elizabeth

Trails: 3 trails; 3 to 9 km; 1.5 to 3 hours; circular.
Permits: Entry free. No permits required.

Maps: Sketch map.
Facilities/Activities: Maitland Resort, with campsites and ablutions, nearby.
Pertinent information: Water in the reserve's streams is not suitable for drinking; carry water.

Situated at the mouth of the river to which it owes its name, the 127-ha Maitland Nature Reserve provides protection to a fine stand of coastal forest, and bush consisting of, amongst others, yellowwood, milkwood and boer bean trees.

Among the animals you may chance upon are the bushbuck, blue duiker and grey mongoose, and the forest is also home to the Knysna lourie, paradise flycatcher and emerald-spotted wood dove.

Starting from the entrance gate, all three trails initially follow the old wagon road to the long-abandoned lead mine at the top of the hill, outside the reserve.

1. Sir Peregrine Maitland Trail This trail follows the old wagon road and then loops back down the slope through coastal forest to the De Stades River, with its dense canopy of overhanging trees. **3 km; 1.5 hours; circular.**

2. Igolomi Trail From the turnoff onto the Sir Peregrine Maitland Trail continue for a short way along the wagon road to where the Igolomi Trail splits off to the right. The return leg goes through low bush and small trees and along the way there are fine views across the coast. **4 km; 2 hours; circular.**

3. De Stades Trail branches off to the left, opposite the Igolomi Trail turnoff, and then runs along the ridge of a forested dune, from where there are expansive views of the Maitland River valley and the high sand dune at the river mouth. **9 km; 3 hours; circular.**

45. THE ISLAND NATURE RESERVE
Port Elizabeth

Trails: Network of several trails; 1.5 to 16 km; 30 min to 5 hours; circular.
Permits: The Officer-in-Charge,

The Island Nature Reserve,
P O Box 50634, Colin Glen 6018,
tel: (041) 378 1634, fax: 378 1607.
Maps: Sketch map.
Facilities/Activities: Picnic sites; covered
braai and eating area.
Pertinent information: Precautions against
ticks are advisable.

The Island Nature Reserve stretches over some 500 ha. It is interspersed with pine and eucalyptus plantations, and also provides protection to a patch of Alexandria Forest. It is typically very dense, with a height of about 10 m, and represents the southwestern extension of the more tropical coastal forests occurring further east. It is composed of more plants specially adapted for dry areas than the coastal forests further east, but also contains species typical of the temperate forests further west.

Bushbuck Walk In addition to the antelope after which the walk is named, you might also chance upon common duiker and vervet monkey, while a variety of small mammals also live in the reserve. Among the bird species to look out for are the olive bush shrike, Narina trogon, Knysna lourie, forest weaver and olive woodpecker.

Trees along the network of trails have been marked and can be identified by referring to the list on the trail brochure. Along the Bushbuck Walk, some fine examples of hard pear, cheesewood, Outeniqua yellowwood, veld fig, Cape teak and Cape chestnut can be seen.

The Alexandria Forest is on an ancient vegetated dune, which forms part of a series of dunes in this area of the Island Nature Reserve with a height of up to 282 m above sea level. On the full circuit there are two good vantage points on the dune. At the 8.5-km point trailists can climb up an iron ladder to the top of a beacon, and at the 10.4-km mark there is a fire lookout. From here there are extensive views over the forest and the ocean beyond, with Jeffrey's Bay and Cape St Francis clearly visible on a clear day. **Bushbuck Walk consists of a number of interlinked loops: 1.5 km; 30 min, 3.4 km; 45 min, 7.6 km; 2 hours, and 16 km; 5 hours; all circular.**

46. SARDINIA BAY NATURE RESERVE
Port Elizabeth

Trails: 8 km; 3 hours; circular.
Permits: Not required.
Maps: Sketch map.
Facilities/Activities: Picnic facilities; toilets.
Pertinent information: For your own safety it is advisable to walk in a group.

Covering 320 ha, this reserve was established in 1980 to protect the coastal dune fynbos vegetation and its associated fauna. From near Schoenmakerskop, westwards, to Bushy Park, the Sardinia Bay Marine Reserve extends 1 km out to sea.

As a result of the strong coastal winds, the milkwoods are stunted and low, sometimes only knee-high. In spring, numerous dusky pink sand onions (*Veltheimia viridifolia*) can be seen flowering under the coastal bush, and the gazania and red hot poker flowers add colour to the rocks along the coast.

Sacramento Trail is named after the Portuguese galleon that ran aground just off Schoenmakerskop on 30 June 1647. Only nine of the 72 survivors reached Delagoa Bay (today Maputo) after a six-month, 1,300-km walk. A bronze cannon, salvaged from the wreck in 1977 and mounted on the coast just west of Schoenmakerskop, is a reminder of the disaster.

From the western end of Schoenmakerskop the trail follows the coast past the Sacramento Monument, and at the far end of Cannon Bay the ruins of a mill used to crush sea shells can be seen. Beyond Cannon Rocks there are numerous gullies where trailists can explore the local marine life or cool off. The return leg from Sardinia Bay follows a ridge linked to the reserve's network of bridle paths.

47. CAPE RECIFE NATURE RESERVE
Port Elizabeth

Trails: 9 km; 3 hours; circular.
Permits: No fee if vehicles are left outside gate. No permit required for walks.

Maps: Sketch map and information sheet.
Facilities/Activities: Informaion centre;
birdhide; toilets.

This reserve, at the western-most point of Algoa Bay, encompasses 336 ha of coastal dune flora and rocky shores. Dominating the reserve is a 24-m-high octagonal lighthouse, which has warned ships of the dangers of Recife Point and Thunderbolt Reef since 1851.

A variety of waterbirds, such as the black-winged stilt, avocet, purple gallinule and waterfowl, are attracted to the water reclamation works, and a large number of terns roost on Recife Point. A rocky promontory has been set aside as a sanctuary for the endangered African penguin, and it is hoped that rescued and injured birds released here after rehabilitation will form a mainland breeding colony.

Trail of the Roseate Tern was named after a tern species occurring along the coast. The trail leads from the reserve gate to the water reclamation works, where a birdhide provides good birding opportunities. The route then follows the coastline, past the lighthouse and the African penguin sanctuary, before swinging away from the coast to the remains of World War II military barracks. A short climb brings you to an observation post, built in 1940 as part of the city's harbour defences, from where you look out over the reserve, Algoa Bay and the notorious Thunderbolt Reef.

48. SETTLERS PARK
Port Elizabeth

Trails: 2 to 7.5 km; 1 to 3.5 hours; network.
Permits: No permit required.
Maps: Sketch map and information sheet.
Facilities/Activities: Flower display house;
toilets; water.
Pertinent information: Don't drink water
from the Baakens River.

Situated in the heart of Port Elizabeth, Settlers Park is a 54-ha greenbelt in the steep-sided Baakens River valley. Amid the natural, mixed woodland are manicured lawns, pathways, benches and water features.

Jan Smuts Walk From the main entrance gate off Howe Street, the trail leads down into the valley with its high cliffs, springs, groves of exotic trees, and collections of proteas and cycads. There are numerous footpaths to follow, and along the way good birding can be enjoyed. The 120 species to be seen include the olive woodpecker, red-necked francolin, yellow-breasted apalis, forest canary and tambourine dove. Keep an eye out for peregrine falcon in the vicinity of Lovers' Rock.

49. GUINEAFOWL TRAILS
Port Elizabeth

Trails: 2 trails; 6 and 7.5 km; 2 and
2.5 hours, with shorter options; open-ended.
Permits: No permit required.
Maps: Sketch map with information sheet.
Facilities/Activities: Flower display house,
toilets and water in Settlers Park.
Pertinent information: The Baakens
River water is not drinkable, so you will
need to carry your own water for each
hike. For your own safety it is advisable
to walk in a group.

The Guineafowl Trails follow the course of the Baakens River along its entire length, from the N2 freeway to Brickmakerskloof. The trail goes along a greenbelt, which passes below city suburbs and through a variety of vegetation types.

1. Upper Guineafowl Trail starts from the car park at the Third Avenue Dip in Newton Park. Heading up the Baakens Valley you cannot fail to notice the infestation of invasive trees in the valley. Fortunately, though, they are being eradicated, by means of biological controls, and in time the indigenous vegetation will be able to re-establish itself here. On the climb towards Fer10 and below Overbaakens the trail passes through fynbos, and valley-bushveld vegetation can be seen on the steep slopes below the Knife Edge, which is a steep-sided ridge. The Upper Guineafowl Trail ends at the bottom end of Hawthorne Avenue. **6 km; 2 hours; open-ended.**

2. Lower Guineafowl Trail stretches from the Third Avenue Dip in Newton Park, downstream, to Settlers Park and Brickmakerskloof. The trail initially follows the course of the river, where alien vegetation is much in evidence. However, where the path climbs out of the valley it makes its way through fynbos and valley-bushveld. You reach Settlers Park about 5 km from the starting point of the trail, and the hike can be terminated either at the main car park, off Howe Avenue, or at Brickmakerskloof. 7.5 km; 2.5 hours; open-ended.

50. ZWARTKOPS NATURE RESERVE
Port Elizabeth

Trail: 10 km; 3 hours; circular.
Permits: No permit required.
Maps: Sketch map with information sheet.
Facilities/Activities: None.
Pertinent information: For your own safety it is advisable to walk in a group.

The Zwartkops Nature Reserve was established to protect the valley-bushveld, salt marshes, tidal flats and pans of the Zwartkops estuary, 15 km north of Port Elizabeth. The vegetation is characterised by boer bean, cabbage, white milkwood and porkbush trees. The reserve also contains aloes, which are especially attractive in June and July when they are in flower.

The wetlands and valley-bushveld attract a diversity of birds, and to date some 220 bird species have been recorded in the Zwartkops estuary. At times up to 1,000 flamingo congregate on the pan, and in summer a variety of waders and terns can be ticked. In the valley-bushveld, keep an eye out for the Knysna woodpecker, grey-wing francolin, southern tchagra and white-throated robin.

The valley-bushveld vegetation here in the Zwartkops Nature Reserve is home to Cape grysbok, blue duiker and bushpig, while the Cape clawless otter favours rank vegetation along the river.

Flamingo Trail starts at the Motherwell stormwater channel in the Zwartkops Nature Reserve, a few kilometres north of the city centre. From here the trail climbs through valley-bushveld vegetation to the escarpment, from where there are fine views over the Zwartkops estuary. It then descends along a kloof to the saltpan and follows a track along the base of the escarpment for a while, before climbing to the top of the escarpment once more. A final descent to the salt pan is followed by a walk along the river to Redhouse, before the trail runs close to the edge of the saltpan.

51. ALOE TRAIL
Bluewater Bay, Port Elizabeth

Trail: 7 km; 2.5 hours; circular.
Permits: No permit required.
Maps: Sketch map with information sheet.
Facilities/Activities: None.

Aloe Trail is named for the profusion of aloes at the start of the trail, the outward leg of which runs along the escarpment above Zwartkops Estuary. Just before the 1-km mark the Yellow Trail (a 2-km circuit) branches off, while the longer Red Trail makes a detour inland a short way on. It then returns to the escarpment from where there are great views over the estuary, Zwartkops Nature Reserve further upstream, and the distant Cockscomb Peak. The trail then swings away from the escarpment and makes its way through valley-bushveld vegetation on the plateau, where it winds through a series of old wallows. These depressions are the only evidence that elephants once roamed the area. The last 1 km follows the return leg of the Yellow Trail. The trail starts at the top end of Tippers Creek Road, between Amsterdamhoek and Bluewater Bay.

52. VAN DER KEMP'S KLOOF TRAIL
Bethelsdorp

Trail: 8 km; 3 hours; circular.
Permits: No permit required for walks.
Maps: Sketch map and information pamphlet.
Facilities/Activities: None.

This trail starts in the heart of the historic settlement of Bethelsdorp, which was established in 1803 by Dr Johannes van der Kemp of the London Mission Society. Among the places of historic interest in the town are the Almshouse (1822), Van der Kemp's Church, built in 1903 on the site of the first church, which was destroyed by a fire in 1890, Church Square, and the Mission Bell, erected in 1815. Another noteworthy building that you can see here is Livingstone Cottage where the missionary and explorer is said to have stayed.

From the village centre the trail makes its way along the Little Zwartkops River in Van der Kemp's Kloof for about 3 km and then climbs onto the plateau, with its grassy fynbos vegetation. Along the way there are views over Port Elizabeth's western suburbs, the kloof, Zwartkops valley and Algoa Bay. A steep descent into the kloof, followed by a short walk, concludes the trail.

53. ZUURBERG
Addo Elephant National Park

> **Trails:** 1 or 4 hours; 2.5 or 12 km; circular.
> **Permits:** Entrance fee. No permit required for walks.
> **Maps:** Sketch map.
> **Facilities/Activities:** Zuurberg Inn near start of trail or self-catering accommodation in the main camp of the Addo Elephant National Park, 20 km to the south.

Addo Elephant National Park was set aside in 1931 to protect the last remaining elephants in the Eastern Cape, and since then the park's elephant population has increased from 11 to over 300. It is also a sanctuary for black rhino and, at one stage, was home to the only population of foot-and-mouth-disease-free buffalo in southern Africa. Red hartebeest, eland, kudu, bushbuck and grysbok are amongst the antelope found in the park. Also of interest is the flightless dung beetle, which is endemic to the Eastern Cape.

The Zuurberg section of the Addo Elephant National Park covers 35,000 ha of rugged mountain peaks and wild river valleys in the Klein Winterhoek Mountains. It was proclaimed a national park in 1985 and was subsequently linked to the Addo National Park when land in between the two reserves was acquired.

Zuurberg is home to a variety of animals, including kudu, mountain reedbuck, grey rhebok, bushbuck, common and blue duiker and bushpig. Since the proclamation of Zuurberg as a national park, Cape mountain zebra, black rhino and a family of hippo have been reintroduced here.

The valley-bushveld vegetation of the area is considered the most pristine in the whole of the Eastern Cape. Fynbos dominates the higher altitudes, while patches of indigenous forest occur in the more sheltered kloofs. Noteworthy among the plants are three cycad species, as well as the grass aloe (*Aloe micracantha*) and the succulent cushion bush (*Ruschia rigens*).

The short option of the trail leads along the edge of a kloof, while the long trail meanders down into the Doringnek Kloof, with its riverine vegetation, and then climbs back to an open fynbos ridge, which you then follow back to the start.

54. ALEXANDRIA HIKING TRAIL
Alexandria

> **Trail:** 36 km; 2 days; circular.
> **Permits:** The Reserve Manager, Woody Cape Nature Reserve, P O Box 50, Alexandria 6185, tel: (046) 653 0601, fax: 653 0302.
> **Maps:** Sketch map.
> **Facilities/Activities:** Two overnight huts, with bunks, mattresses, water and ablutions.
> **Pertinent information:** No fires are permitted at Woody Cape hut. Use water at Woody Cape for drinking and washing cooking utensils only, as the only water available is rainwater collected from the hut's roof. All refuse must be brought back from Woody Cape.

Woody Cape Nature Reserve contains the largest tract of Alexandria Forest in the country and the largest coastal dunefield in southern Africa.

The Alexandria Forest consist of low to medium (10-m-high) trees and often looks more like a thicket than a forest. Taller trees grow in the valleys. Alexandria Forest has an interesting composition, as it contains a mixture of coastal, tropical species, typically occurring further east, temperate montane and Cape forest species.

Covering some 110 square kilometres, the Alexandria dunefield has evolved over the last 6,000 years. It ranks among the best examples of a mobile dune system in the world, and the influx of sand into the system is estimated at 375,000 cubic metres a year.

The forest is the habitat of bushpig, bushbuck and blue duiker, and the dune thickets are inhabited by grysbok, common duiker, tree dassie and vervet monkey. Leopard, caracal, black-backed jackal and a variety of smaller mammals also occur here. The Alexandria dunefield is an important breeding habitat of the Damara tern and the African black oystercatcher. Bird Island, the largest of a group of offshore islands, is home to some 140,000 Cape gannets (the largest colony in the world) and some 5,000 African penguins. Species to look out for in the forest include crowned and trumpeter hornbills, Narina trogon, chorister robin, terrestrial bulbul and forest weaver.

The first day's hike (19.5 km; 6 hours) alternates between plantations and indigenous forest for 4 km to the Waterboom (the 'Water Tree'), so named because early travellers were said to have used rainwater that collects at the hollow in the base of the tree. From here the trail goes through magnificent Alexandria Forest before traversing private property and crossing a buffer dune. After this it reaches the coast at Woody Cape Resort and then follows the magnificent coast, with its white beach, westwards to the dune cliffs. At high tide you will have no option but to take the 'high route' on the cliffs, but at lowtide you can continue along the coast to a rope ladder, which provides access to the top of the cliffs. The last section of both routes runs along the top of the cliffs, with fine views of the coast.

The second day's hike (16.5 km; 5.5 hours) leads through the dunes. The small 'islands' of bush pockets in the dunes are particularly striking. Beyond the dunefield the trail enters private property, where it traverses a large grassy plateau. You will pass a chicory roasting stack, used in the 1920s. The last section of the trail is once again through indigenous forest.

55. BOSBERG HIKING TRAIL
Somerset East

> *Trail:* 15 km; 1 or 2 days; circular.
> *Permits:* The Reserve Manager,
> Blue Crane Route Municipality,
> P O Box 21, Somerset East 5850,
> tel: (042) 243 1333, fax: 243 1548.
> *Maps:* Sketch map and reserve brochure.
> *Facilities/Activities:* Overnight hut with bunks, mattresses, tables, benches, fireplaces, water and toilets; camping sites; picnic sites.

Set against the southern slopes of the Bosberg, the Bosberg Nature Reserve is renowned for its well-preserved Döhne sourveld vegetation, which occurs at higher elevations. The vegetation of the plains is characterised by Karoo-like shrubs and grasslands, while patches of indigenous forests, consisting of wild olive, white stinkwood, Outeniqua yellowwood and wild peach, occur in sheltered kloofs.

Animals you may chance upon include Cape mountain zebra, bushbuck, bushpig, steenbok, baboon, vervet monkey and rock dassie, and a variety of birds can also be ticked.

The first day's hike (5 km; 3 hours) begins with a steep climb, but after the 2-km mark the trail gradient eases slightly. Between the 2 and 3-km markers the trail winds through a fine patch of forest. Slagbos, with its massive dolerite rocks and shady trees, makes for a welcome rest stop. At the 3.5-km mark the overnight trail swings west, but for day hikers there is a circular loop back to the start. Some 700 m is gained in altitude to the overnight hut, but the views are great: on a clear day one can see up to 120 km southwards.

The second day's hike (10 km; 3 hours) initially traverses the plateau area and along the way there are breathtaking views of the Bestershoek Valley. From Bloukop, at 1,620 m the highest point in the reserve, the trail descends steeply before levelling out, with the final section leading through the game enclosure.

56. COMMANDO DRIFT NATURE RESERVE
Tarkastad

See no. 57 (below) for hiking trail.

> *Trail:* 6 km; 2 hours; out-and-return.
> *Permits:* Entrance fee. No permits required.
> *Maps:* Sketch map.
> *Facilities/Activities:* Self-catering accommodation; camping sites; birdhide; mountain biking; picnicking; boating; freshwater angling (permit required).
> *Pertinent information:* Summer temperatures can be very high.

The Commando Drift Dam is the focal point of this 5,983-ha nature reserve, which is characterised by low, undulating hills. The reserve was proclaimed in 1980 and one of the management objectives is to restore the Karoo veld to its original state.

Game that occurred in the area historically has been reintroduced and includes Cape mountain zebra, black wildebeest, red hartebeest, blesbok and springbok. Also found here are kudu, steenbok, mountain reedbuck, caracal, baboon and vervet monkey. To date over 200 bird species have been recorded in the reserve.

Bushman Trail leads from the restcamp along the shores of the dam and then follows a jeep track up Palingkloof (*paling* is Afrikaans for 'eel'). The open water and the shore attract a variety of waterfowl and waders, making this trail an ideal one for birding enthusiasts.

57. ENDURANCE TRAIL
Commando Drift Nature Reserve

See no. 56 (above) for walks.

> *Trail:* 28 km; 2 or 3 days; circular.
> *Permits:* The Manager, Commando Drift Nature Reserve, P O Box 459,

Cradock 5880, tel: (048) 881 3925, fax: 881 3119.
> *Maps:* Sketch map and information brochure.
> *Facilities/Activities:* Overnight hut with bunks, mattresses, cold shower and fireplace; self-catering accommodation; camping sites; birdhide; mountain biking; picnicking; boating; freshwater angling (permit required).
> *Pertinent information:* Summer temperatures can be very high.

Despite its rather daunting name, Endurance Trail is actually relatively easy. On day one (16.5 km; 5.5 hours) the trail winds along the lower slopes of Rooiberg, crossing several stream beds. A visit to the game-viewing hide overlooking a dam, close to the overnight hut, is especially rewarding in the late afternoon or early morning when animals are most likely to be about.

On the second day (11.5 km; 4 hours) the trail traverses Springbokvlakte, an area frequented by game, before swinging back to follow a contour along the western slopes above the dam. A short detour leads to the Tarka River hide, reached just before the end of the trail.

The trail can be extended to a three-day route by booking an extra night at the trail hut. This will enable you to do some game- and bird-watching and to enjoy the natural swimming pool at nearby Ratelshoek.

58. TSOLWANA GAME RESERVE
Whittlesea

> *Trails:* Guided trails; distance and duration variable (4 km to 20 km; 2 hours to 2 days), depending on fitness and interest of group; circular.
> *Permits:* Entrance fee. For overnight trails, book with East Cape Tourism Board, P O Box 186, Bisho 5606, tel: (040) 635 2115, fax: 636 4019.
> *Maps:* Sketch map of reserve.
> *Facilities/Activities:* Two trail camps with

bunks, mattresses and hot and cold water
ablutions; luxury self-catering farm-style
lodges; self-guided or guided game-drives;
horse-riding; picnic sites.

Covering 8,500 ha at the edge of the Winterberg
Mountains the landscape of Tsolwana Game Reserve
is characterised by grassy plains dissected by deep
valleys. The reserve is named after the 1.877-m-high
conical-shaped hill, which reminded the Xhosa of a
spike, *tsolwana* meaning 'spike' in Zulu.

Nestling against the northern slopes of the
Winterberge on the edge of the Karoo, the vegetation ranges from Karoo dwarf shrub to thornveld
and grassland. The plains and slopes are roamed by
a variety of game, among them white rhino, giraffe,
Cape mountain zebra, eland, gemsbok, blesbok,
springbok, mountain reedbuck and grey rhebok.

Trails follow game tracks and gravel roads, and
routes are tailor-made to suit the requirements of
the group. Since all walking takes places under the
guidance of game rangers, the trails are an ideal
opportunity to learn more about the fauna, flora
and ecological processes of the reserve. Trails can
range from short two-hour walks to a two-day
overnight trail in the western section of the reserve.

Another option is to take a guided walk up Ntaba
Themba, which dominates the Hinana Resource
Area in the north of the park. The resource area provides many benefits to the people living in the area,
such as income from taking guided tours and meat
from trophy animals. Steeped in Xhosa legend, the
table-top mountain features prominently in poetry
and was painted by the British artist Thomas Baines.
The steep cliffs of the mountain (which is known in
Afrikaans as Tafelberg – not to be confused with the
famous Tafelberg, or Table Mountain, in Cape Town)
are home to a Cape vulture colony.

59. MPOFU GAME RESERVE
Fort Beaufort

Trails: Guided trails; distance and
duration variable.
Permits: Entrance fee. Walks can be

booked in reserve.
Maps: Sketch map of reserve.
Facilities/Activities: Self-catering lodges;
picnic sites; self-guided or guided game-
drives; night-drives.

Overlooking the Katberg to the south, the landscape of the Mpofu Game Reserve is characterised
by steep cliffs and slopes falling away to forested
valleys. One of several game reserves in the former
homeland of Ciskei, the reserve is home to a variety of game including buffalo, giraffe, white rhino
and Burchell's zebra. Among the antelope are
springbok, red hartebeest, eland, bushbuck, kudu
and mountain reedbuck.

The vegetation ranges from Döhne sourveld, at
the higher altitudes, to valley-bushveld and
indigenous forests lower down. Guided game-
viewing trails in the Fort Fordyce section of the
reserve and along the river, which dissects Fort
Fordyce, can be arranged.

60. DOUBLE DRIFT GAME RESERVE
Peddie

Trails: Guided day walks; distance
and duration variable.
Permits: Entrance fee. Walks can be
booked in reserve.
Maps: Sketch map of reserve.
Facilities/Activities: Self-catering lodges;
self-guided and guided game drives; guided
night drives; picnic sites; freshwater angling.

The Double Drift Game Reserve, which is bounded
by the Great Fish River, protects one of the best
examples of valley-bushveld vegetation in South
Africa. Covering 23,000 ha, the reserve forms a
combined conservation area of 44,000 ha with the
adjoining Andries Vosloo Kudu Reserve and the
Sam Knott Nature Reserve.

In the northern part of this reserve is a fenced-
off game-viewing area. Two of the Big Five, namely
both black and white rhino, as well as buffalo, have
been reintroduced. Other species occurring here

include giraffe, kudu, eland, blue wildebeest, red hartebeest, waterbuck, Burchell's zebra and impala, as well as numerous small mammal species. Hippo have been released in the Great Fish River.

The area is rich in the legacies of the frontier wars fought here between the early white settlers and the Xhosa. Reminders of this turbulent era include the ruins of several forts that once formed part of the Cape Colony's defences.

Guided day walks, tailored to suit the group, are conducted, and include game-viewing, hippo-viewing and a walk along the Great Fish River.

61. HOGSBACK WALKS
Hogsback

Trails: *3 to 20 km; 1 to 6 hours; network.*
Permits: *Not required.*
Maps: *Piggy Books (see below) on sale in the village.*
Facilities/Activities: *Hotels; guest houses; camping site.*
Pertinent information: *Snakes (boomslang, cobras and puff-adders) are plentiful, so you must be alert, especially in spring and summer.*

Situated below the three ridged peaks of Hogsback, to which the mountain village owes its name, Hogsback is renowned for its beautiful indigenous forest, mountain streams, cascades and numerous magnificent waterfalls. The village is also well known for its masses of azaleas, rhododendrons and crab-apple trees, which burst into bloom in spring.

A network of trails traverse the indigenous Auckland Forest along footpaths signposted with pig emblems. The pigs were emblazoned in different colours along the various walks years ago by the Hogsback Inn and are described in what are known as Piggy Books, on sale in the village.

Among the numerous attractions along these walks are waterfalls, with alluring names, and Hogsback's famous Big Tree. Also known as the Eastern Monarch, this ancient Outeniqua yellow-wood towers 34 m above the forest floor. Among the splendid waterfalls are the 39 Steps, Madonna

and Child, Swallowtail, Bridal Veil and Kettlespout. The last is so named because, when the southeaster wind blows strongly, water falling down the natural spout of the cliffs is blown back, creating what looks like steam.

Other trails lead through pine plantations to Tor Doone (1,565 m high) and if you are prepared for a full day's hike it is a steady climb to the summit of the 1,963-m-high Gaika's Kop. Another option is to hike to the base of the three Hogsback peaks.

62. AMATOLA HIKING TRAIL
King William's Town and Keiskammahoek

Trails: *100 km; 6 days; open-ended; several shorter (2-day) loops.*
Permits: *Keiskamma Ecotourism, 9 Chamberlain Street, King William's Town 5601, tel: (043) 642 1747, fax: 642 2571.*
Maps: *Printed map with information on the hiking trail.*
Facilities/Activities: *Overnight huts with bunks, mattresses, braai facilities, firewood, showers and toilets.*
Pertinent information: *The full trail from Maden Dam to Zingcuka Forest Station covers long distances on most days. This, together with some steep ascents, makes the Amatola Hiking Trail a demanding one, which should only be attempted by fit hikers.*

The Amatola Hiking Trail traverses the slopes and high peaks of the Amatola Mountains through the most beautiful scenery imaginable. The route alternates between indigenous forests, grasslands and patches of pine plantations. Outstanding features of the trail are the numerous waterfalls, cascades and inviting swimming pools tucked away in the enchanting forests. Some legs of the trail involve strenuous climbs, but efforts are always rewarded with stupendous views.

The diversity of habitats makes for interesting birding: among the species you may tick are

TOP: The *Storms River suspension bridge* marks the end of the Tsitsikamma Hiking Trail.

ABOVE: The *Otter Hiking Trail* follows the spectacular Tsitsikamma coastline down near the sea, while the Tsitsikamma trail meanders along the cliffs above.

LEFT: *Hogsback is renowned for its splendid cascades.*
BELOW: *On the Tsitsikamma trail you'll pass through a variety of strikingly different fynbos types – a highlight of this hike. The vegetation here is also interspersed with delightful patches of indigenous forest.*

TOP: Make sure you include the Coffee Bay to Mbashe River hike on any trip to the Wild Coast, so you don't miss seeing the famous, natural landmark of Hole in the Wall.

ABOVE This is one of the basic shelters at Helderfontein where you'll sleep after your first day on the Boosmansbos trail.

RIGHT: The Wild Coast is a very isolated area, where people still live quite traditionally, and many young, urban men return here for their initiation into manhood.

TOP: *Walk in the Drakensberg from May to August and you're likely to see the high peaks of the area covered in snow and ice.*
ABOVE: *Hikers can visit the area's many open-air rock art galleries, containing over 35,000 rock paintings.*
LEFT: *The Tunnel Walk is one of the most popular with visitors to the Royal Natal National Park.*

RIGHT: *To take a detour around The Tunnel and get to the Tugela River you need to climb up a chain ladder, on the Drakensberg's Tugela Tunnel and Gorge hike.*

BELOW: *The Amphitheatre forms an impressive backdrop to the Royal Natal National Park, and you'll see it from a number of different vantage points on the various trails through this hikers' mecca.*

ABOVE: In the Little Berg the rivers and streams have carved striking gorges through the soft sandstone of the Clarens Formation, such as this one you can hike down in the Royal Natal National Park.
BELOW: The rare bearded vulture, or lammergeier, is easily identified in flight by its distinctive wedge-shaped tail. The vulture 'restaurant' in the Giant's Castle reserve offers great opportunities to spot this majestic bird.
OPPOSITE TOP: This footbridge takes hikers over the Bushman's River on the River Walk, one of the 25 walks (ranging from 1.9 km to several days) in the Giant's Castle Game Reserve.
OPPOSITE BOTTOM: You can explore this magnificent gorge, hollowed out of Oribi Flats by the Mzimkhulwana River, on several beautiful walks through the Oribi Gorge Nature Reserve.

ABOVE: *Hikers on the Imboma Trail at Cape Vidal, in the Greater St Lucia Wetland Park, can look out over beautiful wetland scenery.*
LEFT: *On the Dugandlovu Trail, also in St Lucia, accommodation is in charming thatched overnight camps.*

RIGHT: *There's a map board for trailists at the start of the Mvubu hike at Cape Vidal.*

ground and trumpeter hornbill, Knysna lourie and Cape parrot. There are also Cape and Gurney's sugarbirds, which are attracted to proteas in the grassland. Raptors include species such as black and crowned eagles.

Among the large animals you may see are bushbuck and bushpig, and you might also spot several rare and endangered amphibians and fish, which are endemic to the Amatola Mountains. These include the Amatola toad, Hogsback frog, and two small fish species – the Border barb and the Amatola barb.

1. Amatola Hiking Trail

The full trail is a 100-km hike over six days. Daily distances range between 15 km and 22.5 km and, as there are some steep ascents, hikers should be fit. However, the magnificent views, tranquil streams with inviting swimming pools, numerous waterfalls, and delightful patches of indigenous forest are ample reward for the exertion required. **100 km; 6 days; open-ended.**

In addition to the Amatola Hiking Trail there are several two-day, circular loops for hikers to try:

2. Dontsa Loop Trail

starts at the Dontsa Forest Station and offers an easy hike through magnificent indigenous forest, as well as stretches through pine and wattle plantations. Highlights of the first day's trail include beautiful rock pools and the overnight hut. Situated in a pine plantation above a waterfall, the hut offers lovely views of the surroundings. **11 km; 2 days; circular.**

3. Cata Loop Trail

Few trails can offer hikers so much natural beauty, with streams, pools, waterfalls and picturesque forests, over only 11 km. Starting at the Dontsa Forest Station, the trail ascends steeply through the appropriately named Waterfall Forest with its numerous splendid cascades. There are also rock pools within 1 km of the Cata overnight stop, where hikers are accommodated in Xhosa rondavels. The second day's hike is an easy descent through Waterfall Forest along a route at a higher elevation than the outward one. **11 km; 2 hours; circular.**

4. Evelyn Valley Loop

Day one's hike (15 km; 6 hours) follows the route of the original Amatola Hiking Trail. Starting at Maden Dam the trail winds through the Pirie Forest, where the cement foundations of a sawmill and the track of a logging railway line bear testimony to the exploitation of the forests in the 1890s. From Timber Square the trail ascends through indigenous forest to the plateau behind McNaughten's Krans. The last 5 km follows a forestry track through pine plantations to the Evelyn Valley Hut. On the second day (12 km; 4 hours) the trail follows an easy descent along a ridge to Evelyn Stream and then passes through indigenous forest along the Buffalo River. **27 km; 2 days; circular.**

5. Zingcuka Loop Trail

starts 3 km from Hogsback on the Wolf Ridge Road, at the western end of the Amatola Hiking Trail. The first day's hike (19.7 km; 7 hours) climbs out of the Tyume River, ascending steadily to a nek between the Hogsback peaks. The route then winds down the Mnyameni River, where hikers can refresh themselves in the inviting mountain pools. Leaving the Mnyameni valley, the trail ascends and then goes along the edge of Zingcuka Krantz before dropping down steeply to the overnight hut. On the return leg (16.5 km; 6 hours) the same route is followed as on day six of the Amatola Hiking Trail, namely a demanding climb to the rocky ridge of Hogsback Peak, followed by a descent to the Tyume River/Wolf Ridge Road. **36.2 km; 2 days; circular.**

6. Wolf River Trail

It alternates between patches of splendid indigenous forest and grasslands and, since the distance covered by each leg is far less than on the full Amatola Trail, hikers will have ample time to enjoy the spectacular scenery. Overnight facilities are planned, but tents might be used initially. Also planned is a lockable storage facility enabling parties to enjoy day walks without the burden of a heavy backpack. Other activities include trout-fishing, horse-riding and guided walks to local villages by appointment. **60 km; 5 days; circular.**

63. PIRIE FOREST
King William's Town

> **Trails:** 2 trails; both 9 km; both 3 hours; circular and out-and-return.
> **Permits:** Not required.

Maps: Available from Department of Forestry, Private Bag X7485, King William's Town 5601, tel: (043) 642 4984.
Facilities/Activities: Picnic sites at Maden Dam; information kiosk.

Situated in the transitional zone between the indigenous forests of the southern Cape and the more sub-tropical forests of the northern part of the Eastern Cape and KwaZulu-Natal, the Pirie Forest is an excellent example of typical Eastern Cape, indigenous high forest. These forests, far more species-rich than the southern Cape forests, are composed of some 250 woody species (nearly double that of the Knysna/Tsitsikamma forests). Also, on account of the dense canopy and sub-canopy there is little undergrowth.

Exploitation of the forest began in 1819 when trees were felled to build Fort Willshire on the Keiskamma River. In the late 1890s the sole right to extract wood from the forest was granted to Mr J E Howse and reminders of this era can still be seen more than a century later (see under 'Pirie Walk', below).

Both walks start at the information kiosk above Maden Dam, reached 11 km off the King William's Town/Stutterheim road.

1. Pirie Walk follows the track of the 4-km-long narrow-gauge railway line that linked Howse's sawmill to Timber Square, where, between 1910 and 1917, the logs were loaded onto a 5-ton locomotive and transported to the mill. Still to be seen here are a section of the original track, hand-hewn lemonwood sleepers, and a trestle bridge across the Hutching's Stream. At Timber Square the trail splits off the Amatola Hiking Trail (see p. 129) and after crossing the Buffalo River meanders along the banks of the river, through indigenous forest, back to the start. **9 km; 3 hours; circular.**

2. Sandile Walk honours the Paramount Chief of the amaRharhabe clan of the Xhosa nation, Sandile, who led his people in three frontier wars against the British military. During the 1877–8 frontier war Sandile used the Pirie Forest and a deep cave at the base of what became known as Sandile's Krantz as a refuge from pursuing British and colonial forces. He was shot dead in a skirmish with the volunteer forces of Captain Lonsdale in May 1877 and buried with full military honours at the foot of Mount Kemp on 9 June 1878.

Sandile's Walk leads along the western bank of Maden Dam and after crossing the Buffalo River and Artillery Stream steadily ascends through indigenous forest to Sandile's Cave. The same route is followed back. **9 km; 3 hours; out-and-return.**

64. WILD COAST AMBLE
Qolora River to Glen Garriff

Trails: 56 km; 4 days; open-ended.
Permits: Wild Coast Holiday Reservations, P O Box 8017, Nahoon 5210, tel: (043) 743 6181, fax: 743 6188, email: meross@iafrica.com
Maps: Trail brochure with Strandloper Trail map.
Facilities/Activities: Hotel accommodation for five nights.
Pertinent information: Fully inclusive package including transfers from and back to East London, hotel accommodation with all meals for five nights and the services of a guide. Porters can be hired to carry hikers' backpacks, which must be kept below 10 kg each.

Starting at either Trennery's or Seagulls Beach Hotel, the first day's hike of 12 km ends at Morgan Bay. The Amble is operated with the approval of the Strandloper Board (the trail is managed by a Board of Directors consisting of representatives of outdoor and conservation bodies) and from Morgan Bay the trail follows the same route as the Strandloper Hiking Trail (see no. 66, p. 131). Overnight accommodation is provided at Morgan Bay, Haga Haga, Cintsa East and Glen Garriff.

65. WILD COAST MEANDER
Kob Inn to Morgan Bay

Trails: 56 km; 4 days; open-ended.
Permits: Wild Coast Holiday Reservations, P O Box 8017, Nahoon 5210,

*tel: (043) 743 6181, fax: 743 6188,
email: meross@iafrica.com*
Maps: *Trail brochure with map.*
Facilities/Activities: *Hotel accommodation for five nights.*
Pertinent information: *Fully inclusive package including transfers from and back to East London, hotel accommodation with all meals for five nights and the services of a guide. Porters can be hired to carry hikers' backpacks, which must be kept below 10 kg each.*

The section of the coastline between the Qora River and Morgan Bay has been a popular holidaying and angling destination for many years and this packaged hike allows hikers to explore this section of the Wild Coast in real luxury.

The trail alternates between beach walking and hiking over grassy headlands with a number of river crossings. Daily distances are generally short, between 6 km and 14 km, leaving ample opportunity for enjoying the superb scenery. The area is also of great historic interest as it was at the enchanted pools in the Gxara River where Nongqawuse heard the voices that prompted the slaughter of livestock and resulted in the national suicide of the Xhosa people in 1856–7.

Hotel accommodation is provided at Kob Inn, Mazeppa Bay, Wavecrest, Trennery's or Seagulls Beach and Morgan Bay Hotel.

66. STRANDLOPER HIKING TRAIL
Kei Mouth to Gonubie

Trail: 54 km; 5 days; open-ended.
Permits: Wild Coast Holiday Reservations, P O Box 8017, Nahoon 5210, tel: (043) 743 6181, fax: 743 6188, email: meross@iafrica.com
Maps: *Colour trail map and information brochure.*
Facilities/Activities: *Overnight huts with bunks, mattresses, fireplaces and water.*
Pertinent information: *Many rivers are crossed; carry a tide table and plan to cross at the turn of lowtide or beginning of an incoming tide.*

On this trail you follow in the footsteps of the ancient Khoikhoi and Bushmen who exploited the marine resources along the coast, and in those of the hapless mariners who were cast ashore after their vessels ran aground. Among the shipwrecked vessels is thought to be the famed *Santo Alberto*, wrecked off Cintsa East in March 1593. The route takes you along rocky shores, and through grassland, patches of coastal bush and sandy beaches.

The trail starts at the Cape Morgan Ecotourism Centre, with the first day's hike offering an 8.75-km circuit incorporating the town of Kei Mouth, the Kei River, and coastal walking.

The second day (7 km; 3 hours) is over uneven, rocky terrain and a long sandy beach to Morgan Bay. From here the trail heads through grassland above the Morgan Bay Cliffs before returning to the coastline, which you follow to Double Mouth hut.

Soon after setting off on day three (15.5 km; 7 hours) you cross the Quko River estuary and the trail then passes Bead Beach, named after the beads washed ashore here from shipwrecks. Beyond Haga Haga, the coastline is characterised by a wave-cut platform and there are numerous opportunities for snorkelling in the gullies.

From the Cape Henderson Hut, the first 10 km of the fourth day's hike (13 km; 5 hours) is along a wide sweep of sandy beach, with four estuaries to be crossed. You will reach Beacon Valley hut a short way beyond Cintsa East and Cintsa West.

The final day's hike (14.5 km; 5 hours) makes its way to Gonubie, mainly along the rocky coastline.

67. WILD COAST
Mtamvuna River to Kei River

Trails: 5 trails; 44 to 100 km; 4 to 9 days; open-ended.
Permits: East Cape Tourism Board, P O Box 186, Bisho 5606, tel: (040) 635 2115, fax: (040) 636 4019.
Maps: *Obtain relevant topographical maps.*
Facilities/Activities: *None.*
Pertinent information: *It is essential to carry tents, as overnight huts are not being maintained and in some cases no longer exist.*

Numerous rivers have to be crossed and you should time crossings for lowtide. A survival bag is useful for floating packs across in the event of a compulsory swim. Keep an eye out for sharks in estuaries, especially during an incoming tide. Wear sandals that fit snugly on your feet when crossing rivers and treat all cuts sustained on rocks along the estuary shores with an antiseptic ointment. Microbes living on the rocks cause small but nasty infections that do not heal very easily.

Until about a decade ago, the Wild Coast was synonymous with the 280-km stretch of coastline between the Mtamvuna River and the Great Kei River, an area formerly referred to as the Transkei. However, the name Wild Coast now also includes the coastline stretching down to Glen Garriff, east of East London. This is without doubt one of the most beautiful coastal areas in the world, and the scenery is characterised by dramatic cliffs, rolling hills, tranquil lagoons, unspoilt beaches and fascinating rock formations.

Set against the grassy slopes and ridges of the rolling hills dropping down to the sea are the typical rondavel homesteads of the Xhosa-speaking people of the Eastern Cape. Where the coast becomes impassable, the trail heads inland and passes by villages and homesteads, providing a fascinating insight into the rural way of life of traditional Xhosa people.

The vegetation here is dominated by coastal grasslands, extending down to the sea in places, with patches of coastbelt and dune forest. Along the Wild Coast there are 18 mangrove communities, and the one at Mngazana is considered to be the finest in southern Africa. Other large communities are found at the Mtamvuna, Mbashe and Kobonqaba rivers.

Among the more than 200 bird species recorded here are uncommon species such as the bald ibis, Delegorgue's pigeon and Cape parrot. Also to be seen are the African fish eagle, trumpeter hornbill, red-billed woodhoopoe, several kingfisher species and a variety of sea birds.

1. Mtamvuna River to Port St Johns

On this trail you will retrace the footsteps of hundreds of survivors shipwrecked along this rugged coastline. Among the numerous ships that ran aground on the coast is the famed HMS *Grosvenor*, wrecked here in 1782. Of particular interest are the fossil beds at Mzamba, close to the start, and the Pondo coconut, which only grows on the northern banks of the Msikaba River. From Port Grosvenor the trail leads through some of the most breathtaking coastal scenery in the world – impressive waterfalls cascading into the sea, towering cliffs, rock formations and unspoilt stretches of beach. **100 km; 9 days; open-ended.**

2. Port St Johns to Coffee Bay

This section of the trail follows the coastline, with its secluded beaches and coves, unspoilt estuaries and patches of coastal forest. When the coastline gets too rugged, the route ascends grassy hills and swings inland, where you will pass Mpondo and Bomvana villages and homesteads. Excellent examples of mangrove communities can be seen at the Mngazana and Mtakatye rivers. **60 km; 6 days; open-ended.**

3. Coffee Bay to Mbashe River

This section of the coast is not as rocky as that east of Coffee Bay. The trail makes its way through an area inhabited mainly by the Bomvana clan, although there are large remaining areas that are sparsely inhabited. The gentle hills of Bomvanaland make for a relaxing trail that takes you along long stretches of deserted beaches, across rolling hills, and past beautiful estuaries and unspoilt lagoons. Hole in the Wall, one of the most fascinating rock formations along the Wild Coast, is a highlight of this trail. **44 km; 4 days; open-ended.**

4. Mbashe River to Qolora Mouth

This trail stretches from the Nqabara Estuary, the southern boundary of Dwesa Nature Reserve, to Qolora Mouth, north of the Great Kei River. Along the way hikers can see the wrecks of the *Jacaranda*, which ran aground between Kobonqaba Point and Qolora Mouth in 1971, and the *Frontier*, which ran into trouble south of the Shixini Estuary in 1939. Kobonqaba is the southernmost large mangrove community along the east coast and, interestingly, only the white mangrove occurs here. Overnight stops are at Nqabara Point, Shixini Estuary, Mazeppa Point, Cebe and Kobonqaba. **80 km; 5 days; open-ended.**

68. PONDOLAND PORTAGE HIKING TRAIL
Lusikisiki

Trail: 4 multi-directional day walks; 15 to 24 km per day; 5 to 10 hours per day; circular.
Permits: Wild Coast Holiday Reservations, P O Box 8017, Nahoon 5210, tel: (043) 743 6181, fax: 743 6188, email: meross@iafrica.com
Facilities/Activities: Accommodation at Mbotyi River Lodge, inclusive of meals, guides and transfers to and from certain sections; optional Xhosa village visit, horse-riding, canoeing and angling.

Using Mbotyi River Lodge as a base, guided walks are undertaken to some of the most dramatic sights along the Pondoland Coast.

The first day's hike covers 24 km (10 hours) to Waterfall Bluff and back, although a shorter option is available. Extending for about 6 km along the coast and up to 5 km inland, the near-vertical sandstone cliffs of Waterfall Bluff tower some 100 m above the ocean. Among the trail's many attractions are the Mlambomkulu River, with its series of pools and its waterfall that plunges directly into the sea, and the 80-m-high Mfihlelo Falls, also falling right into the sea. Other interesting attractions are Cathedral Rock, a huge rock formation with waves pounding through its arches, and the Citadel rock formation. This part of the route can be shortened, as the trail is not fixed and can be tailored to suit a particular group.

On day two (16 km; 5 hours) you hike along a valley and through sections of forest to the top of the escarpment. The route continues through tea plantations to the 125-m-high Magwa Falls. Situated in a tributary of the Mzintlava River, the falls cascade over a sheer cliff into a forested gorge created by a fault. Hikers are met at the falls and taken back to the hotel.

On the third day (15 km; 6 hours) the hike heads southwards along the coast to Collier's Point, alternating between sandy beaches and rocky sections. The return route makes its way inland over grassy hills and past villages, and along the way trailists are rewarded with stunning views of the coast, valleys and patches of indigenous forest.

Day four heads north along the coast to Drew's Camp, where there is a beautiful lagoon. The trail then continues into Fraser's Gorge, with its pristine indigenous forest. The full hike is 16 km (6–7 hours), but the day's programme is flexible.

69. LAMMERGEIER PRIVATE NATURE RESERVE
Lady Grey

Trails: 6 trails; 11 to 22 km; 5 hours to 2 days; out-and-return, circular.
Permits: Lammergeier Private Nature Reserve, P O Box 123, Lady Grey 9755, tel. and fax: (051) 603 1114, email: margot@eci.co.za
Maps: The trails are indicated on a copy of a 1:50,000 topographical map.
Facilities/Activities: Overnight huts with bunks, mattresses, hot showers, flush toilets and braai facilities; trout-fishing; tubing; swimming; horse trails; greywing shooting.

The 7,500-ha Lammergeier Private Nature Reserve lies in the Witteberg, the southwestern spur of the southern Drakensberg. The vegetation is typically grassland, and among the reserve's 282 bird species is the bearded vulture or lammergeier (after which the nature reserve is named), black eagle, Cape vulture and jackal buzzard. A 'vulture restaurant' (feeding station) offers good opportunities for ticking raptors.

The trail network consists of several interlinked loops, offering a choice of hikes:

1. Black Eagle Trail leads into the Karringmelkspruit Valley, with its inviting pools, and further along offers great views of Olympus Gorge. From the Karringmelkspruit and Olympus Gorge junction the trail ascends to Olympus Hut. **11 km; 5 hours; out-and-return.**

2. Witteberg Sky Walk offers a strenuous walk to the summit of the Witteberg. Starting at Olympus Hut, the route ascends steeply up the mountain slopes, but the far-reaching views over the area north of the Kei River and Lesotho make this a worthwhile walk for fit hikers. **12 km; 6 hours; circular.**

3. Cheese Factory Trail is named after a cheese factory, which operated until 1929. From Olympus Hut the trail follows the krantzes above the Karringmelkspruit and continues along the Five Oaks Valley past the Roman Baths (a lovely pool) to Upper Pelion Hut. **Distance and type not available; 5–6 hours.**

4. Pelion Valley Walk leads from Upper Pelion Hut along Pelion Valley, with its rich diversity of flora, pools and waterfalls. The Main Waterfall plunges 45 m into a pool, and a short detour leads to the nearby Hidden Waterfall. **11 km; 5 hours; out-and-return.**

5. Table Mountain Traverse From the Upper Pelion Hut the route descends into the Keiskamma Valley and then rises steeply to the summit of the flat-topped Table Mountain (not to be confused with the famous Table Mountain of Cape Town). After stopping to enjoy the views of the landscape south towards Barkley East and Lesotho, you follow the trail down the mountain's western slopes to the starting point at Tempe. An alternative, easier option skirts the mountain. **Distance not available; 5–6 hours; open-ended.**

6. Snowdon Peak offers a challenging walk to the peak's 2,750-m-high summit. Cape and bearded vultures are often seen, high up in the mountains. There are no facilities here and hikers must provide their own tents. **2 days; 22 km; out-and-return.**

70. BEN MACDHUI HIKING TRAIL
Rhodes

> **Trail:** *51 or 66 km; 3–4 days; circular.*
> **Permits:** *G van Zyl, Ben Macdhui Hiking Trail, P O Box 299, Barkly East 9786, tel. and fax: (045) 971 0446.*
> **Maps:** *Colour trail map and brochure.*
> **Facilities/Activities:** *Exodus NG Church camp in Rhodes; overnight huts on trail, with beds, mattresses, gas stove, coal stove, pots and toilets.*

This trail is laid out against the southern slopes of the 3,001-m-high Ben Macdhui, the highest peak in the Eastern Cape, and traverses private farmland.

The high, mountain vegetation is characterised by grassveld, which is especially attractive in spring when a profusion of flowers are in full bloom. Among the 191 bird species recorded to date are the rare bearded vulture and Drakensberg 'specials' such as the Drakensberg siskin, yellow-breasted pipit and orange-breasted rockjumper.

The first day's hike (17 km; 8 hours) initially follows the course of the Bell River and then ascends the slopes above the Kloppershoek Valley, before dropping down to the overnight stop at Mavis Bank.

Day two (18 km; 10 hours) begins with a steady climb to the 2,670-m-high Lesotho View, the trail's highest point. You gain about 700 m in altitude to the viewpoint. A steep descent to the Kloppershoekspruit is followed by a slightly undulating walk to Hooggenoeg Hut, overlooked by Ben Macdhui.

An alternative for fit and experienced hikers is to follow the road from Lesotho View to the marker indicating the path to Ben Macdhui. The trail ascends steeply, gaining some 400 m in altitude to the summit, which you will reach after a two-hour climb.

Day three (approx. 15 km; 8 hours; out-and-return) offers the option of ascending Ben Macdhui, with Hooggenoeg serving as a basecamp. The route follows the road via Tiffendel Ski Resort and then ascends to the summit of Ben Macdhui, returning to Hooggenoeg Hut.

Day four (16 km; 7 hours) descends to Carlisle's Hoek with its 40-m-high falls and then continues along the Carlisle's Hoek Spruit through spectacular scenery past Goatfell Gorge. The last 8 km to Rhodes is along a gravel road.

71. TELLE FALLS HIKE
Rhodes

> **Trail:** *Approximately 13 km; 6–8 hours; out-and-return.*
> **Permits:** *Advanced reservations not required. Arrangements for a guide can be made on arrival at Tiffendel Ski Resort.*
> **Maps:** *Trail indicated on photocopy of 1:50,000 topographical map.*
> **Facilities/Activities:** *Tiffendel Ski Resort: accommodation ranging from chalets with en*

suite facilities to campsites with communal ablutions; restaurant; skiing; snowboarding.
Pertinent information: *Check weather conditions the night before the planned hike. Beware of strong winds and crumbling rock at the cliff edge near the waterfall.*

Starting at Tiffendel Ski Resort on the slopes below Ben Macdhui, this difficult but rewarding trail leads to the 200-m-high Telle Falls, a spectacular waterfall seen by few people, owing to its remote location. From the resort the trail gains 280 m in altitude to the summit of the Drakensberg and then descends along the slopes above the Telle Valley. A pool below a small waterfall marks the half-way mark. The trail continues its descent along the western slopes of the valley to the waterfall. The return journey consists of a steep walk back to the Drakensberg summit.

72. WOODCLIFFE CAVE TRAIL
Maclear

Trail: *54 km; 5 days; circular.*
Permits: *Phyll Sephton, P O Box 65, Maclear 5480, tel. and fax: (045) 932 1550.*
Maps: *Photocopy of 1:50,000 map of area.*
Facilities/Activities: *Overnight huts and cave; water; firewood at Tok's Cave.*

Situated in the lovely Joelshoek Valley, this circular trail traverses a sheep and cattle farm, with scenery ranging from steep grassy hills and sandstone cliffs to mountain streams, with natural pools, and patches of indigenous forest. Cave rock paintings are reminders of the original inhabitants, the Khoikhoi and Bushmen.

There is a checklist of 170 bird species, and among those to be ticked are the crowned crane, Cape and bearded vultures, black eagle, sunbird, mountain and mocking chats and paradise flycatcher. Two antelope species you may spot are the grey rhebok and mountain reedbuck, while porcupine, caracal and other species also occur, but are seldom encountered.

The first day's hike (5 km; 1.5 hours) is an easy walk along a 4x4 track along the Little Pot River to Tok's Cave, an overhang with four huts built inside.

On the second day (13 km; 7 hours), you backtrack to Woodcliffe farmhouse and follow a circular route to Redcliffe Pool. From here the trail ascends to a saddle above a waterfall and then descends to Skinny Dip Pool before returning to Tok's Cave.

Day three (13 km; 7 hours) follows a jeep track to the base of the Drakensberg and climbs steeply along a ridge to Vlak Nek at the top of the High Berg. Then it is a gentle descent to the Reed Park overnight stop.

The fourth day's hike (13 km; 7.5 hours) begins with a steep climb to the escarpment where hikers are rewarded with spectacular views of the landscape far below. The remainder of the day's hike follows Sephton's 4x4 Pass down to Wide Valley Hut.

Day five (10 km; 3 hours) follows a 4x4 track for 2 km and then climbs along a path to the top of a ridge before dropping down into Woodcliffe Valley.

73. VREDERUS HIKING TRAIL
Maclear

Trail: *18 km; 2 days; circular.*
Permits: *J Naude, P O Box 296, Maclear 5480, tel. and fax: (045) 932 1572.*
Maps: *Sketch map.*
Facilities/Activities: *Self-catering accommodation; trout-fishing; mountain biking; horse-riding.*

Situated in the foothills of the Eastern Cape Drakensberg, Vrederus is renowned for its trout-angling. The lake and two dams on the farm are stocked with rainbow trout and a limited number of brown trout, and river fishing is also possible.

The farm lies at an altitude of 2,000 m and the vegetation is dominated by grasslands. Birders will find Vrederus rewarding: among the more than 100 bird species recorded to date are the bearded vulture, booted eagle, black harrier, yellow-breasted and mountain pipits, as well as the black stork. Also recorded, but less frequently seen, are the crowned and blue cranes, Cape vulture and ground woodpecker.

The trail leads from the Boatman's Cottage to the Luzi River and there are several caves with rock paintings in the area. Tents must be pitched at the overnight campsite, where firewood is provided. The second day's hike leads back to the start.

DRAKENSBERG & KWAZULU-NATAL

From the challenging mountain peaks of the Drakensberg and the rolling grasslands of the Midlands, to the pristine beaches of the Maputaland coast and the mosaic of wetlands that is St Lucia, KwaZulu-Natal offers an incredible diversity of landscapes and attractions. So, it is perhaps not surprising that two of the first four World Heritage sites to be declared in South Africa, the Greater St Lucia Wetland Park and the uKhahlamba-Drakensberg Park, are situated in the province.

The uKhahlamba-Drakensberg Park covers some 243,000 ha and stretches over a distance of 150 km, from Royal Natal in the north to the Mkhomazi Wilderness Area in the south. The park was created in 1986 when five former Natal Parks Board reserves were amalgamated with four wilderness areas and state-owned forestry land. The Drakensberg was proclaimed a World Heritage Site in 2000 and is one of only 23 'mixed' sites (one with cultural and natural significance) on the World Heritage List. Another exciting development involving the Drakensberg is the recent creation of the Maloti-Drakensberg Transfrontier Conservation Area (TFCA) with Lesotho. Of the TFCA's total 8,113 km², 5,170 km² (64 per cent) falls within Lesotho, while the remaining 2,943 km² (36 per cent) lies within South Africa. The TFCA aims to conserve the biodiversity and cultural resources of the Maloti-Drakensberg area and will be managed as an undivided ecosystem. It will also promote the economic development of the transfrontier area.

Part of the Southern African Escarpment, the Drakensberg is South Africa's highest and most spectacular mountain range. Several peaks reach over 3,000 m above sea level and the Zulu name for them, *uKhahlamba*, means 'barrier of spears'. In winter the high peaks are often covered in snow.

These mountains were once the stronghold of the Bushmen who left a rich legacy of rock art on the walls of caves and overhangs in the 'Berg,' as the mountains are affectionately known to outdoor enthusiasts. With over 35,000 individual rock paintings it has one of the largest concentrations of rock art in the world. Well-known sites include Battle Cave in Injisuthi, Main Caves in Giant's Castle, and Ndedema Gorge.

Those accustomed to the floral wealth of the Western Cape fynbos are often disappointed by the flora of the Drakensberg. However, to date more than 1,600 flowering plants and 72 fern species have been recorded here. Many species are obscured in the grasslands, or grow in protected places, and so are easily missed. Spring, though, is full of surprises, as brown grass is brought to life, with numerous plants bursting into flower. Delightful patches of yellowwood forests occur in protected valleys and kloofs. In August the Natal bottlebrush, with its magnificent red flowers, is conspicuous amongst the Clarens sandstone cliffs.

Of great natural significance is the Berg's unique wetland system of marshes, lakes, vleis and numerous networks of streams and rivers. At least 36 plant species are unique to the 11 wetland plant communities occurring in the Drakensberg.

For birding enthusiasts the Drakensberg offers several specials among the 246 species recorded to date. Heading the list is the rare bearded vulture, a species that has its last stronghold here. Its distinctive wedge-shaped tail and wingspan of 2.5 to 3 m make it easily identifiable in flight, and an unforgettable sight. It has extremely powerful wings, and gliding speeds of 105 km/h have been measured. The cliffs of the Drakensberg also serve as a refuge for the rare bald ibis and Cape vulture, while the wetlands provide a habitat for rare and endangered species such as the wattled crane and the striped flufftail. Other specials include the Drakensberg siskin and the orange-breasted rockjumper, as well as the yellow-breasted and mountain pipit.

The Drakensberg is undoubtedly the country's most popular walking and backpacking destination. Options range from numerous self-guided and interpretative walks in the Little Berg to overnight trails in remote wilderness areas. Several passes link the Little Berg to the Escarpment, and there are spectacular hikes between the two. The

Little Berg consists of the many lower mountains and hills, below what is known as the High Berg.

Another unique area of KwaZulu-Natal is the Greater St Lucia Wetland Park, awarded World Heritage status in 1999. It covers some 260,000 ha and has as its focal point Lake St Lucia, Africa's largest saltwater lake and home to the highest concentration of hippo and crocodile in South Africa.

The park consists of five distinct ecosystems: the marine ecosystem, with its sandy beaches and the southernmost coral reefs in the world; the forested dunes of the Eastern Shores; the 38,000-ha Lake St Lucia; the Western Shores with their sand forests and marine fossils; and the Mkuze swamps.

With a bird checklist of 521 species, the Greater St Lucia Wetland Park offers exceptional birding. The lake supports large breeding colonies of pelicans, herons, storks, terns and a wide variety of waterfowl, while the patches of sand forest harbour species such as Neergaard's sugarbird, the yellow-spotted nicator and Rudd's apalis.

Four of the Big Five species (rhino, elephant, buffalo and leopard) occur in the park, and among the other mammals to be seen are reedbuck, blue wildebeest, waterbuck, nyala, impala, Burchell's zebra and red duiker. Cheetah and a variety of smaller predators are also well represented.

Visitors can explore the park on foot, along many self-guided, interpretative walks laid out near the various restcamps, join a guided day walk or undertake a wilderness trail in the Tewate Wilderness Area along the Eastern Shores of the park.

In the northeastern corner of KwaZulu-Natal lies another unique tract of land, Maputaland. Bounded by the Ubombo and Lebombo mountains in the west, this fascinating region covers some 8,000 km² and encompasses the coastal plains from just south of the Mfolozi River, northwards, right up to the border with Mozambique.

Maputaland is a patchwork of forested dunes, swamp forest, marshes, lakes, grasslands, and miles and miles of pristine beaches. Among its many outstanding features is the Kosi Lake system with its raffia palms and palmnut vultures. The unique mangrove community of the Kosi Estuary is the only place in South Africa where five mangrove species occur together. Other attractions include Lake Sibaya, the country's largest freshwater lake, the unique sand forests of Tembe Elephant Park and Ndumo Game Reserve. For those seeking an encounter with the Big Five, the Hluhluwe-Umfolozi Park offers a top-class wildlife experience. Hluhluwe and Umfolozi were proclaimed in 1897 as two separate parks. These parks, together with St Lucia Park, are the three oldest conservation areas in Africa. The first wilderness area in South Africa was set aside in Umfolozi in 1959, and it was in many respects a pioneer. It was here, for example, that the first guided wilderness trails were conducted. Umfolozi also played a crucial role in saving the white rhino from becoming extinct, and the park has one of the largest populations of black rhino in the world today. Opportunities to explore the park on foot range from guided game walks to overnight trails in the wilderness area.

Other scenic highlights of KwaZulu-Natal include the magnificent Mtamvuna and Oribi gorges in the south of the province. There are also several small, but worthwhile, nature reserves and green spaces within the densely populated urban areas of Pietermaritzburg and Durban.

Although KwaZulu-Natal enjoys a warm subtropical climate, altitude has a marked influence on local climatic conditions. Summers are hot and very humid along the coast, while the winter months are pleasant. Further inland, however, winter days are generally pleasant, but at night temperatures often drop to below 5 °C. Summer days in the interior are pleasant, as are the night-time temperatures.

In the Drakensberg foothills summer temperatures range between 13 and 32 °C. In winter they are generally between 5 and 16 °C, although they do often drop to well below freezing.

KwaZulu-Natal has summer rain and most of the rainfall is recorded between October and March in the form of heavy thunderstorms. The average rainfall over most of the Drakensberg is 1,250 mm, but as a general rule the rainfall increases from the valleys to the upper part of the Little Berg.

During summer the Little Berg and summit are often blanketed by heavy cloud and mist, which can take up to two weeks to lift. Frost occurs about 150 nights a year, snowfalls six to 12 times a year. Although snow can be expected any time of year, it generally falls between April and September. In the southern Berg snowfalls are more frequent and heavier than in the northern Berg. Although usually restricted to the summit and near summit, snow occasionally reaches down to the 1,800-m level.

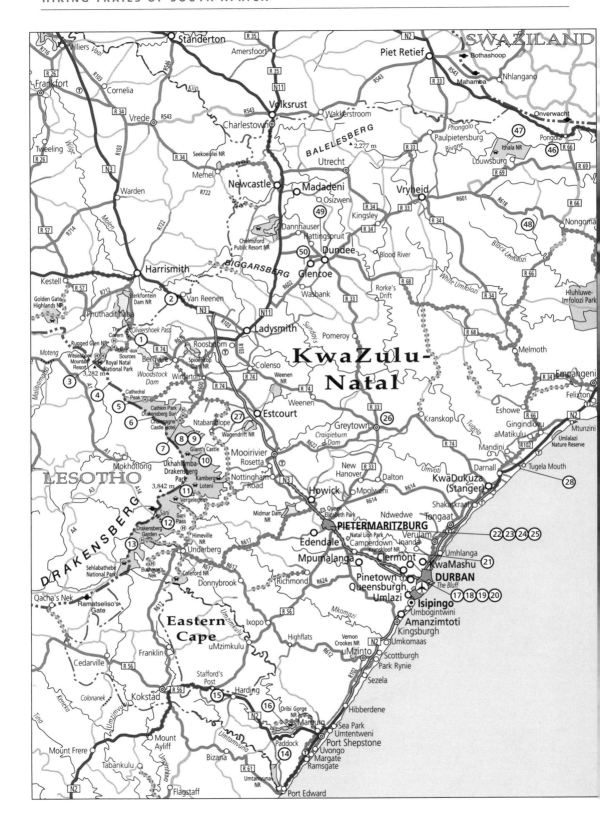

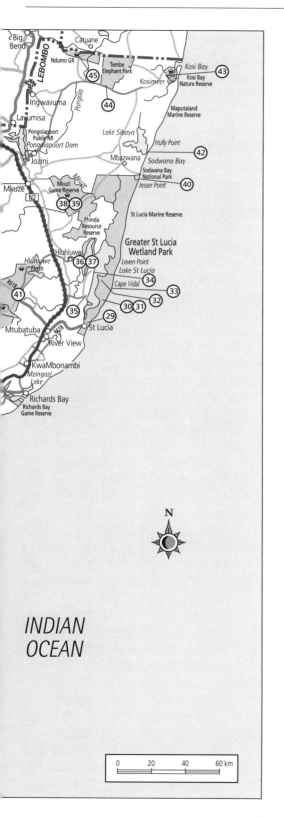

INDIAN
OCEAN

N

| 0 | 20 | 40 | 60 km |

HIKING TRAILS

1 **Vergezient Berg Trails** p.141
2 **Black Wildebeest Hiking Trail** p.141
3 **Royal Natal National Park** p.142
4 **Mont-aux-Sources to Cathedral Peak Hike** p.143
5 **Cathedral Peak and Mlambonja Wilderness Area** p.144
6 **Cathedral Peak Two Passes Hike** p.145
7 **Cathkin Peak and Mdedelelo Wilderness Area** p.146
8 **Injisuthi** p.147
9 **Injisuthi Wilderness Trails** p.148
10 **Giant's Castle** p.148
11 **Mkhomazi Wilderness Area and Kamberg, Lotheni and Vergelegen nature reserves** p.150
12 **Mzimkhulu Wilderness Area and Mzimkhulwana Nature Reserve** p.152
13 **Giant's Cup Hiking Trail** p.153
14 **Umtamvuna Nature Reserve** p.153
15 **Ingeli Forest Lodge** p.154
16 **Oribi Gorge Nature Reserve** p.155
17 **Burman Bush Nature Reserve** p.156
18 **Silverglen Nature Reserve** p.156
19 **Palmiet Nature Reserve** p.157
20 **Kenneth Steinbank Nature Reserve** p.157
21 **Krantzkloof Nature Reserve** p.157
22 **Ferncliffe Nature Reserve** p.158
23 **Natal National Botanical Garden** p.158
24 **Greenbelt Trails** p.159
25 **Dorp Spruit Trail** p.159
26 **Blinkwater Hiking Trails** p.160
27 **Moor Park Nature Reserve** p.160
28 **Harold Johnson Nature Reserve** p.169
29 **St Lucia Game Park** p.169
30 **Mziki Trail** p.170
31 **Emoyeni Trail** p.171
32 **St Lucia Wilderness Trail** p.172
33 **Cape Vidal** p.172
34 **Fanie's Island** p.173
35 **Charter's Creek** p.173
36 **False Bay Park** p.174
37 **Dugandlovu Trail** p.174
38 **Mkuzi Game Reserve** p.175
39 **Mkuzi Bushveld Trail** p.175
40 **Sodwana Bay** p.176
41 **Hluhluwe-Umfolozi Park** p.176
42 **Lake Sibaya Nature Reserve** p.177
43 **Amanzimnyama Trail** p.178
44 **Tembe Elephant Park** p.179
45 **Ndumo Game Reserve** p.180
46 **Mkhaya Trail** p.180
47 **Ithala Game Reserve** p.181
48 **Ntendeka Wilderness Area** p.182
49 **Mpati Mountain Hiking Trail** p.182
50 **Izemfene Hiking Trail** p.183

DRAKENSBERG

Weather conditions here can change rapidly, and this range has probably claimed more lives than any other in South Africa. Always be prepared for adverse weather conditions and bear the following in mind when doing walks longer than a few hours, or overnight hikes:

• Groups for overnight hikes are limited to a maximum of 12 persons.

• Do not venture into the High Berg if you are unfamiliar with the area.

• A good map is essential. The best one is the three-part, 1:50,000 recreational map of the entire Drakensberg from Mont-aux-Sources in the north to Sehlabathebe in the south. Useful features include a safety grid, enabling you to pinpoint your exact position very quickly, and a numbering system at the intersections of footpaths. It is standard practice for backpackers completing the mountain register to state the junction numbers of their intended routes.

• It is compulsory to complete the mountain register upon entering any of the mountain areas. Do this as accurately as possible as this information will speed up assistance or rescue operations, should these be necessary.

• On completion of your hike, note the time and date of your return in the register and inform the Officer-in-Charge.

• You can find yourself trapped in heavy mist, the visibility reduced to a few metres, with very little warning. Do not attempt to descend from the Escarpment. Rather pitch your tent and stay put until the mist lifts.

• Never pitch camp close to streams or rivers, as flash floods are not uncommon after heavy thunderstorms. These thunderstorms might break high in the catchment areas of rivers and you may not even be aware of them.

• In the event of snow, try to move as soon as possible to lower ground but, if the snow is too deep, try to get to the nearest cave or improvise an emergency shelter.

• Always carry at least two-days' worth of high-energy spare rations in case you become trapped by mist or snow.

• There are certain caves that can be booked for the exclusive use of one group. Reservations should be made with the relevant KwaZulu-Natal Wildlife office.

• Even if you have booked a cave, you must always carry a tent, as bad weather or other factors may prevent you getting to it and cause you to spend a night in the open.

• No open fires are permitted on trails in the Drakensberg, so trailists must carry a lightweight backpacking stove and fuel.

• Other essentials for overnight hikes in the Berg are a good down sleeping bag, rated at least -5 °C, a high-density groundpad, waterproof rain gear and cold-weather clothing.

• A valid passport is required for excursions beyond the Escarpment into Lesotho.

ST LUCIA & MAPUTALAND

• Trailists visiting St Lucia and Maputaland are advised to take anti-malaria precautions.

• Swimming and wading are forbidden in all the lakes, because of hippo and crocodile.

• In addition to these two animals, there are also shark in the St Lucia Estuary.

• Hippo usually leave the water in the late afternoon to graze, returning in the early morning. When walking near vleis, lakes and marshes, look out for hippo, and remember that they sometimes rest in forested areas during the day, especially on overcast days. If confronted by an aggressive hippo, retreat as fast as possible, or climb a decent size tree. If the hippo does not appear aggressive, stand still and withdraw quietly.

1. VERGEZIENT BERG TRAILS
Bergville

Trails: Up to 13.5 km and overnight;
1 hour to 2 days; network.
Permits: Jacana Marketing and Reservations,
P O Box 95212, Waterkloof 0145,
tel: (012) 346 3550, fax: 346 2499,
email: info@jacanacollection.co.za
Maps: Trail map incorporated in trail pamphlet.
Facilities/Activities: Basecamp with bunks/
beds, mattresses; kitchen with fridge, microwave,
three-plate cooker, pots, cooking utensils, crockery and cutlery; braai areas; showers and toilets.

Located on the edge of the Drakensberg Escarpment, these trails at Vergezient Mountain Retreat offer stunning views of the Amphitheatre, Cathkin Peak and Champagne Castle to the southeast, the Maluti Mountains to the southwest, and Colenso to the east.

The trail network passes through open short grassland interspersed with proteas, kloofs with delightful patches of indigenous forest, tranquil streams, and two 40-m-high waterfalls. Hidden behind one of the waterfalls is an overhang decorated with rock paintings. Also of interest is a huge ancient landslide, which provides the setting for a rather unusual wetland.

Mountain reedbuck and blesbok count among the animals you may see, while a rich diversity of birds is attracted by the varied habitats. For those interested in history, Retief Pass (along which the Voortrekkers first entered what is now KwaZulu-Natal in 1838) and the Retief Rock are situated nearby.

Trail possibilities include short strolls, three rambles ranging from one to three hours and two 13.5-km routes, which can be combined into an overnight trail from the basecamp.

2. BLACK WILDEBEEST HIKING TRAIL
Van Reenen

Trails: 2 day trails; 4 and 10 km;
1.5 and 3.5 hours; circular. 28.5-km
hiking trail; 2 or 3 days; circular.

Permits: Jacana Marketing and Reservations,
P O Box 95212, Waterkloof 0145,
tel: (012) 346 3550, fax: 346 2499,
email: info@jacanacollection.co.za
Maps: Trail map incorporated in the
trail brochure.
Facilities/Activities: Two overnight camps
with bunks, mattresses, two-plate gas stove,
gas fridge, pots, pans, fireplace, showers
and flush toilets.
Pertinent information: Should the Sandspruit
be in flood, hikers on day two (of the
three-day trail) must walk out to Andrews
Motel, where they will be collected.

1. Crystal Falls Trail follows the same route as the first leg of the overnight trail, along the Crystal Stream Kloof to Dassie Pass, where there are ladders, which provide access to the plateau. Beyond Fig Tree Island the trail splits off to the right and descends back to the start at Siggy's Camp. **4 km; 1.5 hours; circular.**

2. Blouaap Trail mainly follows sections of the first and second or third (if you stayed for two nights at the River Camp) day's hike of the overnight trail. **10 km; 3.5 hours; circular.**

3. Black Wildebeest Hiking Trail This trail in the Sandspruit Conservancy, south of Van Reenen, offers hikers the opportunity to view a variety of game on foot. In addition to a large population of black wildebeest, hikers may also chance upon red hartebeest, blue wildebeest, Burchell's zebra, eland, blesbok and kudu.

The first day's hike (14 km; 5 hours) leads along a kloof to Dassie Pass, where ladders provide access to the plateau. The trail now traverses the undulating hills and the vegetation alternates between grassland and patches of indigenous trees. Along the way several streams are crossed and the trail passes dams where game may be encountered. An inviting swimming spot awaits hikers in the Lost Valley Gorge, and from here it is an easy walk along the Sandspruit to the River Camp.

Using the River Camp as a base, an optional 6.5-km trail can be done on the second day. The trail ascends a ridge and then winds along a contour and after crossing Ribbok Spruit continues to Eagle's View. From here the path doubles back to cross the Ribbok Spruit once more before heading back to the hut.

Day three (8 km; 3 hours) – day two if you left out the optional day trail – begins with a steep climb and then follows an easy route along the plateau, passing through several indigenous forest patches. The path then descends along a valley and the remainder of the hike is an easy walk. **28.5 km; 2 or 3 days, circular.**

3. ROYAL NATAL NATIONAL PARK
uKhahlamba-Drakensberg Park, Bergville

Trails: *24 walks; 3 to 45 km; 45 min to 2 days; circular, out-and-return, open-ended.*
Permits: *Entrance fee. No permit required for walks.*
Maps: *Excellent guidebook with map.*
Facilities/Activities: *Self-catering accommodation; campsites at Mahai and Glen Reenen; picnic sites; trout-fishing; swimming; horse-riding.*

Covering 8,094 ha in the northern Drakensberg, the Royal Natal National Park is dominated by the awe-inspiring Amphitheatre, a sheer basalt wall that rises over 700 m above the Little Berg. This imposing natural wonder stretches from the Eastern Buttress, westwards, for 8 km to the Sentinel. The 500-m-high Tugela Falls plunge over the edge of the Amphitheatre in five gigantic leaps and are among the highest in the world. Other well-known attractions in the area include a sandstone formation, appropriately named the Policeman's Helmet, and the spectacular tunnel carved by the Tugela River.

The Amphitheatre wall forms an impressive backdrop to the Clarens sandstone formations of the Little Berg. At the lower elevations the vegetation is typically grasslands, with scattered stands of proteas, while indigenous forests of yellowwood, Cape beech, assegai and white stinkwood occur in sheltered valleys and kloofs. From the upper edge of the Little Berg to just below the summit, the vegetation

is characterised by grasslands, with the alpine belt occurring above altitudes of 2,865 m. In this belt the grasslands are interspersed by *Erica* and *Helichrysum* species.

The park's bird list of over 130 species features several noteworthy species, including the bearded vulture, peregrine falcon, crowned crane, orange-breasted rockjumper, grassbird and Gurney's sugarbird. Among the other species to keep an eye out for are the Cape vulture, black eagle, Swainson's francolin, ground woodpecker, sentinel rock thrush, starred robin and orange-throated longclaw.

Mammals are mainly small and nocturnal and thus easily overlooked. Among the more conspicuous species are grey rhebok, mountain reedbuck, klipspringer, common duiker, baboon and dassie. Carnivores include caracal and serval.

The park is traversed by a network of trails covering over 100 km, including six short walks, with a total duration of two hours or less.

Mahai Car Park

1. Cascades and McKinlay's Pool The trail follows the road past the trout hatchery and after about 15 minutes you will reach the Cascades, with its delightful setting against the backdrop of a patch of indigenous forest. The trail now continues along the left bank of the Mahai River to reach McKinlay's Pool at the junction of the Mahai and Gudu rivers, about 15 minutes beyond the Cascades. From here you can either retrace your tracks or continue with the path, which ascends steeply to Lookout Rock, where you join the Tiger Falls path. **8 km; 3 hours; circular.**

2. Fairy Glen and the Grotto Cross the Mahai River at the eastern end of the camping site and follow the Fairy Glen and Sunday Falls path. Just before the path crosses the Golide Stream, the Fairy Glen route turns off to the left, ascending gently to Fairy Glen, a popular picnic spot. From here the trail ascends steadily to below the Plowman's Kop cliffs, where you turn right. A short way on the path zigzags steeply and then levels off before reaching a split. The left-hand path leads to the head of the Grotto, where a waterfall plunges over the cliffs. Despite the name, the Grotto is not a cave, but two impressive gorges eroded through the sandstone. **10 km; 4 hours; out-and-return.**

3. Gudu Falls, The Crack and Mudslide Initially this trail follows the Tiger Falls path, which you join behind the hotel, and passes below the sandstone cliffs of Dooley. It then drops down to Gudu Bush where a path leads along the right-hand bank of the Gudu River to the falls at the head of the valley.

Continuing up the Mahai River valley along the Basotho Gate path, you reach the turnoff to the Crack after about 1.2 km. Here a steep climb along a crack in the sandstone cliffs has to be negotiated and at one difficult section there is a chain ladder. The trail now traverses the high ground and crosses the Gudu River about 50 m upstream of the falls; an excellent spot for a refreshing dip and a lunch stop. After traversing Plowman's Kop the route continues down the Mudslide where a short chain ladder assist trailists at the start. Owing to the steep gradient and loose surface, which becomes very slippery after rain, the Mudslide is not suitable for young children and those with a fear of heights. From the base of the cliffs follow the Gudu Bush path to the first turnoff on your left and make your way back to the car park. **11 km; 5 hours; circular.**

4. Sunday Falls, Surprise Ridge and Cannibal Cave This walk follows the route to the Fairy Glen turnoff, where you turn right instead, continuing to Sunday Falls, which you reach about an hour after setting off. The turnoff to the falls is signposted and after crossing above the falls keep an eye out for a track leading to the base of the falls.

Continuing along the main path, the trail crosses the Sunday Falls Stream and then the Sigubudu River. A short climb brings you to Surprise Ridge, with its unexpected views that extend as far as Cathedral Peak, Cathkin Peak and Champagne Castle in the south. Cannibal Cave lies outside the park boundaries, and is reached after a short walk westward along the ridge.

Instead of retracing your tracks, you can return via the Grotto and Fairy Glen trails; a full day's hike, but very rewarding. **22.5 km; 8 hours; circular.**

Gorge Car Park

5. Tugela Tunnel and Gorge This is without doubt the most popular and scenic walk in the park. From the car park the path follows the right-hand bank of the Tugela River past a sandstone ridge dominated by the Policeman's Helmet. The trail passes through several patches of forest and as you continue you become increasingly aware of being enclosed by the gorge. Over the last 1.5 km of the hike you cross the river three times and then reach the Tunnel a short distance beyond a chain ladder on the right-hand bank of the river.

Depending on the level of the river, you can either walk up the Tunnel for about 65 m or use the chain ladder to skirt it and boulder-hop up the Tugela River for about 800 m.

On the left-hand bank of the river, almost directly opposite the chain ladder there is a steep path leading to Tunnel Cave, from where you overlook the Tunnel, with the Amphitheatre forming an impressive backdrop. **22.5 km; 7 hours; out-and-return.**

6. Devil's Hoek Valley From the car park follow the Gorge path to the signposted turnoff to the right. The trail now climbs out of the valley and after a short while there is a split, where you turn left to bypass Thendele Camp. From here the path continues along the right-hand bank of the valley, passing through two delightful patches of forest. The path ends at Second Bush. **9 km; 4 hours; out-and-return.**

7. Vemaan Valley This path follows the Devil's Hoek Valley route for about 1.6 km to a split where you turn left. After crossing the Devil's Hoek River the trail makes its way around to the Vemaan Valley, which you follow to a small patch of forest. From here the trail doubles back along the Policeman's Helmet Ridge, which can be ascended from further back. **9 km; 4 hours; out-and-return.**

4. MONT-AUX-SOURCES TO CATHEDRAL PEAK HIKE
uKhahlamba-Drakensberg Park, Bergville

Trail: 60 km; 5 days; open-ended.
Permits: The Officer-in-Charge,
Cathedral Peak, Private Bag X1,
Winterton 3340,
tel: (036) 488 1880, fax: 488 1677.

Maps: The area is covered by map one in the Drakensberg Recreational Series: Drakensberg North – Mont-aux-Sources to Cathedral Peak.
Facilities/Activities: Campsite at Cathedral Peak; caves.

Starting at the Sentinel car park, this traverse features some of the most dramatic scenery in the whole of the Drakensberg. The first day's hike (12 km) ascends along a chain ladder to the top of the Amphitheatre and then heads south to the Kubedu River. From here the trail ascends gently along a tributary of the Kubedu and, after skirting the Ifidi Pinnacles, you reach Ifidi Cave, which is your overnight stop.

On the second day (11 km) the route heads inland, in order to avoid the deep cutback between Ifidi and Icidi buttresses, before swinging to the Escarpment. From the Stimela Ridge there are breathtaking views over Mbundini Buttress, and Mbundini Abbey also offers impressive vistas of the Fangs, as well as Madonna and her Worshippers. Continuing along the Escarpment, you reach Fangs Pass. Here there is accommodation available for trailists in Fangs Cave, which is found a short way down the pass.

The third day's walk (11 km) offers magnificent views of the Mweni Pinnacles and the Mweni area far below. The path then detours inland around the Mweni Cutback and crosses the Senqu River, the sources of the Gariep (Orange) River. From the headland on the Escarpment edge you can see imposing views of the Mweni Needles and the Rockeries Tower. Mponjwane Cave, a short distance to the north of the Rockeries Pass, is a popular overnight stop.

Day four's hike (15 km) takes you to the head of the Rockeries Pass, from where there are stunning views of the eight peaks of the Rockeries. At the top of the pass there is a path that leads to a waterfall in the Senqu River, which is some 4 km away. You then follow the Kokoatsan River upstream from the waterfall. After a steep climb up a ridge the trail descends steeply to the head of the Ntonjelana Pass. From here the route follows the Escarpment above the Cathedral range to the Mlambonja Pass. Twins Cave, the overnight stop, is just a short way down the pass.

On the final day of the hike (11 km) the route descends along the Mlambonja Pass to the Cathedral Peak Hotel. The route is scrubby and you will lose some 1,500 m in altitude over the course of your descent to the hotel.

5. CATHEDRAL PEAK AND MLAMBONJA WILDERNESS AREA
uKhahlamba-Drakensberg Park, Winterton

Trails: 120-km network of footpaths; 1 to 18 km; 30 min to overnight hikes; circular, out-and-return and open-ended.
Permits: The Officer-in-Charge, Cathedral Peak, Private Bag X1, Winterton 3340, tel: (036) 488 1880, fax: 488 1677.
Maps: This area is covered by map two in the Drakensberg Recreational Series: Drakensberg North – Cathedral Peak to Injisuthi.
Facilities/Activities: Campsite with ablution facilities; certain caves can be reserved in advance for the exclusive use of a group.

Covering 31,500 ha, Cathedral Peak and the adjoining Mlambonja Wilderness Area are among the most favoured Berg destinations for outdoor enthusiasts. Bounded to the north and northwest by the Upper Tugela and to the south by the Mdedelelo Wilderness, the area is dominated by the Cathedral range. The 4-km-long row of free-standing peaks, also known as the Ridge of the Horns, includes some of the most spectacular peaks in South Africa; among them Cathedral Peak (3,004 m), Bell (2,930 m), Outer Horn (3,005 m), Inner Horn (3,005 m) and the Chessmen. In addition to these tall, free-standing peaks are those of the Escarpment here, which are all over 3,000 m.

There are numerous opportunities for short walks in the Little Berg and extended overnight hikes in the Mlambonja Wilderness Area.

1. Ndedema Gorge is reached about 2.5 km beyond the Organ Pipes turnoff. The gorge, about 8 km long, is internationally renowned for its rock art, and 3,909 rock paintings at 17 sites were painstakingly recorded by the late Harald Pager in the 1960s. Sebayeni Cave, the first shelter in the sandstone band on the southern side of the valley, is the largest of the painted shelters in the gorge and contains over 1,100 paintings. Other well-known rock art sites in the gorge include Poacher's Cave and Leopard Cave. The gorge has one of the most extensive patches of indigenous forest to be found in the Drakensberg. **9.5 km; 3 hours, to start of the gorge; open-ended. Guided walks only.**

2. Tarn and Tryme Hills This pleasant walk starts at the Cathedral Peak Hotel and ascends fairly steeply to the Mushroom Rock, from where it climbs along a ridge to Tarn Hill, named after the small tarn on the plateau. After about 4 km you will join a jeep track, along which you ascend steadily for about 1 km before turning left. The trail then winds down the slopes, crosses a stream and then ascends the slopes of Tryme Hill before dropping down into the forested valley of the Mhlonhlo River, which you follow back to the start. There are also worthwhile detours, which can be made to the Ribbon, Albert and Doreen falls. **10 km; 4 hours; circular.**

3. Organ Pipes Cathedral Peak is the only Berg area from which you can drive to the top of the Little Berg. Access is via the 10.5-km-long Mike's Pass, which gains some 500 m in altitude to Arendsig Gate, the starting point of the route to the Organ Pipes and the Escarpment. The start of the ascent is signposted, about 6.5 km from Arendsig. Over the next 7 km the path gains more than 900 m in altitude, passing an assembly of spires and buttresses known in Zulu as *Qolo la Masoja*, or the Ridge of Soldiers. This is either due to apparent resemblance of the fluted columns to a regiment of soldiers standing to attention or the name could be derived from a tradition associated with military action; the origins of the name are not certain. **13.5 km; 7 hours; open-ended.**

From the top of Organ Pipes Pass you can do a traverse along the Escarpment to Gray's Pass, ending at Monk's Cowl office. **50 km; 5 days; open-ended.**

4. Rainbow Gorge Starting at the Cathedral Peak Hotel, this delightful walk follows the deep gorge carved by the Ndumeni River, which has its source below the Organ Pipes. From the hotel the path skirts the base of Tryme Hill and after about 4 km descends into the Ndumeni Valley. As you make your way up the forested valley you reach a beautiful pool into which two waterfalls cascade. The going now becomes more difficult as you have to cross the river several times before reaching the gorge, which can be explored by crawling underneath a boulder jammed in the gorge. From the head of the gorge you can either retrace your tracks or clamber up the steep right-hand bank of Tryme Hill to join a footpath at the top of the hill. Turn right here and follow the path back to the hotel. **11 km; 5 hours; out-and-return or circular.**

5. Cathedral Peak An ascent of Cathedral Peak involves a strenuous 18-km round-trip, for which an entire day should be set aside. The final ascent to the summit of Cathedral Peak involves a C-grade scramble and is, therefore, not recommended for inexperienced hikers. On a clear day the view from the summit is magnificent, with Cathkin Peak to the south and Eastern Buttress to the north clearly visible. To the southeast the scenery is dominated by the deep valley carved by the Mlambonja River. **18 km; 10 hours; out-and-return.**

6. CATHEDRAL PEAK TWO PASSES HIKE
uKhahlamba-Drakensberg Park, Winterton

Trail: 37.5 km; 3 days; open-ended.
Permits: *The Officer-in-Charge, Cathedral Peak, Private Bag X1, Winterton 3340, tel: (036) 488 1880, fax: 488 1677.*
Maps: *This area is covered by map two in the Drakensberg Recreational Series: Drakensberg North – Cathedral Peak to Injisuthi.*
Facilities/Activities: *Campsite at Cathedral Peak; certain caves can be reserved in advance for the exclusive use of a group.*

This is a demanding, but very rewarding hike that should only be attempted by fit and experienced hikers. From the Arendsig Gate at the end of Mike's Pass, the route continues for 3 km along a jeep track to the Contour Path, where you turn left, continuing for 3.5 km to the turnoff to Organ Pipes Pass. Over the next 7 km you will gain over 900 m in altitude as you make your way past the imposing Organ Pipes. The wide valley between Ndumeni Dome and Castle Buttress, reached after the day's strenuous 13.5-km hike, is a good place to stop overnight in a tent or to continue to the Ndumeni Caves, two small shelters high up on Ndumeni Dome.

On account of the undulating terrain an early start is recommended for the second day's hike (12.5 km). For the best views, follow the watershed over Castle Buttress and Cleft Peak (at 3,281 m, the highest point between Mont-aux-Sources and Cathedral Peak). Further along, the path traverses the watershed close to the edge of the Escarpment, revealing awe-inspiring views. Prominent landmarks include the Column, Pyramid, Cockade and Elephant, and beyond Xeni Pass you look down onto the Cathedral Range. The overnight stop, Twins Cave, is situated a short way from the head of the Mlambonja Pass.

Day three's hike (11.5 km) involves a steep descent along the Mlambonja Pass. On account of the steep gradient and the loose scree in the rock bands near the head of the pass, as well as the slippery grass, caution must be exercised and you would be well advised to take your time.

7. CATHKIN PEAK AND MDEDELELO WILDERNESS AREA
uKhahlamba-Drakensberg Park, Winterton

Trails: 185-km network of footpaths; 1 to 58 km; 30 min to overnight hikes; circular, out-and-return; open-ended.
Permits: The Officer-in-Charge, Monk's Cowl, Private Bag X2, Winterton 3340, tel. and fax: (036) 468 1103.
Maps: This area is covered by map two in the Drakensberg Recreational Series: Drakensberg North –

Cathedral Peak to Injisuthi.
Facilities/Activities: Campsite with ablution facilities at Monk's Cowl; certain caves can be reserved in advance for the exclusive use of a group.

Monk's Cowl and the adjoining 29,000-ha Mdedelelo Wilderness Area are characterised by deep valleys, impressive peaks and caves with rock paintings. Familiar landmarks include Cathkin Peak, Gatberg and the Dragon's Back, an impressive range of free-standing, block-shaped peaks. Backpacking is made easier by a contour path that links popular destinations and passes to the Escarpment. The area is bordered in the north by Cathedral Peak and in the south by the Injisuthi section of the Giant's Castle Game Reserve.

1. Contour Path via the Sphinx One of the most popular routes onto the Little Berg from Monk's Cowl is via the Sphinx and Verkykerskop. This is the usual route onto the Contour Path and hence also to the higher peaks and passes. Some 450 m is gained in altitude before the gradient levels off at Breakfast Stream, beyond which the trail ascends gently to the Contour Path. Dominating the scenery ahead is Cathkin Peak (3,149 m), from which the area's name, Mdedelelo, is derived. *Mdedelelo* is Zulu for 'make room for him', and refers to the appearance that Cathkin Peak has pushed aside the other peaks to make space for itself. **5.5 km; 3 hours; open-ended.**

2. Gray's Pass is reached by following the path via the Sphinx to the Contour Path where you turn right, continuing for 2.5 km to Hlatikulu Nek. Remain on the Contour Path for another 1.5 km and turn left to reach Keith Bush Camp after a steady climb of about 4 km. It is a beautiful campsite, situated at the head of the Mhlawazini River and surrounded by cliffs on three sides. Although only 2.5 km long, Gray's Pass is not only eroded and exposed, but also steep, and you will gain some 700 m in altitude.

Shortly after starting the climb up the pass you will get your first uninterrupted view of Monk's Cowl (3,234 m). Nkosazana Cave, near the top of the pass, is a good place to spend the night on the

Escarpment. From the top of the pass it is an easy walk of about 3 km to Champagne Castle (3,377 m). You can either backtrack down Gray's Pass, or descend along Ship's Prow Pass, immediately south of Champagne Castle. Do not attempt to descend along the northern fork of Ship's Prow Pass, which is extremely dangerous, but take the south fork. Loose scree makes this a difficult descent, so take care. **45 km; 3 days; circular.**

3. Monk's Cowl to Ndedema Gorge

Another option when joining the Contour Path via the Sphinx and Breakfast Stream is to hike to Ndedema Gorge. This is a strenuous walk, which takes you through two river valleys with long descents followed by steep ascents. Gatberg, a peak with a hole (estimated to be 9 m in diameter) through its base, is a prominent landmark along this route. The Zulu name, Intunja, is variously translated as 'the eye of the needle' and 'the hole in the mountain through which the shepherds can creep'. Further along the scenery is dominated by the Dragon's Back, an impressive range of block-shaped peaks. Some 400 m in altitude is lost over the last 4 km to Ndedema Gorge, reached about 28 km from the Monk's Cowl Office. From here you can either continue to Cathedral Peak, or hike down Ndedema Gorge (8 km) and return to Monk's Cowl along the Mhlawazini River and Hlatikulu Nek (23 km) or via Hospitalspruit and Stable caves (19 km).

8. INJISUTHI
uKhahlamba-Drakensberg Park, Estcourt

Trails: 5 trails; 2.5 to 15 km; 1 hour to overnight hikes; circular, out-and-return, open-ended. 6-hour guided walk to Battle Cave.
Permits: *Entrance fee. No permit required for walks. For overnight hikes and caves: The Officer-in-Charge, Injisuthi Camp, Private Bag X7010, Estcourt 3310, tel. and fax: (036) 431 7848.*
Maps: *The area is covered by map three in the Drakensberg Recreational Series: Drakensberg Central – Injisuthi, Giant's Castle, Highmoor.*
Facilities/Activities: *Self-catering cabins; campsite; guided walks to Battle Cave; trout-fishing (permit required).*

South Africa's two highest peaks, Mafadi (3,446 m) and Injisuthi Dome (3,379 m) form an impressive backdrop to the wild Injisuthi Valley in the north of the Giant's Castle Game Reserve. Other prominent peaks to be seen in this area include Old Woman Grinding Corn, The Injisuthi Triplets and The Molar. Dominating the skyline to the northwest of the Injisuthi Valley are three particularly impressive peaks – Champagne Castle, Monk's Cowl and Cathkin Peak.

1. Grindstone Caves owe their name to a grindstone that was placed there many years ago. The trail leads to a delightful yellowwood forest and then meanders up mountain slopes towards the sandstone cliffs before levelling off. **3 hours; out-and-return.**

2. Van Heyningen's Pass is a favourite walk to the top of the Little Berg. After passing through a patch of forest the route ascends along Van Heyningen's Pass to a viewpoint, where trailists are rewarded with spectacular views of Monk's Cowl and Champagne Castle. Looking southwards along the line of jagged peaks, the view extends as far as the impressive wall of Giant's Castle. **8 km; 3 hours; out-and-return.**

3. Cataract Valley is reached by continuing from Grindstone Caves down to the Old Woman Stream, which you cross above a waterfall. The path then climbs to the top of a ridge and drops down into Cataract Valley, crossing Cataract Stream three times before reaching Delmhlwazine River. From here the trail veers back to the camp. **13 km; 5 hours; circular.**

4. Battle Cave can only be visited if you join a guided walk. The cave owes its name to a scene depicting a battle between two feuding Bushmen clans. Also depicted are a small group of lions, animals superimposed on humans, eland, rhebok and masked figures. **15 km; 6 hours; out-and-return.**

5. Wonder Valley is reached by hiking to the top of Van Heyningen's Pass. From here, continue heading up the path towards a ridge, which is crossed further along. The route now descends gradually and there are some fine views of Wonder Valley. Continue to Wonder Valley Cave, from where it is best to retrace your tracks. **15 km; 5 hours; out-and-back.**

9. INJISUTHI WILDERNESS TRAILS
uKhahlamba-Drakensberg Park, Estcourt

Trails: Guided wilderness trails; distances vary from 10 to 15 km per day; 2 nights; walks from basecamp cave.
Permits: KwaZulu-Natal Wildlife, P O Box 13069, Cascades 3202, tel: (033) 845 1000, fax: 845 1001, email: trails@kwazulu-natalwildlife.com
Maps: The area is covered by map three in the Drakensberg Recreational Series: Drakensberg Central – Injisuthi, Giant's Castle, Highmoor.
Facilities/Activities: On trail: accommo-dation in cave. Injisuthi Camp: Self-catering cabins; campsite; guided walks to Battle Cave; trout-fishing (permit required).
Pertinent information: Trail season is from the beginning of October to the end of May. The minimum age for trailists is 16 years old.

On these guided trails, you will explore the wild Injisuthi area of Giant's Castle on foot. The land-scape ranges from remote valleys and grassy hill-sides, to the high peaks dominating the Escarpment. A rich diversity of habitats attracts an equally diverse variety of birds, and trailists may also see herds of eland and other game. No less spectacular is the grassland flora, which is especial-ly eye-catching in spring and early summer.

The emphasis of these trails is on enjoying the spec-tacular setting and appreciating the complex envi-ronment through which you are hiking. The two nights of the trail are spent in a cave.

10. GIANT'S CASTLE
uKhahlamba-Drakensberg Park, Estcourt

Trails: 285-km network of footpaths; 3 to 30 km; 1 hour to overnight hikes; circular, out-and-return, open-ended.
Permits: Entrance fee. No permit required for day walks. For overnight hikes, mountain huts and caves: The Officer-in-Charge, Giant's Castle, Private Bag X7055, Estcourt 3310, tel: (036) 353 3718, fax: 353 3775.
Maps: The area is covered by map three in the Drakensberg Recreational Series: Drakensberg Central – Injisuthi, Giant's Castle, Highmoor.
Facilities/Activities: Three mountain huts; self-catering cottages, restaurant, guided walks to Main Cave rock paintings; vulture restaurant; horse-riding at Hillside.

Situated on a grassy plateau among deep valleys and below the dramatic, sheer cliffs of the Escarpment, the Giant's Castle area is a hiker's par-adise. The Escarpment here is dominated by a number of well-known natural landmarks such as Giant's Castle, the Long Wall, Carbineer Point, The Thumb and Bannerman Face.

Giant's Castle Game Reserve, proclaimed in 1903 to protect the declining population of eland, extends from Giant's Castle Ridge, northwards, for 25 km to the Injisuthi River. In addition to eland, the reserve is also home to blesbok, mountain reedbuck, southern reedbuck, grey rhebok, grey duiker and baboon.

With an extensive bird checklist of some 160 species, Giant's Castle offers birding enthusiasts exciting opportunities. Topping the list of note-worthy species is the rare bearded vulture, which is often seen flying overhead. Not to be missed is a guided walk to the vulture hide at Bamboo Hollow, where carcasses are placed between May and September especially to supplement the diet of the bearded vultures. Other raptors you might see at the hide include Cape vulture, black eagle, lanner falcon and jackal buzzard.

The bald ibis has been recorded in the area, and among the other species you may tick here are orange-throated longclaw, ground woodpecker, orange-breasted rockjumper, Drakensberg siskin and Gurney's sugarbird.

There are in excess of 25 walks in the reserve (excluding the Injisuthi area), ranging from a 1.9-km round trip from Giant's Castle Camp to Main Ridge, to a four-day hike.

Short Walks

1. River Walk The outward leg takes the Main Caves path to Rock 75 and then doubles back through grassveld and light bush along the eastern bank of the Bushman's River. **3 km; 1 hour; out-and-return.**

2. Bushman's River Trail, an interpretative walk starting at the hutted camp, is one of the most popular walks in the reserve. Points of interest along the way include Sandstone View and the historic Rock 75, where the camp cook of the 75th Regiment on Foot carved the figure 75 into a boulder during the Langalibalele rebellion in 1874. The highlight of the trail are the Main Caves. One of the best-known rock art sites in South Africa, the two large overhangs contain some 540 individual paintings. A recorded commentary on the Bushmen is given hourly, and the site museum provides an invaluable insight into the life of these early inhabitants of the Drakensberg. **3.2 km; 2 hours; out-and-return.**

3. Grysbok Bush Trail follows the path past Main Caves and then ascends steadily through grassland and oldwood. Further along, the valley closes in and becomes more densely wooded with oldwood and wild olive trees. About 4 km after setting off from the Main Camp you will reach the first pool and Grysbok Bush, a delightful patch of indigenous forest. **8 km; 4 hours; out-and-return.**

Longer Walks

4. Giant's Hut via Giant's Ridge Follow the path past the Main Caves turnoff for about 500 m. The trail climbs steeply out of the Bushman's River Valley and two short but steep ascents, with more gentle terrain in between them, have to be negotiated.

The path then follows the spine of a ridge and traverses the slopes of another ridge before joining the Contour Path. Turn left here and follow the Contour Path as it winds below Giant's Castle to reach Giant's Castle Hut after 2 km. The return leg along Two Dassie Stream is reached a short way on and initially follows the stream's western bank. Lower down you will cross the stream a number of times, and there are several inviting pools. After 8 km the trail joins the path to the Main Caves and the remainder of the walk is an easy stroll back to Main Camp. **20.5 km; 9 hours; circular.**

5. Langalibalele Pass is reached by taking the Main Caves and Grysbok Bush paths (see 'Short Walks', this page). From the lower end of Grysbok Bush the trail ascends steadily along the spine of a ridge, gaining some 400 m in altitude over 2 km to the Contour Path. A 1-km walk along the Contour Path brings you to the turnoff to Langalibalele Pass, which gains some 670 m in altitude over 3 km. At the top of the pass a short walk to the south leads to a simple stone cairn that marks the spot where three carbineers of Major Durnford's forces and two auxiliaries were killed in a skirmish with Chief Langalibalele's Hlubi (the Sotho-speaking people of Zululand) on 4 November 1873. Five of the peaks to the south of the pass – Erskine, Bond, Potterill, Kambule and Katana – were named in honour of those killed. The same route is followed back. **21 km; 10 hours; out-and-return.**

6. Giant's Pass and Giant's Castle From the Main Camp follow the path up Giant's Ridge to the Contour Path where you turn right, continuing for 2 km to the turnoff to Giant's Castle Pass. Over the next 2 km you will gain some 770 m in altitude to the top of Giant's Castle Pass. The last section is steep, so beware of landslides and avoid gullies branching off to the left as they are impassable. From the pass a path leads eastwards for about 2 km, and reaches the summit of Giant's Castle (3,314 m) after a gentle ascent of about 230 m. Return to Main Camp along the same route. **30 km; 2 days; out-and-return.**

Overnight Hiking

7. This route has no particular name, but offers a rewarding, circular, four-day hike, incorporating two of the mountain huts. On the first day (10.5 km; 4 hours) you hike from Main Camp via Two Dassie Stream to the Contour Path and Giant's Hut.

Giant's Hut is the ideal base for an ascent of Giant's Castle (18 km; 9 hours) on day two. From the hut, follow the Contour Path for about 2 km beyond the Giant's Ridge path until you reach the foot of Giant's Castle Pass. A steep 2-km climb brings you to the top of the pass, where a path leads eastwards for about 2 km to the summit of Giant's Castle. You return along the same route to the hut.

Day three's hike (17.5 km; 7 hours) to Bannerman Hut follows the Contour Path, at an altitude of about 2,300 m. Except for numerous mountain stream crossings, where the terrain becomes more difficult, the walk is fairly easy. Dominating the Escarpment are several prominent landmarks: the Long Wall, Katana, Carbineer Point, Kambule, Mount Durnford, Potterill, Bond and Erskine. About 9.5 km after setting off you will reach the base of Langalibalele Pass. Further along, the path passes below the Thumb and Bannerman Face, before reaching Bannerman Hut at the foot of Bannerman Pass.

On the fourth day, backtrack for 4 km to join the Secretary Bird Ridge path, or continue for another 500 m to join a more direct route back to the Main Camp. The total distances for this day are 12 km (4 hours) and 10.5 km (3.5 hours) respectively. **56.5 km or 58 km; 4 days; circular.**

11. MKHOMAZI WILDERNESS AREA AND KAMBERG, LOTHENI AND VERGELEGEN NATURE RESERVES
uKhahlamba-Drakensberg Park, Nottingham Road

Trails: 465-km network of footpaths; 3 to 80 km; 1.5 hour to overnight hikes; circular, out-and-return, open-ended.
Permits: *Entrance fee. No permit required for day walks. For overnight hikes and caves: The Officer-in-Charge, Mkhomazi, P O Box 105, Nottingham Road 3280, tel. and fax: (033) 263 6444. The Officer-in-Charge, Highmoor, P O Box 51, Rosetta 3301,*

tel. and fax: (033) 263 7240. The Officer-in-Charge, Lotheni, P O Box 14, Himeville 3256, tel. and fax: (033) 702 0540. The Officer-in-Charge, Vergelegen, P O Box 53, Himeville 3256, tel: (033) 702 0712.
Maps: *The area is covered by map four: Drakensberg Central – Highmoor, Mkhomazi, Loteni, and map five: Southern Drakensberg – Vergelegen, Cobham, Garden Castle, in the Drakensberg Recreational Series.*
Facilities/Activities: *Highmoor: campsites. Kamberg: self-catering accommodation; trout-fishing. Lotheni: self-catering accommodation; campsite; trout-fishing; Settlers' Museum. Vergelegen: self-catering accommodation.*

Mkhomazi Wilderness Area

Proclaimed in May 1973, the Mkhomazi Wilderness Area of some 54,000 ha is not as well known as the areas further north. The spurs of the Little Berg extend further east from the Escarpment than they do towards the north and the deeply incised valleys give the landscape a rugged appearance and a sense of isolation and tranquillity. Soaring buttresses and several unnamed peaks of over 3,000 m dominate the Escarpment.

The area is rich in history, and was the scene of many bitter clashes between the Bushmen and the early white settlers. Some routes to the Escarpment are the original passes used by the Bushmen and Basotho across the Drakensberg.

Highmoor

To the north and east of the wilderness area is Highmoor, which has the largest breeding colony of bald ibis in the whole of KwaZulu-Natal. The dams and wetlands at Highmoor are also an important habitat for the wattled crane, African rail and red-chested flufftail.

Kamberg, Lotheni and Vergelegen, which serve as convenient access points for the Mkhomazi Wilderness Area, adjoin the wilderness area to the south and east. Despite the rugged terrain there are numerous footpaths, but they are mainly restricted to the occasional spur and to river valleys, often making it necessary to boulder-hop up a valley to reach higher ground.

Kamberg

This reserve, on the northeastern boundary of the Mkhomazi Wilderness Area, covers 2,232 ha and is renowned for its scenery, as well as for its excellent trout-fishing. Game to be seen include mountain reedbuck, reedbuck, blesbok, eland, grey rhebok and oribi.

1. Mooi River Trail takes its name from the Mooi River, which has its source in the adjoining Mkhomazi Wilderness Area. This walk consists of a main trail, with three 1-km loops and has been designed as a wheelchair trail. **7 km, with shorter options; 2 to 3.5 hours; circular.**

Lotheni

Lotheni covers 3,984 ha and has some of the most spectacular scenery in the Drakensberg, including a number of waterfalls. Among these are Jacob's Ladder Falls, which cascade down the mountain slopes in several tiers. Prominent peaks, such as the Tent, Hawk and Redi peaks, are clearly visible on the Escarpment.

2. Gelib Tree Trail is a self-guided, interpretative trail that serves as a reminder of an incident during World War II near the settlement of Gelib in Ethiopia. An officer of the 1st Royal Natal Carbineers, Captain Charles Eustace, who fought in what was then Italian Somaliland, collected a few seeds of an acacia tree. Eustace planted the seed years later on his farm (which became part of the Lotheni Nature Reserve) in memory of 13 carbineers who were ambushed during the military campaign to take the village of Gelib, which was held by the Italian military forces. The 11 points of interest along the trail include the area's rivers and fish, its geology, a termite mound, alien trees and a soil reclamation project. **5.5 km; 2.5 hours; circular.**

3. Yellowwood Cave From Simes's Cottage the trail follows the left-hand bank of the Lotheni River

upstream past the eMpophomeni Falls. Further along it continues along Ka-Masihlenga Stream, flanked by indigenous forest, to a cave situated on the right-hand bank of the stream. **10.6 km; 4 hours; out-and-return.**

4. Emadundwini Trail starts at the Lotheni Camp huts, from where it ascends steadily to just below Sheba's Breasts, gaining some 770 m in altitude. A short way on you join the Contour Path to Giant's Hut and from here you continue in a northwesterly direction until you reach the Taylor's Path junction. Turn left and follow Taylor's Pass, which descends steadily and crosses a tributary of the Elandshoek River. The trail winds above the Elandshoek River, and a short walk along the Lotheni River returns you to the start. **11.5 km; 5 hours; circular.**

5. Eagle Trail leads from the Lotheni Campsite past the 12 points of interest that are discussed in the trail brochure. Aspects covered include the geology of the region, the Drakensberg as a water catchment area, sandstone formations, grasslands and fire, as well as tree ferns. The terrain is moderate, but you will encounter one or two fairly steep gradients. **12 km; 5 hours; circular.**

6. Bhodla River Canyon From the Lotheni Camp huts the trail initially follows the Gelib Tree Trail and then continues towards the game guard huts below Ka-Zwelewle. However, before reaching the huts, the path splits off to the right, continuing to the magnificent canyon carved by the Bhodla River. **12.6 km; 6 hours; out-and-return.**

7. Hlathimbe Pass Ascending the Escarpment via the historic Hlathimbe Pass you will gain 880 m in altitude over 9 km to the Contour Path linking the Hlathimbe and Ka-Masihlenga passes. You follow the contour path for about 3.5 km, and over the last 4 km the trail gains 440 m in altitude up the Hlathimbe Pass. **35 km; 2 days; out-and-return.**

Vergelegen

Cradled by the Mkhomazi and Mlahlangubo rivers, this Y-shaped reserve covers 1,159 ha of deep valleys and steep grassy hillsides. It is a sanctuary to eland, mountain reedbuck, reedbuck, grey rhebok and oribi.

5. Mohlesi Pass should only be attempted by trailists who are physically fit as it is a demanding hike with an altitude gain of about 1,600 m to the top of the pass. The 3,482-m-high Thabana Ntlenyana, the highest point in Africa south of Kilimanjaro, lies about 5 km away in Lesotho. **50 km; 2 days; out-and-return**.

12. MZIMKHULU WILDERNESS AREA AND MZIMKHULWANA NATURE RESERVE
uKhahlamba-Drakensberg Park, Himeville

Trails: 220-km network of footpaths; 3 to 35 km; 1.5 hours to overnight hikes; circular, out-and-return, open-ended.
Permits: The Officer-in-Charge, Cobham, P O Box 168, Himeville 3256, tel. and fax: (033) 702 0831.
The Officer-in-Charge, Garden Castle, P O Box 378, Underberg 3257, tel: (033) 701 1823, fax: 701 1822.
Maps: The area is covered by map five: Drakensberg South – Vergelegen, Cobham, Garden Castle, and map six: Drakensberg South – Garden Castle, Bushman's Nek, Sehlabathebe, in the Drakensberg Recreational Series.
Facilities/Activities: Campsites at Cobham and Garden Castle; certain caves can be reserved in advance for the exclusive use of a group.

The southern uKhahlamba area is characterised by spectacular sandstone formations, numerous streams and rivers. Those seeking to escape from the more popular areas further north will find Mzimkhulu a haven of tranquillity. Although the area lacks a well-defined contour path, the northern section has an extensive network of trails, while in the southern section you can ascend the Escarpment along several passes.

The Mzimkhulu Wilderness Area extends from Sani Pass in the north to Griqualand East in the south, and is bounded to the east by the Mzimkhulwana Nature Reserve. The two areas

cover a total of 57,000 ha. Despite the absence of prominent free-standing peaks, which are so characteristic of the central and northern Berg, several unusual buttresses and rock formations create some quite stunning scenery. Access to the greatest concentration of the area's footpaths is from the Cobham office.

1. Rhino Peak (3,051 m) juts out from the Escarpment for about 2 km and is one of the most conspicuous peaks in the southern Drakensberg. The Zulu name, Ntabangcobo, means 'rhino's horn peak'. The peak is reached by following a well-defined path from the Garden Castle office along the Mlambonja River. From Pillar Cave, reached 2 km from the start, the path climbs 500 m in altitude over 3.5 km, and then by another 400 m over the final 1.5 km along the Mashai Pass. Once you reach the Escarpment, the path swings eastwards, and after about 2 km you come to Rhino Peak, which is easily ascended. To the south lies Wilson's Peak (3,267 m), Mashai (3,313 m), Walker's Peak (3,306 m) and the Devil's Knuckles, also known as Baroa-Ba-Bararo or The Three Bushmen. **12 km; 8 hours; out-and-return**.

2. Sipongweni Shelter is reached, from the Cobham office, by following the course of the Pholela River upstream for about 7 km before turning left. You will come to the shelter about 1 km on. It is regarded as one of the best rock art sites in the entire Drakensberg, taking into consideration the number of paintings found here, their state of preservation and the interesting themes depicted. It is best known for the scene depicting men spearing fish from small canoes. **16 km; 4 hours; out-and-return**.

3. Hodgson's Peaks Captain Allen Gardiner noted the 'singularly indented outline' of the twin peaks just south of Sani Pass when he first saw them in 1835, and this prompted him to name them the Giant's Cup. The peaks were later renamed in memory of Thomas Hodgson, who was accidentally wounded during a punitive expedition organised in 1862 to take back cattle and horses from the Bushmen. He died of his wounds a day later and was buried at the top of the pass. A cairn was erected on the site a year later. The trail from Cobham office follows the Pholela River upstream, and the final ascent is along the Masubashuba Pass. About 1,400 m is gained in altitude to the top of the pass. **36 km; 2 days; out-and-return**.

13. GIANT'S CUP HIKING TRAIL
uKhahlamba-Drakensberg Park, Himeville

Trails: *59.3 km; 5 days; open-ended.*
Permits: *The Reservations Officer, KwaZulu-Natal Wildlife, P O Box 13069, Cascades 3202, tel: (033) 845 1000, fax: 845 1001, email: trails@kwazulu-natalwildlife.com*
Maps: *Colour trail map with information on the reverse.*
Facilities/Activities: *Five overnight huts with bunks, mattresses, cold water and toilets.*
Pertinent information: *There is no overnight hut at the start of the trail. Arrangements must be made for transport at the end of the trail, as it is open-ended.*

This relatively easy trail traverses the foothills of the southern Berg and is an ideal introduction for those unfamiliar with the Berg. Stretching from the foot of the Sani Pass in the north to Bushman's Nek in the south, the trail winds past eroded sandstone formations, across grassy plains and through spectacular valleys with inviting pools. Herds of eland are sometimes encountered, while raptors such as the bearded and Cape vultures are occasionally seen overhead.

The first day's hike (13.3 km; 6 hours) traverses easy terrain and you will reach Ngenwa Pool after 5 km. Although short of the halfway mark, the pool is an ideal lunch stop, especially on a hot day. From here the trail ascends gently and then levels off as it skirts the base of Ndlovini, before dropping down to the first overnight hut in the Pholela Valley.

Day two (9 km; 3.5 hours) begins with a gentle climb before plateauing at the Tortoise Rocks – round flattened rocks resembling prehistoric tortoises. Further along you will reach Bathplug Cave, named after the small waterfall that cascades after rain through the cave's roof and then disappears

through a natural drain-hole, before reappearing a little further along. The walls of the cave are decorated with several hundred small paintings of stick-like human figures, horses and animals. From here the trail descends to the overnight hut in the Mzimkhulwana Valley.

The third day's hike (12.2 km; 5.5 hours) begins with an easy ascent towards the Little Bamboo Mountains, and after about 4 km reaches its highest point at Crane Tarn. A short way on, the trail passes an interesting site where the remains of petrified trees can be seen exposed in the Beaufort Group. The trail then follows Killiecranckie Stream, and halfway between the 5-km and 6-km markers you come to a beautiful pool beneath a massive boulder. A gentle descent brings you to the Mzimkhulu Valley, and from here it is an easy 2-km walk to the overnight hut.

A short, but steep climb up the slopes of Garden Castle awaits hikers at the start of day four of the hike (12.8 km; 6 hours). The trail then levels off just above the 1,900-m contour and further along you will find yourself looking down onto the Drakensberg Gardens Hotel. After about 8 km the trail descends steeply, and the remainder of the day's hike is over level terrain.

On the final day's hike (12 km; 5 hours) the trail takes you up an easy climb to Bucquay Nek and then descends to the Mzimude River, which you can cross by means of a suspension bridge. Over the next 2 km you will gain some 200 m in altitude to Langalibalele Cave on the western slopes of Langalibalele Peak. The remainder of the trail to Bushman's Nek Hut is mostly downhill.

14. UMTAMVUNA NATURE RESERVE
Port Edward

Trails: *6 trails; 2 to 12 km; 1 to 8 hours; circular and open-ended.*
Permits: *Entrance fee. No permit required.*
Maps: *Comprehensive brochure with sketch maps of trails.*
Facilities/Activities: *Braai facilities; toilets at Beacon Hill entrance.*
Pertinent information: *Accommodation is*

available at the adjoining Clearwater Chalets, P O Box 111, Port Edward 4295, tel. and fax: (039) 313 2684, email: tabbott@venturenet.co.za

Situated on the northern bank of the Mtamvuna River, which forms the boundary between the Eastern Cape and KwaZulu-Natal provinces, the Umtamvuna Nature Reserve covers 3,257 ha of spectacular scenery. Highlights of the reserve include the deep gorge carved by the Mtamvuna River, its riverine forest, steep rocky cliffs, waterfalls and magnificent views.

The reserve is said to contain more species of rare trees than anywhere else in southern Africa and, despite its small size, a staggering 1,250 flowering plants, ferns, mosses and lichens have been recorded. The Pondoland coastal grassland above the gorge is especially eye-catching in spring, when flowers in different hues come into bloom.

Umtamvuna's bird checklist stands at 259 and includes species such as crowned eagle, secretary bird, green pigeon, Knysna woodpecker, Cape rock thrush and Gurney's sugarbird. The cliffs are also home to a steadily increasing population of Cape vulture, and there are good views from the vulture hide.

Antelope you may chance upon include blue and common duiker, bushbuck and reedbuck. Other mammals to keep an eye out for are the samango and vervet monkey, thick-tailed bushbaby, baboon, rock dassie and Natal red hare.

The trails have been laid out in the vicinity of the Pont and Beacon Hill entrances.

Pont Entrance

1. Lourie Trail, an easy walk, meanders above the Mtamvuna River before swinging away to ascend partly the slope on the eastern bank of the Mtamvuna River. The trail then works its way back through a forest, where there is a possibility of seeing blue duiker and bushbuck. **2 km; 1 hour; circular.**

2. Fish Eagle Trail follows the course of the Mtamvuna River upstream for some 3 km, before taking the Dog's Leg to ascend steeply to the grassland. It continues along the krans edge, and there

are some spectacular views over the gorge and the landscape south of the Mtamvuna River further along. The path then descends back to the start. **8 km; 4 hours; circular.**

Beacon Hill Entrance

3. Ingungumbane Trail involves a steep climb down to the Bulolo River, which you cross twice before the trail ascends steeply through magnificent forests back to the grasslands. Despite its steep gradients the trail is regarded as one of the most delightful walks in the reserve. **4 km; 3 hours; circular.**

4. uNkonka Trail drops down to the Bulolo River, which is followed downstream to its junction with the Mtamvuna River. Although the terrain along the river is difficult in places there are numerous good swimming spots. A steep climb (with an altitude gain of over 300 m) along the Razorback takes you back to the grassland, from where there are excellent views over the gorge. **8 km; 6 hours; circular.**

5. iMpunzi Trail leads through grassland along the eastern boundary of the reserve and later links up with the Fish Eagle Trail to end at the Pont Entrance. Along the way there are sweeping views across the gorge. **8 km; 4 hours; open-ended.**

6. iMziki Trail This trail descends to the Bulolo River and then gains some 200 m in altitude on the ascent to the Western Heights, the largest grassland area in the reserve. Along the way you will explore hidden kloofs, streams, forests and a pristine vlei, and enjoy spectacular views. **12 km; 8 hours; circular.**

15. INGELI FOREST LODGE
Harding

Trails: 3 trails; 3.3 to 18 km;
1 to 6 hours; circular, out-and-return.
Permits: No permit required for walks.
For accommodation at Umsilo Hut,
book with: Ingeli Forest Lodge,

Private Bag X502, Kokstad 4700,
tel: (039) 553 0600, fax: 553 0609,
email: i-hotel@venturenet.co.za
Maps: *Sketch map.*
Facilities/Activities: *Ingeli Forest Lodge:*
rooms with en suite facilities; swimming pool;
mountain biking; horse-riding; tennis. Umsilo
Hut: bunks with mattresses; water; firewood.

The Ngele area is a mosaic of pine plantations (the Weza Plantation here is the largest in South Africa), patches of indigenous forest and mountain grasslands. Typical forest species to be seen in the Ngele Forest include lemonwood, knobwood, Outeniqua yellowwood, red stinkwood and sneezewood.

The grasslands are the habitat of myriad flowers belonging to the lily, orchid, iris and aster families. Among them are brunsvigias, nerinas, watsonias, wild dagga, red hot pokers and a variety of herbaceous plants. The Christmas bell (*Sandersonia aurantiaca*) with its bright orange-yellow bell-shaped flower is frequently seen near vleis.

The forest patches and plantations are inhabited by one of the largest populations of bushbuck in South Africa, while the common vervet and samango monkey also occurs here. The Ngele Forest is home to a large population of the rare serval, although they are seldom seen because of their shy nature. Mountain reedbuck, grey rhebok and baboon occur in the more mountainous areas.

Among the nearly 200 bird species recorded in the Weza/Ngele area are Delagorgue's and green pigeon, Cape parrot, long-crested eagle, forest buzzard, Knysna lourie, Narina trogon, Knysna woodpecker and yellow-throated warbler. Grassland species include secretary bird, crowned crane and orange-throated longclaw.

1. Narina Trogon Trail alternates between indigenous forest, plantation and grassland in the Mackton Plantation, close to the lodge. **3.3 km; 1 hour; circular.**

2. Glen Ives Trail starts with a steep climb through the Ngele Forest to a fire lookout point. From here the route follows the upper edge of the forest, with expansive views over the patchwork of plantations, indigenous forests and grasslands. Dominating the scenery to the southwest is the 2,268-m-high Ngele Peak. The return leg is mainly through the forest. **9 km; 3 hours; circular.**

3. Ngelipoort Trail This route initially winds through the Ngele Forest and then cuts through the Ngelipoort Plantation. The trail then meanders through grassland along the slopes of Ngele Mountain to Breekkrans. From here it is an easy walk to Umsilo Hut. **18 km; 6 hours; out-and-return.**

16. ORIBI GORGE NATURE RESERVE
Port Shepstone

Trails: *5 walks; 1 to 9 km; 30 min to 5 hours; circular, out-and-return.*
Permits: *Entrance fee. No permit required for walks.*
Maps: *Sketch map.*
Facilities/Activities: *Self-catering cottages and huts; picnic sites.*
Pertinent information: *The river water is not fit for human consumption. On account of the danger of bilharzia it is inadvisable to swim in the river.*

In its wanderings across the Oribi Flats, the Mzimkhulwana River has carved a 24-km-long gorge to create one of South Africa's least-known natural wonders, Oribi Gorge. It has a depth of up to 500 m and a width of up to 5 km, and the scenery along the gorge changes from indigenous forest and bushveld to towering sandstone cliffs. The most scenic section lies in the 1,873-ha Oribi Gorge Nature Reserve.

The reserve has an excellent example of evergreen coastal scarp forest, with typical species such as forest bushwillow, Cape beech, red quince, rock ash and tarwood. The striking large-leaved dragon tree and the Drakensberg cycad are also found here.

Animals you may see on the walks include blue and common duiker, bushbuck, common reedbuck, baboon and samango monkey. Leopard do occur here, but are seldom encountered.

With a bird checklist of over 220 species, birding can be rewarding. Species to look out for include Narina trogon, trumpeter hornbill, Delagorgue's pigeon, cinnamon dove, green pigeon and Knysna lourie. The variety of habitats also attracts several raptor species, among them the booted, martial and crowned eagle, African marsh harrier and lanner falcon.

1. Nkonka Walk Starting at the Gorge Picnic Site, this route passes through the forested slopes above the Mzimkhulwana River. It then continues along the base of the drier west- and north-facing slopes, with their valley bushveld vegetation. **5 km; 2.5 hours; out-and-return.**

2. Hoopoe Falls Walk follows an easy route from the Gorge Picnic Site along the northern banks of the Mzimkhulwana River for about 1.5 hours. Flanked by majestic sandstone cliffs and forested slopes, the trail then follows the Mbabala Stream to where the Hoopoe Falls plunge into a deep pool. **7 km; 4 hours; out-and-return.**

3. Mziki Walk owes its name to the Zulu word for the reedbuck. Starting at the Gorge picnic site, the route ascends along a narrow gully to the top of the cliffs. From here it makes its way through grassland, with wonderful views over the gorge. It can also be started at the restcamp. **9 km; 5 hours; out-and-return.**

17. BURMAN BUSH NATURE RESERVE
Durban

Trails: 3 trails; 1.68 km (in total); 10 min to 1 hour; circular.
Permits: Entrance fee. No permit required.
Maps: Enquire at the reserve.
Facilities/Activities: Picnic sites; public toilets; parking.

Burman Bush Nature Reserve, 8 km north of the city centre, provides protection to 50 ha of coastal dune bush, regarded as one of the best preserved relic patches of coastal bush in the Durban area. Typical tree species to be seen include the flat-crown, forest fever-berry, Natal mahogany, pigeon-wood, white stinkwood and red beech.

Among the birds to look out for are the lanner falcon, red-billed woodhoopoe, fork-tailed and square-tailed drongo, Natal robin, yellow-breasted apalis and paradise flycatcher. Also to be seen are the orange-breasted bush shrike, forest weaver, green twinspot and pin-tailed whydah.

Animals found here include the blue duiker, known in Zulu as *pithi*, common duiker and vervet monkey. The banded and slender mongoose, and the porcupine also occur here.

The trail network consists of three interlinked, circular trails: the **Pithi Trail** (180 m), **Hadeda Trail** (500 m) and the **Umgeni Trail** (1 km). A highlight of the Umgeni Trail is a viewing platform at canopy level from where there are sweeping views of the Umgeni River, from the Connaught Bridge downstream to its mouth at the Blue Lagoon.

18. SILVERGLEN NATURE RESERVE
Durban

Trails: 2 hours; 4 km; circular.
Permits: Entrance fee. No permit required.
Maps: Enquire at reserve.
Facilities/Activities: Picnic site; resource centre; medicinal plant nursery.

Situated to the south of the Durban city centre on the northern bank of the Mlazi River, the Silverglen Nature Reserve provides protection to a variety of grassland, forest and riverine vegetation.

Among the trees to be seen are the red-stem corkwood, forest milkberry, red beech, Natal fig, forest bushwillow, black monkey orange, and the flat-crown and silver oak. In moist grassland areas the waterberry, also known as the umdoni, is a conspicuous species.

Along the trail you may tick the long-crested eagle, the Knysna and purple-crested lourie, Narina trogon, Burchell's coucal and a variety of kingfisher species. Also recorded in the reserve are the tambourine dove, black-collared barbet and buff-spotted flufftail.

Silverglen Trail starts at the picnic site near to the southern end of Clearwater Dam and initially wanders through coastal bush, which later gives way to grasslands. On reaching a junction, the trail continues in a clockwise direction, passing through grassland, clumps of coastal bush and coastal forest. Along the course of the trail there are wonderful panoramas stretching from the inland portion of the Bluff, to the Nwabe Plateau in the east, and Umlazi. Further along, the trail joins up with a tarred road, which you then follow back to the start. **4 km; 2 hours; circular.**

19. PALMIET NATURE RESERVE
Westville, Durban

> *Trails: Network of 4 interlinked trails; 700 m to 2.7 km; 15 min to 1 hour.*
> *Permits: Entrance fee. No permit required for walks.*
> *Maps: Trail booklet.*
> *Facilities/Activities: Picnic sites and braai facilities at Cascades.*

This 90-ha nature reserve, in the heart of Westville and a mere 10 km northwest of Durban, provides protection to the rugged Palmiet River Valley, which is home to blue duiker, bushbuck and vervet monkey.

Among the interesting birds to keep an eye out for are Narina trogon and lanner falcon, while the Natal robin is common. In the forested parts of the reserve you may catch a glimpse of the blue duiker. The trail network alternates between coastal and riverine forests, the Nkawu cliffs, grassland and the course of the Palmiet River. Although the routes are not difficult there are some steep ascents.

20. KENNETH STEINBANK NATURE RESERVE
Durban

> *Trails: Red Trail; 5 km; 2 hours; circular. Several short rambles also available.*
> *Permits: Entrance fee. No permit*

> *required for day walks.*
> *Maps: Sketch map.*
> *Facilities/Activities: Campsite; picnic site with braai facilities; toilets; cycling trails.*

Situated in the southwestern suburbs of greater Durban, this nature reserve provides protection to 211 ha of coastal forest and grassveld.

Along the trails you may come upon common reedbuck, bushbuck, red and blue duiker, impala, nyala and vervet monkey. There is also a rich diversity of smaller mammals, among them the Cape clawless otter and banded mongoose.

Birding here can be rewarding – among the noteworthy species to be seen are the white-eared barbet, green coucal and spotted thrush. Other species you may tick include the long-crested eagle, golden-tailed woodpecker, various species of kingfisher and the green-backed heron.

Red Trail This route initially winds through grassland past a dam, where antelope are often seen drinking. Further along the grassveld gives way to indigenous coastal forest and the trail then follows the Little Umhlatuzana River, which you cross twice before the trail loops back to the start. **5 km; 2 hours; circular.**

21. KRANTZKLOOF NATURE RESERVE
Kloof

> *Trails: 6 trails; distances unavailable; 45 min to 6 hours; out-and-return, circular, open-ended.*
> *Permits: Entrance fee. No permit required for walks.*
> *Maps: Reserve information brochure with map.*
> *Facilities/Activities: Picnic sites; small interpretative centre.*

The Krantzkloof Nature Reserve, which nestles against the coastal Escarpment, was proclaimed in 1950 to protect the spectacular forested gorges created by the Molweni and Nkutu rivers. The reserve is renowned for its breathtaking views of the gorge, which is up to 350 m deep, orange-red sandstone cliffs, the Ipithi and Nkutu waterfalls and the 90-m-high Kloof Falls on the Molweni River.

Despite its small size (584 ha), the reserve boasts a great diversity of flora, including several rare species. Among these is one of South Africa's rarest trees, the Natal quince, which occurs only in a few scattered localities. Other interesting species include the Pondo rose-apple, tarwood, rock ash and the Natal flame bush.

The reserve is home to the thick-tailed bushbaby, bushbuck, blue and red duiker, and the tree dassie. Noteworthy species that birders may tick include the crowned eagle, Wahlberg's eagle (the reserve is home to the southernmost known breeding sites of this species) and the African broadbill. Also recorded are the Knysna and purple-crested lourie, Narina trogon, brown robin and trumpeter hornbill.

1. Nkutu Falls Trail starts at the Nkutu picnic site and meanders mainly through grasslands along the cliffs above the Nkutu River. A detour, reached about 1 km after setting off, leads to the base of the first waterfall. After retracing your tracks to the main trail, the route continues along the cliff edge, and further along you reach another detour to the second waterfall. Still further on there are spectacular views into the lower gorge. **1.5 hours. or 3 hours if visiting both falls; out-and-return.**

2. Molweni Trail has three starting points: Kloof Falls Road picnic site, Uve Road car park and Nkutu picnic site. All three trail options begin with a descent of some 350 m into the gorge and an equally strenuous climb out. This is the only trail that provides access to the bottom of the Kloof Falls. Trailists are advised not to walk downstream of Splash Rock, owing to the troublesome behaviour of residents outside the reserve. **5 hours; open-ended.**

3. Beacon Trail Starting at the Kloof Falls picnic site, this route initially follows the Molweni Trail, and then passes through grassland to a trigonometric beacon. The trail winds down into the gorge to Splash Pool. From here you follow the Molweni Trail back to the start. **6 hours; circular.**

22. FERNCLIFFE NATURE RESERVE
Pietermaritzburg

Trails: *7 walks; 10 km (in total); 10 min to 1 hour; circular, out-and- return.*
Permits: *Not required.*
Maps: *Enquire at reserve.*
Facilities/Activities: *Picnic sites; parking.*

Ferncliffe lies just below the Escarpment, about 12 km northwest of Pietermaritzburg, and covers some 250 ha of exotic plantations and indigenous forest, with species such as lemonwood, forest fig and clivia. The reserve's network of short trails takes in scenic attractions such as Breakfast Rock, with its fine views over Pietermaritzburg, a cave, which houses four species of bat, Boulder Dam, tranquil streams and the Maidenhair Falls. A variety of birds are attracted to the plantations and forests, and you may come across bushbuck, provided you move about quietly.

23. NATAL NATIONAL BOTANICAL GARDEN
Pietermaritzburg

Trails: *Network of footpaths; each no longer than 1 hour.*
Permits: *Entrance fee. No permit required.*
Maps: *Map of botanical garden available.*
Facilities/Activities: *Restaurant; public toilets; nursery.*

One of a network of eight National Botanical Institute gardens, the Natal National Botanical Garden dates back to 1874. A focal point of the garden is the magnificent plane tree avenue planted in 1908, while stately camphor, magnolia, tulip and swamp cypress trees testify to the early Victorian influence. Also of interest is a traditional Zulu hut, surrounded by an indigenous medicinal garden that forms part of a *muthi* (medicine) plant display.

The garden specialises in plants from the eastern grasslands of South Africa and the grassland project contains fine collections of red-hot pokers (*Kniphofia*), *Watsonias* and *Dieramas*. The north-eastern section of the garden is characterised by indigenous scrub forest with a mixture of thicket, thornveld and mist-belt species and consequently attracts a wide variety of birds. A section of the forest forms part of the garden's clivia conservation project where four species of clivia are cultivated under irrigation.

To date over 130 bird species have been recorded in the garden. Among the species to be seen are the crowned eagle, black crake, cinnamon dove, black-headed oriole, pied and giant kingfisher, chorister robin and forest weaver. Careful searching may yield species such as buff-spotted flufftail, tambourine dove and green twinspot.

1. Turraea Trail makes its way along the shores of Kingfisher Lake and through indigenous forest, thickets and tangled scrub. The trail is especially rewarding for birding enthusiasts and includes a section planted with indigenous plants that attract birds and butterflies.

2. Forest Footpath offers wonderful views over the garden, and provides good chances to tick typical forest species such as the crowned eagle, African goshawk and forest weaver.

24. GREENBELT TRAILS
Pietermaritzburg

Trails: 6 trails; 1.1 to 10.3 km; 30 min to 4 hours; out-and-return; open-ended.
Permits: Not required.
Maps: Enquire at Pietermaritzburg Publicity Association, P O Box 25, Pietermaritzburg 3200, tel: (033) 345 1348.
Facilities/Activities: Picnic sites and parking at World's View.

Rising some 350 m above Pietermaritzburg, the Escarpment to the northeast of the city has, quite appropriately, been named World's View. Covering over 20 km, the network of greenbelt trails here wanders through plantations and patches of natural vegetation, and along the way trailists can enjoy the wonderful, expansive views of the city below.

1. World's View Trail Starting at Voortrekker Road, the World's View Trail climbs steadily and you gain 250 m in altitude. The trail closely follows the wagon road used by the Voortrekkers when they first settled in what was then Natal. From World's View trailists are rewarded with a magnificent panorama of the city. **4.8 km; 2 hours; out-and-return.**

2. Upper Linwood Trail starts in Celtis Road and after a steady climb of about 1 km the trail joins the outward leg of the Telekulu Trail. The remaining 2.4 km of the trail follows the railbed of a deviation from the main railway line. It was opened in 1916, to ease the climb out of Pietermaritzburg, and closed in 1960. Along the trail you will pass through a 100-m-long tunnel, where a torch is essential. The trail ends about 700 m from the World's View parking area. **7 km; 3 hours; out-and-return, or 4.2 km; 2 hours; open-ended.**

3. Lower Linwood Trail winds along the lower slopes of World's View through eucalyptus plantations, with starting points at Celtis Road and Linwood Drive. From the junction of these two paths, the trail climbs steadily, gaining 100 m in altitude before following a contour. **7.4 km; 3.5 hours; out-and-return.**

4. Telekulu Trail From the World's View parking area, walk along World's View Road for about 800 m to the signposted turnoff. The trail now heads in a southwesterly direction across a plateau and then descends along the spine of a ridge, before swinging sharply northwest to join the Upper Linwood Trail. From here you take the path alongside the old railway line to Celtis Road, which you follow for 1.7 km before you begin the climb back to the start. **10.3 km; 4 hours; out-and-return.**

25. DORP SPRUIT TRAIL
Pietermaritzburg

Trail: 4 km; 2 hours; out-and-return.
Permits: Not required.
Maps: Enquire with Pietermaritzburg Publicity

Association, P O Box 25, Pietermaritzburg
3200, tel: (033) 345 1348.
Facilities/Activities: None.

The first of a series of spruit trails planned for Pietermaritzburg, the Dorp Spruit Trail was opened to commemorate World Environment Day in 1987. The trail starts at the Voortrekker Bridge in Roberts Road, from where it follows the Dorp Spruit past old local industries and the old city quarry. Here a route branches off to De Villiers Drive, which provides a link with the World's View Trail. The main route, however, crosses the Dorp Spruit and then follows Tomlinson Road, which fronts on the spruit.

26. BLINKWATER HIKING TRAILS
Greytown

Trails: 100 km (in total); 2 to 6 days;
network of trails.
Permits: Blinkwater Trails,
P O Box 573, Greytown 3250,
tel. and fax: (033) 507 0047.
Maps: Trail pamphlet with map.
Facilities/Activities: Four overnight huts
with bunks, mattresses, hot showers at
three of the overnight huts, toilets, fireplaces
and firewood; mountain bike trails.

Situated in the KwaZulu-Natal Midlands, this magnificent trail is a joint venture between the Umvoti Branch of the Wildlife and Environment Society of South Africa, two timber companies (Sappi and Mondi) and KwaZulu-Natal Wildlife.

The area is dominated by commercial plantations, but patches of indigenous forest occur in the river valleys and on the southern slopes, while grasslands are found at higher elevations. Typical forest species occurring here include real, Outeniqua and Henkel's yellowwoods, knobwood, Cape chestnut, sneezewood, pompom tree and tree fuchsia. Ferns, begonias and *Streptocarpus* plants provide a touch of colour to the forest floor, while clivia grow in the forks of trees. The common tree fern is conspicuous along stream banks in the grasslands.

Among the animals you may see in the grasslands are the endangered oribi and mountain reedbuck. Most noteworthy among the birds are the endangered blue swallow, which breeds in the area, and the wattled crane, an endangered species that breeds in the vicinity of Island Dam. Raptors are represented by some 21 species, including the Cape vulture, martial and crowned eagle, forest buzzard and African marsh harrier. Among the other species you may tick are buff-spotted fluff-tail, cinnamon dove, Cape parrot, grass owl, trumpeter hornbill, Natal and starred robins, grassbird and orange-throated longclaw.

The trail network consists of two sections: the Southern Section, which is accessed through Mondi's Seele Estate, and the Northern Section, which starts at Mountain Falls in Sappi forests. All the trails are circular and interlinked, providing hikers with several options. The trails follow forestry roads, boundary firebreaks and footpaths, passing through plantations, indigenous forests and grasslands. Adding to the diversity of landscapes are tranquil streams, waterfalls and dams. There are also lovely views of the Albert Falls Dam.

As much as possible of the area's local history has been incorporated into the trail network. Reminders of the early settlers include an old grave site of the Wesleyans, who came from Yorkshire to KwaZulu-Natal to practise their religion without fear of persecution. Also to be seen is an old railway line, constructed at the start of the 20th century to extract timber from the indigenous forests and sawpits. Each of the trail huts has its own character and atmosphere: one is a renovated cottage next to an old farmhouse and another is a replica of the original homestead, built in 1905 by the owner of what was then farmland. There is a third hut situated next to a stream and a fourth one on high grassland.

27. MOOR PARK NATURE RESERVE
Estcourt

Trail: 6 km; 3 hours; out-and-return.
Permits: Entrance fee. No permit
required for walks.

ABOVE: *The Mngobozeleni Trail, at Sodwana Bay, takes you down to Lake Mngobozeleni – named after Chief Mngobo, who used to live on its shores.*

ABOVE: *There are great birding opportunities on the Bay Camp Trail at Lake Sibaya.* **RIGHT:** *This is an easy river crossing for hikers on the Umfolozi Primitive Trail.*

ABOVE: *A 4x4 makes its way down the beach on the remote coast of Maputaland at Kosi Bay. Since this photograph was taken a total ban was placed on driving along South Africa's beaches, to prevent damage to sensitive dune areas.*

THIS PAGE: *On day one of the Amanzimnyama Trail you'll see traditional Thonga fish-traps in Lake Makawulani (below), which is the first of the four interconnected lakes making up the Kosi system. At the start of the fourth and last day of the hike you'll cross the Sihadla River on a raft, made by the local residents from poles and raffia leaves (above).*

LEFT and BELOW: *One of the two beautiful waterfalls (left) hikers will see on the first day of the Koranna trail, which meanders through the rural Free State (below). The vegetation here is typified by short, dense grassveld, with flowering plants only noticeable in spring.*
OPPOSITE: *You'll come to the Little Caledon River on the third day of the Brandwater Hiking Trail, also in the Free State.*

THIS PAGE: *The spectacular scenery (top) of the Golden Gate Highlands National Park makes it a wonderful hiking destination. There are many striking, natural features, such as the Sentinel, or Brandwag (above), and caves, like this one (right), which you can explore on the Holkrans Trail.*

ABOVE: *This wooden bridge helps trailists up a sheer rock face on the Holkrans Trail.*

ABOVE and BELOW: *The imposing roof of Cathedral Cave (above) is another of the amazing rock formations at Golden Gate, as are the incredible, stratified Mushroom Rocks (below).*

THIS PAGE: *You can enjoy beautiful hikes in Mpumalanga: along a grassy ridge overlooking the Sabie Valley (above) on the Loerie Walk; past Lone Creek Waterfall (left) on one of the Fanie Botha hikes; and to the famous Bourke's Luck Potholes (below) – the highlight of the Blyderivierspoort Hiking Trail.*

Maps: *Trail booklet.*
Facilities/Activities: *Picnic site; education centre; campsite at adjacent Wagendrift Dam Resort.*

This small nature reserve, which covers 264 ha and lies at the head of the Wagendrift Dam, is dominated by Makabeni Hill. The landscapes range from exposed cliffs and deep gullies to a high plateau and the Bushman's River, which forms the reserve's southern boundary.

The vegetation is a patchwork of bushveld, thornveld, tall grassland and highveld sourveld, and among the game that have been introduced are Burchell's zebra, blesbok, mountain reedbuck, black wildebeest and impala. The reserve has a bird checklist of over 190 species.

Archaeological excavations on Makabeni Hill have provided evidence that Iron Age people lived here some 1,000 years ago. Of more recent historical interest is Veglaer, where the Voortrekkers fought a three-day battle against a large Zulu force from 13 to 15 August 1838. The site has been flooded by the Wagendrift Dam.

Old Furrow Trail is a self-guided, interpretative trail that leads along a historic irrigation furrow built by the Moor family between 1900 and 1903 to divert water from the Bushman's River to land that became submerged after the completion of the Wagendrift Dam in 1964. Marked points of interest along the trail include the area's history, vegetation types, trees and the ecology of the Bushman's River and are described in the trail booklet.

28. HAROLD JOHNSON NATURE RESERVE
Darnall

Trails: *2 trails; 1.8 to 5 km; 1 to 3 hours; circular.*
Permits: *Entrance fee. No permit required.*
Maps: *Information booklet on Remedies and Rituals Trail and map of Bushbuck Trail available from reserve office.*
Facilities/Activities: *Campsites with ablution facilities; picnic sites; education centre.*

Situated on the southern bank of the Tugela River, the Harold Johnson Nature Reserve covers 104 ha of grassland, bush and well-preserved tracts of coastal bush. The reserve is noted for its rich variety of epiphytic orchids. Among the trees commonly found here are the wild date palm, brackthorn, small knobwood, white milkwood, Kei-apple and black monkey orange.

The reserve is home to Burchells's zebra, impala and smaller mammal species such as the common, red and blue duiker, bushbuck and bushpig. Among the typical coastal birds you may tick are the forest weaver, Narina trogon, Natal robin, purple-crested lourie and white-eared barbet.

In addition to its natural attractions and scenic views over the Tugela River, the area is also rich in history. Of historic significance are the ruins of Fort Pearson, which served as a launching point when British troops invaded Zululand in 1879, and the Ultimatum Tree, where the British ultimatum to Cetshwayo was read out to his chiefs on 11 December 1878.

1. Remedies and Rituals Trail is a self-guided, interpretative trail focusing on the early white settlers, as well as on the Zulu people and the way they used some of the trees in the area for medicinal and other purposes. Sixteen trees along the trail have been marked and are described in the trail booklet. **1.8 km; 1 hour; circular.**

2. Bushbuck Trail wanders down the steep slopes above the Tugela River to a streambed and then ascends to a ridge overlooking the Tugela River Valley. **5 km; 3 hours; circular.**

29. ST LUCIA GAME PARK
Greater St Lucia Wetland Park, St Lucia village

Trails: *4 trails; 5 km (Imvubu Trail), other distances not available; 40 min to 3 hours; circular, out-and-return.*
Permits: *Entrance fee. No permit required for walks.*
Maps: *Information booklet with map.*

*Facilities/Activities: Three campsites;
Crocodile Centre; tours of St Lucia estuary
by motor launch.*
*Pertinent information: The trails may
only be hiked in daylight hours, as hippo
leave the estuary in the late afternoon to
feed in the grasslands, returning in the
early morning. Take care when walking
close to the estuary shore or pans, and
do not wade through open water, as
these areas are inhabited by crocodile.*

This small game park is situated just north of the
village of St Lucia and the St Lucia Estuary, the
mouth of the St Lucia lake system. The vegetation
is typical of the eastern shores of St Lucia, and
ranges from dune forest, grassland and Umdoni
parkland to marshes, reed swamps and mangroves
along the St Lucia Estuary.

Among the large game species to be seen are blue
wildebeest, reedbuck, Burchell's zebra, waterbuck,
impala and bushbuck. Smaller species to look out
for include red and common duiker, vervet monkey
and side-striped jackal. Hippo and crocodile can
often be seen from the banks of the estuary.

Not to be missed is a visit to the Crocodile Centre,
which aims to educate visitors about the importance
of crocodiles in nature. Interesting displays provide
a fascinating insight into their biology and the way
of life of these misunderstood reptiles. In addition to
Nile crocodiles of different ages, two other African
species (the dwarf and long-snouted crocodile) and
the American alligator can be seen.

With its rich diversity of habitats, St Lucia offers
excellent birding possibilities. Species you may tick
include the pygmy goose, African fish eagle, crested
guineafowl, Burchell's coucal and trumpeter hornbill. Keep an eye out in the grassland for the yellow-
throated longclaw.

Imvubu Trail meanders from the Crocodile Centre
through grassland before reaching a delightful patch
of swamp forest, with fine examples of the swamp
fig and powder-puff tree. After passing through protea veld, the route continues through marsh before
reaching the estuary shores, with its mangrove
community. **5 km; 1 hour 15 min; out-and-return.**

The Imvubu Trail is linked to the trail network
east of the Cape Vidal road by a 35-minute trail.

Trail options here include the **Ihlathi Trail**, which
traverses the dune forest to the coast and back
(40 min; out-and-return), and the **Iphiva Trail**, a
circuit featuring grassland, marsh and the dune
forest edge (60 min; circular). The **Iphothwe Trail**
passes mainly through grassland with sections
skirting swamps (50 min; circular).

30. MZIKI TRAIL
Greater St Lucia Wetland Park, Mission Rocks

*Trail: 38 km; 3 days; network
from basecamp.*
*Permits: The Officer-in-Charge,
Mfabeni/Mission Rocks,
P O Box 52, St Lucia Estuary 3936,
tel: (035) 590 9002, fax: 590 9090.*
*Maps: Sketch map of trail. Colour
tourist map of park.*
*Facilities/Activities: Mount Tabor: basecamp
with bunks, mattresses, kitchen facilities, gas
fridge, gas stove, bucket shower, toilets and
fireplace. Mission Rocks: picnic sites and toilets.*
*Pertinent information: Since four of the
Big Five animals occur in the area, an
armed field ranger has to be booked to
accompany trailists to protect them from
the potentially dangerous animals.*

This trail is situated along the eastern shores of Lake
St Lucia in the park's Mfabeni section, about 16 km
north of St Lucia village. Although the vegetation
is dominated by grasslands, the most outstanding
feature of the Eastern Shores is the magnificent
dune forest. Said to be the tallest forested coastal
dunes in the world, these dunes reach heights of
nearly 200 m above sea level and from a distance
can be easily mistaken for large hills. In actual fact,
they consist of wind-blown sand that accumulated
on the underlying rock bed during the past 12,000
to 20,000 years. Typical tree species found here
include thorny rope, water ironplum, poison olive
and white milkwood.

St Lucia is home to four of the Big Five, with only
lion still not having been reintroduced. The most

recent introduction of a Big Five species took place in August 2001, when the first group of elephants were released into a boma in the Eastern Shores section of the park. Lake St Lucia is also an important habitat for hippos and crocodile.

With a population of between 4,000 and 5,000 reedbuck, the Eastern Shores section of the park supports one of the largest concentrations of this species in Africa. Other mammals include waterbuck, kudu, impala, bushbuck, warthog and bushpig. The large predators are represented by leopard and cheetah.

Noteworthy among the more than 245 bird species occurring in the area are Rudd's apalis, Woodward's batis and the brown robin. Forest species you may tick include the tambourine dove, Knysna lourie, white-eared barbet, golden-tailed woodpecker and square-tailed drongo.

Although the hike was originally designed as a self-guided trail, the reintroduction of elephants into this section of the park has made it necessary for groups to be accompanied by an armed field ranger, for safety reasons. The trail consists of three routes, hiked as day walks from the Mount Tabor basecamp, an old World War II radar station. Situated about 130 m above sea level, the hut offers a spectacular view of Lake St Lucia to the west and the Indian Ocean to the east.

1. South Coast Loop, hiked on day one, passes from open grassland to dune forest, after which there is a 2-km section of walking along the rocky coastline. The coastal rocks consist of sea sand that was cemented together by calcium carbonate, derived from seashells, about 80,000 years ago, and these rocks provide the base on which the coastal dunes developed. At Mission Rocks the trail turns inland, ascending through dune forest back to the camp. **10 km; 4 hours; circular.**

2. Lake Loop heads westwards through indigenous forest to a hide overlooking Mfazana Pan. Hippo, crocodile and a variety of waterfowl can be observed from the hide. From here the trail continues through grassland to the shores of Lake St Lucia, which you follow for about 1.5 km before returning through grassland and Umdoni parkland to Mount Tabor. **10 km; 4 hours; circular.**

3. North Coast Loop initially follows Mount Tabor Ridge northwards and then drops into Bokkie

Valley, which takes its name from the large number of reedbuck found here. The last 4 km of the outward section of the trail winds through indigenous forest and forested dunes, where you may see samango monkey and red squirrel. After descending to the beach, the trail follows the unspoilt coastline southward for about 8 km, alternating between sandy beaches and rocky shores. The final section of the trail climbs steeply back to Mount Tabor. **18 km; 7 hours; circular.**

31. EMOYENI TRAIL
Greater St Lucia Wetland Park, Mission Rocks

Trail: Guided trail; 63 km; 5 days; circular.
Permits: The Officer-in-Charge, Mfabeni/Mission Rocks, P O Box 52, St Lucia Estuary 3936, tel: (035) 590 9002, fax: 590 9090.
Maps: Colour tourist map of the park.
Facilities/Activities: On trail: rustic campsites with a table, benches, cold bucket shower and toilet. Mission Rocks: picnic sites and toilets.
Pertinent information: Tents have to be carried, as facilities on the trail are limited to basic campsites.

This five-day trail passes through a variety of landscapes in the Eastern Shores section of the park and offers great views of Lake St Lucia and Lake Bhangazi.

Starting from Mission Rocks, the first day's hike (7 km; 3 hours) leads to the Eastern Shores of Lake St Lucia, passing through dune forest, wetland margins and forest patches. It heads along the lake shore to the overnight stop, Jock's Mess, at Catalina Bay, named after the *Catalina* aquaplane, which crashed into the bay shortly after take-off on 25 June 1943. The *Catalina* was deployed on the Eastern Shores during World War II to do anti-submarine patrols.

Day two (18 km; 9 hours) follows the lakeshore closely in a northwesterly direction and passes through forest patches and grasslands. A highlight of the day's hike is the swamp forest of the Nkamaza Stream with its unique vegetation. The second overnight stop is at Jumangoma.

On day three (11 km; 5 hours) the trail leads mainly through grassland, interspersed with forest patches and wetlands, to the southern boundary of the Tewate Wilderness Area, where Umdoni parkland predominates. Before reaching the third overnight stop near the shores of Lake Bhangazi the trail wanders past the edge of the eDuyini Stream and its swamp forest.

Early on day four (16 km; 8 hours) the trail skirts the southern edge of Lake Bhangazi and continues along the eastern edge of the Mfabeni Swamp. It then ascends the forested dunes south of Cape Vidal to the overnight camp at Banel's Folly.

The final day's hike (11 km) winds down to the rocky coastline, which you follow to Mission Rocks, from where the trail heads inland to the start.

32. ST LUCIA WILDERNESS TRAIL
Greater St Lucia Wetland Park,
Cape Vidal

> **Trail:** *Guided wilderness trail; 4 nights; distance varies from 10 to 12 km per day; walks from basecamp.*
> **Permits:** *KwaZulu-Natal Wildlife, P O Box 13069, Cascades 3202, tel: (033) 845 1067, fax: 845 1001, email: trails@kwazulu-natalwildlife.com*
> **Maps:** *Colour tourist map of the park.*
> **Facilities/Activities:** *Tented basecamp: tents containing mattresses, pillows, sheets and blankets; fully equipped kitchen, limited fridge facilities and a camp cook to cater for the trailists; communal lounge; hot shower and toilet. On trail: tents with same facilities as basecamp; cooking over open fire; hot-water bucket shower. Cape Vidal: self-catering accommodation; campsites; angling; snorkelling.*
> **Pertinent information:** *Owing to high summer temperatures, trails are only run from the beginning of April to the end of September. Anti-malaria precautions are essential. Tackies (sneakers) or sandals are recommended, as a fair amount of wading is done in the pans. Trails are conducted from a Friday afternoon to a Tuesday morning.*

This trail is conducted in the Tewate Wilderness Area to the northwest of Cape Vidal. On the first evening trailists are accommodated in the Bhangazi basecamp, which is situated on the western shores of Lake Bhangazi South. Trailists set off the following morning and the following two nights are spent in a tented camp on the Eastern Shores of Lake St Lucia.

From the tented camp the lake shore, wetlands, grasslands, dune forests and dunes are explored under the guidance of an armed ranger. No set routes are followed, but expect to cover about 10 km each day.

In addition to walking, there is also an opportunity to canoe along the shoreline of Lake St Lucia and to go snorkelling along the coast.

33. CAPE VIDAL
Greater St Lucia Wetland Park,
Cape Vidal

> **Trails:** *2 trails; 1.5 and 3 hours; 3.5 and 7 km; circular.*
> **Permits:** *Entrance fee. No permit required for walks.*
> **Maps:** *Colour tourist map of park.*
> **Facilities/Activities:** *Cape Vidal: self-catering log cabins; campsites; angling; snorkelling.*

Situated some 35 km north of St Lucia village, Cape Vidal nestles on the edge of magnificent dune forest alongside the coast.

1. Imboma Trail traverses parkland, wetlands and indigenous dune forest to the south of Lake Bhangazi South. Sections of the trail follow hippo paths, and the wetlands offer great opportunities for birding. Reedbuck frequent the area and trailists are advised to keep an eye out for hippo and buffalo. **3.5 km; 1.5 hours; circular.**

2. Mvubu Trail From the restcamp, the Mvubu (Zulu for 'hippo') Trail climbs steadily through dune forest and then descends to the shores of Lake Bhangazi South. After following the lake shore for a while, the trail passes through *Acacia* woodlands before ascending through the dune forest back to the start.

Wildlife to be seen includes reedbuck, waterbuck, bushbuck, bushpig and samango monkey. Along the shores of Lake Bhangazi, keep an eye out for hippo and crocodile. The trail also offers good birding opportunities. **7 km; 3 hours; circular.**

34. FANIE'S ISLAND
Greater St Lucia Wetland Park, Mtubatuba

Trails: 5 km; 2 hours; circular.
Permits: Entrance fee. No permit required for trails.
Maps: Trail brochure with map. Colour tourist brochure of park.
Facilities/Activities: Self-catering accommodation; campsite; swimming pool; angling.
Pertinent information:
Since hippo leave the lake in the late afternoon to feed and return only in the early morning, the trail may only be walked during daylight hours. Be on the lookout for hippo on cool overcast mornings, when they occasionally rest in the forest.

Situated on the western shores of Lake St Lucia, Fanie's Island is named after the large reed island overlooking the restcamp. It is a popular birding and angling destination, with a peaceful and relaxed atmosphere.

Umkhiwane Trail This trail, which features the trumpeter hornbill as its emblem, passes through coastal bush, coastal forest, a swamp forest and grassland, returning parallel to the shores of Lake St Lucia. Trees and other points of interest along the trail have been marked and are described in the trail booklet, giving you a chance to learn about the flora along the way and making this a very worthwhile walk.

On the trail you can see the Lowveld toad tree, coast silver oak, forest mahogany, powder-puff tree, water berry and the torny rope. Also to be seen are the common coral tree, which has beautiful scarlet flowers between July and October, green and black monkey orange trees, wild medlar and the wild date palm.

Along the way you might chance upon red duiker, reedbuck, bushbuck and vervet monkey, while hippo are also present. Birdlife is prolific and includes species such as the white-eared barbet, trumpeter hornbill, green pigeon, Narina trogon, purple-crested lourie and crested guineafowl.

35. CHARTER'S CREEK
Greater St Lucia Wetland Park, Mtubatuba

Trails: 2 trails; 5 and 7 km; 2 and 3 hours; circular.
Permits: Entrance fee. No permit required for walks.
Maps: Brochures, but no trail maps. Colour tourist map of park.
Facilities/Activities: Self-catering huts; kitchen blocks; laundry; hot-water showers; swimming pool; playground; picnic sites; angling; boat trips on lake.
Pertinent information: Although it is unlikely that you will encounter them, it is still advisable always to keep a sharp lookout for hippo. Do not paddle or swim in the lake.

The relaxing and tranquil atmosphere of Charter's Creek, on the Western Shores of Lake St Lucia, has long been a favourite with those seeking to escape the frenetic pace of city living.

The vegetation along the Western Shores is a mosaic of coastal forest, grassland, swamp forest and reedbeds. Among the many species along the two trails that have been labelled are the pigeonwood tree, Natal mahogany, white stinkwood, flat crown and the Natal wild banana.

There are a variety of mammals that you may see along the trails, including the red duiker, bushbuck, nyala, reedbuck, bushpig and vervet monkey. The birdlife here is prolific and among the many species that you might tick are green coucal, purple-crested lourie, Narina trogon, yellow-spotted nicator and pink-throated twinspot.

1. Umkhumbe Trail takes its name from the Zulu word for red duiker, which is the most common antelope in the area. Interesting information is provided in the trail pamphlet on 12 points of interest, among them several species of trees, the red duiker, the nest of the cocktail ant, and the bushbuck. **5 km; 2 hours; circular.**

2. Isikhova Nature Trail A special feature of this trail, winding through coastal forest, is the Isikhoveni Stream, after which the trail is named. Logs have been placed at two places along the walk, so you can sit here and take a rest. On the return leg the trail wanders along the lake shore before returning to the start. There are 17 points of interest marked along the trail and described in the trail pamphlet. **7 km; 3 hours; circular.**

36. FALSE BAY PARK
Greater St Lucia Wetland Park, Hluhluwe village

> *Trails: 2 trails; 6 and 10 km; 3 and 4.5 hours; circular.*
> *Permits: Entrance fee. No permit required for day walks.*
> *Maps: Information brochure with trail maps.*
> *Facilities/Activities: Campsites with hot-water ablutions; swimming pool; picnic sites; angling.*

False Bay forms the northwestern arm of the H-shaped Lake St Lucia and lies on the lake's Western Shores. It offers good game-viewing and birding possibilities, and one of its outstanding features is its sand forest, a dry forest type, which occurs discontinuously in northeastern KwaZulu-Natal. Found only on deep white sand, it is characterised by species such as the Lebombo wattle and false tamboti.

A noteworthy antelope species to look out for is the suni, which occurs only in sand forest. Other antelope you may happen upon are the common and red duiker, waterbuck, reedbuck, nyala and impala. Also keep an eye out for Burchell's zebra, bushpig, warthog, vervet monkey, black-backed jackal and leopard.

Over 160 bird species have been recorded in the False Bay area to date, among them sand forest specials such as Neergaard's sunbird, yellow-spotted nicator and Rudd's apalis. Other species to look out for include African broadbill, green coucal, pink-throated longclaw and scaly-throated honeyguide.

1. Ingwe Trail owes its name to the regular sightings of leopard (*ingwe* in Zulu) in the area. The trail stretches from one side of the Lister Peninsula to the other and moves from the shores of Lake St Lucia to woodland, thickets and sand forest. Of interest along the lake shore are the fossils of marine animals and fossil corals that are exposed when the level of the lake is low. **6 km; 3 hours; circular.**

2. Mphophomeni Trail has been laid out in the northern part of the False Bay section of the park. The trail winds through woodland, thicket and sand forest and there are 27 numbered points of interest, mainly trees, along the route. A picnic site near the halfway mark provides an ideal resting spot. **10 km; 4.5 hours, or 7 km; 3 hours; circular.**

37. DUGANDLOVU TRAIL
Greater St Lucia Wetland Park, False Bay

> *Trails: 16 km; 6 hours, or overnight hiking trail; circular.*
> *Permits: The Officer-in-Charge, False Bay, P O Box 222, Hluhluwe 3960, tel. and fax: (035) 562 0425.*
> *Maps: Information brochure with trail maps. Colour tourist map of park.*
> *Facilities/Activities: Dugandlovu rustic camp: four huts equipped with beds and mattresses, gas cooker, deep freezer, fireplaces, bucket showers and toilets. False Bay: campsites; swimming pool; picnic sites; angling.*
> *Pertinent information: Mosquitoes can be a problem at the overnight camp, making it advisable to take a mosquito repellent along. Be wary of crocodiles when walking along the lake shore.*

Novices and families will find the Dugandlovu, or Lost Elephant, Trail ideal because of the easy terrain and the short distances. A short way beyond the start, the trail splits and trailists can opt to continue along the management track, which passes through *Acacia* and *Terminalia* woodlands, or follow the Warburgia Loop, named after the pepper-bark tree (*Warburgia* is the scientific name of the genus to which this species belongs). After the Warburgia Loop rejoins the main trail, the path swings to the shore of Lake St Lucia, which you follow to the overnight camp. Ammonites and other marine fossils can be seen along the lake shore, providing evidence that ocean waves once lapped these shores. The rustic overnight camp is situated on a high cliff just to the north of the Hluhluwe River floodplain. Two viewing platforms provide expansive views over the lake and the floodplain, which, under favourable conditions, attracts large flocks of waterbirds, including the pink-backed and white pelicans, greater flamingo and African spoonbill. Herds of antelope are also attracted to the good grazing in the area.

A short circular route close to the camp, the **Wild Camphor Loop**, can be explored before you set off on the second day's hike. From the camp, the trail initially follows a route through woodlands and thickets before joining the outward leg of the first day's hike.

38. MKUZI GAME RESERVE
Greater St Lucia Wetland Park,
Mkuze village

Trails: 1 self-guided walk; 3 km; 1 hour; circular. Guided walks; 2 to 3 hours; 4 to 5 km; circular.
Permits: Entrance fee. No permit required for walks. Guided walks must be booked in advance at the office.
Maps: Trail brochure with map of Fig Forest Walk. Colour tourist map of park.
Facilities/Activities: Self-catering accommodation; tented camp; campsites; self-drive game-viewing; night drives; traditional Zulu cultural village; picnic sites.

Proclaimed as a game reserve almost a hundred years ago in 1912, the 36,000-ha Mkuzi section of the Greater St Lucia Wetland Park is linked to the main body of the park by means of the Mkuze Swamps. Bounded by the Ubombo Mountains in the west, its spectacular landscapes include pristine bushveld, riverine forests dominated by sycamore figs, fever tree forests and Nsumo Pan.

Game is abundant and includes three of the Big Five (black and white rhino, elephant and leopard), as well as hippo, giraffe, Burchell's zebra and warthog. Antelope are represented by the red and common duiker, nyala, kudu, reedbuck and impala, while suni occur in the sand forest east of the restcamp.

Mkuzi has an excellent reputation for birding. Among the species you may find are the African broadbill, crested guineafowl, Neergaard's sunbird and the pink-throated twinspot. The hides alongside Nsumo Pan offer good opportunities for spotting waterbirds, especially when the water level is low.

1. Mkuzi Fig Forest Walk leads past stands of fever trees and then goes through a magnificent patch of sycamore fig forest in the southeastern section of Mkuzi. This type of forest is extremely rare in South Africa and, of the 1,800 ha remaining in KwaZulu-Natal, 1,400 ha are located in Mkuzi. Seven points of interest have been numbered along the trail and correspond to the numbered text in the trail pamphlet. **3 km; 1 hour; circular.**

2. Guided Walks conducted from Mantuma Hutted Camp offer a choice of walks for birders and for those primarily interested in viewing game on foot. The early morning birding walk covers about 5 km and, after winding through the sycamore fig riverine forest along the Mkuze River, makes its way to a viewpoint overlooking Nhlonhlela Pan. From here the trail winds back to the restcamp. **4 to 5 km; 2 to 3 hours; circular.**

39. MKUZI BUSHVELD TRAIL
Greater St Lucia Wetland Park,
Mkuze village

Trail: Guided wilderness trail; distances vary from 10 to 15 km per day; 3 nights; walks from basecamp.

Permits: KwaZulu-Natal Wildlife,
P O Box 13069, Cascades 3202,
tel: (033) 845 1000, fax: 845 1001,
email: trails@kwazulu-natalwildlife.com
Maps: *Colour tourist map of park.*
Facilities/Activities: *Trails camp with beds,*
bedding, mattresses, kitchen, communal hot-
water shower and flush toilets. Mkuzi: self-
catering accommodation; tented camp; camp-
sites; self-drive game-viewing; night drives;
traditional Zulu cultural village; picnic sites.
Pertinent information: *The trail season is*
from the beginning of March to the end of
November, as it is too hot during the summer
months. All meals are catered for, but trailists
must provide their own beverages and snacks.

This trail offers the opportunity to explore the varied landscapes of Mkuzi Game Reserve on foot, under the guidance of a trails ranger and a game guard. In addition to its herds of game, the reserve is also known for its excellent birding, with species such as African broadbill, crested guineafowl, Neergaard's sunbird, bearded robin, white- and pink-backed pelicans, pygmy goose and African fish eagle.

Trailists are accommodated for three nights at the trails camp in the south of the reserve, and two full days are spent walking through a diversity of landscapes and vegetation types. After an early morning walk on the last day, trailists return to the trails camp for brunch, after which the trail ends.

40. SODWANA BAY
Greater St Lucia Wetland Park

Trail: 5 km; 2.5 hours; circular.
Permits: *Entry fee. No permit required.*
Maps: *Trail brochure with map.*
Facilities/Activities: *Self-catering accommo-*
dation; campsite; shop; filling station; scuba
diving; angling; snorkelling; guided turtle
nesting night tours (December and January).

The name Sodwana is synonymous with exceptional deep-sea angling, especially game fishing. Offshore

are the southernmost coral reefs in the world and an incredible diversity of colourful fishes, making Sodwana the prime scuba-diving spot along the South African coast.

Proclaimed in 1950 as a national park, Sodwana consists of 413 ha of coastal dune forest, Lake Mngobozeleni and a small mangrove forest in the estuary just north of Jesser Point. To the south, Sodwana borders on Ozabeni, also part of the Greater St Lucia Wetland Park.

Wildlife found here includes reedbuck, red and common duiker, suni and bushpig, and a rich diversity of birds. Species to look out for are the purple-crested lourie, Narina trogon, Rudd's apalis, yellow-spotted nicator and Woodward's batis.

The beaches of Sodwana are an important breeding ground for the leatherback turtle. The nesting season stretches from October to February, during which time the females come ashore at night to lay their eggs in holes dug above the high-water mark.

Mngobozeleni Trail initially moves through grasslands before heading down to Lake Mngobozeleni, named after Chief Mngobo who used to live on the shore of the lake. A resting place is provided shortly before you reach Lake Mngobozeleni, which forms part of a small coastal lake system. The steep banks of the lake are covered by dense forest, extending right to the water's edge, so that from the viewpoint you can catch only a glimpse of the lake. Along the trail there are 10 marked points of interest, which are explained in the trail brochure. **5 km; 2.5 hours; circular.**

41. HLUHLUWE-UMFOLOZI PARK
Mtubatuba and Hluhluwe villages

Trails: Guided day walks; 4 to 5 km;
2 to 3 hours; circular. Guided
wilderness trails; distances vary from
12 to 15 km per day; 2 to 4 nights;
walks from basecamp.
Permits: *KwaZulu-Natal Wildlife,*
P O Box 13069, Cascades 3202,
tel: (033) 845 1000, fax: 845 1001,

email: trails@kwazulu-natalwildlife.com
Maps: *Colour tourist map of park.*
Facilities/Activities: *Self-catering accommodation; restaurant at Hilltop; self-drive game-viewing; guided night drives; picnic sites.*

The Hluhluwe-Umfolozi Park is without doubt one of South Africa's most celebrated parks. Hluhluwe and Umfolozi were proclaimed, in 1897, as two separate game reserves, and, together with St Lucia, are the oldest game reserves in Africa. Umfolozi is the birthplace of the wilderness concept in South Africa, pioneered by visionary conservationist Ian Player. (This concept is to take an intrinsically wild area and conserve it in its natural state, with minimal human interference, such as the building of roads and other structures.) The first wilderness area was set aside in the southern part of the reserve in 1959 and it was here, too, that South Africa's first wilderness trails were conducted. Umfolozi has also played an important role in the conservation of South Africa's white rhino population.

Originally separated by a strip of land known as the Corridor, the two reserves were amalgamated when the Corridor Reserve was proclaimed in 1985, and now form a 96,000-ha game park.

Home to the Big Five, the park is especially renowned for its large population of white rhino, and it also has one of the highest concentrations of black rhino in the world. Other species found here include cheetah, leopard, wild dog, Burchell's zebra, giraffe and hippo. Antelope are represented by kudu, waterbuck, nyala, impala, blue wildebeest and reedbuck.

1. Umfolozi Wilderness Trails are conducted under the guidance of an armed trail ranger and a game guard. The trail is not an endurance test and, although tracking game on foot is an integral part of the daily programme, the overall objective is to provide trailists with an enjoyable wilderness experience. The first and, optional, last night are spent at the Mdindini basecamp, while the second and third nights are spent in a trails camp in the wilderness. As all equipment is taken to the trails camp, you need carry only a small daypack. **Distances vary from 12 to 15 km per day; 4 nights; walks from basecamp.**

2. Umfolozi Primitive Trail This guided trail will appeal to outdoor enthusiasts with a sense of adventure, as no facilities are provided. Since trailists must carry their backpacks, with food, equipment and clothing, the trail is more demanding than a traditional wilderness trail. The route is selected by the trails officer and depends on factors such as the fitness of the group and weather conditions. You sleep under the stars or in caves. **Distances vary from 12 to 15 km per day; 4 nights; walks from basecamp.**

3. Umfolozi Weekend Wilderness Trail This guided trail starts just after lunch on Friday afternoon and trailists must carry their equipment for 7 km to the trails camp. The two nights of the trail are spent in a tented camp, and the walks begin from here. Distances of between 12 and 15 km are covered each day, but trailists carry only a light pack with a water bottle and their lunch. The trail ends on Sunday afternoon. **Distances vary from 12 to 15 km per day; 2 nights; walks from basecamp.**

4. Guided Day Walks are conducted under the guidance of a game guard from Hilltop and Mpila camps. These informative walks last from two to three hours and are a wonderful way of experiencing nature at its best. **Distances vary from 4 to 5 km; 2 to 3 hours; circular.**

42. LAKE SIBAYA NATURE RESERVE
Mbazwana

Trail: *3.4 km; 2 hours; circular.*
Permits: *Entrance fee. No permit required for walk.*
Maps: *Sketch map with information about the trail.*
Facilities/Activities: *Rustic thatched huts with cold water hand basins; communal dining area; communal ablutions.*

This small nature reserve is a wetland of international importance and Lake Sibaya, the country's largest freshwater lake, is its focal point. The lake's surface area varies between 6,600 ha and 7,000 ha, depending on the water level. The average depth is 13 m, but in places it has a maximum depth of 43 m. Separating the lake from the sea are high forested dunes that are called isiBayo, which means 'a cattle kraal' in Zulu.

The coastal dune forest around the lake is home to the common and red duiker, bushpig, samango and vervet monkey, thick-tailed bushbaby and red squirrel, and the lake is home to healthy hippo and crocodile populations.

With its diversity of habitats, Sibaya offers excellent birding opportunities. Among the nearly 300 bird species known to occur in the area are the crowned and trumpeter hornbill, yellow-spotted nicator, gorgeous bush shrike and brown robin. In the moist grasslands, look out for pink-throated longclaw, while great-crested grebe should be sought in the inlets along the lake shore.

Baya Camp Trail passes through a variety of plant communities ranging from coastal forest and coastal woodland to Umdoni parkland, named after the dominant water berry tree (called umdoni in Zulu). Two hides along the trail provide excellent opportunities for birding enthusiasts. Mdoni Hide overlooks a pan situated in Umdoni woodland, while Amadada Hide, at the turn-around point, overlooks an open pan. **3.4 km; 2 hours; circular.**

43. AMANZIMNYAMA TRAIL
Kosi Bay Nature Reserve,
KwaNgwanase

Trail: Guided trail; 35 km; 4 days; circular.
Permits: KwaZulu-Natal Wildlife,
P O Box 13069, Cascades 3202,
tel: (033) 845 1000, fax: 845 1001,
email: trails@kwazulu-natalwildlife.com
Maps: Sketch map.
Facilities/Activities: Four overnight huts
with beds, mattresses, kitchen with two-plate
gas cooker, pots and kettle, and ablution
facilities. Kosi Bay: campsites. Kosi Mouth:
community campsite; snorkelling.
Pertinent information: Water purification
tablets are recommended, as drinking

water here is limited and trailists may
need to use water from the lakes for
cooking and drinking.

Kosi Bay is a fascinating area. Extending over a distance of about 18 km, the Kosi system consists of a string of four interconnected lakes and an estuary, which links the system to the sea. Surrounding the lakes is a mosaic of swamps, marshes and pans, while a strip of high dunes separates the lakes from the sea.

Nhlange, or Third Lake, is the largest of the four lakes, covering an area of between 3,000 and 3,700 ha, and, with a maximum depth of 31 m, is also the deepest. Mpungwini, or Second Lake, has less than 10 per cent of the surface area of Nhlange, while Makawulani (First Lake) is the smallest, with a surface area ranging between 800 and 1,000 ha. Amanzimnyama, or Fourth Lake, the southernmost lake in the system, is in many respects unique. In addition to its swamp forests it has the most extensive occurrence of the rare raffia palm in South Africa. This species is confined to KwaZulu-Natal, and there are scattered groups near Manguzi (a small settlement outside the reserve). The palms at Mntuzini (south of Richards Bay) were established from seed. Also of interest here, from a botanical point of view, is Kosi Mouth, which is the only place in South Africa where five mangrove species occur together.

Among the more than 250 bird species recorded in the area is South Africa's rarest breeding bird, the palmnut vulture – a fantastic tick for any birder. The breeding and feeding habits of the palmnut vulture are closely associated with oil palms. Another noteworthy species, Pel's fishing owl, occurs in the swamp forest of Lake Amanzimnyama. Other species found here include the African fish eagle, white-faced duck, pygmy goose, green coucal, broad-billed roller, African broadbill and Stierling's barred warbler.

The coast of Maputaland is the most important breeding ground of the leatherback turtle in the southern Indian Ocean. Between October and February the females come ashore at night to lay their eggs on the beach.

Of cultural interest here is the complex system of fish traps at Lake Makawulani. These traps, which consist of wooden and reed fences designed to trap the fish in funnel-shaped baskets, have been used by the local Thonga people for over 500 years.

Starting at Nhlange Hikers' Camp on the northwestern shore of Nhlange, the first day's hike (7 km; 3 hours) passes through magnificent coastal forest to Lake Makawulani (First Lake) with its fascinating complex of Thonga fishing kraals. After wading across, it is a short walk to the overnight camp. Kosi Bay mouth lies a mere 2 km to the north and offers excellent snorkelling.

On the second day (10 km; 4 hours) there is a choice between walking along the beach and following the dune ridge to Banga Nek. *Encephalartos ferox*, a cycad with brilliant scarlet cones, is conspicuous amongst the dune forest. Banga Nek is a breeding ground of the leatherback turtle and between October and February they can be observed at night when the females come ashore to lay their eggs.

On the third day (7 km; 3 hours) the trail veers away from the coast as it heads inland for Lake Amanzimnyama, with its black, peat-stained water, swamp forests and raffia palms. The overnight camp is situated on the southern shores of the lake next to the Sihadla River.

At the very beginning of day four's hike (11 km; 5 hours) you will cross the Sihadla River on a raft made from poles and raffia palm leaves by the local Thonga people. The trail continues through the swamp forests, and then makes its way back to the starting point.

44. TEMBE ELEPHANT PARK
KwaNgwanase

Trail: 1 trail with 2 routes; 2.2 and 3.5 km; 1 and 2 hours; circular.
Permits: Entrance fee. No permit required for walk.
Maps: Sketch map.
Facilities/Activities: Luxury tented camp; guided game-viewing.
Pertinent information: On account of the very high temperatures, especially in summer, and the soft sand, it is advisable to do the trail either in the early morning or in the afternoon. If you opt to do the trail in the afternoon you need to ensure that you leave enough time to complete the trail before dark.

Bounded in the north by Mozambique, the 29,000-ha Tembe Elephant Park lies within the sand forest zone and is home to several rare animal, plant and bird species. The park was proclaimed in 1983 to protect the last remaining herds of free-ranging elephants in South Africa. The elephants used to migrate seasonally from the Maputo Elephant Reserve in southern Mozambique to Tembe along the Futi Channel, but as a result of the civil war in Mozambique, as well as poaching, their numbers declined from an estimated 350 in the early 1970s to a mere 120 by the late 1980s. Fearing that the entire population would be wiped out, the then KwaZulu conservation authorities fenced off the northern boundary of the park in 1989. The population in Tembe now stands at over 150 animals and it is hoped that in the future the park will once again be linked to the Maputo Elephant Reserve, to enable the elephants to migrate freely.

The park's vegetation is a mosaic of sand forest, woodlands, grassland, palmveld and swamp. Of special conservation importance is the sand forest, a dry forest confined to the deep white sand of the coastal belt of KwaZulu-Natal and only extensive in the northeast of the province. Characteristic tree species include the Lebombo wattle, pod mahogany, false tamboti, green apple, bastard tamboti and sand canary-berry.

Sand forest is associated with rare animal species such as the suni, Tonga red squirrel and four-toed elephant shrew. In addition to elephant, the park is also a sanctuary to white rhino, leopard, buffalo, hippo, giraffe, waterbuck, reedbuck, blue wildebeest, nyala, kudu, impala, Burchell's zebra and red duiker, as well as crocodile. The last of the Big Five species, lion, were reintroduced into the park in the first half of 2002, when six lions were translocated from the Madikwe Game Reserve in North West Province to Tembe.

The prolific birdlife is also one of the park's main attractions, as several species reach the southern limit of their distribution in Maputaland. Noteworthy species include Rudd's apalis, Neergaard's sunbird, yellow-spotted nicator and pink-throated twinspot. Also recorded here are African broadbill, Woodward's batis, gorgeous bush shrike, Narina trogon, purple-banded sunbird and lemon-breasted canary.

Ngobozana Sand Forest Trails provide an opportunity for trailists to explore Tembe's unique sand forest, with its rare birds, small mammals and interesting vegetation. The trails wind through a patch of sand forest near the tented camp that has been fenced off to keep out elephants without restricting the movement of smaller animals. It offers excellent birding opportunities, so make sure that you take binoculars along. **There is a choice of a short or long loop. Nhlengane Trail: 3.5 km; 2 hours or Umgqulo Trail: 2.2 km; 1 hour; both circular.**

45. NDUMO GAME RESERVE
Ndumo

> **Trails:** *5 guided day walks; 4 to 6 km; 2 to 3 hours; circular.*
> **Permits:** *Entrance fee. Walks can be booked at reception.*
> **Maps:** *Sketch map.*
> **Facilities/Activities:** *Self-catering accommodation; luxury tented camp; picnic sites; community campsite just outside reserve; guided drives to the pans; self-drive game-viewing.*

Bounded by the Usutu River in the north and the Lebombo Mountains to the west, the Ndumo Game Reserve is known for its excellent birding. The reserve covers 12,420 ha and contains a wide variety of vegetation and scenery, including sand forest, floodplains, wetlands, riverine forest, woodlands and the dense Mahemane bush. A prominent feature of the reserve is the system of seasonal and permanent pans, fringed by the distinctive fever tree, and vleis. Well-known pans include Nyamithi and Banzi in the east of the reserve and Shokwe Pan in the west.

Established in 1924 as a sanctuary for the declining number of hippos, the park now has a healthy hippo population, as well as large numbers of crocodile. The nyala is the most common antelope in the park – Ndumo has one of the highest concentrations of nyala in South Africa. Also well represented are black and white rhino, giraffe, kudu, reedbuck, bushbuck, blue wildebeest, Burchell's zebra, red duiker, bushpig and spotted hyaena. Of special interest in the sand forest are the diminutive suni and the Tonga red squirrel. Buffalo occur, but as they favour the rank grass of the floodplains they are seen only occasionally.

Ndumo is a birding hotspot. With over 420 bird species it is, considering its size, undeniably South Africa's top birding destination. At least 17 of the 21 species that reach the southern limit of their distribution in Maputaland have been recorded here. Exciting species you may tick include yellow-spotted nicator, white-eared barbet, Stierling's barred warbler, Woodward's batis, purple-banded sunbird and pink-throated twinspot. Of special interest is the system of wetlands, with a rich diversity of waterfowl and waders. Among these are pygmy goose, lesser moorhen, Baillon's crake, white and pink-backed pelicans, and the African finfoot. Raptors are also well represented.

Guided Walks Five guided walks are conducted through different landscapes and vegetation types in the reserve, ensuring that each trail offers a totally different experience, including the chance to see game.

The **Manzimbomvu Walk** explores the southwestern corner of the park, and the **Shokwe Pan Walk** is conducted in the vicinity of the seasonal pan of that name. Two walks focus on the Pongolo River with its interesting riverine vegetation: **North Pongolo Walk** and **South Pongolo Walk**, and the **Nyamithi Pan Walk** leads to a birdhide overlooking a small reed-fringed pan that lies on the northeastern corner of Nyamithi Pan. **4 to 6 km; 2 to 3 hours; circular.**

46. MKHAYA TRAIL
Pongola

> **Trail:** *30 or 40 km; 2 or 3 days; circular. Shorter options available.*
> **Permits:** *Mrs M de Swardt,*

P O Box 734, Pongola 3170,
tel. and fax: (034) 414 1076.
Maps: Sketch map of trail.
Facilities/Activities: Rondavels at start
and huts at the end of first day's hike.
Beds, mattresses, fireplaces, firewood, hot
water showers and toilets are provided.

in Ntshondwe Camp. Colour tourist
map of park.
Facilities/Activities: Ntshondwe Camp: fully
equipped self-catering chalets; restaurant; curio
shop; swimming pool. Ntshondwe Lodge:
rustic campsites; self-drive game-viewing,
morning, afternoon and night game-drives.

Situated between Vryheid and Pongola, this circular route winds through the bushveld of northern KwaZulu-Natal on a private farm. The vegetation is typical northern KwaZulu-Natal bushveld, and among the game to be seen here are mountain reedbuck and red duiker. The birdlife is prolific and you may tick raptors such as the black, crowned and tawny eagles.

Places of interest on the first day's hike (18 km; 7 hours) include the spot where Dingane is said to have slept when he fled to Swaziland in 1840, as well as the stone cairns and underground granaries of the area's early Zulu inhabitants. Also of interest is a paperbark thorn tree with a crown spread of 30 m. Known in Afrikaans as the Wonderboom it is believed to be the largest specimen of this species in South Africa. The trail ascends to the 951-m-high KwaVundla Mountain, with its commanding view over the surrounding countryside, before descending to the overnight camp.

On the second day (12 km; 5 hours) the trail traverses the low-lying areas and crosses the Mkhaya Stream, after which the trail has been named. Conspicuous along the stream is the lala palm, one of two species of fan palms occurring in South Africa.

There is the option of a third day's circuit of 10 km.

47. ITHALA GAME RESERVE
Louwsburg

Trails: Self-guided walks; 1 to 4 hours;
network from restcamp. Guided walks;
4 to 5 km; 2 to 3 hours; circular.
Permits: Entrance fee. No permit required
for walks. Guided walks can be booked
at the reserve office.
Maps: Sketch map of self-guided walks

Bounded by the Pongola River in the north, the Ithala Game Reserve covers 29,653 ha of rugged countryside, ranging from Drakensberg highlands to typical lowveld. The reserve is renowned for its excellent game-viewing and the superb facilities offered by Ntshondwe Camp.

To date over 900 plant species have been recorded in the reserve, including approximately 320 tree species, one of the greatest diversities of trees in KwaZulu-Natal. The vegetation over much of the reserve is dominated by sweet and scented thorn woodlands, ranging from open savannah to dense thickets. The woodlands are interspersed with patches of tall grassland, consisting mainly of thatch grasses, while the plateau areas are characterised by short grassveld.

The many different habitats support a variety of animals and birds. Ithala is a sanctuary to rhino (both black and white), elephant, giraffe, kudu, eland, waterbuck, nyala, impala, red hartebeest, blue wildebeest, mountain reedbuck, bushbuck and klipspringer. It is also home to the rare roan and to the only population of tsessebe in KwaZulu-Natal.

With a checklist of over 314 bird species, Ithala offers good birding and counts among its noteworthy species the bald ibis. Raptors are represented by 29 species, including the white-backed vulture, the black, martial, crowned and African fish eagles, the bateleur, and the gymnogene. Also recorded are the brown-headed parrot, purple-crested lourie, several kingfisher species, ground hornbill, blue swallow, yellow-spotted nicator, plum-coloured starling and red-billed oxpecker.

1. Self-guided Walks have been laid out below the cliffs in the Ntshondwe Camp. The **Plum-coloured Starling Walk** and **Porcupine Walk** both take about an hour to hike, while the **Klipspringer Walk** takes 90 minutes. About four hours must be set aside for the longest route, the **Bushpig Walk**. Hikers are cautioned to keep a sharp lookout for dangerous animals such as leopard, black rhino and snakes.

2. Guided walks are conducted twice daily; in the early morning and in the mid-afternoon. Trailists are accompanied by a game guard. **4 to 5 km; 2 to 3 hours; circular.**

48. NTENDEKA WILDERNESS AREA
Ngome State Forest, Vryheid

Trails: Network of several trails; 57 km (in total); 3 hours to full day; circular and open-ended.
Permits: State Forester, Ngome State Forest, Private Bag X9306, Vryheid 3100, tel. and fax: (034) 967 1404.
Maps: Wilderness area brochure with map.
Facilities/Activities: Campsite with fireplaces, firewood and ablutions.
Pertinent information: Camping is not permitted in the wilderness area.

Ntendeka, a Zulu name meaning 'place of precipitous heights', is a wonder-world of spectacular cliffs, tropical indigenous forest and grassland. The wilderness area is rich in the history of the Zulu nation and was used as a refuge by Mzilikazi when he was pursued by Shaka. In 1879 the Zulu king Cetshwayo took refuge in a cave at the base of one of the cliffs, following the defeat of the Zulu by the British.

Just under half of the 5,230-ha wilderness area consists of grasslands, while indigenous forest covers the remaining 2,635 ha. The Ngome Forest is considered one of the most beautiful in KwaZulu-Natal and is the habitat of more than 60 fern species, including *Didymochlaena truncatula*, a fern with 2.5-m-long dark green fronds, and forest tree ferns reaching up to 8 m tall. The forest is also home to 19 ephipytic orchid species and the giant-leaved *Streptocarpus*, which has leaves up to 1 m long. Typical forest species include the real yellowwood, lemonwood, thorny rope, red alder, forest elder and some large specimens of forest waterwood. Of particular interest is the forest fig, also known as the strangler fig.

Among the 200-odd bird species recorded in this wilderness area are several noteworthy ones, among them the bald ibis, Delagorgue's pigeon, wattled crane, green twinspot and blue swallow. Other species to look out for include the crowned and martial eagles, trumpeter hornbill and Narina trogon.

The wilderness area is traversed by a network of interlinking footpaths, which can be explored as day walks from the campsite. The shortest circuit is 8 km, and the detour to Cetshwayo's Refuge will add another 5 km to the trail distance. A full-day circular route of 19 km meanders below and over the Ntendeka cliffs. **57 km (in total); 3 hours to a full day; circular and open-ended.**

49. MPATI MOUNTAIN HIKING TRAIL
Dundee

Trail: 18 km; one day or overnight trail; circular.
Permits: Dundee Municipality, P O Box 76, Dundee 3000, tel: (034) 212 2121, fax: 212 3856.
Maps: Comprehensive trail brochure with map.
Facilities/Activities: Accommodation is available in the Dundee Caravan Park, where the trail starts. Chase Cottage on Mpati Mountain: bunks and beds with mattresses, communal room with fireplace, braai places, hot shower, toilet.

A project of the Biggarsberg branch of the Wildlife and Environment Society of South Africa and the Dundee Municipality, this trail has been developed to encourage awareness of the environment, and to provide an educational and recreational resource. The trail traverses Mpati Mountain, an *inselberg* in the Biggarsberg, which stretches from the Free State Drakensberg to the Buffalo and Tugela rivers. The vegetation is mainly grassland interspersed with *Acacias*, and the Natal bottlebrush, common cabbage tree and the kranz aloe are common on the slopes of Mpati.

Among the antelope you may chance upon are kudu, mountain reedbuck, springbok, steenbok and common duiker. Also to be seen are Natal red rock rabbit, Cape hare, porcupine, black-backed jackal and Cape fox. Leopard, African wild cat, serval and aardwolf are also known to occur here, but are seldom encountered.

Some 170 bird species have been recorded in this area to date, and among these are the bald ibis, black and martial eagles, green pigeon, grass owl and arrow-marked babbler. Also recorded here are Ayres's cisticola, the orange-throated longclaw and spectacled weaver.

Mpati Mountain featured prominently during the first days of the South African War. Following the invasion of what was then Natal by the Boers in early October 1899, a force under General Erasmus, a Boer General, occupied Mpati Mountain with a 40-lb Long Tom field artillery gun, while General Meyer, another Boer General, occupied nearby Talana Hill. The opening shots of the war were fired from Talana Hill and after the withdrawal of the Boer forces from the hill, the town of Dundee came under bombardment from Mpati.

The first day's route (13 km; 5 hours) ascends to the 1,590-m-high summit of Mpati, from where there are wonderful all-round views. To the east of Dundee is the flat-topped Talana Hill, and to the southeast Isandlwana, where the British suffered a crushing defeat during the Anglo-Zulu War of 1879, can be seen. The trail then wanders down to Chase Cottage, which is situated next to a stream.

From Chase Cottage hikers can undertake an optional 6-km out-and-return hike to two dams in a tributary of the Sterkstroom. The return leg (5 km; 2 hours) to the starting point is an easy walk along the outward route of the first day's hike.

50. IZEMFENE HIKING TRAIL
Glencoe

Trail: 22.5 km; 2 days; circular.
Permits: Jacana Marketing and Reservations, P O Box 95212, Waterkloof 0145, tel: (012) 346 3550, fax: 346 2499, email: info@jacanacollection.co.za
Maps: Trail map incorporated in trail pamphlet.
Facilities/Activities: Basecamp: thatch hut with bunks, mattresses, lounge/dining room,

kitchen with gas cooker, pots, fireplaces, hot showers and toilets. Dipkraal Camp: tents, kitchen with gas cooker, pots, fireplaces, hot showers and toilets.

This trail in the Biggarsberg takes its name from the Zulu word *izemfene*, which translates as 'place of the baboons'. The area's elevation ranges from 700 to 1,750 m, while the vegetation changes from bushveld in the lower-lying areas and patches of indigenous forests in the kloofs to grasslands at higher altitudes.

The area is rich in culture and history. Along the trail you can see reminders of the early Voortrekkers who passed through here. Wasbank River, for example, got its name after the Vootrekkers washed their clothes in the river in 1838, and a viewpoint on the first day's hike overlooks the spot where the Boers positioned one of their Long Tom field artillery guns to ambush the British troops retreating from Talana to Elandslaagte. Also to be seen are the remains of a pioneer farmyard dating back to between 1850 and 1890, traces of old coal mine shafts and a Hindu temple.

The first day's hike (12 km; 6 hours) ascends steadily and about 1,000 m is gained in altitude to the overnight stop. Along the way you pass an area ravaged by a tornado in 1996, an orchard of old pomegranate trees and a pioneer house. The trail follows a stream with several swimming spots and as you climb towards a saddle, which marks the halfway point, the bushveld vegetation gives way to grasslands. From here the trail continues to climb to the plateau, from where there are magnificent vistas, and then follows a contour before descending through indigenous forest to the overnight stop.

Day two's hike (10.5 km) begins with a short climb and then descends into a valley, where you will pass the ruins of an old stone house and the Piano House. You continue down the valley and follow a stream, with several inviting swimming places, to a saddle, from where you can enjoy panoramic views of the Wasbank Valley and the Drakensberg. The remainder of the trail winds down the mountain slopes, through grasslands, past old mine shafts, an incomplete multi-storeyed concrete structure dubbed the Jungle Gym, and the ruins of a Hindu temple.

FREE STATE

Bounded by the Gariep (Orange) River in the south and by the Vaal River in the north, the Free State lies on the great southern African central plateau, or Highveld. This province's landscape is predominantly flat, although sometimes gently undulating, and it is characterised by maize farms and extensive grasslands, where cattle are reared. In the east and northeast of the Free State, however, the grasslands give way to dramatic sandstone rock formations, rugged mountains, challenging peaks and deep valleys, all of which create numerous opportunities for hikes, walks and other outdoor activities.

Situated at an altitude of between 1,000 and 1,800 m, the Highveld has a severe climate, with temperatures ranging from below freezing point during winter to 30 °C in summer. Under these extreme conditions only the hardiest plant and tree species can survive, so the vegetation found here is mainly grasslands, with few trees and shrubs, although proteaveld sometimes occurs on the slopes below sandstone cliffs.

Among the many prominent landmarks in the northeastern Free State are formations shaped like a camel and the profile of Queen Victoria, and Lesoba, a Sotho name referring to a hole eroded through the mountain. Well-known formations in the Golden Gate Highlands National Park include Brandwag, also known as the Sentinel, the spectacular Mushroom Rocks and Gladstone's Nose, a formation resembling the profile of a former British Prime Minister.

The rock paintings on the walls of many of the holkranse (overhangs) in the northeastern Free State bear testimony to the Bushmen who once lived here. Also of interest is Salpeterkrans, which lies near Fouriesburg, where many women bring offerings to the spirits in the belief that it will increase their fertility.

After the harsh winter months the grasslands are brown and uninviting, but in spring a variety of flowering plants provides a touch of colour. Among these plants are *Gladiolus*, *Agapanthus*, *Hypoxis*, *Watsonia* and *Brunsvigia* species, as well as pineapple flowers (*Eucomis*), red-hot pokers (*Kniphofia*) and berg lilies (*Galtonia*).

In the more mountainous eastern and northeastern parts of the province, oldwood trees are conspicuous along the river courses. Wild sage

trees, wild peach, Cape myrtle, small-leaved guarri, and bladder nut, as well as nana berry can all be found in sheltered valleys and ravines. Cabbage trees can be seen in rocky outcrops.

Typical game species of the Highveld include Burchell's zebra, black wildebeest, blesbok, eland and smaller antelope such as common duiker and steenbok. Also found here are springbok and oribi, while the grey rhebok and mountain reedbuck favour the mountainous areas. Smaller mammals found here include baboon, black-backed jackal, caracal, African wild cat and Cape hare.

For birding enthusiasts the eastern parts of the province and the northeastern highlands offer the opportunity to tick several noteworthy species. Amongst these are bearded and Cape vultures, bald ibis and yellow-breasted pipit. Typical grassland species that you should be on the look out for include the sentinel rock thrush, buff-streaked chat, blue korhaan and crowned crane. Ground woodpecker and orange-breasted rockjumper favour the rocky, higher elevations, while Gurney's sugarbird can be spotted in proteaveld. Rudd's and Botha's larks are two threatened species to look out for in the high-altitude grasslands of the northeastern corner of the Free State.

The landscape of the northeastern highlands is dominated by imposing cliffs, buttresses and outcrops of the Clarens Sandstone Formation, which forms the upper part of the Karoo Supergroup. The sandstone cliffs were formed by fine windblown sand that was deposited in a huge basin, when climatic conditions became increasingly dry during the Karoo times.

The many striking sandstone formations were shaped by a combination of several processes. The spectacular Mushroom Rocks in the Golden Gate Highlands National Park, for example, were created as a result of the calcification of the sandstone at different levels, which in turn resulted in differences in resistance to weathering. Another process, salt weathering, was also at work here. This takes place when salt solutions seep out near the base of a cliff and crystalise, gradually eroding the cliff surface. In addition, groundwater is forced to seep out near the base of the sandstone when it reaches the impermeable mudstone, undermining the base of the sandstone cliff.

The Drakensberg Formation is another arresting natural feature in this area, and reaches a thickness of 600 m at Ribbokkop in the Golden Gate Highlands National Park. It was formed some 190 million years ago, when vast flows of lava covered large parts of southern Africa. The lava subsequently solidified to form thick layers of basalt, which are today the high mountains of the park.

A number of fossils have been discovered in the Golden Gate Highlands National Park and in the surrounding area of Clarens. The most exciting discovery to date has been that of a clutch of six dinosaur eggs (the first record of fossil eggs of the Upper Triassic period), which date back to between 185 and 195 million years ago.

Over much of the Free State summer days are warm, and evening temperatures are pleasant. In the northeastern highlands, however, temperatures are typically a few degrees lower and evenings can be cool. Winter days are generally mild, but can be bitingly cold when the southerly winds blow from the Drakensberg and the Malutis. At night temperatures frequently drop below freezing point and heavy frost is not uncommon. Mid-winter snow occasionally falls on the high mountains in the northeast.

Rainfall ranges from 600 mm in the northwestern Free State to 900 mm in the northeastern highlands. Most rain is recorded between November and March with January and February being the wettest months, and June, July and August being the driest. The rains are typically accompanied by dramatic thunderstorms and displays of lightening, usually in mid-afternoon.

Opportunities for walks and hikes in the Free State range from easy rambles amongst the dolerite hills in the Free State National Botanical Gardens to day walks along the Gariep River, which demarcates the province's southern boundary. In the east and northeast of the Free State there is an extensive network of hikes and walks on private farms and in conservancies. Hikers can also explore the high mountains of the Golden Gate Highlands National Park, or undertake a fairly demanding hike to the top of the Amphitheatre and the summit of Mont-aux-Sources.

IMPORTANT INFORMATION

• When planning a winter hike, bear in mind it can become extremely cold, so ensure you pack enough warm clothing. A good-quality sleeping bag, rated below zero degrees, is essential.

• Lightning poses a threat in summer. Start walking early in the morning and aim to get to the overnight stop before the thunderstorm breaks. If caught in a thunderstorm, try to avoid exposed high ground, boulders and trees.

• Thunderstorms also pose the risk of flash floods on trails where rivers have to be crossed. Do not try to cross a river that is flowing strongly, but wait until it has subsided to a safe level.

• Firewood is not provided on some hikes, so check with the relevant trail authority when making reservations. Woody vegetation is in short supply and you should never collect firewood unless this has been authorised.

• Make fires only where permitted. Smokers must take great care – matches and cigarette ends may not be discarded on the trail. The risk of fire is very high during the winter months when the dry grass is extremely flammable.

• Many streams are dry in winter, so it is essential to set off with a full waterbottle (of at least 2 litres) and use water sparingly until you can fill up again.

• Most Free State trails traverse private farmland and you must always use stiles where provided. Gates found closed must be shut behind you, and open gates left open. Visit a farmhouse only by invitation from the owner, or in cases of extreme emergency.

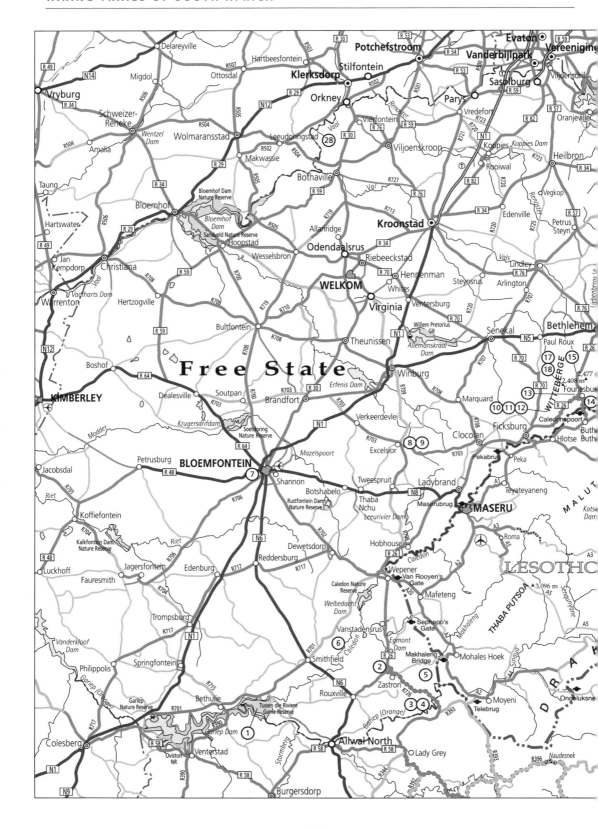

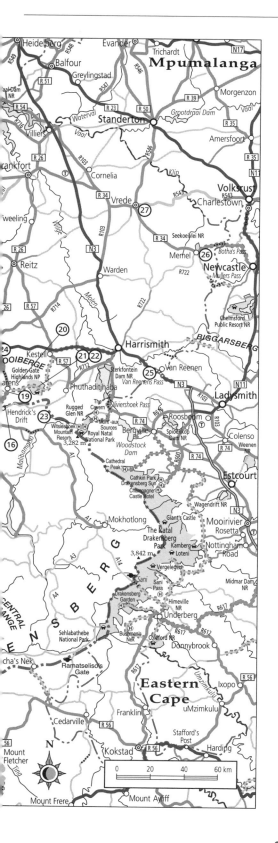

1. TUSSEN-DIE-RIVIERE GAME RESERVE
Bethulie

> **Trail:** 7 km; 3 hours; circular.
> **Permits:** Entrance fee. No permit required for trail.
> **Maps:** Reserve brochure with sketch map.
> **Facilities/Activities:** Self-contained cottages.

Nestling between the Gariep (Orange) and Caledon rivers, the Tussen-die-Riviere Game Reserve covers 22,871 ha of rocky ridges and open plains. Erosion of dolerite intrusions has resulted in fascinating piles of precariously balanced rocks.

The vegetation of the plains is typically grass and low Karoo bushes such as bitterbos (*Chrysocoma ciliata*), persaarbos (*Walafrida geniculata*), kapokbossie (*Eriocephalus*) and vaalkaroo (*Pentzia globosa*). Wild olive, white stinkwood, karee and cabbage trees dominate the dolerite hills, while the riverine vegetation is characterised by sweet thorn, white stinkwood, Cape willow and Karoo bluebush.

Both black and white rhino have been reintroduced into the reserve, which is also home to Burchell's zebra and a rich diversity of antelope species. Amongst these are kudu, eland, black wildebeest, red hartebeest, impala, springbok, blesbok and mountain reedbuck. Smaller mammals found here include bat-eared and Cape foxes, baboon, vervet monkey and aardwolf.

Among the more than 220 bird species known to occur here are the Cape vulture, African fish eagle, blue korhaan, Karoo and sickle-winged chats and Namaqua warbler. Several lark and cisticola species have also been recorded. A variety of waterbirds is attracted to the Gariep Dam, and to the Gariep and Caledon rivers.

Middelpunt Trail From the reserve office the trail meanders along the base of a ridge to a point close to the confluence of the Gariep and Caledon rivers. The route then doubles back from high on the slopes of the ridge. Along the way there are extensive views over the Caledon River and the reserve's hilly landscape, and alert hikers may spot some of the game species roaming the reserve.

Two other walks, the Klipstapel and Orange River trails, had to be closed following the reintroduction of black rhino into the reserve. **7 km; 3 hours; circular.**

2. AASVOËLBERG HIKING TRAIL
Zastron

> **Trail:** 23 km; 2 days; circular.
> **Permits:** Mr L Alberts, P O Box 24, Zastron 9950, tel: (051) 673 1323, fax: 673 2100.
> **Maps:** Brochure and sketch map.
> **Facilities/Activities:** Accommodation available at the start in the Zastron municipal caravan park or the Maluti Hotel. Overnight hut with bunks, mattresses, braai area, shower and toilet.

Located in the southeastern Free State, this hiking trail traverses the Aasvoëlberg west of Zastron. It is renowned for its scenic mountain vistas, waterfalls and sandstone overhangs. Among the interesting rock formations found here are the Mushroom Rock, Face Rock, the Tunnel and Die Oog, a hole eroded through a rocky outcrop.

Large mammals you may chance upon include grey rhebok and mountain reedbuck, and baboon, rock dassie, springhare, porcupine and a variety of rodents are among the small mammals found here. The carnivores are represented by caracal, African wild cat, Cape fox and black-backed jackal.

To date some 136 different bird species have been recorded in the Zastron area, amongst them the endangered Cape vulture, after which Aasvoëlberg is named (*aasvoël* being the Afrikaans word for vulture). The vultures use the western cliffs of Aasvoëlberg as a nesting and roosting site, and these birds make up the only such colony in the southern Free State. A 'vulture restaurant' (feeding station) has been established on the northwestern slopes of the mountain to supplement their diet. Other raptors to look out for include black and booted eagles, yellow-billed kite, black harrier and gymnogene. Also recorded are ostrich, Orange River francolin, four lark species, Cape rock thrush and orange-throated longclaw.

The Aasvoëlberg Hiking Trail passes through forested kloofs, grasslands and along the base of sandstone cliffs. Owing to the rugged terrain traversed by the original route of 37 km, over two days, the trail gained a reputation for being difficult. This prompted the owner to redesign and shorten the route in 2002. However, the highlights of the old trail have all been incorporated into the new route.

3. BERGKLOOF HIKING TRAIL
Zastron

Trails: 2 trails; 6 to 10 km; 3 to 5 hours; network from basecamp.
Permits: Snyman, P O Box 145, Zastron 9950, tel: (05542) 1922 (first dial just the area code to be connected to the operator, then give them the four-digit number).
Maps: Sketch map.
Facilities/Activities: Basecamp: farmhouse with bed and mattresses, fully equipped kitchen, thatched lapa with braai facilities, bathroom with hot water and toilet.

These trails traverse grassland, as well as wooded countryside on a farm some 32 km from Zastron. There are two circular day walks, which can be hiked from the basecamp, an old farmhouse, so you need only carry a daypack for these hikes.

Rooikop Route traverses the high-lying areas of the farm and ascends to the summit of Rooikop after which it is named. Here trailists are rewarded with far-reaching views of the Malutis, in Lesotho, and the Witteberg at Lady Grey. The trail covers 8 km, but a shorter 6-km option is also available. **6 or 8 km; 3 or 4 hours; circular.**

River View Route winds along kloofs and over hills in the lower-lying section of the farm. Along the way trailists will enjoy scenic views of the meandering Gariep (Orange) River. This trail offers good birding possibilities. **10 km; 5 hours; circular.**

4. QUAGGAFONTEIN HIKING TRAIL
Zastron

Trails: 2 trails; 3 to 13 km; 1.5 to 6.5 hours; network from basecamp.
Permits: Rits Agency, P O Box 8871, Bloemfontein 9300, tel: (082) 429 3711, fax: (051) 405 5044, email: derekrits@mweb.co.za
Maps: The trail is indicated on a copy of a 1:50,000 topographical map.
Facilities/Activities: Farmhouse with beds, bedding, fully equipped kitchen with gas stove, fridge and deep freeze, dining room, lounge with fireplace, bathroom with hot water, paraffin lamps and braai facilities.

This trail, with its figure-of-eight design, allows hikers to explore the fascinating landscape of the southern Free State. It is laid out in the vicinity of the Gariep (Orange) River, near the border between South Africa and Lesotho, where the scenery is varied and the trails offer spectacular mountain views. A renovated farmhouse dating back to 1912 serves as a basecamp.

The Quaggafontein Hiking Trail passes mainly through grassland, but it also makes its way through wooded ravines and kloofs. The most conspicuous large mammal found here, which you may chance upon during the hike, is the mountain reedbuck, and there is a rich diversity of waterbirds, which are attracted to the Gariep River and farm dams.

River Trail Along this route, with 7- and 13-km options, trailists will enjoy fine views of the Gariep River. There are also good birding opportunities. **7 or 13 km; 3.5 or 6.5 hours; circular.**

Mountain Trail As the name implies, this 10.5-km route traverses mountainous terrain that is characterised by wooded kloofs and rocky slopes. There is rock art here, which can be viewed along the trail. A shorter, 3-km option is available. **3 or 10.5 km; 1.5 or 5 hours; circular.**

5. CHAMPAGNE TRAIL
Zastron

> *Trails:* 4 trails; 30 min to 5 hours;
> network from basecamp.
> *Permits:* Rits Agency,
> P O Box 8871, Bloemfontein 9300,
> tel: (082) 429 3711, fax: (051) 405
> 5044, email: derekrits@mweb.co.za
> *Maps:* The trail is indicated on a
> 1:50,000 topographical map that
> was specially drawn for this hike.
> *Facilities/Activities:* Farmhouse with beds
> and mattresses, kitchen with a coal stove,
> gas cooker, fridge and cooking utensils, hot
> showers, toilet, braai facilities and firewood.

Situated to the east of Zastron, this scenic farm is characterised by grasslands, forested kloofs, interesting rock formations, hills and ridges. The trail network offers four circular day walks, ranging from an easy 2-km ramble to a moderately difficult 10-km route from the basecamp up to the summits of the highest peaks on the farm. A highlight of nearly all these routes is the wonderful views of the south-eastern Free State, the Malutis, in Lesotho, and the Witteberg at Lady Grey.

6. STOKSTERT HIKING TRAIL
Smithfield

> *Trail:* 22 km; 2 days; network
> from basecamp.
> *Permits:* Mr Jan le Roux Pieterse,
> P O Box 71, Smithfield 9966, tel: (05562)
> 2104 (dial the exchange code and give the
> operator the four-digit phone number).
> *Maps:* Sketch map of trail.
> *Facilities/Activities:* Overnight hut with
> beds, mattresses, shower, toilet, braai
> place and firewood.

Named after the suricate, known in Afrikaans as the stokstert meerkat, this trail traverses a farm in the Caledon River Conservancy, which lies just to the west of the Caledon River, between Wepener in the north and Smithfield in the south. Dominating the surrounding scenery is the 1,704-m-high Burnetskop with is sheer cliffs.

To date some 105 bird species have been recorded in the area, among them black, martial and African fish eagles, black stork and several lark and chat species.

Designed as a figure-of-eight route from a central basecamp, the two-day walk passes through grasslands, wooded ridges and scenic kloofs. Highlights include a walk along the Caledon River and Mosselgat (a tributary of the Caledon River with freshwater mussels). Also of interest are the ruins of the French mission station founded at Beersheba in 1828 and used until 1856.

7. FREE STATE NATIONAL BOTANICAL GARDEN
Bloemfontein

> *Trails:* 4 km; 1.5 hours; network.
> *Permits:* Entrance fee. No permit for walks.
> *Maps:* Available at entrance.
> *Facilities/Activities:* Picnic areas;
> tea kiosk; plant sales.

The Free State National Botanical Garden straddles a valley between three dolerite koppies on the outskirts of Bloemfontein. Ranging from tall grassland and woodland, characterised by species such as buffalo thorn, karee and white stinkwood, to succulent Karoo-like vegetation, the natural flora has largely been left undisturbed, and only seven of the garden's 70 ha have been developed. Special plant collections include the grass and bulb gardens and a fine collection of South African wild currant and karee trees. The garden is especially attractive between November and March when a rich variety of trees are in full leaf.

Of special interest is a traditional Basotho homestead, while a stone wall, patrol path on one of the koppies, and the main dam, left by British troops, are reminders of the South African War of 1899–1902. There are two demonstration gardens: a medicinal plant and a 'water-wise' garden.

The garden is traversed by a network of footpaths that winds around the dolerite koppies and to rocky outcrops, from where there are stunning views over the valley, with its three dams, and the cultivated section of the garden.

8. KORANNA HIKING TRAIL
Marquard

See no. 9 (this page) for walks.

Trail: 28 km; 2 days; circular.
Permits: Jacana Marketing and Reservations, P O Box 95212, Waterkloof 0145, tel: (012) 346 3550, fax: 346 2499, email: info@jacanacollection.co.za
Maps: Trail pamphlet with map available.
Facilities/Activities: Merrimetsi Barn: 33 bunks with mattresses, electricity, gas cookers, gas fridge, cooking utensils, fireplace and hot-water ablutions. Merrimetsi Farmhouse: accommodates 10 people, and has electricity, fridge, gas stove, cooking utensils, cutlery, crockery, fireplace, hot-water ablutions. Waenhuiskrans cave, on the trail.
Pertinent information: A torch is essential for the detour through Magul se Gat on the second day's hike.

Rising some 400 m above the surrounding plains, the Korannaberg is like an island amongst a patchwork of farmlands. The trail traverses a mountain, which forms the focal point of the 7,000-ha Korannaberg Conservancy, and along the route the scenery varies from well-wooded kloofs and waterfalls to interesting sandstone formations and grasslands.

The vegetation of the plains and mountain plateau is dominated by short, dense grassveld, with a variety of flowering plants that are only conspicuous in spring. A variety of trees and shrubs occur on the closely wooded mountain slopes and river valleys. They include wild olive, oldwood, karee, tree fuchsia, Cape holly and sagewood trees.

Bird species occurring in the area number around 150 and among the species you may tick are black and martial eagles, Richard's and yellow-breasted pipits, ground woodpecker, black korhaan and grey-winged francolin. Four lark species (rufous-naped, clapper, red-capped and pink-billed) have also been recorded.

The first day's hike (18 km; 7 hours) ascends steeply along Boskloof to a magnificent waterfall, reached about 15 minutes before the head of the kloof. From the top of the kloof the route continues to climb steadily through grassland and beautiful rock formations to the base of the sandstone cliffs, where a waterfall that cascades over the lip of a large overhang provides an ideal lunch spot. Continuing through grasslands, hikers are rewarded with far-reaching views of the Maermanshoek Valley and Wonderkop. A descent to Olienhoutbos is followed by a steep climb to the Waenhuiskrans, a large two-chambered overhang divided by a rock pillar.

The second day's hike (10 km; 4 hours) is mainly downhill and leads past imposing rocky outcrops before reaching the highlight on this section, Magul se Gat. In 1858, the Koranna chief, Gert Taaibosch, and his followers were besieged in the cave by the white settlers, but managed to escape through a tunnel under cover of darkness. Packs can be left at the entrance if you want to explore the cave, but remember to take a torch along. At the far end of the overhang the tunnel becomes narrower and you are forced to crawl underneath a huge boulder to a wide chamber where you must clamber up some large rocks before emerging into the open. An easy climb is followed by a descent to the Albaster Rocks, named after their resemblance to giant marbles. The remainder of the day's hike is all downhill.

9. MERRIMETSI HIKING TRAILS
Marquard

See no. 8 (this page) for hiking trail.

Trails: 3 trails; 6 to 10 km; 3 to 6 hours; network from basecamp.
Permits: Jacana Marketing and Reservations, P O Box 95212, Waterkloof 0145,

---

tel: (012) 346 3550, fax: 346 2499,
email: info@jacanacollection.co.za
Maps: Trail pamphlet with map available.
Facilities/Activities: Merrimetsi Barn:
33 bunks with mattresses, electricity,
gas cookers, gas fridge, cooking utensils,
fireplace and hot-water ablutions. Merrimetsi
farmhouse: accommodates 10 people,
and has electricity, fridge, gas stove,
cooking utensils, cutlery, crockery, fireplace,
hot-water ablutions.
Pertinent information: A torch is essential
for the detour through Magul se Gat on
the Blue Route.

This network of day walks caters for those wanting to explore the flora and fauna of the Korannaberg unencumbered by a backpack.

1. Yellow Route begins with a steep climb to Lion's Head, but then levels off as it continues across the plateau to an overhang with rock paintings. From here the trail heads in a northerly direction to the Albaster Rocks. The remainder of the route is downhill. **6 km; 4–6 hours; circular.**

2. Green Route From Merrimetsi this trail heads off in a southerly direction and then ascends steeply, gaining about 200 m in altitude to the plateau of the Korannaberg. Highlights along the course of the hike include Cannibals' Cave, stands of the rare voetangel (a plant species occurring in only three places on the Korannaberg) and a magnificent overhang that makes a good stopping place for tea. The trail then descends back to Merrimetsi. **10 km; 4 hours; circular.**

3. Blue Route ascends steeply to the plateau and then continues to Waenhuiskrans, a cave that serves as overnight accommodation on the Koranna Hiking Trail. Further along Magul se Gat is reached and the final section of the trail follows the return leg of the Green Route. Over 40 indigenous tree species have been marked along the Blue Route, which provides an ideal opportunity to discover the flora of the area. Of particular interest is a white stinkwood tree with an unusually massive trunk. **10 km; 6 hours; circular.**

10. WATERKLOOF HIKING TRAIL
Ficksburg

See nos. 11 and 12 (p. 193) for other trails.

Trails: 21 km; 2 days, or 26.7 km;
3 days; circular.
Permits: Jacana Marketing and Reservations,
P O Box 95212, Waterkloof 0145,
tel: (012) 346 3550, fax: 346 2499,
email: info@jacanacollection.co.za
Maps: Trail pamphlet with map available.
Facilities/Activities: Waterkloof basecamp:
30 beds with mattresses, two-plate gas
stove, pots, pans, kettle, braai facilities and
hot-water ablutions. Barolong Overnight
Camp: three wattle-and-daub rooms, or sleep
in cave (bring own ground sheets or pads),
braai facilities, cast-iron pots, water and pit
toilets. Sphinx Mountain Hut: 22 beds,
mattresses, braai facilities, pots, cast-iron
potjie, cold-water showers and pit toilets.

This trail lies in the Visierskerf Private Nature Reserve near Ficksburg in the eastern Free State. The vegetation ranges from typical grassland to wooded kloofs, and some of the nearly 90 tree and shrub species occurring in the area have been marked along the trail.

Game you might encounter includes grey rhebok, springbok, mountain reedbuck and common duiker, as well as numerous small mammals. The trail environs are home to an estimated 200 bird species.

Overlooked by the 2,410-m-high Visierskerf, the first day's route (10.5 km; 5 hours) ascends along a well-watered kloof with magnificent pools and then follows a contour at the base of the sandstone cliffs, passing several large overhangs. An optional detour takes hikers to the summit of the 2,312-m-high Sekonyela Peak, a climb involving a 240-m gain in altitude. From here the trail continues to the second kloof, where there is an inviting rock pool, perfect for a lunch stop. The path then wanders down to the Bamboeskloof, situated close to the overnight stop.

The second day's hike (10.5 km; 5 hours) initially rambles along the sandstone cliffs to a junction, where there is an option of ascending the Visierskerf. This 4-km out-and-return detour leads to the highest point in the Free State outside of the Malutis. From here the trail continues to a kloof with a delightful series of seven pools, where the route splits. The two-day route passes the pools and then descends through grasslands back to the start, while the three-day route continues along a contour on the slopes of Jacobsberg to the Sphinx overnight hut.

The third day's hike (5.7 km; 2 hours) winds below the Second and First Pyramids and then passes through ancient oak trees and along a willow tree lane to a large swimming pool. The remainder of the hike is mainly through cultivated lands.

the slopes of Jacobsberg. A ladder leads down into a ravine and for the next 1 km the route is through dense indigenous forest. The Sphinx overnight hut overlooks a natural swimming pool, and a nearby dam provides good birding possibilities.

The second day's hike (5 km; 2 hours) traverses the contours below the two Pyramid Mountains. Local lore has it that the overhang was also used as an arsenal during the South African War (1899–1902). The trail then descends to a swimming pool and a dam, with a reed bird-watching hide, before reaching the basecamp.

11. SPHINX HIKING TRAIL
Ficksburg

See nos. 10 (p. 192) and 12 (this page) for other trails.

> *Trail:* 15.5 km; 2 days; circular.
> *Permits:* Jacana Marketing and Reservations, P O Box 95212, Waterkloof 0145, tel: (012) 346 3550, fax: 346 2499, email: info@jacanacollection.co.za
> *Maps:* Trail brochure with map.
> *Facilities/Activities:* Moolmanshoek basecamp: farmhouse with 22 beds, mattresses, two-plate gas stove, pots, pans, kettle, braai facilities and hot-water ablutions. Sphinx Mountain Hut: hut with 22 beds, mattresses, braai facilities, pots, cast-iron potjie, cold-water showers and pit toilets.

This trail takes in a number of well-known rock formations, such as the Sphinx and the Pyramids, in the Visierskerf Private Nature Reserve.

From the Moolmanshoek Valley the first day's trail (10.5 km; 4 hours) gradually ascends the slopes of the Witteberg through grassveld and then follows a contour to Spiraalgat. Shaped like an upside down ice-cream cone, the 4.5-m-deep pool is an ideal place for a tea stop. A short way on, the trail passes another inviting swimming hole, Witgatbad, and, still further on, the detour to the summit of the 2,410-m-high Visierskerf is reached. From here the route continues behind the Sphinx and then follows the contours on

12. LANGESNEK HIKING TRAIL
Ficksburg

See nos. 10 (p. 192) and 11 (this page) for other trails.

> *Trail:* 22 km; 2 days; network from basecamp.
> *Permits:* Jacana Marketing and Reservations, P O Box 95212, Waterkloof 0145, tel: (012) 346 3550, fax: 346 2499, email: info@jacanacollection.co.za
> *Maps:* Trail brochure with map.
> *Facilities/Activities:* Basecamp: old farmhouse with bunks, mattresses and fully equipped kitchen with fridge, two-plate gas cooker, pots, pans, lapa with braai facilities, bathrooms and toilets.

From the basecamp on the farm Langesnek, in the Visierskerf Private Nature Reserve, the first day's trail (11.5 km; 5 hours) leads past an old mill, once used for the milling of maize and wheat. A short way on you will reach Swallows' Nest, a pink sandstone overhang, and later a sheep dip carved out of sandstone. The trail climbs to Pulpit View, passes layered brown sandstone formations, and then comes to a plateau. On descending to a saddle you can enjoy the first good views of the Malutis, and, further on, Visierskerf and Sekonyela's Hat come into view. The trail takes you to Crater Pools (natural pools eroded into the sandstone) and a dam, where you can stop for lunch. A steady climb to the Klipkoppie is followed by an easy walk over exposed sandstone and a descent to Photographer's Rock, a massive sandstone formation, which is a good spot for taking photographs. From here it is a short walk back to the basecamp.

The second day's route (10.5 km; 4 hours) makes its way to a slippery natural rockslide appropriately named Supertube Gorge. The path then climbs to the Moolmanshoek Valley viewpoint, where there is an optional 2-km out-and-return walk to the summit of the First Pyramid. The trail then traverses the slopes below First and Second Pyramids before descending to the Sphinx overnight hut. The return leg follows the route of the Sphinx Hiking Trail to Mrs Mitchell's High Tea Rock, where one of the first owners of Moolmanshoek used to enjoy her traditional English high tea every afternoon. A short way on the trail splits, with the Langesnek Trail climbing steeply to sandstone ridges and an overhang. The final section of the trail descends gradually to the basecamp.

13. BRANDWATER HIKING TRAIL
Fouriesburg

> **Trail:** 61 km; 5 days; circular.
> **Permits:** Fouriesburg Cultural Association, Reverend J Mostert, P O Box 24, Fouriesburg 9725, tel: (058) 223 0050.
> **Maps:** Trail indicated on photocopy of 1:50,000 topographical map sections 2828 AC 2828 AD, 2828 CA and 2828 CB.
> **Facilities/Activities:** Three caves and a barn with no facilities.

This fairly demanding trail west of Fouriesburg, in the eastern Free State, will soon dispel any preconceived ideas that the province is flat and uninteresting. The trail meanders through grassland and beautiful mountain kloofs, as well as past white sandstone formations and green meadows.

The vegetation is dominated by sour grassveld, with patches of scrub forest in the river valleys and on valley slopes. The grassveld is interspersed with everlastings (Helichrysum), red heath (Erica cerinthoides), red-hot pokers (Kniphofia), gazanias and a variety of other flowering plants. On the first day of the hike you will see the particularly striking Euphorbia clavarioides, a succulent resembling a round termite mound.

Birdlife is typical of the highland grassveld of the eastern Free State. Keep an eye out on the third day's hike for the bearded vulture, which is often seen in the vicinity of Snymanshoekberg. Other species you might tick include the ground woodpecker, Cape and sentinel rock thrush, orange-breasted rock-jumper, orange-breasted longclaw and rock pipit.

The first day's hike (14 km; 7 hours) is the most difficult and an early start is advisable. Starting at the Meiringspoort Restcamp, the trail follows Meiringskloofspruit until it ends in a narrow chasm, where a chain ladder provides the only way out. From here the trail ascends steadily to the old Ventersberg farmstead and then climbs steeply to the Maluti viewpoint. For the next few kilometres the route is mainly level or downhill, winding in and out of several kloofs. A short uphill stretch to a nek follows, and from here it is about an hour's walk to the overnight stop, Waterfall Cave.

Day two (14 km; 6 hours) follows an undulating course to reach a large overhang less than two hours after setting off. After a gentle climb the trail descends, only to ascend again, and finally make its way down steeply, crossing a stream with small potholes eroded into the sandstone. You follow a farm road down a valley with lush pastures to the old Paterimo farmhouse, built from orange sandstone rock. The trail then continues along a valley reminiscent of Yellowstone Park in the United States of America, and climbs sharply through proteaveld to Protea Ridge Cave.

The third day's hike (13 km; 6 hours) starts with a steep 40-minute climb up the Snymanshoek Mountain before the gradient eases off, as the path traverses the mountain slopes for about 30 minutes. After you cross to the southern side of the mountain at a nek, you will see the Maluti Mountains come into view, and then, over the next few kilometres, the trail loses some 500 m in altitude. Keep an eye out for Salpeterkrans, the landmark that you are headed for. You descend to the Little Caledon River and after a short uphill walk you will reach the enormous Salpeterkrans cave, said to be the largest overhang in the southern hemisphere. The cave is a place of pilgrimage for many women, who bring offerings to the spirits in the belief this will increase fertility.

If the cave is occupied, greet the sangoma and worshippers politely before proceeding. The remaining hour of the day's hike follows the banks of the Little Caledon River to the overnight stop, an old barn.

Day four (10 km; 4 hours) is an easy walk, first along a gravel road and then along the Little Caledon River. A short way beyond Middenin Farm you pass an old Voortrekker cemetery, and the trail then winds up a hill before descending into a valley, at the head of which the overnight cave is situated.

The final day's hike (10 km; 4 hours) begins with a sustained uphill climb and about 300 m in altitude is gained to Ventersberg. A short descent follows and at the old Ventersberg farmhouse you join the outward route of the first day. From here retrace your tracks to Meiringskloof.

14. CAMELROC HIKING TRAIL
Fouriesburg

Trails: *2 day-walks (can be combined into a 2-day hike); 9 and 4 km; 4 and 1.5 hours; network from basecamp.*
Permits: *Jacana Marketing and Reservations, P O Box 95212, Waterkloof 0145, tel: (012) 346 3550, fax: 346 2499, email: info@jacanacollection.co.za*
Maps: *Trail brochure with map.*
Facilities/Activities: *Basecamp: hut with bunks and mattresses accommodating 16 people; tents accommodating 12 people; cooking facilities; fireplace; ablutions; 6-km 4x4 route.*

Named after a sandstone rock formation resembling the head of a camel, this trail near the Caledonpoort border post is hiked as two day-walks. Its attractions include far-reaching views of Lesotho and the Malutis, interesting rock formations and sandstone overhangs.

Although the first day's hike is short (9 km; 4 hours), it should not be underestimated as there are several steep climbs. From the basecamp the trail climbs steeply to God's Window, a sandstone cave with splendid views of the landscape below. Adventurous hikers can approach the cave via The

Ledge, which traverses a sandstone ridge with steep slopes, while the Chicken Run offers a safer alternative for the less adventurous. There is a steep ascent to the plateau, where a wooden bridge spans the gorge between the mountain and the freestanding Camel Head rock formation. From here the trail continues across the plateau and then descends into a shady gorge. There are pools near the end of the day's hike, ideal for cooling off on a hot day.

A highlight of day two's hike (4 km; 1.5 hours) is an overhang with rock paintings, reached by means of a bridge across the Caledon River. The trail follows the course of the Caledon River and there are numerous opportunities for a swim, or you can combine the hike with tubing downstream.

15. SPOREKRANS HIKING TRAIL
Fouriesburg

Trail: *16.5 km; 2 days; network from basecamp.*
Permits: *Discovery Trails, P O Box 149, Paul Roux 9800, tel. and fax: (058) 471 0551, email: retastrydom@worldonline.co.za*
Maps: *Rough trail map.*
Facilities/Activities: *Basecamp with bunks, mattresses, kitchen with fridge, hot-plate, pots, pan and electric kettle, lapa with braai facilities, hot showers and toilet; horse-riding; abseiling; sunset game-drives.*

Laid out on Bergdeel Private Nature Reserve, this trail wanders through forested kloofs, across mountain streams and through grassland, in the heart of the Witteberg. The reserve is home to a variety of game species, among them eland, blue and black wildebeest, kudu, red hartebeest, blesbok and Burchell's zebra. Noteworthy among the birds is the rare bald ibis, which breeds in the sandstone cliffs of Bergdeel.

On the first day's hike (12 km; 5 hours) you walk along Stinkhoutkloof, with its white stinkwood trees, and then ascend a ladder to Angel's Corner and God's View, where you are rewarded with wonderful views. About 1 km on, you reach the scenic Bushman Baths and, further along, the trail follows Kudupoort before reaching two of the trail's main attractions: the scenic Bamboeskloof and Mermaid Pool, where you can take a refreshing swim. From here is a 4-km walk to the overnight stop, Bushmen's Cave.

The second day of this route (4.5 km; 1.5 hours) retraces the last section of the previous day's hike to Sporekrans, after which the trail is named, and then takes trailists in an anti-clockwise direction, back to the start.

16. LESOBA HIKING TRAIL
Fouriesburg

> **Trails:** *26 km; 2 days; network from basecamp, with an additional 6-km; 2-hour day hike available.*
> **Permits:** *Mrs A Viviers, 6 Bougainvilla, Orchid Crescent, Gardeniapark, Bloemfontein 9301, tel: (051) 522 8659 or (058) 223 0444.*
> **Maps:** *Sketch map.*
> **Facilities/Activities:** *Huts with beds, kitchen with two-plate stove, fridge, kettle, hot showers, toilets and braai facilities.*

The Lesoba Hiking Trail traverses the mountains between Clarens and Fouriesburg, on the border between South Africa and Lesotho. It takes its name from the Sesotho term for the prominent hole that has been eroded through a mountain dominating the area.

The vegetation is mainly grassland, interspersed with proteas and mountain cabbage trees. Oldwood are also found here, occurring alongside the stream banks. The grasslands are especially eye-catching in spring when watsonias and a variety of other bulbous plants and orchids can be seen in full bloom. The stands of Lombardy poplar found here look beautiful in autumn.

The first day's hike (14 km; 6 hours) ascends to the summit of a mountain, where trailists are rewarded with far-reaching views over the Caledon River and the distant Maluti Mountains in Lesotho, as well as Lesoba. The trail then strikes westwards across the plateau and descends to the Church Door, an overhang with red and black rock paintings. On the return leg the trail passes a site where the fossilised remains of a dinosaur femur bone and shoulder blade can be seen, and the Queen Victoria rock formation, named after its resemblance to the former British monarch.

The second day's hike (12 km; 5 hours) makes its way past Lesoba and then climbs steeply to the top of a mountain, where hikers can once again enjoy stunning views of the surrounding landscape. On the descent, the trail passes another hole in the mountain and then skirts a grassy basin, where blesbok can usually be seen.

A shady day hike (6 km; 2 hours) is also available for those seeking more exercise or who would like to extend their stay.

17. TEPELKOP HIKING TRAIL
Bethlehem

> **Trail:** *17 km; 2 days; network from basecamp.*
> **Permits:** *Discovery Trails, P O Box 149, Paul Roux 9800, tel. and fax: (058) 471 0551, email: retastrydom@worldonline.co.za*
> **Maps:** *Sketch map.*
> **Facilities/Activities:** *Sandstone house with 20 beds and mattresses, fireplace, gas stove, fridge, cutlery, crockery, hot showers and toilets.*

Situated on the southeastern slopes of the Witteberg range, the farm Tepelkop owes its name to a hill resembling a breast (*tepel* is Afrikaans for 'nipple'). The first 3 km of the first day's hike (10 km; 4 hours) is a steep ascent to Tepelkop (2,023 m), from where a contour is followed. After passing through several kloofs with dense riverine bush, the trail circles back to the basecamp.

The second day's hike (7 km; 2.5 hours) winds around Mushroom Mountain, which is the dominant feature of the scenery behind the basecamp. Of interest along the hike is Mapieta's Cave, which served as a refuge for the wife and children of Tepelkop Farm's original owner during the South African War (1899–1902).

18. UITZICHT HIKING TRAIL
Bethlehem

Trails: Various options; 16 to 26 km;
2 days; network from basecamp.
Permits: Discovery Trails, P O Box 149, Paul
Roux 9800, tel. and fax: (058) 471 0551,
email: retastrydom@worldonline.co.za
Maps: Enquire when making reservation.
Facilities/Activities: Basecamp with bunks
and mattresses, kitchen with gas cooker,
pots, pan and kettle, fireplace, hot showers
and toilets; horse-riding; game-drives.

Situated in the Witteberg Mountains 50 km south
of Bethlehem, this trail traverses a private game
reserve stocked with 15 species of game. The landscape is characterised by grasslands, lightly wooded
slopes and magnificent sandstone formations. The
trail's surroundings are especially attractive between
November and February, when the proteas on the
farm Suikerboschrand are in bloom. Along the trail
there are far-reaching views of the Maluti
Mountains in Lesotho. The first day's hike offers
options of 11, 15 and 18 km, while there is a choice
of 5 or 8 km on the second day.

19. ST FORT HIKING TRAIL
Clarens

Trail: 17 km; 2 days; circular.
Permits: Discovery Trails, P O Box 149, Paul
Roux 9800, tel. and fax: (058) 471 0551,
email: retastrydom@worldonline.co.za
Maps: None.
Facilities/Activities: Basecamp: restored
dairy room with bunks and mattresses,
electricity, kitchen with stove, fridge, pots,
pan and kettle, fireplace, hot showers and
toilets. Mike's Cave: mattresses, fireplace,
firewood, pot, kettle and toilet.

Laid out on the farm Letsoana Stad, 5 km south of
Clarens, this trail is overlooked by the 1,824-m-high
peak, The Fort. This easy to moderate route wanders
below imposing sandstone outcrops, along densely
wooded ravines and across grassveld.

The first day's hike (10 km; 4 hours) follows a route
along the base of the sandstone cliffs, past five overhangs. These caves were once the home of the
Bushmen, and some of their walls have been decorated with rock paintings. The route incorporates
four ravines, and there are numerous wooden bridges
and ladders to assist hikers. A swimming hole at the
halfway mark makes an ideal place to stop for tea.

The second day's hike (7 km; 3 hours) affords
hikers splendid views of the high peaks of the area,
including George's Pimple, Wodehouse, Generaalskop and Visierskerf. Further along the 125-step
Step Ladder leads down to the Little Caledon River,
which is crossed by means of a wooden bridge. The
trail follows the course of the river, with an optional
ascent to the Mushroom Rocks before you cross the
river for the second time.

20. BOKPOORT HIKING TRAIL
Clarens

Trail: 14 km; 2 days; circular.
Permits: Jacana Marketing and Reservations,
P O Box 95212, Waterkloof 0145,
tel: (012) 346 3550, fax: 346 2499,
email: info@jacanacollection.co.za
Maps: Trail pamphlet with sketch map.
Facilities/Activities: Basecamp: 24 beds
and mattresses, electricity, fireplace, cast-iron
pots, kettles and ablutions. Mountain camp:
two huts sleeping six people each (bring
own ground sheets or pads), coal stove,
fireplace, cold shower and toilet.

An amphitheatre in the foothills of the Rooiberg
range, west of Golden Gate, provides the setting for
this trail, with spectacular sandstone scenery.

The first day's hike (7 km; 2.5 hours) follows an
easy route, and along the way you will cross nine
streams. Highlights include a chain and tyre ladder
and The Eye, an impressive tunnel carved by the
wind. From the overnight hut there is an optional
4-km loop to the summit of George's Pimple, the

highest peak in the area (2,540 m). Although steep, this option is highly recommended on account of the breathtaking views over Lesotho and the Malutis.

The second day's hike (7 km; 2.5 hours) follows an old horse trail back to the basecamp. About 1 km before the trail ends it crosses a stream with a lovely swimming pool.

21. RHEBOK HIKING TRAIL
Golden Gate Highlands National Park, Clarens

See no 22 (p. 199) for walks.

> **Trail:** 29 km; 2 days; circular.
> **Permits:** South African National Parks, P O Box 787, Pretoria 0001, tel: (012) 428 9111, fax: 343 0905, email: reservations@parks-sa.co.za
> **Maps:** Trail pamphlet with sketch map.
> **Facilities/Activities:** On the trail: overnight hut with bunk beds and mattresses, basic kitchen utensils, fireplace, hot shower and toilet. Glen Reenen Restcamp: semi-equipped stone rondavels with shower; campsites with hot-water ablutions, scullery and braai places; shop. Brandwag Restcamp: single and double rooms with en-suite facilities, telephone and television; chalets with bedroom, living room, semi-equipped kitchen, braai places and bathroom; short self-drive game-drives; guided night-drives; guided walks to Cathedral Cave; vulture hide.

Laid out in the foothills of the Malutis, the Rhebok Hiking Trail traverses the Golden Gate Highlands National Park. The trail winds through open grassland, passing impressive sandstone formations, which are especially attractive in the late afternoon when they are transformed from pink and yellow to a glowing golden colour.

Since it was proclaimed in 1962, the Golden Gate Highlands National Park has nearly doubled in size from its original 4,792 ha. It is renowned for its spectacular sandstone formations, among them the Golden Gate (after which the park is named), the Sentinel or Brandwag, the imposing Mushroom Rocks and Cathedral Cave. There are also numerous *holkranse* or overhangs along the base of the Clarens Sandstone Formation.

The park has one of the largest herds of black wildebeest in the country. Other game species typical of the highlands include eland, blesbok, Burchell's zebra, mountain reedbuck and grey rhebok, and oribi and springbok also occur here.

To date some 160 bird species have been identified, among them the black eagle and the bald ibis, which breeds in the park, while the rare bearded vulture is sometimes seen soaring overhead. Other species you may tick include orange-throated longclaw, grey-wing francolin, sentinel rock thrush and orange-breasted rockjumper.

When you are walking through flat or gently sloping grasslands, keep an eye out for the tunnels of the giant girdled lizard, also known as the sungazer because of its habit of staring into the sun for hours. The park has a surprising diversity of butterflies, and among the 78 species recorded are several endemic and rare species.

The vegetation is characterised by dense montane sour grasslands and to date some 65 grass and over 200 flowering plant species have been identified. Trees and shrubs are scarce in the grasslands and are dominated by oldwood, while woody vegetation is restricted to the Little Caledon River Valley, sheltered ravines and sandstone crevices.

The first day's hike (16 km; 7 hours) ascends to the well-known Sentinel, overlooking the Little Caledon River Valley. It then climbs steadily up the slopes of Wodehouse Peak before winding to Boskloof (not to be confused with Boskloof in the cliffs above Glen Reenen). From Tweelingskop the trail drops down to Wilgenhof, and then follows an easy route to the overnight hut in Oudehoutskloof.

On day two's hike (13 km; 6 hours) the trail ascends along the Ribbokspruit, passing interesting rock crevices and an impressive waterfall. You gain about 700 m in altitude to the 2,732-m-high summit of Generaalskop, the park's highest point. The trail then descends along a spur, which offers dramatic views over the Little Caledon River Valley and the Mushroom Rocks. The slopes attract several game species, such as black wildebeest, blesbok and Burchell's zebra. From Langtoon Dam it is a short walk past a natural rockslide and pool to the Glen Reenen Restcamp.

22. GOLDEN GATE HIGHLANDS NATIONAL PARK
Clarens

See no 21 (p. 198) for hiking trail.

Trails: 4 trails; 2 to 7 km; 1 to 2.5 hours; circular, out-and-return.
Permits: Entrance fee. No permit required for walks. Reservations for guided walks to Cathedral Cave can be made at the reception office of the Glen Reenen Restcamp.
Maps: Sketch map.
Facilities/Activities: Glen Reenen Restcamp: semi-equipped stone rondavels with shower; campsites with hot-water ablutions, scullery and braai places; shop. Brandwag Restcamp: single and double rooms with en-suite facilities, telephone and television; chalets with bedroom, living room, semi-equipped kitchen, braai places and bathroom; short self-drive game-drives; guided night-drives; guided walks to Cathedral Cave; vulture hide.

Glen Reenen Restcamp

1. Wodehouse Kop is reached by following the path to the top of Brandwag. From here you follow the Rhebok Hiking Trail across a plateau before it climbs steeply up a grassy slope. Just beyond a band of dolerite the route splits off to the right, following a faint footpath to the 2,438-m-high Wodehouse Kop. **4 km; 2 hours; out-and-return.**

2. Golden Gate Highlights From Glen Reenen Restcamp you can undertake several short walks under an hour to well-known features such as Echo Ravine, Boskloof, the Brandwag (Sentinel) and Mushroom Rocks, or do a longer hike combining all of these.

From the restcamp take the footbridge over the Little Caledon River and climb to the base of the sandstone cliffs and Echo Ravine, a deep gorge, which can be explored. Backtrack to the base of the split to Echo Ravine, turn right and continue to a right-hand fork, which leads deep into the wooded

Boskloof. Once again you need to backtrack to the split (as the trail to Boskloof eventually peters out) where you turn right, continuing through boulders to the base of Brandwag. A chain ladder has been provided to help you negotiate the last 20 m of the cliffs. From the top of Brandwag there are fine views over the Little Caledon River and the park surroundings. You now have to backtrack to the first split to Echo Gorge, from where the trail hugs the base of the sandstone cliffs beneath the Mushroom Rocks until it eventually joins the park road. From here you can either backtrack, or follow the road back to the restcamp. **5 km; 2.5 hours; circular or out-and-return.**

3. Cathedral Cave is a guided walk that should not be missed, but is only conducted outside the June to September breeding season of the bald ibis. The cave is one of the most spectacular examples of sandstone weathering in South Africa. From a narrow opening in the roof at the end of the cave a stream plunges some 30 m to the floor, and below the lip of the waterfall the ceiling has been weathered into a magnificent dome, hence the name. Walks are conducted as part of the park's holiday programme but can also be arranged on request. Reservations can be made at the reception office of the Glen Reenen Restcamp. **Approximately 7 km; 2.5 hours; out-and-return.**

Brandwag Restcamp

Brandwag, the park's main restcamp, nestles below an imposing sandstone outcrop, which provides the setting for one of the most interesting walks in the park.

4. Holkrans From the restcamp the trail ascends steeply to the base of the sandstone cliffs behind the restcamp. The trail now hugs the base of the cliffs, leading to some spectacular caves, eroded into the sandstone over countless aeons. Wooden steps provide access to the caves, which are a delight to photographers as the rounded entrances provide perfect frames for the vistas across the valley. Where the trail eventually breaks away from the cliffs, a long wooden ladder provides access to a valley, which you follow back to the restcamp. **2 km; 1 hour; circular.**

23. SENTINEL TRAIL AND MONT-AUX-SOURCES
Phuthaditjhaba

Trails: 12 km; 2 days; out-and-return, with an optional ascent of Mont-aux-Sources available.
Permits: Entrance fee. No permit required for trail.
Maps: The area is covered by map one in the Drakensberg Recreational Series: Drakensberg North – Mont-aux-Sources to Cathedral Peak.
Facilities/Activities: Overnight hut with bunks and mattresses for 12 people, cold shower and toilet at parking area at the end of the Mountain Road. No facilities on Escarpment.
Pertinent information: Weather conditions on the Escarpment can change very rapidly. Keep an eye out for possible weather changes, especially mist, which can set in with little warning. In winter, you must pack warm clothing, as a snowfall is always a possibility, and a tent must be carried if you plan to spend a night on the summit.

Starting at the car park at the end of the Mountain Road, the path zigzags uphill and you pass the Witches, from where there are magnificent views of Eastern Buttress (3,047 m) and the Devil's Tooth (3,019 m). You will reach the Contour Path at the foot of the Sentinel after gaining some 300 m in altitude, and you then follow it below Western Buttress (3,121 m).

At Kloof Gully there is a steep, rocky route that leads to Beacon Buttress (2,899 m) on the Escarpment, providing an alternative route for those wishing to avoid the chain ladders about 1 km on. However, in winter, Kloof Gully is often blocked by snow and ice. In the early days this gully was the usual way to the top and climbers often slept in Sentinel Cave, a short way beyond the gully.

Two chain ladders, anchored by the then Natal Section of the Mountain Club of South Africa in 1930, provide access to the Escarpment. The first ladder scales near vertical cliffs for about 17 m and has approximately 50 rungs, while the second ladder has approximately 45 rungs over about 13 m.

From the top of the ladders it is roughly 1.5 km to the Escarpment edge, with the Tugela River crossed en route. From the precipitous edge there are awesome views over the Royal Natal National Park, the Tugela Falls, Eastern Buttress, the Devil's Tooth and the Devil's Toothpick.

On the Escarpment you can sleep in Crow's Nest Cave, situated about 1 km southwest of the ruins of the old Natal Mountain Club hut. There are several peaks on the Escarpment that can be reached from the summit plateau, among them Mount Amery, Western Buttress and Mont-aux-Sources.

Mont-aux-Sources (3,282 m), the highest point of the Drakensberg Amphitheatre, is situated about 5 km southwest of the ruin. It is reached by following the Tugela River upstream to its source and then to the beacon that marks the boundary between Lesotho, the Free State and KwaZulu-Natal.

The summit was first ascended by two French missionaries, Thomas Arbousset and François Dumas, while they were exploring the highlands of Lesotho in 1830. Realising the importance of the peak as the source of five major rivers, they named it the 'Mountain of Sources'. The Bilanjil and the Tugela rivers flow eastwards into KwaZulu-Natal, while the Western and Eastern Khebedu form the upper source of the Gariep (Orange) River. The Elands River, which flows into the Free State, can be seen tumbling over a precipice near the chain ladders.

24. WOLHUTERSKOP HIKING TRAIL
Bethlehem

Trail: 19 km; 2 days; circular.
Permits: Jacana Marketing and Reservations, P O Box 95212, Waterkloof 0145, tel: (012) 346 3550, fax: 346 2499, email: info@jacanacollection.co.za
Maps: Sketch map.
Facilities/Activities: Farmhouse at start: equipped with beds and mattresses,

electricity, two-plate stove, fridge, pots, pans, cast-iron pot, hot-water shower and toilet. Overnight hut: beds, bunks, mattresses, kitchen with gas cooker, pots, pans, cast-iron pot, cutlery, crockery, fireplace, hot shower and toilets.

This trail in the 1,200-ha Wolhuterskop Nature Reserve, 2 km south of Bethlehem, provides hikers with an opportunity to explore the scenic beauty of the reserve on foot. An added attraction is the possibility of seeing game such as springbok, blesbok, gemsbok, impala and common duiker.

The first day's hike (12 km; 5 hours) ascends towards Wolhuterskop with extensive views of the reserve, the surrounding farms and, further afield, the Malutis. Beyond Barbersbaai Dam the route winds through interesting sandstone formations to the overnight hut, situated close to a dam, which attracts a variety of waterbirds and game.

The second day's hike (7 km; 2.5 hours) leads to the Gerrands viewpoint and, after following a jeep track for a short distance, drops down to Loch Athlone. Whilst descending, keep an eye out for the giant girdled lizards, also known as ouvolk or sungazers, inhabiting the grassy slopes.

25. BALD IBIS HIKING TRAIL
Swinburne

Trail: 26.7 km; 2 days; network from basecamp.
Permits: Jacana Marketing and Reservations, P O Box 95212, Waterkloof 0145, tel: (012) 346 3550, fax: 346 2499, email: info@jacanacollection.co.za
Maps: Trail brochure with map.
Facilities/Activities: Basecamp: barn with beds, mattresses, kitchen with pots, kettles, pans, two-plate gas cooker, covered dining area, lapa with braai facilities, hot showers and toilets. Overnight cave: bed platforms (supply own mattresses), water (can be heated for a shower), braai grid and toilet.

The Bald Ibis Hiking Trail in the Harrismith and Van Reenen's Pass area is dominated by one of the best-known landmarks in the northeastern Free State, Rensburgkoppie.

As well as bald ibis and Cape vulture, birders may tick black and crowned eagles. Also keep an eye out for Abdim's stork and typical grassland species such as orange-throated longclaw and rufous-naped lark.

Soon after the start of the first day's hike (17.7 km; 7 hours) the trail reaches a natural hide amongst the boulders overlooking a 'vulture restaurant' (feeding station). After passing through a delightful patch of indigenous forest, the trail follows a steep zigzag path up the mountain. Cathedral Cave, a magnificent overhang with a roof resembling that of a Gothic Cathedral, is reached 3.2 km from the start. Other highlights include the Miracle Fountain, imposing sandstone formations, clumps of indigenous forest and a cave with well-preserved rock paintings. Just over 12.5 km from the start, a detour ascends steeply to the 2,205-m-high summit of Rensburgkoppie, gaining some 220 m in altitude over 400 m. Continuing through forests of oldwood and yellowwood, the trail crosses the Bald Ibis Flats, where this rare bird species is frequently seen. A gentle descent is followed by a climb up a hill, and the trail then follows an easy gradient on the hillside past the Mushroom Rock to the overnight cave.

Shortly after setting off on day two's hike (9 km; 4 hours), you reach the sheer Swallow Cliffs, where caution must be exercised, especially in misty conditions. The trail then follows an undulating course, through grassland dotted with proteas and oldwood trees, to the Lost Valley viewpoint and past impressive sandstone boulders. A farm dam, about 7 km from the start, provides an ideal chance to cool off during the summer months. The remaining 2 km is an easy walk along a contour, followed by a gentle descent.

26. SEDIBA HIKING TRAIL
Memel

Trail: 16.5 km; 2 days; network from basecamp.
Permits: Discovery Trails, P O Box 149, Paul Roux 9800, tel. and fax: (058) 471 0551,

email: retastrydom@worldonline.co.za
Maps: *Sketch map.*
Facilities/Activities: *Basecamp with
bunks, mattresses, kitchen with gas fridge,
hot-plate, pots, pan, kettle, hot showers
and lapa with braai facilities; kiosk with
braai packs and farm produce.*
Pertinent information: *Hikers must bring
their own wood or charcoal.*

This trail is situated in the northeastern Free State near Memel, and the basecamp is very scenic, situated close to a magnificent waterfall. The Sotho word *sediba* means 'fountain water', a reference to the abundance of water in the area. With 15 Red Data bird species occurring in the area and a checklist of some 230 species, the trail offers good birding opportunities. Among the noteworthy birds recorded here are crowned, blue and wattled cranes, as well as Rudd's and Botha's larks.

Day one's hike (10.5 km; 4 hours) leads through Dassie Skeur, a deep crevice carved through the sandstone rock, and then continues to Khwela Kloof with its cascades. Further along you reach Ipikiniki, where the inviting pools offer an ideal lunch stop and a refreshing dip. Before the end of the day's hike the trail meanders past Fairy Falls and then continues to the Alpha and Omega falls. The second day's hike is a short, but delightful circuit (6 km; 2.5 hours).

27. LANGBERG HIKING TRAIL
Vrede

Trail: *22 km; 2 days; network
from basecamp.*
Permits: *Jacana Marketing and Reservations,
P O Box 95212, Waterkloof 0145,
tel: (012) 346 3550, fax: 346 2499,
email: info@jacanacollection.co.za*
Maps: *Sketch map.*
Facilities/Activities: *Overnight hut: double-
storey building with bunks, mattresses,
lounge, dining area, electricity, fridge, cooking utensils, fireplace and ablutions; mountain biking; rock climbing, abseiling; caving.*

This trail on Koefontein Farm traverses the slopes of the Langberg Mountains and the easy terrain makes it an ideal introduction for novice hikers. The first day's trail (14 km; 6 hours) alternates between winding above and below the sandstone cliffs. Highlights of the first day include the Waenhuis (Coach House), an enormous cave where women and children hid during the South African War (1899–1902), and a second cave with numerous passages.

The second day's hike (8 km; 3 hours) makes its way along an easy route across the lower slopes of the mountain. The trail partly follows the course of the Spruitsonderdrif, with its delightful natural pool, where you can enjoy a swim to cool off. There are also good birding opportunities.

28. WAG-'N-BIETJIE HIKING TRAIL
Bothaville

Trail: *15 km; 2 days; network
from basecamp.*
Permits: *Discovery Trails,
P O Box 149, Paul Roux 9800,
tel. and fax: (058) 471 0551,
email: retastrydom@worldonline.co.za*
Maps: *Enquire when making reservation.*
Facilities/Activities: *Basecamp with beds,
mattresses, kitchen with fridge, hot plate,
pots, pan, electric kettle, braai facilities,
hot showers and toilet.*

This trail is laid out on a farm in the northwestern Free State, north of Bothaville, and is named after the buffalo-thorn, which is known in Afrikaans as the blinkblaarwag-'n-bietjie. Starting at the basecamp, situated a mere 300 m from the river, both legs of the trail (11 km on day one and 4 km on day two) wind mainly through lush riverine forests, which are characterised by buffalo-thorn, karee tree and wild raisin bush. Along the course of the hike there are delightful resting spots and glimpses of the river. The open water and riverine forest provide good opportunities for birding enthusiasts. Among the birds that you should look out for are various kingfisher, heron and duck species.

Salpeterkrans, on the Brandwater trail, is a place of pilgrimage for many women. Hikers here may meet worshippers bringing offerings to the ancestral spirits in the hope of increasing their fertility.

Mpumalanga & Limpopo Province

Situated in the northeastern and northern part of South Africa, Mpumalanga and Limpopo Province are renowned for their diverse landscapes, magnificent scenery and numerous other natural attractions. Mpumalanga shares a border with Swaziland to the southeast, while the Lebombo Mountains form a natural boundary with Mozambique to the east. Limpopo Province also borders on two countries; the Limpopo River forms the northern border with Zimbabwe, and to the west the province borders on Botswana.

There are numerous opportunities for outdoor enthusiasts to explore natural attractions of these two provinces. These range from short, easy interpretative walks and overnight hiking trails to guided walks in the Kruger National Park and the Wolkberg wilderness where backpackers can blaze their own trails.

Most of Mpumalanga lies on the Highveld, an upland region ranging in altitude from 900 m in the west to 2,277 m at the top of Mount Anderson in the Mpumalanga Drakensberg. The vegetation of the Highveld is characterised by grassland, ranging from almost pure grassveld with few trees and shrubs, to grassveld interspersed with patches of woodland in the valleys and against hill slopes. Large areas that were formerly grassland are now planted with maize, wheat, sorghum and sunflowers, and additional vast stretches have been planted under pine and eucalyptus plantations. In addition, little remains of the large herds of game that once roamed the Highveld plains.

The Mpumalanga Drakensberg Escarpment is an area of scenic grandeur, featuring many waterfalls and well-known attractions such as the Blyde River Canyon, Bourke's Luck and God's Window. In the 1880s fortune seekers flocked to the area in search of gold, and the historic gold-mining towns of Pilgrim's Rest and Kaapschehoop serve as reminders of this era.

The vegetation of the Escarpment is characterised by mountain grassland, punctuated by rocky outcrops, weathered into fascinating shapes. In spring a variety of flowering plants provides a touch of colour to the grasslands.

Except for the indigenous forests of Mount Sheba only small patches of montane forests are found, in sheltered kloofs and ravines, on the Mpumalanga Escarpment. Typical species include Outeniqua and real yellowwood, lemonwood, Cape beech, white stinkwood and forest bushwillow.

Large mammals are neither abundant nor spectacular on the Escarpment. Antelope occurring naturally include grey rhebok, mountain reedbuck, klipspringer, common duiker, oribi and bushbuck. Also to be found are all five South African primates (baboon, vervet monkey, samango monkey, thick-tailed bushbaby and lesser bushbaby), bushpig, as well as a variety of small carnivores and rodents.

The montane grasslands near Graskop and Kaapschehoop are an important habitat of the endangered blue swallow, and southeastern Mpumalanga is home to several grassland specials such as Botha's and Rudd's lark, yellow-breasted pipit and crowned crane, as well as the largest bald ibis breeding colonies in the world. Other grassland species found here include Cape rock thrush, Swainson's francolin, Gurney's sugarbird, striped flufftail and buff-streaked chat. Among the forest species are crowned eagle, Knysna lourie, paradise flycatcher, chorister robin, sombre bulbul and olive woodpecker.

Minimum temperatures of below freezing point are not uncommon in winter, while days are cool. Frost can occur from May to September, and summer temperatures are moderate. Most of the Highveld's rainfall is recorded between November and March and is usually accompanied by violent mid-afternoon thunder storms and lightning. Annual rainfall varies from less than 400 mm in the west to over 2,600 mm at God's Window, where the moisture-laden easterly winds are forced into an updraught, causing the formation of heavy mist and rain. Mist is especially common between December and March.

The Escarpment falls away to the Lowveld, a landscape of low-lying plains with altitudes ranging from 150 m to 600 m above sea level. These dry woodlands contain a wealth of trees, with over 300 species recorded in the Kruger National Park alone. Typical species include mopane, bushwillow, leadwood, umbrella and knob thorns, apple-leaf, marula, Lowveld and silver cluster-leaf, baobab and fever trees.

Often regarded as 'the essential Africa', the Lowveld is synonymous with large herds of game and the Big Five (elephant, rhino, buffalo, lion and leopard). Stretching southwards from the Limpopo River for 350 km to the Crocodile River is the world-renowned Kruger National Park. This wildlife sanctuary of nearly 2 million ha is home to some 147 mammal species, 114 different reptile species and over 500 bird species.

The Lowveld enjoys a subtropical climate. Winter days are mild, but in mid-winter minimum temperatures can drop to about 5 °C. During mid-summer maximum temperatures can be unbearably hot, reaching up to 35 °C in January. Rainfall varies between 350 and 600 mm per year, the months between November and February being the wettest. Heavy thunderstorms and lightning are common during this period.

Limpopo Province is a region of plains and hills, punctuated by the Soutpansberg in the north, the Waterberg in the west and the northern Drakensberg Escarpment in the east. The vegetation of the Escarpment is typically montane grasslands with small patches of indigenous forest in sheltered kloofs. Grootbosch near Magoebaskloof and the Wonderwoud in the Wolkberg wilderness area are the only two places where extensive patches of indigenous forests have survived.

Except for the Escarpment and the Lowveld, the vegetation over the rest of Limpopo Province consists of bushveld – a landscape of mixed trees and shrubs lower than 10 m and generally with their canopies touching. It is composed of, amongst others, a variety of bushwillow and euphorbia tree species, marula, red syringa, buffalo-thorn and vast stands of mopane.

On many farms in Limpopo Province cattle farming has been phased out in favour of game ranching, and the once prolific herds of game have begun to re-establish themselves. The Waterberg is a stronghold of the rare roan, while sable, kudu, reedbuck and impala are among the antelope species found here.

Birdlife is prolific and ranges from woodland species such as white-throated and Kalahari robins, yellow-billed hornbill, barred warbler and Burchell's glossy starling, to the exceptionally rich diversity of birds attracted to the Nylsvley wetlands. One of South Africa's top birding hotspots, Nylsvley has a bird checklist of 426 species, including breeding populations of several rare and threatened species. On occasion the wetlands attract up to 80,000 birds at a time. The cliffs of the Waterberg are home to the largest breeding colony of the Cape vulture in the world.

Winter temperatures in the bushveld are generally quite mild, but in mid-summer they often exceed 40 °C, especially in the low-lying areas. Mpumalanga and Limpopo Province lie within the summer-rainfall region.

PERTINENT INFORMATION

• Minimum temperatures on the Highveld and at high altitudes on the Escarpment can be extremely low, especially in winter, so hikers must pack sufficient warm clothing and a good sleeping bag.

• Mist is common along the Escarpment between September and April. If it is very thick you should wait until it has lifted (usually around mid-morning) or you could easily miss trail markers and get lost.

• Heavy thunderstorms occur in both Mpumalanga and Limpopo Province during summer, and are often accompanied by lightning. Plan to reach the overnight stop by mid-afternoon to avoid being caught in a thunderstorm or trapped by a river in flood.

• Always be aware of the risk of fire when walking through grassland. Smokers should be very cautious and fires must be made only where permitted.

• Ticks can be a problem in summer. It is advisable to take precautions, such as treating your socks with a tick repellent.

• Malaria is endemic in the Lowveld, while most of the rest of Mpumalanga and Limpopo Province fall within an epidemic malaria area. Consult a doctor about anti-malaria medication before you set off for the area.

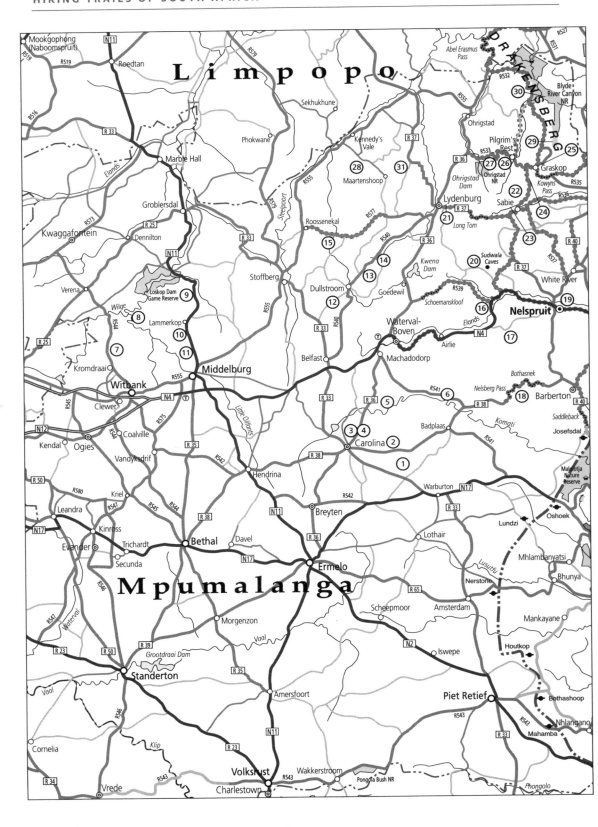

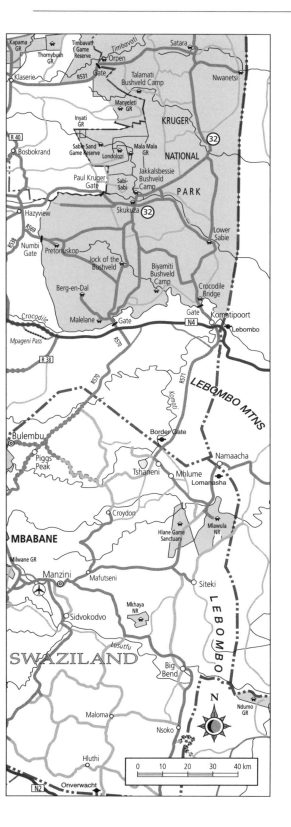

Continued on pp. 208–209

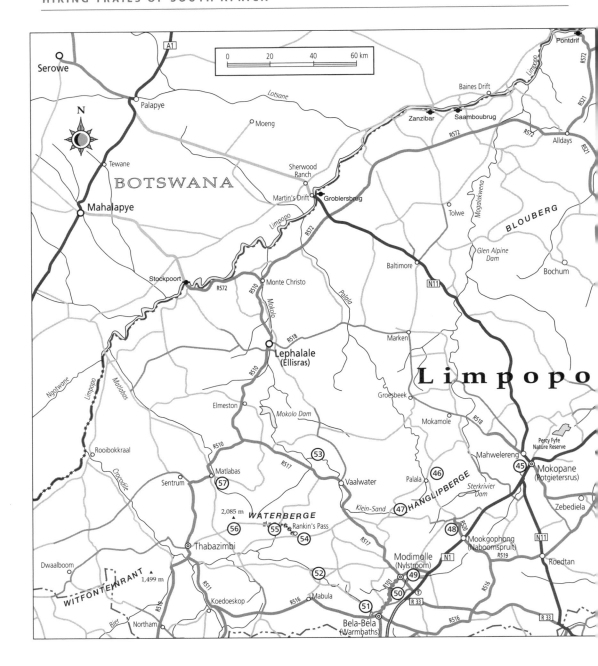

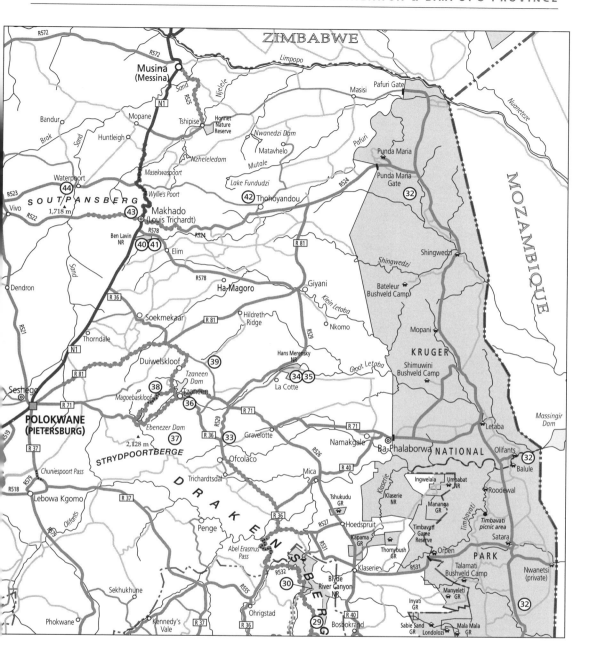

1. THE BROOK/MONDI HIKING TRAILS
Warburton

Trails: 3 trails; 5 to 11 km; 2.5 to 5 hours; network from basecamp.
Permits: Jacana Marketing and Reservations, P O Box 95212, Waterkloof 0145, tel: (012) 346 3550, fax: 346 2499, email: info@jacanacollection.co.za
Maps: Trail pamphlet with map.
Facilities/Activities: Muzentu Hut: restored farmhouse with beds, mattresses, kitchen with gas stoves, fridge, pots, pans, kettles, braai facilities, hot showers and toilets; trout-angling.

This trail traverses an area of southeastern Mpumalanga where the Highveld gives way to valleys that form the start of several eastward-flowing rivers. The numerous cascades and streams here inspired one of the original Scottish settlers, in what was then known as the New Scotland Development, to name his farm The Brook. Rising on the Highveld, the numerous streams tumble down the mountain slopes to the northern valley of the Komati Basin and eventually combine to form the Muzentu Stream.

Typical Highveld grassland, with a rich diversity of flowering plants such as dieramas, watsonias and six species of aloe, is characteristic in this area. Among the larger mammals to be seen are blesbok, Burchell's zebra and mountain reedbuck, and some 80 different bird species have been recorded here.

The trail network consists of a full-day walk of 11 km, which traverses the slopes of the Muzentu Stream, and two half-day routes of 5 km and 5.5 km respectively.

1. Moon Rock Trail descends to cross a stream and then wanders up to the rock formation to which it owes its name. From here the trail drops down to cross Daisy Creek, where it follows a contour to another stream. Further along it links up with a road, which you follow back to the start. **5 km; 2.5 hours; circular.**

3. Waterfall Trail From the basecamp the trail climbs steadily up the western slopes above the Muzentu Stream, gaining some 200 m in altitude.

It then zigzags down to the river, where a pool provides an ideal lunch spot. After lunch the trail winds past a magnificent waterfall and then ascends steeply up the eastern slopes of the valley. The trail then traverses the top of the valley before winding around Aalwynspruit and Grasklokkies Klippe back to the start. **11 km; 5 hours; circular.**

2. Boulder Canyon Trail is a lovely half-day walk that meanders down into the Muzentu Valley, passing enormous rocks, and then makes its way along a boulder-strewn canyon before returning to the start. **5.5 km; 3 hours; circular.**

2. EL DORIAN HIKING TRAIL
Carolina

Trail: 27 km; 2 days; circular.
Permits: Anvie Ventures, P O Box 60035, Pierre van Ryneveld 0045, tel. and fax: (012) 662 1140.
Maps: Sketch map.
Facilities/Activities: Basecamp: house with mattresses, lounge with fireplace, kitchen with fridge, pots, pans, braai area, hot showers and toilets. Overnight camp: house with bunks and mattresses, covered braai area with pots, pans, lanterns, showers and toilets.
Pertinent information: Smoking is not permitted on the trail. Fires allowed only at demarcated places.

This trail traverses a 20,000-ha mountainous area, 22 km east of Carolina, featuring kloofs with indigenous forests, plantations, fountains and panoramic views. The Buffelspruit, which drains the area, is crossed several times over the course of the trail.

On day one (15 km; 6 hours) the trail initially goes eastwards and then passes above the Little Buffelspruit to a delightful waterfall, where you can stop for lunch. The trail crosses the river and ascends to a plateau, and then re-crosses the Buffelspruit, before reaching the overnight hut. About 1 km after setting off on the second day's hike (12 km; 5 hours) the trail reaches the Buffelspoort Dam, from where it climbs to the highest point on the trail. Further along it reaches another dam, where hikers can cool off before tackling the last section of the trail back to the start.

3. SUIKERBOSCHFONTEIN HIKING TRAIL
Carolina

Trail: *19.5 km; 2 days; circular.*
Permits: *Jacana Marketing and Reservations, P O Box 95212, Waterkloof 0145, tel: (012) 346 3550, fax: 346 2499, email: info@jacanacollection.co.za*
Maps: *Trail pamphlet with map.*
Facilities/Activities: *Rooikrans Camp: huts with beds, mattresses, kitchen with kettle, pots, pans, braai facilities, hot showers and toilets. Oom Japie's House: house with beds, mattresses, kitchen with kettle, pots, pans, braai facilities, hot showers and toilets.*

Situated on the Escarpment, 20 km northeast of Carolina, the Suikerboschfontein Hiking Trail traverses grassland interspersed with patches of common sugarbush, also known as the Highveld sugarbush. Patches of indigenous forest, with yellowwoods, occur in sheltered kloofs, while common tree ferns are conspicuous along stream banks. Of historical interest are the ruins of shrines, temples and other structures built by Dravidian (Indian) gold-seekers who prospected and traded gold with the Khoikhoi, and later the Nguni people, during the first millennium and early second millennium.

From Oom Japie's House the first day's hike (9.3 km; 4 hours) descends steadily to the Yellowwood Cliffs and then passes some good examples of rock art. Further on you will reach some ruins, dating back to the era of the Dravidian gold-seekers, and the route then continues to Dassiekrans, where more ruins can be viewed. After following a contour the trail winds around a kloof and comes to the Dying Sun Chariot Temple, a Dravidian temple with an upright stone aligned with the summit of Doornkop, where the 'dying sun' sets at about 16:50 on 21 June, the winter solstice. The remaining 2 km to Rooikrans Camp is steadily uphill.

The second day's hike (10.2 km; 4 hours) from Rooikrans Camp passes through narrow gorges and then leads to a shrine, the starting point of the way to the Dying Sun Chariot Temple. Grootkloof and the 23-m-high Mooifontein Waterfall are reached just over 2 km from the start. From here the trail follows a contour to S-bend Kloof and then leads along a stream, with beautiful waterfalls and pools. The trail makes its way through Gladdekloof, which makes a good lunch stop. After negotiating Gladdekloof (a rope assists hikers up the wet cliffs) you follow the trail across Suikerbosrand, with its profusion of common sugarbushes, and then head for the Rooirant. The descent into Oom Japie's Gorge, with its magnificent tree ferns, is followed by a steady climb to Oom Japie's House.

4. STRIKDAS HIKING TRAIL AND HEBRON TRAILS
Carolina

Trails: *Overnight trail; 19 km; 2 days; circular. 4 day walks; 4 to 12 km; 2 to 6 hours; circular and open-ended.*
Permits: *Anvie Ventures, P O Box 60035, Pierre van Ryneveld 0045, tel. and fax: (012) 662 1140.*
Maps: *Sketch map.*
Facilities/Activities: *Basecamp: stone cottage and hut with bunks and mattresses, braai place with pots, pans, kettle, firewood, hot showers and toilets. Overnight camp: log cabin and stone hut with mattresses, braai areas, pots, pans, kettle, hot shower and toilet.*

1. Strikdas Hiking Trail follows the Hebron and Bosvark trails to reach the overnight camp 11 km (5 hours) after setting off. (Hikers can leave their backpacks here while they go on the 12-km Kiepersol Route (see p. 212), named after the Afrikaans term for the mountain cabbage tree.) Highlights along the trail include Die Venster, a viewpoint with panoramic vistas over the Komati Valley, and the ruins of structures, built by Indian gold-diggers, dating back to the 6th century BC.

Further along the trail follows the course of a stream, with inviting pools and exciting rapids. The second day's hike (8 km; 3 hours) initially follows the course of a stream along a kloof and then joins the return leg of the Waterfall Route. **19 km; 2 days; circular.**

2. Hebron Trail Network consists of four trails: **Bosvark** (4 km; 2 hours; open-ended), **Hebron** (7 km; 3.5 hours; open-ended), **Kiepersol** (12 km; 6 hours; circular) and the **Waterfall Route** (7.5 km; 4 hours; circular). As the name suggests, the Waterfall Route features delightful waterfalls and swimming pools, and a quartz mushroom-shaped rock formation is another highlight. **4 to 12 km; 2 to 6 hours; circular and open-ended.**

5. KRANSKLOOF HIKING TRAIL
Carolina

Trails: 1 hiking trail; 18.5 km; 2 days; circular. 4 day walks; 3.5 to 5 km; 2 to 3 hours; circular and out-and-return.
Permits: Jacana Marketing and Reservations, P O Box 95212, Waterkloof 0145, tel: (012) 346 3550, fax: 346 2499, email: info@jacanacollection.co.za
Maps: Trail pamphlet with map.
Facilities/Activities: Kranskloof: stone huts with bunks and mattresses, kitchen with two-plate gas stove, pots, pans, braai facilities, hot showers and toilets. Suikerkrans: timber huts with the same amenities as Kranskloof.

1. Kranskloof Hiking Trail The first day (10 km; 4 hours) of this trail, also known as the Grey Rhebok Route, steadily ascends along the edge of a kloof, passing through a stand of milkplum trees. On reaching a waterfall, which plunges over a cliff edge, the trail climbs through interesting rock formations and grassveld before descending gently to the overnight stop, Suikerkrans.

Day two's hike (8.5 km; 3 hours), the Oribi Route, climbs out of Kleinklofie, with its huge tree ferns, to the plateau and then ascends gently to the waterfall, where the outward route of the first

day's hike is reached. From here you retrace your tracks back to the start. **18.5 km; 2 days; circular.**

2. Ruins Day Walk can also be done here. **3.5 km; 2 hours; circular.**

3. Cliff Route follows the outward route of the overnight trail to the waterfall, from where you can retrace your steps. **4.5 km; 2 hours; out-and-return.**

4. Gully Route can be combined with the Cliff Walk by descending into the valley from the waterfall. The descent is steep, and you lose some 100 m in altitude on your way down to the river, with its waterchute and lovely pools. **5 km; 3 hours; circular.**

6. BERMANZI HIKING TRAIL
Machadodorp

Trails: 2 trails; 8 and 12 km; 4 and 6 hours; circular.
Permits: Anvie Ventures, P O Box 60035, Pierre van Ryneveld 0045, tel. and fax: (012) 662 1140.
Maps: Sketch map.
Facilities/Activities: Luxury thatched stone house: three bedrooms, bathroom, kitchen with gas stove and fridge, solar lighting, electricity, lounge with fireplace, and braai area. Hikers' huts with bunk beds, mattresses, pots, pan, kettle, small charcoal stove, braai facilities, hot showers and toilets.

The mountains between Machadodorp, Waterval Boven and Badplaas provide the setting for this trail, southeast of Machadodorp.

1. Route 1, also known as the Main Trail, initially follows an old wagon road made by a family who found safety in these valleys during the South African War (1899–1902). After passing through a natural rock crevice, Houtkapperskeur, the route descends to the base of the cliffs overlooking the Komati Valley. It then joins the old wagon road and from here continues steeply down through indigenous bush to the

Bushbuck Trail and the Bankspruit. The trail now ascends sharply to the summit of Rooikrans and then drops down to a delightful pool and rapids. Further along you reach the Uitkoms Waterfall, reputedly the second highest in Mpumalanga, and then climb steadily back to a plateau. The return leg follows the edge of the plateau back to the base-camp. **12 km; 6 hours; circular.**

2. Route 2 consists of a combination of several relatively short secondary trails, such as the **Boerperd, Rooikat, Tarentaal, Tierboskat, Bosvark** and **Duiker** routes. **8 km; 4 hours; circular.**

7. BAKOONDKRANS HIKING TRAIL
Witbank

Trail: 21 km; 2 days; circular.
Permits: Anvie Ventures, P O Box 60035, Pierre van Ryneveld 0045, tel. and fax: (012) 662 1140.
Maps: Trail indicated on photocopy of 1:50,000 topographical map.
Facilities/Activities: Koeistalle Basecamp: renovated cattle shed with bunks, mattresses, braai facilities, pots, pans, kettle and lanterns, shower and toilet. Overnight hut: 'cave' hut with beds, mattresses, braai area with pots, pans, lanterns, shower and toilet.

Traversing the Gouwsberg, 30 km north of Witbank, this delightful trail features cycads (*Encephalartos*), a natural rock bridge, caves and magnificent rock formations.

From the Koeistalle Basecamp the first day's trail (12 km; 6 hours) leads through grassveld to Ras-se-Kloof and meanders through cycads to the top of the mountain, from where there are fine views of the Olifants River. The trail descends along a kloof to the Klipspruit, with its natural rock bridge, pools, rapids and a 3-m-high waterfall, the perfect place for a lunch stop. The trail then ascends to the Mushroom Rocks and Salpeterkrans, and passes a cave that was once the home of Iron Age people. It finally winds down to Bakoondkrans along the Olifants River. The second day's hike

(9 km; 4 hours) follows the Olifants River and continues along Diepkloof, a lush wooded area with common tree ferns. The final 1 km of the trail is through grassland.

8. OLIFANTS GORGE TRAILS
Witbank

Trails: 3 trails; 23 to 27 km; 2 days; circular, which can be combined into longer hikes.
Permits: Anvie Ventures, P O Box 60035, Pierre van Ryneveld 0045, tel. and fax: (012) 662 1140.
Maps: Sketch map.
Facilities/Activities: Kingdom Basecamp: stone huts with bunks, mattresses, shower and toilet; thatched area with kitchen and braai facilities, pots, pan, kettles and lanterns. Slagthoek: farmhouse with bunks, mattresses, braai and kitchen facilities, pots, pan, kettle. Grootdraai: hut with bunks, mattresses, braai facilities, pot, pan and kettle, shower and toilet.

This trail network traverses an area of 15,000 ha at the confluence of the Olifants and Wilge rivers in the Loskop Dam area. The trail network consists of a two-day overnight hiking trail and two trails each composed of two circular routes that can be hiked individually, as day routes, or combined into overnight trails.

1. Slagthoek Hiking Trail traverses the area to the east of the Olifants River. From the Slagthoek Basecamp, the God's Window Loop (12 km; 6 hours) climbs gradually through rocks to a viewpoint overlooking the Hundred Hills. It winds down into a valley with striking rock formations to a viewpoint, where hikers can enjoy stunning vistas of the Olifants River. From here the trail climbs gently to Gif-koppie, with its panoramic views over the rapids and cascades of the Olifants River, and then drops down to the Olifants River. After crossing the river, the route follows a densely wooded kloof back to the basecamp. The Cycad Loop (11 km; 5 hours) follows a track to Boschkloof plateau and then descends along a valley with a natural cycad garden. Further along it ascends gently to a viewpoint overlooking the Olifants River, after which it heads back down to the basecamp. **23 km; 2 days; circular.**

2. Kingdom Hiking Trail Starting at the Kingdom Basecamp, Route 1 (9 km; 4 hours) ascends a kloof with a seasonal waterfall to a plateau, where hikers are rewarded with magnificent views of the Wilge River from the Razor's Edge. After following a contour, the trail descends into the densely wooded Donkerkloof, with its springs and ancient white stinkwood trees. Further along, the path makes its way along the Nyala River to Black Rock Cascade and Kingdom Basecamp. Route 2 (16 km; 7 hours) leads past Black Rock Cascade and then ascends a kloof to a plateau, with a viewpoint that overlooks the Olifants Gorge and Die Hel at the confluence of the Olifants and Wilge rivers. The trail then descends a kloof to the Olifants River, passing a magnificent old fig tree along the way. On the river you will find the Hippo Pool swimming spot, the ideal spot for a swim or just to rest for a while. The trail continues along the river below towering cliffs, crossing the river twice by means of a cable handhold. However, when the river is high, you will have to follow an alternative route, which bypasses the loop where the Olifants River is crossed. After the second crossing, the path ascends gently to Snaaksekrans viewpoint and 1 km on veers sharply to the right to pass through Sheba's Breasts. The final section descends along the valley of the Nyala River back to the basecamp. **25 km; 2 days; circular.**

3. Olifants Gorge Hiking Trail is a two-day hike, which can be extended to a three- or four-day trail by adding any of the circular routes detailed below. Day one (12 km; 5 hours) follows the first 7.5 km of Route 2 of the Kingdom Hiking Trail to the first crossing of the Olifants River. Here the trail splits off to the left to follow a kloof back to Slagthoek. On day two (15 km; 7 hours) the trail heads through the Bamboeskloof and then follows the Olifants River, where there are several enticing swimming spots. At Grootdraai Hut it joins the Paradors Loop and then follows the Nyala River back to the Kingdom Basecamp. **27 km; 2 days; circular.**

9. IDWALA HIKING TRAIL
Loskop Dam

Trails: Network of several routes; 24 km (in total); 1 hour to 1½ days; circular.
Permits: Jacana Marketing and Reservations, P O Box 95212, Waterkloof 0145, tel: (012) 346 3550, fax: 346 2499, email: info@jacanacollection.co.za
Maps: Trail pamphlet with map.
Facilities/Activities: Basecamp: chalets with beds, mattresses, kitchen with two-plate gas stoves, pots, pans, braai facilities (bring your own charcoal), hot showers and toilets.
Pertinent information: The farm Kranskloof, on which the trail is situated, is open to visitors from 15:00 Thursday until 10:00 Monday, with the exception of public holidays, when it is closed.

Overlooking the Loskop Dam, this trail lies in the transitional zone between the Highveld and the Lowveld, and the flora and fauna here are therefore representative of both regions. *Idwala* is a Ndebele word meaning 'big flat rocks', a reference to the rocky ridges in the area. The short distances of these routes make this an ideal trail for beginners and families with children.

The vegetation ranges from extensive grasslands, with a variety of flowering plants and proteaveld, to densely wooded kloofs. Typical tree species found here include the common tree fern, Transvaal milkplum, wild plum, Transvaal bottlebrush and mountain seringa.

Large game species occurring in the area include roan, kudu, mountain reedbuck, blue wildebeest and Burchell's zebra. Also to be seen are klipspringer, common duiker and steenbok. Over 85 different bird species have been recorded here to date, among them the clapper lark, and a variety of waterbirds are attracted to Hannes's Dam, which is on the farm.

The Idwala trail network consists of several easy interlinked loops. The loops on the grassy plains to the south of the basecamp range from a short walk along Varingkloof to the 6-km-long

Hoëveldklappertjie Trail. An interesting feature that you will see on this trail is a conglomerate ridge, formed over 350 million years ago when pebbles were embedded in lava.

To the north of the basecamp the trail ascends along the 9.4-km-long **Mwamasi Trail** to the Suikerbosvlakte. The trail can be extended by linking up with the 3.4-km **Suikerbossingel Trail**. **Haelgeweer Loop**, which splits off Suikerbossingel, can be dangerous (as the trail follows a cliff ledge, which can be slippery in wet weather) and should not be hiked in wet weather, or by unaccompanied children or inexperienced hikers. Along the trails there are wonderful views of the deep valleys and gorges of the area, as well as Loskop Dam, which lies several hundred metres below.

10. BOTSHABELO HIKING TRAILS
Middelburg

> *Trails:* 3 trails; 6 to 12 km;
> 3 to 6 hours; circular.
> *Permits:* Entrance fee. No permit
> required for walks.
> *Maps:* Sketch map.
> *Facilities/Activities:* Restaurant; kiosk;
> curio shop; Botshabelo Site Museum;
> Ndebele Open-Air Museum.

This trail network combines the natural beauty of the area, its history, and the culture of the Ndebele people. Botshabelo, a name meaning 'place of shelter', was established by the Berlin Mission Society in 1865. To protect his followers against attacks from the Pedi leader Sekhukhune, missionary Alexander Merensky built a stone fort. The mission station expanded rapidly and by 1873 there were 1,315 inhabitants. The fort, two churches, Merensky House Museum and numerous other buildings from this era form part of the Botshabelo Site Museum.

Botshabelo lies within a 2,306-ha nature reserve, and among the game species to be seen are eland, blesbok, red hartebeest, black wildebeest, springbok and Burchell's zebra. Smaller species include steenbok, common duiker, oribi, klipspringer, baboon and vervet monkey.

1. Botshabelo Trail focuses on the history of the mission station. Winding past Fort Merensky, it offers excellent views of the settlement. After passing through two kloofs, the trail descends to the Little Olifants River and then makes its way back to Botshabelo, leaving enough time to explore the settlement. **6 km; 3 hours; circular.**

2. Klein Aasvoëlkrans Trail passes through stands of the endemic Olifants River cycad and offers fine views over the Little Olifants River. The outward leg of this trail initially climbs gently and then follows a route above the Little Olifants River Gorge to Aasvoëlkrans. After crossing the river, the trail remains parallel to the Little Olifants River all the way back to the start. **12 km; 6 hours; circular.**

There is also a somewhat shorter option on the Klein Aasvoëlkrans Trail, which descends into the gorge and then continues above the river, before linking up with the outward leg of the hike. **10 km; 5 hours; circular.**

11. CYCAD HIKING TRAIL
Middelburg

> *Trails:* 3 trails; 9 to 21 km; 4 to 8 hours;
> circular, which can be combined into
> longer hikes.
> *Permits:* Cycad Hiking Trail,
> P O Box 1326, Middelburg 1050,
> tel: (013) 282 6101, fax: 282 5752.
> *Maps:* Sketch map.
> *Facilities/Activities:* Scheepersdal
> Basecamp: farmhouse with mattresses,
> water, braai facilities, firewood and
> toilets. On the trail: huts with mattresses,
> braai facilities, firewood and toilets.

Opened in 1975, the Cycad Hiking Trail traverses magnificent scenery in the Olifants River Valley. The trail network wanders through magnificent rock formations and dense stands of cycads, as well as along the Olifants River.

The vegetation is dominated by mixed sourveld, composed of species such as common hook-thorn, strawberry bush, Transvaal beech, velvet bushwillow, common wild pear and common sugarbush. Of special interest are the large populations of two cycad species that occur here: the Olifants River cycad is endemic to the upper reaches of the Olifants River and attains only about 1 m in height, while the Waterberg cycad grows up to 4 m tall.

Among the mammals you might chance upon are kudu, klipspringer, warthog, vervet monkey and baboon. Leopard and brown hyaena also occur here, but are seldom seen.

Along the Olifants River keep an eye out for grey heron, Burchell's coucal and giant kingfisher. Birds of prey you may see include black, martial and African fish eagles, and lanner and peregrine falcons. Swainson's francolin, common quail, stonechat and pied starling are among the bushveld savannah species you may tick.

The trail network consists of three trails, which can be hiked as day routes, or combined into a two- or three-day trail.

1. Suikerbos Trail owes its name to the Afrikaans term for the common sugarbush, which is abundant along the route. The trail makes its way along the upper plateau and then ascends along a kloof to the Olifants River. The return leg mainly follows the bank of the river back to the start at the Scheepersdal farmhouse. Suikerbos Trail can also be hiked as the second leg of a two- or three-day route. **9 km; 4 hours; circular.**

2. Cycad Trail winds along the edge of the plateau, from where there are stunning views over the Olifants River. The trail takes its name from the two cycad species that grow here in abundance. The Eagle's Nest Hut is situated on the trail route at the edge of the cliffs that give way to the Little Olifants River Valley. The Cycad Trail can also be hiked as the first leg of a two-day or three-day route. **14 km; 6 hours; circular.**

3. Baboon Route requires a reasonable degree of fitness, as there are some rocky sections that require hikers to climb and scramble like a baboon – hence the name. The trail initially follows the plateau edge and then descends to the Olifants River, which is followed for 14 km before the trail loops back to the start. Baboon Route can also be hiked in conjunction with the two other trails as the second or third leg. **21 km; 8 hours; circular.**

12. AMA POOT POOT HIKING TRAIL
Dullstroom

> **Trails:** *Trail with two different routes; 6 and 13 km; 3 and 6 hours; network from basecamp.*
> **Permits:** *Anvie Ventures, P O Box 60035, Pierre van Ryneveld 0045, tel. and fax: (012) 662 1140.*
> **Maps:** *Sketch map.*
> **Facilities/Activities:** *Basecamp with bunks, mattresses, kitchen with gas appliances, pots, pans, lounge with fireplace, braai facilities, hot showers and toilets. Trout-angling.*

Laid out on a private game farm near Dullstroom, the two routes of the Ama Poot Poot Hiking Trail meander through grassland, where hikers may spot a variety of game. Hiking can be combined with trout-angling in the dams.

1. Trout Route follows a stream with two waterfalls, past trout dams, to the Witpoort River Gorge. Provided you take rope along, and you are relatively agile and adventurous, the gorge can be explored at your leisure and you can wade up to the falls passed on the Mountain Reedbuck Route. From here the trail continues to a viewpoint overlooking the river and then doubles back to the start. **6 km; 3 hours; circular.**

2. Mountain Reedbuck Route wanders along rocky ridges and above kranses, where hikers are rewarded with beautiful views. After crossing the Witpoort River the trail climbs steeply up the mountain slopes and loops back along a kloof with an abundance of common tree ferns. The highlight of the trail is a 10-m-high waterfall and an enormous pool, ideal for a lunch stop. After re-crossing the Witpoort River the trail climbs out of the gorge and returns to the start. **13 km; 6 hours; circular.**

TOP: *God's Window provides sweeping views of Blyde River Canyon, near the start of the Blyderivierspoort Hiking Trail.*

ABOVE: *The well-known Three Rondavels, overlooking the canyon, make a striking landmark.*

THIS PAGE: *Kruger National Park is the ideal place to hike if you want to see a wonderful variety of animals. You're most likely to spot vervet monkey (above) in wooded country near water. Water holes are a good place to find many animals, such as giraffe (left), which are particularly vulnerable to attack when drinking. You may even see the elusive cheetah (below) on one of the park's many wilderness trails.*
OPPOSITE: *A ladder helps hikers up difficult sections of the Magoebaskloof trail, near Tzaneen.*

ABOVE: *The Forest Falls Walk, near Sabie in Mpumalanga, takes its name from these magnificent falls.*
BELOW: *You'll find numerous reminders of the gold rush era of the 19th century on the Prospector's trails near Pilgrim's Rest.*

ABOVE: *Hikers may see wild horses grazing near Excelsior Hut on the Prospector's hike.*
BELOW: *This is one of the lovely views over the Lowveld on the Kaapschehoop trail.*

NEXT PAGE: *The breathtaking Valley of Desolation is the focal point of the Karoo Nature Reserve and provides a spectacular setting for many of the reserve's hiking trails.*

TOP: *Start out early when you're hiking in the Northern Cape's Richtersveld, so you can avoid the baking heat of the day.*
ABOVE: *The unusual-looking quiver tree is synonymous with Namaqualand and the arid Northern Cape.*

13. WELGEDACHT TRAILS
Lydenburg

> **Trails:** Several trail options; 2 to 20 km; network. All trails can be done as day walks or combined into an overnight hiking trail.
> **Permits:** Jacana Marketing and Reservations, P O Box 95212, Waterkloof 0145, tel: (012) 346 3550, fax: 346 2499, email: info@jacanacollection.co.za
> **Maps:** Trails indicated on aerial photographs of the area.
> **Facilities/Activities:** Basecamp: two houses with bunks, mattresses, two-plate stove, pots, pans, kettle, braai facilities, firewood, hot showers and toilets. Fernkloof Hut: bunks, mattresses, pots, pans, kettle, braai facilities, cold shower and toilet.

A network of trails traverses Welgedacht, a dairy and trout farm, on the edge of the Escarpment, southwest of Lydenburg. The scenery ranges from the picturesque Crocodile River Valley to grassy mountain slopes and the Mpumalanga Drakensberg Escarpment, and unspoilt indigenous forests can also be enjoyed along the trails.

Some 160 bird species have been recorded here to date, including the bald ibis, bateleur, crowned crane, tambourine dove, Cape rock thrush, grassbird, orange-throated longclaw and several sunbird species.

Some of the trails have been laid out along the Crocodile River and the foothills of the Escarpment, while three challenging routes climb to the summit of the Escarpment. Amongst the attractions found here are far-reaching views of the Ratelspruit and Lunsklip waterfalls, Steenkampsberg and the Badsfontein Valley, mountain streams with waterfalls, and archaeological sites of ruined stone-walled houses and enclosures, dating back to the 1600s and the 1900s.

All the Welgedacht trails can be hiked as day walks, and range in length from 2 km to 20 km. Alternatively hikers can use the Varingkloof Hut as a basecamp to explore the plateau area. The shortest route to the hut is, however, an extremely stiff climb involving an altitude gain of over 530 m in just under 5 km.

14. RATELSPRUIT HIKING TRAIL
Dullstroom

> **Trails:** 2 trails; 12 and 13 km; 6 hours; circular.
> **Permits:** Mr and Mrs L Mostert, P O Box 27, Dullstroom 1110, tel. and fax: (013) 254 0831.
> **Maps:** Sketch map.
> **Facilities/Activities:** Basecamp: hut with bunks, mattresses, small kitchen with coal stove, braai facilities, firewood, shower and toilet; tent sites. Fully equipped self-catering cottage and rondavel.

The trail network on this farm northeast of Dullstroom passes through grassveld, which produces a wonderfully colourful display of lilies, *Streptocarpus* and numerous other flowering plants during the summer months. Patches of common sugarbush also occur here, while Natal bottlebrush and cabbage tree are conspicuous among rocky outcrops.

Mammals you may chance upon include the grey rhebok, baboon and honey badger. Among the rich diversity of birds are black eagle, blue crane, secretary bird and African fish eagle.

1. Langklippe Trail traverses grassveld and takes you past a number of interesting features such as old stone kraals and unusual rock formations, which are known locally as the Langklippe (long rocks). **12 km; 6 hours; circular.**

2. Ratelsrus Trail The name of this trail means 'badger's rest' and is derived from the Ratelspruit ('Badger River') – the badger (*ratel* in Afrikaans) also features on the trail brochure. Highlights of this route include Klein Victoria, a waterfall reminiscent (on a small-scale) of the great Victoria Falls, and Die Geut, where the river flows through a narrow chute (*geut* in Afrikaans). Just downstream of Die Geut the river plunges over yet another waterfall, where the trail follows high rocky ridges on the edge of the plateau that affords hikers beautiful views of the ravines and cliffs below. **13 km; 6 hours; circular.**

15. SALPETERKRANS HIKING TRAILS
Roossenekal

> **Trails:** Overnight trail; 25 km; 2 days;
> circular. 3 day-trails; 10.5 to 15 km;
> 4 to 7 hours; circular.
> **Permits:** Jacana marketing and Reservations,
> P O Box 95212, Waterkloof 0145,
> tel: (012) 346 3550, fax: 346 2499.
> **Maps:** Trail pamphlet with map.
> **Facilities/Activities:** Basecamp: huts
> with bunks, mattresses, braai facilities,
> firewood, hot showers and toilets. Finger
> Rock Overnight Camp: bunks with
> mattresses, kitchen area, braai facilities,
> hot showers and toilets.

This trail traverses the Salpeterkrans Mountains, west of the Steenkampsberg range, on the edge of the Escarpment. It owes its name to the Salpeterkrans, so called because, in years gone by, sulphur was excavated here and used to cure biltong. The vegetation consists of Highveld and Escarpment species, and the grasslands are especially attractive from October to January when masses of yellow arum lilies (*Zantedeschia pentlandii*) are in full flower. Also noteworthy are the river crinum (*Crinum macowanii*), blue scilla (*Scilla natalensis*), krantz aloe and *Aloe reitzii*, a rare aloe restricted to the Belfast district in Mpumalanga and northern KwaZulu-Natal.

Of historical interest are the reminders of the South African War (1899–1902) and the war the Boers waged against the Ndebele leader Mabhogo (Mapoch) in 1883.

1. Salpeterkrans Hiking Trail The first day's hike (15 km; 7 hours) follows the Roossekop Trail until it comes to the turnoff to the Otter Swimming Hole. It then crosses the Klip River and continues to the Finger Rock Camp, named after two rock fingers protruding above the indigenous forest. Day two's hike (10 km; 5 km) ascends steadily and then traverses Spitsberg. From here the trail descends and makes its way along the Bokbrug loop past the natural rock bridge, back to the basecamp. **25 km; 2 days; circular.**

2. Bokbrug Trail is followed to the Kingfisher Bridge and continues along a loop to Bokbrug, where the Klip River flows in several channels underneath a natural rock bridge. Here you can have a refreshing swim and explore the small potholes eroded by the fast-flowing river. The trail then loops back past Reitziikop, with its aloes, and Varkoorvlei, with its seasonal display of yellow arum lilies (*varkoor* in Afrikaans). Still further on, the trail reaches the Rotskamer, where the Boers hid horses during the South African War. **10.5 km; 4 hours; circular.**

3. Salpeterkrans Trail winds past Geelbooi's Kraal to Bakenkop, where trailists are rewarded with spectacular views of the Vlugkraal Dam, and the Roossenekal and Draaikraal landscape. A little way on from Salpeterkrans a short 7-km option loops back to the basecamp. The longer of the two routes continues along the Salpeterkrans ridge and then descends to the Otter Swimming Hole, from where the trail loops back to the start. **7 or 13 km; 3.5 or 6 hours; circular.**

4. Roossekop Trail follows the same route as the Salpeterkrans Trail, but instead of descending to the Otter Swimming Hole it continues to the top of Roossekop, named after Boer Field Cornet Roos who was fatally wounded there while attempting to capture the Pedi leader Mampuru. The entrance to the cave where Field Cornet Roos was injured was subsequently dynamited by the Boers and the Pedi defenders inside, who had wounded him, were buried in what was to become their mass grave. The incident resulted in the 1883 war against the Ndebele leader Mabhogo who had given refuge to Mampuru. The trail then loops back and joins the return leg of the Salpeterkrans Trail. **15 km; 7 hours; circular.**

16. ELANDSVALLEI HIKING TRAIL
West of Nelspruit

> **Trails:** Overnight hike; 19 km; 2 days;
> circular. 2 day-trails; 3 and 8 km;
> 1.5 and 4 hours; circular.

Permits: *Jacana Marketing and Reservations,*
P O Box 95212, Waterkloof 0145,
tel: (012) 346 3550, fax: 346 2499,
email: info@jacanacollection.co.za
Maps: *Trail brochure with map.*
Facilities/Activities: *Skooltjie Basecamp*
(at an old school): bunks, mattresses, pans,
pots, kettle, braai facilities, hot shower
and toilet; no gas cooker. Cheeky's Place
(overnight bushcamp): same facilities as
Skooltjie Basecamp.
Pertinent information: *Keep an eye out*
for hippo when walking along or crossing
the Elands River.

The Elands River Valley, between Ngodwana and Nelspruit in the Lowveld, provides the setting for this trail network on the farm Lindenau. Although large areas of the farm have been planted under eucalyptus and pine plantations, indigenous vegetation occurs in the kloofs and gorges. Trees along the route have been labelled, and among the species to be seen are the Graskop aloe, the Barberton Lowveld and the African white sugarbush, common tree euphorbia and several bushwillow species.

Animals that may be seen along the course of the Elandsvallei Hiking Trail include baboon, vervet monkey, bushbuck, mountain reedbuck, blue and common duiker, klipspringer, steenbok and oribi. The spotted hyaena is the largest predator in this area, and there are also hippo, which inhabit the Elands River.

The diversity of habitats and flora here has resulted in prolific birdlife. Among the more than 250 species recorded are Burchell's coucal, giant kingfisher, orange-throated longclaw, Knysna and purple-crested louries, long-billed pipit and black and martial eagles.

The first 3 km of day one's hike (13 km; 6 hours) follows an easy route along the Elands River to a swimming pool and waterfall, which make a great reststop. The trail then passes through a tunnel underneath the N4 and climbs steeply to the top of Sugarloaf, a vantage point overlooking Elands River Valley. From here the trail follows a contour for about 2 km, before ascending along a cleft in the cliffs to the plateau. The remainder of the day's

hike follows a gently undulating course, with a final descent along a forest road to the overnight camp.

Shortly after setting off on day two's hike (6 km; 3 hours), the trail passes an old gold mine and then drops down to a pool beneath a waterfall. A steady climb up the mountain slopes, followed by a gentle descent, leads to the site where the Boers deployed artillery guns in the closing stages of the South African War (1899–1902). Continuing along the upper slopes of the plateau, the trail reaches a point overlooking the saw mills and plantations across the valley. A steep descent along a kloof takes hikers back to the basecamp.

There are also two day-trails of 3 km (1.5 hours) and 8 km (4 hours) both circular.

17. KAAPSCHEHOOP HIKING TRAIL
Kaapschehoop

Trails: *Network of several trails; 111 km*
(in total); 2 to 4 days; circular.
Permits: *SAFCOL Ecotourism,*
P O Box 1771, Silverton 0127,
tel: (012) 481 3615, fax: 481 3622,
email: ecotour@safcol.co.za
Maps: *A4 colour sketch map of trail.*
Facilities/Activities: *Kaapschehoop:*
hut with bunks, mattresses, pots,
pans, kettles, braai area, firewood,
hot showers and toilets. Barretts
Coaches: train coaches, pots, pans,
braai area, firewood, showers and
toilets. Wattles: hut with bunks,
mattresses, pots, pans, kettle, braai
area, firewood, hot showers and
toilets. Coetzeestroom: hut with bunks,
mattresses, showers and toilet.
Pertinent information: *Hikes can be started*
at Kaapschehoop and Barretts Coaches.

The SAFCOL Berlin Plantation on the Drakensberg Escarpment provides the setting for the Kaapschehoop Hiking Trail. Situated on a plateau at the edge of the Escarpment, the landscape here is characterised by deeply eroded valleys, with patches of indigenous forest, sheer cliffs, hills and streams.

The settlement of Kaapschehoop was the focal point of the gold rush in the 1880s and many relics of the early gold-mining days, such as the Gold Commissioner's house, old post office and jail in Kaapschehoop and the gold mine diggings, can still be seen here today. By 1886, a year after the De Kaap Goldfields were proclaimed a public goldfield, the area already had a few thousand inhabitants and several permanent buildings. Following the discovery of gold on the Witwatersrand, however, many diggers left this area and the settlement became a ghost town.

Plantations have replaced much of the natural vegetation, but a few patches of grassveld and indigenous forest have been left untouched. At Coetzeestroom the vegetation changes dramatically to Lowveld bushveld savannah. A noteworthy plant species occurring in the area is the endemic Kaapsehoop cycad, which enjoys protection in the Starvation Creek Nature Reserve.

Mammals to be found here include baboon, vervet monkey, rock dassie, oribi, common and blue duiker, klipspringer, bushbuck and bushpig. Also of interest are the wild horses of Kaapschehoop, variously said to be descendants of pit ponies and/or Boer horses that ran wild during the South African War (1899–1902).

More than 200 bird species have been recorded, among them eight to 12 breeding pairs of the endangered blue swallow. They breed on Blouswawelvlakte, southeast of Kaapschehoop. The area, which has been set aside as the Blue Swallow Natural Heritage Site, holds the third largest breeding population of this species in South Africa. Other species to look out for include chorister and starred robins, Knysna lourie, forest buzzard and olive bush shrike.

This trail network offers trailists several options, ranging from four two-day trails to tailor-made three- and four-day trails. One of the four-day trails, incorporating most of the different options, is described here in detail.

Kaapschehoop Four-day Trail Starting at Barretts Coaches, this trail offers a combination of historical and cultural highlights. The first day's hike (16.5 km; 6 hours) alternates between pine plantations and indigenous forest patches in the upper reaches of Battery Creek. The trail descends steadily to the Starvation Creek Nature Reserve, set aside to protect the Kaapsehoop cycad, and continues to a waterfall in the creek. From here the trail ascends steeply along a stream to the Starvation Creek Falls and then eases off as it continues to the Wattles Hut. On day two (15.4 km; 6 hours) the trail winds up Spitskop and follows an undulating course along the Escarpment edge to the settlement of Kaapschehoop, where some beautiful examples of Victorian architecture can be seen, before continuing to the Kaapschehoop Hut.

Day three (14 km; 6 hours) initially follows an easy route along the Escarpment edge and makes its way down to an indigenous forest and several old mine shafts. The trail ascends to make its way across Blouswawelvlakte and then descends through to the Coetzeestroom Hut. The final day's hike (9 km; 4.5 km) takes hikers back to Barretts Coaches, passing through grassland, plantations and forest patches on the way. **54.9 km; 4 days; circular.**

18. QUEEN ROSE HIKING TRAIL
Barberton

Trail: 20.9 km; 2 days; circular.
Permits: Queen Rose Hiking Trail,
P O Box 1332, Barberton 1300,
tel: (083) 545 0900, fax: (013) 712 6054.
Maps: Sketch map.
Facilities/Activities: Queen's View Hut
at start with hot showers and toilets.
Two overnight huts with bunks, mattresses,
braai facilities, stove and fridge.
Pertinent information: The trail involves
numerous river crossings, during which
caution must be exercised.

Laid out in the mountains west of Barberton, near Nelshoogte, this trail passes through spectacular scenery as it follows the Montrose and Queen's rivers.

From Queen's View Hut the first day's hike (13 km; 6 hours) ascends steadily through pine plantations to the highest point of the trail, which offers wonderful views of the surroundings. The trail descends sharply to the wooded Montrose River

Valley, where the Alvin Falls and a deep pool make an ideal reststop. From here the river is crossed several times, and you reach Marie's Picnic Place in time for lunch. After lunch the trail follows an easy contour path past interesting rock formations to Angel's View. A steep descent leads to Makesh Hut.

Day two (7.9 km; 4 hours) initially follows the Queen's River upstream and climbs steadily for about an hour before reaching a picnic area. There is a detour to a pool with a cable slide, a short way downstream of the picnic area, which is well worth the effort. The trail ascends again and rewards hikers with great views of the Queen's River, its wild kloofs and Kupid Falls. Depending on the level of the river, the top of the falls can be reached along Heaven's Staircase. After the final uphill section at Fountain Forest, it is an easy walk back to the start.

19. LOWVELD NATIONAL BOTANICAL GARDEN
Nelspruit

Trails: Network of paths.
Permits: Entrance fee. No permit required.
Maps: Information brochure with map.
Facilities/Activities: Guided tours by arrangement; restaurant; parking; toilets; plant sales.

Two highlights of the 159-ha Lowveld National Botanical Garden are the deep gorge, carved by the Crocodile River, and the Nels River, which converges with the Crocodile after tumbling over a waterfall. About 600 plant species grow naturally in the garden, and a further 2,000 have been planted here. With over 650 of South Africa's approximately 1,000 tree and shrub species represented, the garden is a delight to tree-lovers. Tree families collected in the garden include those of the corkwood and cabbage tree, wild fig, baobab, bushwillow and legume.

Of specific interest here is the cycad collection, considered to be the best collection of African cycads in South Africa, and the tropical African rain forest, which represents the magnificent tropical rain forests of Central and West Africa.

In addition to the paved footpaths that meander through the garden there is also a 1-km-long walk, the **Riverside Trail**, along the Crocodile River. Interpretative stations along the walk are explained in the trail brochure.

20. UITSOEK HIKING TRAIL
Nelspruit

Trails: Overnight trail; 25.5 km; 2 days; circular. 2 trails; 11 km; 5 hours; circular.
Permits: SAFCOL Ecotourism,
P O Box 1771, Silverton 0127,
tel: (012) 481 3615, fax: 481 3622,
email: ecotour@safcol.co.za
Maps: A4 colour sketch map of trail.
Facilities/Activities: Overnight huts with bunks, mattresses, pots, pans (Uitsoek Hut only), braai facilities, firewood, hot water (Uitsoek Hut), cold water (Lisabon Hut) and toilets.
Pertinent information: Since firewood is not provided at Lisabon Hut, a backpacking stove is essential. Mist is common throughout the year, so take rain gear and waterproof your pack.

This trail in the southeast of Mpumalanga takes the hiker from the foothills of the Drakensberg to the Escarpment and back, traversing deep valleys and high mountains, which offer magnificent views. The route passes through montane grassland, pine plantations and beautiful indigenous forests, which were a source of timber for the first Voortrekkers who began settling in the area in 1848.

The vegetation of the low-lying areas in the south of the Uitsoek Plantation is characterised by patches of semi-deciduous forest and Lowveld sour bushveld. Above 1,200 m this vegetation is replaced by northeastern mountain sourveld, much of which has been cleared for pine plantations. Typical tree species include Transvaal and broad-leafed beeches, wild teak and oldwood. Among the grassland flowers found here are the dwarf red-hot poker (*Kniphofia triangularis*), pineapple flower (*Eucomis humilis*) and no fewer than eight disa species. Extensive patches of montane forest have survived in the Houtbosloop and Beestekraalspruit valleys. About 120 tree species have been recorded in the area.

The only large predator occurring in the area is the leopard. Antelope to be seen here include red and common duiker, oribi, grey rhebok, mountain reedbuck, bushbuck and klipspringer. Among the other mammals you may see are bushpig, baboon and vervet monkey.

To date over 100 bird species have been recorded here. Amongst these are long-crested eagle, Cape rock thrush, white stork, Narina trogon and buff-streaked chat. Grassland bird species you may tick include kurrichane, buttonquail, fan-tailed cisticola and orange-throated longclaw.

1. Uitsoek Hiking Trail

The first day's hike (11 km; 5 hours) begins with a steady 8-km uphill slog, during which you gain 700 m in altitude. The trail now more or less follows the 1,800-m contour on the southern slopes of Makobolwane for about 2 km, and then skirts the upper reaches of the Kwagga River. The steep drop into Clivia Gorge, with its profusion of forest lilies (*Clivia caulescens*), is followed by an exhausting climb to the Escarpment, during which you gain some 180 m in altitude in less than 1 km. The final section of the day's hike follows an easy route across a rocky hill to Lisabon Hut.

Except for two short uphill stretches, day two (14.5 km; 7 hours) is downhill. Near the 3-km mark the trail drops steeply into Grootkloof. In just over 3 km you will lose 500 m in altitude to the Houtbosloop Valley, passing through beautiful indigenous forest. The trail then follows the course of the Houtbosloop, which is criss-crossed numerous times. Near the 9-km mark there is a detour to the Bakkrans Waterfall, where a large pool makes a perfect lunch spot. From here the trail continues along the course of the Houtbosloop, with the final section climbing gradually through proteaveld. **25.5 km; 2 days; circular.**

2. Beestekraalspruit Trail

This route ascends steadily through pine plantations, indigenous scrub forest and grassland to the cliff edge of Beestekraalspruit. It then descends gradually into Beestekraalspruit-kloof, with its indigenous forest. For the next 4 km the trail follows the course of the river, which you cross 20 times by means of wooden bridges. On leaving the stream, the trail climbs gradually to the starting point. **11 km; 5 hours; circular.**

3. Bakkrans Trail

This trail leads to the Bakkrans Waterfall, alternating between pine plantations above the Houtbosloop and indigenous scrub forest in the kloofs. From here the last 4.5 km of the Uitsoek Hiking Trail is followed back to the start. **11 km; 5 hours; circular.**

21. GUSTAV KLINGBIEL NATURE RESERVE
Lydenburg

> *Trails:* 3 trails; 5 to 12 km; 2 to 6 hours; circular.
> *Permit:* Entrance fee. No permit required for trails.
> *Map:* Sketch map.
> *Facilities/Activities:* Museum; toilets.

Situated just outside Lydenburg, the Gustav Klingbiel Nature Reserve covers 2,200 ha of typical Escarpment flora and fauna. The reserve has been stocked with eland, blue wildebeest, blesbok, kudu, grey rhebok, mountain reedbuck, common duiker, steenbok and oribi. Over 200 bird species have been recorded and a 'vulture restaurant' (feeding station) has been established in the reserve.

1. Pedi Route

is named after the Pedi people, who lived here for centuries. The focal point of the trail is an early Pedi settlement, and along the way you will pass terraces, stone-walled paths and the ruins of homesteads. The settlement was abandoned in the 1820s after its inhabitants were attacked by the Zulu leader Mzilikazi. After fleeing from the Zulu king Shaka, Mzilikazi and his followers migrated to the Highveld, where he attacked and conquered the Sotho, Tswana and Pedi inhabitants. **5 km; 2 hours; circular.**

2. Crane Route

leads to a dam, which offers excellent birding opportunities, and then winds around

Aarbeikop to the vulture restaurant (where you might see the Cape vulture) on the slopes of Vyekop before looping back to the start. Pedi ruins are also seen along this route. **9 km; 4 hours; circular.**

3. Protea Route follows Crane Route to Aarbeikop and then gently ascends to a vantage point where the Boers deployed two of their Long Tom artillery guns to delay the British advance of General Buller's troops during the closing stages of the South African War (1899–1902). The return leg of the trail descends along a kloof. **12 km; 6 hours; circular.**

22. FANIE BOTHA HIKING TRAIL NETWORK
Sabie

Trails: 5 trails; 17.7 to 72.4 km; 2 to 5 days; circular and open-ended.
Permits: SAFCOL Ecotourism, P O Box 1771, Silverton 0127, tel: (012) 481 3615, fax: 481 3622, email: ecotour@safcol.co.za
Maps: A4 colour sketch map of trail.
Facilities/Activities: Six overnight huts with bunks, mattresses; covered braai area, firewood, showers (in all except Mac-Mac Hut) and toilets.
Pertinent information: Ceylon Plantation, Graskop Hut and the President Burger Hut at Mac-Mac Plantation can be used as starting points.

Opened in 1973, the Fanie Botha Hiking Trail will always be remembered as one of the pioneer hiking trails of South Africa. Located on the Drakensberg Escarpment, the trail takes in pine plantations, grassland and patches of indigenous forest, offering many splendid views over a mosaic of plantations and the Lowveld below.

Antelope you might encounter include klipspringer, grey rhebok, mountain reedbuck, bushbuck and oribi. Other species to keep an eye out for are bushpig, baboon and rock dassie.

Among the birds recorded on Hartbeestvlakte are blue swallow and broad-tailed warbler. Elsewhere along the trail you may tick jackal buzzard, Swainson's francolin, Cape rock thrush, Knysna lourie and Gurney's sugarbird.

The full course of the trail extends from the SAFCOL Ceylon Plantation to Graskop and then doubles back to Mac-Mac.

1. Maritzbos Trail Starting at the Ceylon Hut, the first day's hike (8.7 km; 4 hours) makes its way steadily uphill through pine plantations for 3 km and then descends, passing the Lone Creek Falls. From here the trail gently ascends to the overnight hut on the edge of Maritzbos. Day two's hike (9 km; 4 hours) initially follows the Lone Creek downstream along its northern bank, before joining the outward leg of the first day's hike, from where you backtrack to Ceylon Hut. **17.7 km; 2 days; circular.**

2. Bonnet and Mac-Mac Pools Trail This trail can be started either at Graskop Hut or the President Burger Hut at Mac-Mac Plantation. From the President Burger Hut the first day's trail (16 km; 7 hours) climbs gently through pine plantations and indigenous forest patches for about 7 km. Further along, it follows an old coach road on the eastern slopes of Stanley Bush Hill to The Bonnet, from where it descends through grassveld to Graskop Hut. On day two (23 km; 9.5 hours) the trail passes through pine plantations and grassland before descending through indigenous forest to the Mac-Mac River, which you cross by means of a suspension bridge. From here the trail climbs steeply to Mac-Mac Bluff and then descends past Mac-Mac Pools and Mac-Mac Falls. The final section ascends gradually through pine plantations to President Burger Hut. **39 km (same distance from both starting points); 2 days; circular.**

3. Hartbeestvlakte Trail leads from the Ceylon Plantation to Maritzbos, a relic patch of indigenous forest, on the first day (8.7 km; 4 hours). On the second day (12 km; 8 hours) the trail ascends along the Lone Creek through Maritzbos. After you leave the forest, the trail climbs steadily up the slopes of Mount Anderson to Hartbeestvlakte. Further along, you follow a mountain stream with pools and waterfalls before the final section of the trail takes you down through a pine plantation to the Stables Overnight Hut. The third day's hike (10 km; 4 hours) is an easy downhill walk through pine plantations and patches of indigenous forest. **30.7 km; 3 days; circular.**

4. Mount Moodie Trail starts at the Ceylon Plantation and follows the first two days of the Hartbeestvlakte Trail. From the Stables the third day's hike (16.4 km; 8 hours) skirts the edge of pine plantations as it climbs steeply to the summit of Mount Moodie (2,078 m), where hikers are greeted with views of the Sabie Valley. From here the trail descends sharply, down the slopes of Baker's Bliss to Mac-Mac Hut. On day four hikers have the option of following the long route via Mac-Mac Pools and the Escarpment (22.3 km; 9.5 hours) to Graskop Hut, or the shorter route via The Bonnet (13 km; 6 hours). **50.1 km, or 59.4 km; 4 days; open-ended.**

5. Fanie Botha Five-day Trail follows the four days of the Mount Moodie Trail. On the fifth day (13 km; 6 hours) hikers follow the trail via The Bonnet to the President Burger Hut at Mac-Mac Plantation. **63.1 km or 72.4 km; 5 days; open-ended.**

23. LOERIE WALK
Sabie

Trails: 13.5 km; 6 hours; circular.
Shorter, 10.5-km option available.
Permits: SAFCOL,
Private Bag X503, Sabie 1260,
tel: (013) 764 2423, fax: 764 2662.
Permits can also be obtained from
the SAFCOL office in Sabie during
office hours.
Maps: Sketch map.
Facilities/Activities: None.

The Loerie Walk follows a route through the valleys of the Sabie River and passes mainly through pine and eucalyptus plantations. It can be started either at Castle Rock Caravan Park or the Ceylon Plantation office. From the Ceylon Plantation office the trail passes through grassveld and pine plantations to reach the Bridal Veil Falls. From

here the trail climbs steeply through and along the edge of indigenous forests past the Glynis and Elna falls to a ridge, from where there are stunning views over the Sabie Valley. After following a gum belt (eucalyptus trees planted between plantation sections as a windbreak) the trail joins a forestry track and then descends to Castle Rock. The remaining part of the trail is an easy walk along the course of the Sabie River.

A shorter trail option branches off from the main route about 7 km before you reach Ceylon Plantation and then winds down to reach the starting point after 3 km.

24. FOREST FALLS WALK
Sabie/Graskop

Trail: 3 km; 1 hour; circular.
Permits: SAFCOL,
Private Bag X503, Sabie 1260,
tel: (013) 764 2423, fax: 764 2662.
Permits can also be obtained from
the SAFCOL office in Sabie during
office hours.
Maps: Sketch map.
Facilities/Activities: Picnic sites at start.

From the Mac-Mac picnic site the trail passes through pine plantations and along the edge of indigenous forest fringing a tributary of the Mac-Mac River, to reach the beautiful Forest Falls after 1.6 km. The return leg follows the eastern bank of the river past several old mines before reaching the starting point.

25. JOCK OF THE BUSHVELD TRAIL
Graskop

Trail: 8 km; 3 hours; circular.
Permits: Not required.
Maps: Sketch map.
Facilities/Activities: Graskop Holiday
Resort at start.

On this route hikers can follow in the tracks of the famous Staffordshire terrier Jock of the Bushveld, a frequent visitor to the area with his master Sir Percy Fitzpatrick during the years from 1885 to 1887. From the Graskop Holiday Resort the path makes its way to Paradise Camp, where Fitzpatrick used to camp. From here the trail continues to the Bathing Pools (mentioned in the book *Jock of the Bushveld*) in the Tumbling Waters Spruit, which cascades over numerous rapids further downstream. At its southern end the trail wanders past the Sandstone Sentinels, quartz rock formations resembling a sea horse, wolf, camel, sitting hen and a vulture. Further along, you cross the Fairyland Spruit and the trail then passes the Window Rock on the way back to the start.

26. PROSPECTOR'S HIKING TRAILS
Pilgrim's Rest

Trails: *4 trails; 20.9 to 63 km; 2 to 5 days; circular.*
Permits: *SAFCOL Ecotourism, P O Box 1771, Silverton 0127, tel: (012) 481 3615, fax: 481 3622, email: ecotour@safcol.co.za*
Maps: *A4 colour sketch map of trail.*
Facilities/Activities: *Four overnight huts with bunks, mattresses, braai facilities, firewood, hot showers and toilets.*
Pertinent information: *The trail can be started at Pilgrim's Rest Hut (1 km from the town) and at the Morgenzon Plantation office, 2.3 km from Morgenzon Hut.*

On this trail hikers follow in the footsteps of the early miners, prospectors and fortune-seekers who rushed to the area after gold was discovered at Pilgrim's Rest in 1873. The trail incorporates many relics of the early gold-mining days, including a water furrow to channel water to an old mine and the village of Pilgrim's Rest itself, and sections also wind through patches of indigenous forest, pine plantations and across grasslands.

The animal life of the trail area is similar to that elsewhere along the Mpumalanga Drakensberg,

including animals such as grey rhebok, mountain reedbuck, oribi, klipspringer, bushbuck, common duiker and baboon. Keep an eye out for the well-known wild horses of Morgenzon, especially in the vicinity of the Excelsior Hut. It has been suggested that they are the descendants of horses abandoned by prospectors during the gold rush of the 1880s or horses that ran wild during the South African War (1899–1902).

1. Peach Tree Creek Trail Starting at the Pilgrim's Rest Hut, the first day's trail (12.6 km; 7 hours) meanders past numerous reminders of the gold-mining era, such as an old coco pan track, the railway line to the mines in Peach Tree Creek and an old abandoned mine. From the hut the trail ascends steadily up Brown's Hill and then winds down to reach the Blyde River about 5 km from the start. After crossing the river, you follow the route of an old railway line that once served the mines in Peach Tree Creek, and climb to an old concrete canal. From here, the trail continues to ascend steeply along an early diggers' path to an abandoned mine, and continues its ascent through grassland to a saddle, where the gradient eases. Further along, the trail passes through a patch of indigenous forest and then descends sharply. The remainder of the day's hike to Morgenzon Hut traverses easy terrain. On day two (8.3 km; 3 hours) the trail makes its way through a patch of indigenous forest and proteaveld before joining the Columbia Race – a furrow used to bring water to the Columbia Mine. A short way further on, you reach the site of the Columbia Mine and the trail then descends steeply down Columbia Hill to Pilgrim's Rest. You should finish the hike relatively early in the day, leaving you with some time to explore this historic town. **20.9 km; 2 days; circular.**

2. Black Hill Trail From the Morgenzon Plantation office the first day's trail (15.6 km; 7 hours) descends into the Clever Valley and then climbs steeply up a ridge opposite the Clever Falls. Further on, the trail enters a kloof, with indigenous forest, and follows a stream to a small waterfall. The trail then follows a road to another forested kloof, where it once again ascends steeply along a stream to beautiful waterfalls. Higher up, the trail emerges into fynbos and comes to the Black Hill Hut a short way on. Over the course of the second day's hike (12.6 km; 6 hours) the trail passes rock formations on its way to the Black Hill viewpoint and then heads downhill through pine plantations, before ascending through grasslands to a viewpoint. The trail descends again through pine plantations and fynbos, which later gives way to grasslands, and comes to a stream with waterfalls and pools, a good stopping place for lunch. From the viewpoint overlooking the Ohrigstad Valley it is a short, steady climb to the Excelsior Hut. The third day's hike (15.7 km; 7 hours) follows an undulating course. Highlights include the view from Themeda Hill, the Clivia Bush and a rocky maze. The final section of the trail ascends steeply through indigenous forest. **43.9 km; 3 days; circular.**

3. Prospector's and Morgenzon Trail The first day's trail (12.6 km; 7 hours) is the same as that of the Peach Tree Creek Trail, ascending from Pilgrim's Rest to Morgenzon Hut, and the remaining three days follow the same route as the Black Hill Trail. **56.5 km; 4 days; circular.**

4. Prospector's Five-day Trail Starting at Pilgrim's Rest Hut, the first two days of this hike follow the same route as the Prospector's and Morgenzon Trail. From Black Hill the third day's hike (10.5 km; 5 hours) ascends to the Black Hill Lookout, from where there are far-reaching views, and then descends before climbing steadily. The trail makes its way down to a stream with waterfalls and pools, after which there is a gentle climb to Excelsior Hut. The fourth day's hike (16 km; 7 hours) is moderately difficult, rambling over undulating terrain. Highlights include Clivia Bush, the view from Themeda Hill and a rocky maze. The final day's hike (8.3 km; 3 hours) is an easy downhill walk via Columbia Hill. **63 km; 5 days; circular.**

27. MOUNT SHEBA NATURE RESERVE
Pilgrim's Rest

> *Trails:* 2 trails; 3 and 5 km; 1.5 and 2.5 hours; circular and out-and-return. Network of 10 other shorter options available.

Permits: Not required by lodge guests.
Maps: Brochure and map available.
Facilities/Activities: Country lodge.

Situated on the slopes of Mount Sheba above Pilgrim's Rest, the 400-ha Mount Sheba Nature Reserve provides protection to one of the last remaining patches of unspoilt indigenous forest in the Mpumalanga Drakensberg. Dominant among the 110 tree species recorded in the forest are some exceptionally large yellowwood, red pear and Cape chestnut trees, and the forest floor has a rich diversity of ferns and mosses.

Baboon, samango monkey, thick-tailed bushbaby, blesbok, grey rhebok, klipspringer, red and common duiker, oribi, bushpig and rock dassie are all found here. The forests offer good birding opportunities.

The reserve is criss-crossed by a network of 12 trails, ranging from easy rambles to demanding routes.

1. Old Digging Walk This walk criss-crosses Kearney's Creek numerous times as it makes its way to old digging sites, dating back to the area's early gold rush days. Along the way you pass several fine yellowwood specimens and lovely pools. **3 km; 1.5 hours; out-and-return (from bridge over Kearney's Creek).**

2. Marco's Mantle Walk has justifiably been described as sensational. The first portion of the trail passes through indigenous forest to Marco's Mantle Falls, in the upper reaches of Kearney's Creek. Here the trail passes behind the falls and then leads down to the pool below the falls. **5 km; 2.5 hours; circular.**

Amongst the other walks that can be done here are the **Waterfall Trail**, which leads to two beautiful waterfalls in the Sheba Spruit, and a walk to the Lost City Viewpoint on Mount Sheba.

28. MATLAPA HIKING TRAIL
Steelpoort

> *Trail:* 18 km; 2 days; circular.
> *Permits:* Hikers Paradise,
> tel: (012) 663 7647, fax: 663 7649.

Maps: *Sketch map.*
Facilities/Activities: *Two overnight huts with bunks, mattresses, braai facilities, firewood, scullery, shower (Maroela Den only) and toilet.*
Pertinent information: *The trail's steep descents and boulder-hopping require caution.*

Laid out on the farm St George, south of Steelpoort, the name of this trail translates as 'Place of the Stones' – a reference to the eroded granite formations dominating the area.

From Maroela Den Camp, at the start of the trail, the first day's route (10 km; 6 hours) leads to the entrance of a valley, where an enormous common cluster fig and a rock with holes gouged into its surface by early inhabitants of the area can be seen. Further along, the trail ascends along a river course, which requires a fair amount of boulder-hopping, before reaching Jacob's Ladder, where hundreds of steps have been chiselled into a granite outcrop. Still further on, the trail meanders along St George's Street, with its interesting geological formations and far-reaching views, and then descends steeply along Russian Roulette Kloof to the Glygat Camp, named after the nearby natural rockslide into a pool.

Day two's hike (8 km; 5 hours) initially follows a river with beautiful pools and waterfalls and then ascends steeply to a viewpoint. From here it is a long descent to the upper reaches of the Fontein, after which the trail then continues down Broekskeurkloof to inviting pools at the base of the kloof. The final section is an easy ramble back to the start.

29. BLYDERIVIERSPOORT HIKING TRAIL
Blyde River Canyon Nature Reserve

See no. 30 (p. 236) for walks.

Trail: *30.1 km; 3 days; open-ended.*
Permits: *Mpumalanga Parks Board, P O Box 1990, Nelspruit 1200, tel: (013) 759 5432, fax: 755 3928.*
Maps: *Sketch map of trail.*
Facilities/Activities: *Two overnight huts with bunks, mattresses, pots, kettles, braai facilities, firewood and toilets.*
Pertinent information: *Parking is available at Paradise Camp at owners' risk. The trail from Bourke's Luck to Swadini is closed and hiking is not permitted on this section.*

The Blyderivierspoort ('Blyde River Canyon' in English) Hiking Trail traverses the southern half of the 30,000-ha Blyde River Canyon Nature Reserve, which contains well-known attractions such as The Pinnacle rock formation, God's Window and Bourke's Luck Potholes.

The vegetation in the high-lying southern reaches of the reserve is dominated by montane sourveld, which consists of open grassveld with small patches of indigenous forest. The grassveld is devoid of tall trees, except for the occasional stunted Transvaal beech, and you can often see common tree fern lining the small streams in the area.

Among the mammals found in the reserve are baboon, vervet monkey, bushbuck, kudu, red and common duiker, grey rhebok, klipspringer and bushpig. Some 227 bird species have been recorded in the reserve. These include 25 bird of prey species, such as black, martial and crowned eagles, black-breasted snake eagle, jackal buzzard, rock kestrel, and peregrine and lanner falcons. Keep an eye out for Shelley's francolin, Stanley's bustard, buff-streaked chat and Gurney's sugarbird, as well as bald ibis, a species that breeds in the cliffs near Bourke's Luck.

Starting at Paradise Camp, on the God's Window Loop Road outside Graskop, the first day's hike (3 km; 1 hour) meanders through weathered quartzite rocks and across grassland to the Watervalspruit Valley. From Paradise Pool the trail rises gently and then descends to Watervalspruit Hut, which is built against a slope.

Shortly after the start of the second day's hike (13.5 km; 5 hours), the trail makes its way past quartzite outcrops that have been eroded into interesting shapes and eye-catching patches of mottled yellow, white and red-brown lichens growing on the rocks. The path then descends to the Clearstream Hut, which is situated just upstream of a magnificent rock pool, where you can spend the afternoon swimming and relaxing.

On day three (13.6 km; 5 hours) the trail closely follows the Treur River, before passing the site from where the Voortrekker leader Hendrik Potgieter is thought to have set off to look for a route to the sea in 1840. The trail continues along the course of the Treur River past the New Chumm Falls and the Belvedere Hydro-Electric Station. It then skirts the Crocodile Valley Estates Plantation, descending gradually to Bourke's Luck Potholes and the Old Mine Hut.

30. BOURKE'S LUCK POTHOLES TRAILS
Blyde River Canyon Nature Reserve

See no. 29 (p. 235) for hiking trail.

Trails: 2 trails; 180 m and 8 km; 30 min and 5 hours; circular.
Permits: Available from Bourke's Luck Potholes Information Office.
Maps: Available from Bourke's Luck Potholes Information Office.
Facilities/Activities: Visitors' Centre; kiosk; picnic and braai facilities.

The famous Bourke's Luck Potholes are one of the main attractions of the Blyde River Canyon Nature Reserve. Here the Blyde River has cut a deep gorge into the rock and at its confluence with the Treur River the swirling waters of the two rivers and waterborne pebbles have eroded spectacular cylindrical potholes into the rock. The potholes were named after a certain Tom Bourke, who predicted that gold would be found in the vicinity. Ironically, Bourke's nearby claim turned out to be unproductive. Good views of the gorge and the potholes can be obtained from the three metal bridges spanning the gorge.

Downstream of Bourke's Luck, the Blyde River has carved a spectacular canyon, which is up to 700 m deep and 32 km long. Overlooking the Blyde River Canyon are the well-known Three Rondavels peaks.

1. Lichen Trail is an interpretive walk with information points about lichens on boards along the trail. Information is also provided in large print, as well as in Braille, and there is a tapping rail for blind visitors. This walk is also suitable for those in wheelchairs. Although under an hour, this trail is still included here as it is one of the few walks available for the blind and physically disabled. **180 m; 30 min; circular.**

2. Belvedere Day Walk leads to the Belvedere Hydro-Electric Power Station at the confluence of the Blyde and Belvedere rivers. Built in 1911 to supply electricity to the 'gold crushers' (machines that crushed ore) at Pilgrim's Rest, it was the largest plant of its kind in the whole of the southern hemisphere at the time. From the Bourke's Luck Visitors' Centre the trail descends steeply into the Blyde River Canyon, losing some 400 m in altitude. The return leg follows a different route back to the start. It is a strenuous trail, which should only be attempted by fit hikers. **8 km; 5 hours; circular.**

31. HADEDA FALLS HIKING TRAIL
Burgersfort

Trails: 5 trails; 4 to 15.8 km; 2 to 9 hours; network from basecamp.
Permits: Jacana Marketing and Reservations, P O Box 95212, Waterkloof 0145, tel: (012) 346 3550, fax: 346 2499, email: info@jacanacollection.co.za
Maps: Trail pamphlet with sketch map.
Facilities/Activities: Basecamp: huts with bunks, mattresses, kitchen with pots, pans, gas cooker, braai facilities, firewood, hot showers and toilets. Leopard Cave: overhang accommodating eight people; tent site; braai facilities, firewood and toilet. Hadeda's Nest: fully equipped self-catering rondavel.

Situated in the Waterfall River Valley, northwest of Lydenburg, this trail network traverses several citrus and vegetable farms, starting from Buffelsvlei Farm. The routes wind through the unspoilt areas of the farms, and among the animals you may chance upon are kudu, grey rhebok, mountain reedbuck, bushbuck, common duiker and baboon.

1. Leopard Loop winds from Three Loop Junction to Hadeda Falls and ascends along the stream, past numerous waterfalls and pools, to Leopard Cave Falls and Leopard Cave. This cave is a popular lunch and overnight stop. **4 km; 2 hours; open-ended.**

2. Krantz Trail follows the same route as the River Trail for about 700 m, but instead of turning left at the first junction it continues straight and climbs to a rock face, thereafter reaching a gorge, where a tyre ladder helps hikers to climb to the top of the first krans ledge. A short walk leads to Three Loop Junction at the top of a waterfall, from where the trail follows the edge of the cliffs to the Hadeda Falls. Here you have the option of taking a 1.6-km out-and-return detour to Leopard Cave or you can have a swim in the pool below the Hadeda Falls before continuing. From this point the trail ascends steeply and crosses the river several times on the way to the basecamp. This trail can also be combined with Leopard Loop to form an overnight trail. **4.5 km; 2 hours; circular.**

3. River Trail is an easy ramble, which follows the same route as the Krantz Trail for about 700 m. It then splits off to the left to ascend a koppie, from where there are lovely views of the fruit and vegetable farms in the valley. After following a contour the trail winds down to the Watervals River, which you follow for a while before ascending a hill and winding back to the basecamp. **5.6 km; 3 hours; circular.**

4. Tree Fern Kloof Trail follows the Krantz Trail to Three Loop Junction, from where it ascends along a stream, the banks of which are lined with numerous common tree ferns. The trail continues its ascent past numerous waterfalls, including six falling into a single pool and another one 40 m high. At the crest this hike joins up with the Ammo Trail, and then follows the Leopard Loop and Krantz Trail back to the basecamp. **7.5 km; 4 hours; circular.**

5. Ammo Trail splits off in an easterly direction from the Gorge Junction and traverses a 500-m section, with a sheer drop, before ascending steeply to the base of Ammo Gorge. Car tyres have been placed in the gorge to help hikers negotiate difficult sections, and once you reach the top of the gorge you can enjoy a bird's-eye view of the Skurings, Steenkamps and Drakensberg. From here the trail continues to Leopard Cave and Hadeda Falls, before traversing to Three Loop Junction, where it backtracks along the Krantz Trail for just over 1 km. The final section follows the River Trail back to the basecamp. You can also do this hike as an overnight trail, ending the first day at Leopard Cave and hiking the remainder of the trail the following day. **15.8 km; 9 hours.**

32. KRUGER NATIONAL PARK
Eastern Mpumalanga

Trails: 7 overnight wilderness trails; variable distances, up to 20 km a day from basecamp; 2 days/3 nights. Guided 2- to 3-hour day walks; 4 to 6 km; circular.
Permits: South African National Parks, P O Box 787, Pretoria 0001, tel: (012) 428 9111, fax: 343 0905, email: reservations@parks-sa.co.za
Maps: General park map.
Facilities/Activities: 12 restcamps with self-catering accommodation; six bushveld camps; four satellite camps; campsites in the park; luxury private camps; restaurants; shops. On the trails: rustic huts with beds, bedding, covered lapa that serves as dining area, reed-walled showers and toilets.
Pertinent information: Groups are limited to eight persons, all of whom must be between the ages of 12 and 60 years. Trails are conducted from Sunday to Wednesday or from Wednesday to Saturday. A reasonable level of fitness is essential, as up to 20 km may be walked in a day. Anti-malaria precautions are essential.

Proclaimed in 1926, the Kruger National Park is one of Africa's great game parks and is renowned worldwide for its superb wildlife. The park covers nearly 2 million ha of unspoilt wilderness and is home to 147 mammal species. For many visitors the park's chief attraction is the Big Five (elephant, rhino, buffalo, lion and leopard), but there is also a wide variety of antelope such as sable, nyala, kudu, waterbuck, tsessebe and impala (the most abundant of the antelope). Also to be seen are wild dog, cheetah, herds of blue wildebeest, Burchell's zebra, giraffe and hippo.

Kruger National Park offers exceptional birding, with a bird checklist of 505 species. Especially rewarding is the northern corner, where several uncommon species can be ticked. More than 50 raptor species have been recorded in the park to date.

In July 1978 Kruger National Park's first hike, Wolhuter Wilderness Trail, was opened in the south of the park. Since then the number of wilderness trails has increased to seven, and they are spread throughout the park.

Trails are conducted by a trained trails ranger and, although game-viewing on foot forms an integral part of the experience, time is also spent learning more about the environment. The trails ranger will interpret the tell-tale signs of nature, and tree identification, bird-watching and appreciating the beauty of nature all form part of the experience. The trail camps are rustic, but comfortable, and serve as a base from where walks are undertaken. Simple, but wholesome, meals are provided.

1. Bushman Trail

is conducted in the southwestern corner of the park in an area boasting over 90 rock art sites, as well as numerous Stone and Iron Age sites. The generally hilly terrain is punctuated by granite outcrops, which afford trailists magnificent views of the area. Among the animals trailists might find are white rhino, elephant, buffalo, mountain reedbuck, kudu, klipspringer, Burchell's zebra and giraffe. The Malelane Gate is the nearest entry point to the Berg-en-Dal Restcamp, from where trailists are transported to the basecamp.

2. Metsi-Metsi Trail

The undulating hills and gorges east of Nwarmuriwa Mountain near Tshokwane provide a glorious setting for this trail, named after the Metsi-Metsi River (meaning 'water-water'). The Nwaswitsonto River, which is one of the few permanent sources of water in the park, attracts a rich diversity of game during the dry winter months. Game occurring in the area includes large numbers of elephant, black rhino, buffalo, lion and several antelope species, and the basecamp overlooks a small waterhole where animals come to drink. Trails depart from Skukuza, the most convenient entrance gate for this camp being Kruger Gate.

3. Napi Trail

traverses the rolling landscape and granite hills midway between Skukuza and Pretoriuskop. The basecamp is situated at the confluence of the Mbayamiti and Napi rivers in an area with a high white rhino population. Trailists may also chance upon black rhino, elephant, buffalo, sable, kudu and reedbuck. Predators such as lion, leopard and wild dog occur in the area, which also supports prolific birdlife. Trailists meet at Pretoriuskop. Numbi is the entrance gate nearest to this camp.

4. Nyalaland Trail

The Punda Maria region in the far north of the Kruger National Park is considered one of southern Africa's most outstanding wilderness areas. The landscape is characterised by mopane trees, extensive baobab 'forests' and stands of fever trees. Although not rich in game it is one of South Africa's birding hotspots, with several Red Data species such as mottled and Böhm's spinetails and the silvery-cheeked hornbill. Punda Maria Restcamp, from where trailists are transported to the basecamp on the banks of the Madzaringwe Stream, is best accessed through Punda Maria Gate.

5. Olifants Trail

is found in the central part of the park, with a basecamp on the southern bank of the Olifants River, 4 km west of its confluence with the Letaba River. Game is plentiful and species to be seen include elephant, buffalo giraffe, blue wildebeest, waterbuck, Burchell's zebra and lion, and hippo and crocodile abound in the river. The landscape is diverse, ranging from plains to the foothills of the Lebombo Mountains, and the potholes in the narrow ravines near the basecamp are a scenic highlight. Trails depart from Letaba Restcamp. Ba-Phalaborwa is the nearest entrance gate.

6. Sweni Trail

On this wilderness trail hikers explore the area near Nwanetsi. The marula and knob thorn savannah supports a rich diversity of game, including elephant, buffalo, black and white rhino, blue wildebeest, Burchell's zebra, giraffe and lion. Trailists are transported from Satara Restcamp, best reached via Orpen Gate, to the basecamp, which overlooks the Sweni Stream, with its exceptional communities of lala palms.

7. Wolhuter Trail honours the legendary Harry and Henry Wolhuter, a father and son, who were in control of the southern section of the park for many years during the first half of the 1900s. The trail is conducted in the area between the Berg-en-Dal and Pretoriuskop restcamps, a landscape characterised by gently rolling bushveld plains punctuated by granite outcrops. This area, in the heart of white rhino country, is also favoured by mountain reedbuck, sable, impala, giraffe, blue wildebeest, leopard and lion. Trailists must report at Berg-en-Dal Restcamp, from where they are transported to the basecamp on the Mavukane River. Malelane Gate is the most convenient entry point for this trail.

8. Day walks are conducted for groups of between four and eight persons under the guidance of two armed field guides. The trails start early in the morning and last between three and four hours. Along the way the guides will track game and share their intimate knowledge of the local animal-, plant- and birdlife with trailists. Walks can be reserved at Berg-en-Dal, Letaba, Lower Sabie, Mopani, Orpen, Pretoriuskop, Satara and Skukuza restcamps, as well as at Bateleur, Biyamiti and Shimuwini bushveld camps. Children under 12 years are not allowed on the day walks. **4 to 6 km; 2 to 3 hours; circular.**

33. DE NECK HIKING TRAIL
Letsitele

Trails: 2 trails with linking routes; 30 km (in total); network from base.
Permits: Jacana Marketing and Reservations, P O Box 95212, Waterkloof 0145, tel: (012) 346 3550, fax: 346 2499,

email: info@jacanacollection.co.za
Maps: Trail pamphlet with map.
Facilities/Activities: Knoppiesdoring Camp: huts with beds, mattresses, gas lamps, hot showers and toilets. Ou Kraal: converted silos with bunks, mattresses, two-plate gas cooker, pots, pans, kettle, braai facilities, firewood, scullery, hot showers and toilets. Murchison View Campsite: sites for tents. Mountain biking.

Nestling between the folds of the Seribane Hills, De Neck Private Nature Reserve near Letsitele is home to a variety of game. Among the species to be seen are sable, giraffe, kudu, reedbuck and Burchell's zebra, and a rich variety of birds have also been recorded in the reserve. Also of interest are Iron Age sites that were inhabited by the ancestors of the Shangaan people, who have lived in the area for centuries.

The trail network consists of two day walks, **Rietbok Round** and **Rooibok Loop**, which are linked by six connecting routes, enabling trailists to tailor-make their own trail combinations. The routes pass through riverine forest, lush kloofs and along the slopes of the Seribane Hills, which have wonderful far-reaching views of the Murchison Range to the east.

34. GIRAFFE HIKING TRAIL
Hans Merensky Nature Reserve, Letsitele

See no. 35 (p. 240) for walks.

Trails: 21 or 32 km; 2 or 3 days; circular.
Permits: The Officer-in-Charge, Hans Merensky Nature Reserve, Private Bag X502, Letsitele 0885, tel. and fax: (015) 386 8633.
Maps: Trail brochure with sketch map.
Facilities/Activities: Overnight camp: thatched A-frame huts with bunks, mattresses, dining area under thatch, fireplace, firewood, cold showers and toilet. Eiland Resort:

self-catering accommodation; swimming pool; Visitors' Centre; self-drive game-viewing; Tsonga Kraal Museum.

Pertinent information: As temperatures can rise up to 40 °C in mid-summer, precautions such as a sunhat and sunscreen are advisable. You need carry only a daypack for the second day's hike, as it is a circular day walk from the overnight hut.

Situated 66 km northeast of Tzaneen, the Hans Merensky Nature Reserve covers 5,300 ha of Arid Lowveld vegetation and is bounded by the Letaba River to the north. The vegetation consists mainly of mopane woodlands, and woodlands of round-leaved teak, red bushwillow and silver cluster-leaf.

The impala is the most numerous of the many antelope species roaming the reserve. Amongst the other antelope found here are kudu, sable, water-buck, reedbuck, bushbuck, blue wildebeest and Sharpe's grysbok. Also occurring in the reserve are a variety of animals, including giraffe, Burchell's zebra, warthog and hippo.

Birdlife is quite prolific in this area, and amongst the more than 280 species that have been recorded here are Arnot's chat, open-billed and saddle-billed storks, hooded vulture, scimitar-billed woodhoopoe, arrow-marked babbler and black-headed oriole.

The first day's hike (9 km; 3 hours) follows an easy, level path through mopane woodlands. On account of the dense vegetation, game-viewing is difficult, but the birdlife compensates amply. The overnight camp is situated near a waterhole, where you may spot some game.

Day two (11 km; 4 hours) wanders through mopane and red bushwillow woodlands to the Black Hills, a dolerite dyke that has forced its way through the granite. Here trailists can enjoy the only panoramic view on the trail before continuing to a large dam, which offers good birding opportunities and the chance of seeing game. From here it is an easy 90-minute walk back to the basecamp.

On day three (12 km; 4 hours) the trail winds in a northeasterly direction to the base of the Black Hills. It then swings west and, after a while, joins the first day's route, along which you back-track to the start.

35. HANS MERENSKY NATURE RESERVE
Letsitele

See no. 34 (p. 239) for hiking trail.

Trails: 3 trails; 1.12 to 11 km; 30 min to 4 hours; circular.
Permits: Entrance fee. No permit required for walks.
Maps: Brochure with sketch maps.
Facilities/Activities: Eiland Resort: self-catering accommodation; swimming pool; Visitors' Centre; self-drive game-viewing; Tsonga Kraal Museum.

1. Mopane Interpretative Trail Although this trail is under an hour, it is included here as it provides an excellent introduction to the trees and other environmental aspects of the area, which are marked with numbered points that are explained in a brochure. The trail starts at the Visitors' Centre. **1.12 km; 30 min; circular.**

2. Letaba Nature Trail has been laid out in the northern part of the reserve and starts at the reserve entrance gate. A 1-km section of the trail, consisting of two loops, makes its way through dense riverine vegetation along the Letaba River. **7 km; 2.5 hours; circular.**

3. Waterbuck Nature Trail Starting at the Visitors' Centre, this route follows a loop through the southern section of the reserve. Over the course of the trail there is ample opportunity for bird-watching, and you may well see some game, provided you move fairly quietly. **11 km; 4 hours; circular.**

36. ROOIKAT NATURE WALK
Tzaneen

Trail: 11 km; 5 hours; circular.
Permits: The Forester, New Agatha Plantation, Private Bag X4009,

Tzaneen 0850, tel: (015) 307 4311,
fax: 307 5926. Permits can be obtained
at the start of the trail during office hours.
Maps: *Trail pamphlet with sketch map.*
Facilities/Activities: *Picnic site and toilets*
at the halfway mark.
Pertinent information: *Arrangements to visit*
the area must be made well in advance.
After heavy rains it is advisable to check
whether the trail is open, as the Bobs River,
which is crossed several times during the
course of the hike, could be in flood.

Haenertsburg 0730, tel: (015) 276 1303.
Maps: *Information pamphlet and sketch*
map. The area is covered by 1:50,000
topographical map sections 2330CC
and 2430AA.
Facilities/Activities: *Campsite at start*
with showers and toilets.
Pertinent information: *The maximum*
group size for overnight visitors is 10,
and there is a limit of 60 people per
day. Fires are strictly forbidden in the
wilderness area. It is essential to carry
a topographical map, as the footpaths
are often indistinct.

This trail meanders through the New Agatha Plantation, 18 km east of Tzaneen, against the backdrop of Krugerkop and Tandberg, two well-known landmarks of the Wolkberg. Although pine and eucalyptus plantations have replaced much of the natural vegetation here, the banks of the Bobs River are lined with magnificent indigenous forest. Some of the trees along the route have been marked with their national tree number and among the species common to this area are Natal mahogany, white stinkwood, mitzeeri, pigeonwood and forest cabbage tree.

In addition to the caracal, a small cat to which the trail owes its Afrikaans name, this area is also home to bushbuck, common duiker, bushpig and baboon, as well as vervet and samango monkeys. Birds you may tick include the rare bat hawk (which breeds here), jackal buzzard, purple-crested lourie, black-headed oriole and brown-throated weaver.

After initially passing through pine plantations, the trail follows the course of the Bobs River. The trail crosses the river a number of times, and passes several cascades, rapids and pools where trailists can cool off. Set among pin oaks, Die Akker picnic site is reached after about 7 km. The final 4 km of the trail is through eucalyptus and pine plantations.

37. WOLKBERG WILDERNESS AREA
Tzaneen

Trails: *No set trails.*
Permits: *The Officer-in-Charge,*
Wolkberg Wilderness, Private Bag X102,

Situated about 80 km southwest of Tzaneen, the Wolkberg forms an arc where the northern extension of the Drakensberg joins the eastern extremity of the Strydpoort Mountain. The wilderness area covers 19,145 ha of high mountain peaks, deep ravines, patches of indigenous forest and grasslands. Dominated by the 2,050-m-high Krugerkop, also known as Serala, the Wolkberg (meaning 'cloud mountain') frequently lives up to its name, especially in summer when the high peaks are often covered in a fine mist.

Most of the vegetation is dominated by montane sourveld interspersed with proteaveld, but the vegetation along the Mohlapitse Valley consists of sour grassveld and bushveld trees. Patches of indigenous forest occur in deep ravines and on the southern and eastern slopes of higher-lying areas. Noteworthy trees include the Transvaal mountain sugarbush and the Modjadji cycad.

The area does not support a rich diversity of large mammals. Species you might see include bushbuck, grey rhebok, reedbuck, klipspringer, common duiker, baboon, samango and vervet monkeys, and lesser bushbaby.

Among the more than 157 bird species recorded here to date are bat hawk, martial eagle, black-fronted bush shrike, crested guineafowl and yellow wagtail. Also keep an eye out for secretary bird, Burchell's coucal, southern boubou, lilac-breasted roller and Marico sunbird.

Except for management tracks and faint footpaths there are no set trails in this wilderness area. From the office a jeep track descends past a spectacular tufa formation in the Ashmole Dales Valley to the Mohlapitse River, which you can follow downstream to its junction with the Mogwatse River. By turning up Mampa's Kloof you can continue to well-known landmarks such as the Devil's Knuckles, the Wonderwoud and the Thabina Falls.

The Devil's Knuckles, a 6-km ridge of quartzite cliffs, are a formidable barrier, which can only be crossed at the highest knuckle. From the summit it is a steep descent to the Wonderwoud, and there are chains to assist hikers at a difficult section. Covering 500 ha, the Wonderwoud is the largest indigenous forest in the wilderness area and has some fine yellowwood specimens, with trunk circumferences of up to 5 m.

From the Wonderwoud you can follow the Shobwe River downstream to a jeep track, which climbs back to the starting point. A short detour off the track leads to the Klipdraai Falls, a good example of a tufa waterfall. The other option from the Wonderwoud is to continue to the Serala Plateau, via Kruger's Nose, which forms part of what looks like the profile of former president Paul Kruger, with the Wonderwoud forming his beard.

38. MAGOEBASKLOOF HIKING TRAIL
Tzaneen

Trails: 65.7 km; 5 days; circular.
4 shorter options; 20.1 to 40.7 km;
2 to 3 days; circular.
Permits: SAFCOL Ecotourism,
P O Box 1771, Silverton 0127,
tel: (012) 481 3615, fax: 481 3622,
email: ecotour@safcol.co.za
Maps: A4 sketch map of trail.
Facilities/Activities: Six overnight huts
with bunks, mattresses, braai facilities,
showers (hot water at De Hoek and
Broederstroom, cold at Dokolewa,
Waterfall, Woodbush and Seepsteen
Mule Stables) and toilets.
Pertinent information: Starting points
are at De Hoek, Woodbush and
Broederstroom huts. Dokolewa Pools
Hut is a 1.5-km walk from De Hoek,

and the distance from Woodbush Hut
to Seepsteen Stables Hut is also 1.5 km.
Since the trail has some steep ascents
and descents (with altitude differences
of 500 m), trailists must ensure they are
fit before attempting this hike.

The indigenous forests of Magoebaskloof are among the most beautiful in South Africa, resembling a fairytale wonderland. Streams cascade down the mountain slopes over moss-covered rocks, while ferns line their banks. Overhead, large masses of clivias (*Clivia* spp.) nestle in the forks of tree branches, and the colourful Knysna lourie can be seen gliding between trees. Some sections of the trail traverse pine plantations.

The forest is the home to red duiker, leopard and bushbuck, as well as vervet and samango monkeys. The latter can be identified by their call, which consists of a loud repeated 'nyah', often followed by a series of chuckles. Although bushpigs are mainly nocturnal, they are often seen in Grootbosch during the daytime.

Grootbosch is the largest indigenous forest north of the Vaal River, covering some 4,600 ha. Among the dominant species here are Outeniqua and real yellowwoods, white stinkwood, lemonwood, forest bushwillow and ironwood. The area is also home to several epiphytic orchids, while forest montbretia (*Crocosmia aurea*), with its yellow-orange flowers, the showy *Streptocarpus parviflorus* and impatients (*Impatiens* spp.) are amongst the flowering species on the forest floor.

Birdlife is prolific, with some 309 species recorded in the De Hoek and Grootbosch areas. Species to keep an eye out for include crowned and long-crested eagles, black-fronted bush shrike, chorister and starred robins, black-eyed bulbul and yellow-throated warbler.

Of historic interest are the Seepsteen Mule Stables, the Woodbush Arboretum (established in 1907) and the oak trees planted along the Broederstroom by Lady Florence Phillips, who bred horses at the Broederstroom Stud Farm in the second decade of the 1900s.

The trail network consists of several sections, which can be combined to form trails ranging from two to five days.

1. Debengeni Trail starts at Woodbush Hut and descends steadily to De Hoek (11.7 km; 6 hours). Shortly before you reach De Hoek, a path leads to a viewpoint overlooking the spectacular Debengeni Falls. The return route (8.4 km; 3 hours) is an uphill haul, involving an altitude gain of some 500 m to Woodbush. Highlights include the Dokolewa Pools, exceptionally tall tree ferns and the walk along the Dokolewa Stream, with its pools and magificent indigenous forest. The trail can also be hiked in the opposite direction, starting at De Hoek. **20.1 km; 2 days; circular.**

2. Dokolewa Pools Trail This option starts at Dokolewa Pools Hut and day one's hike (9 km; 5 hours) ascends along the return leg of the Debengeni Trail before branching off to the Seepsteen Stables Hut near the end of the trail. Day two's hike (12 km; 5 hours) is a steady descent, which leads past Debengeni Falls and then to the Dokolewa Pools Hut. **21 km; 2 days; circular.**

3. Dokolewa Waterfalls Trail (from Woodbush Hut) From Woodbush Hut the first day's hike (13.7 km; 7 hours) leaves the arboretum and winds through pine plantations interspersed with patches of indigenous forest. The trail passes what is reputedly the tallest planted tree in the southern hemisphere, a saligna gum tree with a height of 84.4 m. The trail climbs through indigenous forest and patches of pine plantation, and then descends. Further along it passes through an avenue of oak trees planted in the early 1900s and ascends to a viewpoint overlooking the Dap Naude Dam. After skirting the dam you reach the turnoff to the Broederstroom Hut and Waterfall Camp. The second day's hike (18 km; 7 hours) follows an easy route along a ridge, from where there are spectacular views of the forested valley below. Further along, the trail descends steeply to the top of a series of high waterfalls. Another waterfall is reached a short way on, and the trail then wends its way past tall tree ferns lining the Dokolewa Stream, which you follow past several inviting pools to the Dokolewa Pools. The last 1 km ascends through pine plantations to the Dokolewa Pools Hut. The final day's hike (9 km; 5 hours) is a steady uphill climb back to the parking area at Woodbush Hut. **40.7 km; 3 days; circular.**

4. Dokolewa Waterfalls Trail (from Dokolewa Pools Hut) starts at the Dokolewa Pools Hut, from where the first day's hike (8.4 km) climbs steadily to the Seepsteen Stables Hut. Day two's hike (13.8 km; 6 hours) makes its way to Waterfall Camp, while the third day's hike (18 km; 7 hours) descends to Dokolewa Pools Hut. Highlights include magnificent tree ferns, the walk along the Dokolewa Stream, with its pools and magificent indigenous forest, the arboretum at Woodbush, the waterfalls in Grootbosch and the Dokolewa waterfalls and pools. **40.2 km; 3 days; circular.**

5. Magoebaskloof Five-night Trail This trail combines all the highlights of the Magoebaskloof area. The first three days of the hike follow the same route as the Dokolewa Waterfalls Trail option, which starts at De Hoek parking area. From Dokolewa Pools Hut the fourth day of the Magoebaskloof Five-night Trail (9 km; 5 hours) ascends to Woodbush Hut, and the final day's hike (16 km; 6 hours) makes its way mainly downhill to De Hoek. **65.7 km; 5 days; circular.**

39. MODJADJI NATURE RESERVE
Tzaneen

Trail: 7 km; 3–4 hours; circular.
Permits: Entrance fee. No permit required for walk.
Maps: Sketch map.
Facilities/Activities: Information Centre; museum; picnic sites.

Covering 530 ha, the Modjadji Nature Reserve provides protection to a unique and spectacular forest of Modjadji cycads on the slopes above the Modjadji Valley, 35 km northeast of Tzaneen. This reserve is said to contain the highest concentration of a single cycad species in the world. The Modjadji cycad is the tallest-growing of all the 29 different cycad species indigenous to South Africa, and although their average height ranges between 5 m and 8 m, large specimens can grow up to 13 m tall, and their golden-brown fruit can weigh a staggering 34 kg.

The cycad forest has enjoyed the protection of successive generations of Modjadji, or Rain Queens, the hereditary female rulers of the Bolobedu people, who have lived in the area for over three centuries. A small museum dedicated to the Rain Queen provides a fascinating insight into the Bolobedu people and their mystical rulers.

The trail winds through the cycad forest down to the bushveld below, where trailists may see waterbuck, blue wildebeest, nyala and impala. Over 170 bird species have been recorded in the area, among them black eagle, purple-crested lourie and bush shrike.

40. KHONGONI HIKING TRAIL
Ben Lavin Nature Reserve,
Makhado (Louis Trichardt)

See no. 41 (this page) for walks.

Trail: 17.5 km; 2 days; circular.
Permits: Jacana Marketing and Reservations,
P O Box 95212, Waterkloof 0145,
tel: (012) 346 3550, fax: 346 2499,
email: info@jacanacollection.co.za
Maps: Sketch map.
Facilities/Activities: Muvuvhu Main
Camp: fully equipped thatched lodges
with en-suite bathrooms; fully equipped
thatched huts with toilet and basin;
equipped two-bed tents; campsites with
braai facilities, electrical points, hot
water ablutions; swimming pool; shop
selling groceries, firewood and curios.
Bush Camp: two fully equipped rustic
thatched 10-bed huts with kitchen, braai
facilities and hot-water ablutions (guests need
to supply their own bedding and
towels). Mountain biking; self-drive
game-viewing; guided night-drives; bird-
and game-viewing hides.

The 2,500-ha Ben Lavin Nature Reserve, 12 km southeast of Makhado, provides the setting for this overnight hiking trail. The reserve was donated to the Wildlife and Environment Society in 1970 by Mrs Molly Lavin, following the death of her conservation-minded husband, Ben, so that the land could be developed in his memory.

The reserve is home to a variety of antelope, including sable, blue wildebeest (after which the trail is named; *khongoni* means 'wildebeest' in Venda), tsessebe, red hartebeest, waterbuck, mountain reedbuck, kudu, nyala, impala and bushbuck. Among the other species found here are giraffe, Burchell's zebra, warthog, brown hyaena and a variety of small mammals.

To date over 230 bird species have been recorded, among them Wahlberg's and martial eagles, black-breasted snake eagle, green pigeon, purple-crested lourie and yellow-throated longclaw. Also keep an eye out for Burchell's coucal, broad-billed roller, scimitar-billed woodhoopoe, African golden oriole, yellow-breasted apalis and orange-breasted bush shrike.

The first day's hike (8 km; 4 hours) follows an easy route through grasslands to Tabajwane Koppie, and then continues past the Tabajwane windmill and Mdudzi Dam, to reach the Doring River. A little further on, the path joins the Fountain Trail for a short distance before branching off to the Bush Camp.

On day two (9.5 km; 5 hours) the trail passes through bushveld vegetation past the Makulu Dam and then follows the Klipspruit River to the Tshumanini waterhole and hide. The return leg of trail leads you to a lookout and, further along, links up with the Fountain Trail, which you follow back to the start.

41. BEN LAVIN NATURE RESERVE
Makhado (Louis Trichardt)

See no. 40 (this page) for hiking trail.

Trails: 4 trails; 3 to 8 km; 1.5 to
4 hours; circular.
Permits: Entrance fee. No permit
required for walks.
Maps: Sketch map available at
reserve entrance.
Facilities/Activities: Muvuvhu Main

Camp: *fully equipped thatched lodges with en-suite bathrooms; fully equipped thatched huts with toilet and basin; equipped two-bed tents; campsites with braai facilities, electrical points and hot-water ablutions; swimming pool; shop selling groceries, firewood and curios. Bush Camp: two fully equipped rustic thatched 10-bed huts with kitchen, braai facilities and hot-water ablutions (guests need to supply their own bedding and towels). Mountain biking; self-drive game viewing; guided night-drives; bird- and game-viewing hides.*
Pertinent information: *Group size is limited – a maximum of six people is allowed per trail.*

1. Waterbuck Trail

Starting near Muvuvhu Main Camp, this trail passes the Waterbuck, Steenbok and Marsh dams and then follows Camp Road back to the start. In addition to waterbuck, trailists may spot impala and kudu. **3 km; 1.5 hours; circular.**

2. Fountain Trail

meanders through grassland to the Doring River, with its lush riverine vegetation. Game you might encounter here includes nyala, reedbuck and bushbuck. After following the banks of the river the trail links up with Camp Road. **4 km; 2 hours; circular.**

3. Tshumanini Springs Trail

traverses the northern section of the Ben Lavin Nature Reserve, an area favoured by Burchell's zebra, impala, kudu and warthog. The trail starts at Zebra Dam and winds to the Tshumanini waterhole and hide. **5 km; 2.5 hours; out-and-return.**

4. Tabajwane Trail

From Muvuvhu Main Camp the trail stays close to the reserve's southern boundary on the way to Tabajwane Koppie, from where trailists can enjoy beautiful views over the surrounding bushveld and the Soutpansberg. The trail then continues on past the Tabajwane windmill and Mpunzi Dam, and the return route follows the Doring River back to the start. **8 km; 4 hours; circular.**

42. MABUDASHANGO HIKING TRAIL
Thohoyandou

Trail: *53 km; 4 days; circular.*
Permits: *Department of Forestry, Private Bag X2413, Makhado 0920, tel: (015) 516 0201, fax: 516 1062.*
Maps: *Sketch map.*
Facilities: *Two overnight stops on trail: basic thatched open shelters, fireplace, firewood, water, refuse bin and toilet.*
Pertinent information: *After heavy rains river crossings can be difficult, especially on day three.*

This hiking trail in the eastern reaches of the Soutpansberg leads through pine-scented plantations and dank, unspoilt indigenous forests. The area is rich in the lore of the Venda people, and the trail winds through the Thathe Sacred Forest, as well as providing you with a glimpse of the sacred Lake Fundudzi. Various vantage points afford splendid views of golden-green tea plantations, typical Venda villages, interlocking pine plantations and indigenous forests.

The indigenous forests are composed of species such as broom cluster and Natal fig, lemonwood, Cape holly, common onionwood, forest fever tree, Transvaal wild banana and large-leaved dragon tree. Trees to be seen in the Thathe Sacred Forest include real yellowwood, Transvaal pock ironwood, common wild elder, lemonwood, wild loquat and red bird-berry.

Mammals you might spot in the forests include samango monkey, bushpig, bushbuck and red duiker, while leopard also occur, but are seldom seen, owing to their secretive habits. Look out for vervet monkey on the forest fringes and baboon in rocky mountain areas. Common duiker and mountain reedbuck also occur in the area.

Birdlife is prolific and you should keep an eye out for crested guineafowl, olive bush shrike, crowned hornbill, black-headed oriole, Knysna and purple-crested lourie. Birds of prey include crowned and black eagles, as well as African goshawk. Burchell's coucal and long-tailed wagtail might also be ticked.

The first day's hike (14 km; 7 hours) initially follows plantation roads and then climbs steeply through indigenous forest to a vantage point with splendid views over the Tshivase tea estate, the Vondo Dam and Lwamondo Kop, which is revered by the Venda people. The trail then drops down to the Nzhelele River and ascends steeply through indigenous forest to a plateau. The remainder of the day's hike to Fundudzi Camp is mainly along forestry roads through pine plantations.

Day two (13 km; 6 hours) starts with a walk along the Mutale River and then follows a fire-break, from where you will get your first glimpse of the sacred Lake Fundudzi. The lake is the source of many beliefs among the Venda, who believe that its southwestern shore is the 'spirit gardens' where their ancestral spirits still cultivate their crops. From here the trail ascends steadily to the Thathe Sacred Forest, which is the traditional burial ground of chiefs of the Netshisivhe family. Continuing its ascent, the path reaches the beacon at the 1,438-m-high Vhulambanngwe, the highest point of the trail. The trail then descends steeply through indigenous forest, where wooden ladders assist hikers at difficult sections. The final part of the day's hike follows forestry roads through pine plantations to Mukumbani Camp, situated just above Mukumbani Dam.

Day three's hike (15 km; 7 hours) leads to the Mahovhohovho Waterfall, from where it follows forestry roads through pine plantations and a patch of dry forest, where some impressive common tree ferns (some up to 5 m tall) are a high-light. Further along, the trail crosses the Tshirovha River and, after recrossing it, makes its way through dry scrub to the Tshatsingo Potholes, which was used as a place to execute killers and people accused of bewitching others, many genera-tions ago. Here the river cascades about 4 m into a pothole, resembling a cauldron of boiling water, and then re-appears in a smaller pothole several metres downstream. From here you retrace your tracks back to Mukumbani Camp.

After walking along the Mukumbani Dam wall at the start of day four (11 km; 5 hours) you climb sharply to a lookout. After enjoying the all-round views, you descend through pine plantations and indigenous forest. Further along the trail skirts a typical Venda village and then swings into pine plantations. The remainder of the hike follows forestry roads through pine plantations.

43. SOUTPANSBERG HIKING TRAIL
Makhado (Louis Trichardt)

Trail: 20.5 km; 2 days; circular.
Permits: SAFCOL Ecotourism, P O Box 1771, Silverton 0127, tel: (012) 481 3615, fax: 481 3622, email: ecotour@safcol.co.za
Maps: A4 colour sketch map of trail.
Facilities/Activities: Two overnight huts with bunks, mattresses, braai facilities, firewood, hot (Soutpansberg Hut) and cold (Hanglip Hut) showers, and toilets.

Laid out on the slopes of the Soutpansberg, South Africa's northern-most mountain, this trail follows the first day's route of the original Soutpansberg Hiking Trail. Although most of the trail is through pine and eucalyptus plantations, sections wind through beautiful indigenous forest.

Among the dominant tree species are real yellow-wood, lemonwood, forest bushwillow, forest water-wood and Cape beech. Other species found here include knobwood, Cape chestnut, Transvaal plane, assegai and forest elder.

Three primate species occur in the Soutpansberg (vervet and samango monkeys, and baboon), and antelope are represented by bushbuck, klipspringer, oribi and common duiker. Also inhabiting the range is the shy and secretive leopard.

Birdlife is prolific and includes the black spar-rowhawk, long-crested and crowned eagles, red-eyed dove, Narina trogon and Knysna lourie. You might also tick chorister and starred robins, olive bush shrike and crested guineafowl.

From Zoutpansberg Hut the first day's hike (13 km; 6 hours) ascends steeply through pine plan-tations for the first 5.5 km, gaining some 300 m in altitude. The trail passes through a patch of beauti-ful indigenous forest along Bobbejaanskraal and then ascends gradually along the lower slopes of Hanglip to the overnight hut.

Day two's hike (7.5 km; 2 hours) climbs gently for about 1 km to a small hill, from where there are great views of Makhado, the surrounding farms and Albasini Dam. The trail then descends through bushveld for about 5 km, before entering pine plan-tations and descending for the final 1.5 km.

44. LESHEBA WILDERNESS
Makhado (Louis Trichardt)

Trails: 10 trails, self-guided or guided;
1.5 to 6 hours; circular and out-and-return.
Permits: Lesheba Wilderness,
P O Box 795, Makhado 0920,
tel. and fax: (015) 593 0076.
Maps: Sketch map.
Facilities/Activities: Three fully
equipped self-catering camps; fully
catered farmhouse accommodation;
game-drives; guided walks.

Situated on the summit of the western Soutpansberg, the unspoilt Lesheba Wilderness forms part of the Western Soutpansberg Conservancy and has been declared a Natural Heritage Site.

With a checklist of over 340 tree species, Lesheba offers excellent opportunities for amateur botanists. The vegetation ranges from bushveld to magnificent patches of montane forest, and several endemic succulents also occur on Lesheba. Among the trees recorded are Outeniqua and real yellowwoods, 12 acacia and nine fig species, common wild pear, marula, Transvaal milkplum and common star chestnut.

Lesheba is a sanctuary for white rhino, giraffe, Burchell's zebra, bushpig and warthog, while large antelope are represented by amongst others sable, kudu, eland, red hartebeest, waterbuck, mountain reedbuck and impala. Common and red duiker, Sharpe's grysbok and klipspringer count among the small antelope species. Also occurring here are leopard and brown hyaena.

Birdlife is prolific and includes Cape vulture, black and martial eagles, tambourine dove, crested guineafowl, and Knysna and purple-crested louries. Yellow-spotted nicator, Heuglin's robin, lilac-breasted roller and Cape rock thrush have also been recorded here.

Visitors can opt to do Lesheba's 10 well-marked trails either as self-guided routes or with a knowledgeable guide. Although the guided walks usually follow the various marked routes, specific tree, bird and rock art trails, that do not necessarily follow the marked routes, are also offered.

The longest walk is about 6 km, and takes between 5 and 6 hours. Special features of the trails include baobab trees (in some areas), rock pools where you can enjoy a refreshing swim after the summer rains, deep gorges framed by high cliffs, and rock paintings. On some of the trails hikers are rewarded with incredible vistas from vantage points on the edge of sheer cliffs.

A three-day hiking trail from the foothills of the Soutpansberg to the highest point in the range, the 1,746-m-high Lejume, is planned. The hike will be known as the Old Salt Trail and, since meals and accommodation will be provided at three stopovers, hikers will need to carry only personal belongings.

45. THABAPHASWA TRAIL
Mokopane (Potgietersrus)

Trails: 3 trails; 38 km (in total); circular.
Permits: Jacana Marketing and Reservations,
P O Box 95212, Waterkloof 0145,
tel: (012) 346 3550, fax: 346 2499,
email: info@jacanacollection.co.za
Maps: Trail pamphlet with map.
Facilities/Activities: Dome Rock
Basecamp and Kanniedood Camp:
huts with beds, mattresses, braai
facilities, two-plate gas stove, fridge,
pots, pans, kettle, washing-up area,
showers and toilets. Thabaphaswa
Campsite: tents with beds and
mattresses; hikers can pitch own tents.
Mountain bike trails.

Overlooked by Thabaphaswa (which means the 'black and white mountain'), Groenkop Farm lies in a lush basin just 16 km from the town of Mokopane. This network of three trails offers a number of different options, including a hike up the mountains behind the Kanniedood Camp, along the valley running through the farm, and across the flats in the western part of the farm. The various trail options are connected by links, which makes it possible to plan a route to suit trailists' particular level of fitness.

46. UBUMANZI HIKING TRAIL
Mookgophong (Naboomspruit)

Trail: Guided trail; 24 km; 2 days;
network from basecamp.
Permits: Anvie Ventures, P O Box 60035,
Pierre van Ryneveld 0045,
tel. and fax: (012) 662 1140.
Facilities/Activities: Converted cattle
dip with bunks, mattresses, braai
facilities, firewood, hot shower and
toilet; guided horse trails.

This guided trail traverses three different farms in the Palala Conservancy, north of Mookgophong, in the Waterberg. Game you might encounter while walking the trial include elephant, white rhino, giraffe, Burchell's zebra, bushpig and warthog. Among the antelope to be found here are kudu, eland, gemsbok, red hartebeest, blue wildebeest, waterbuck, mountain reedbuck, bushbuck, blesbok and impala. Other species that you should look out for include leopard, brown hyaena, aardwolf and caracal.

The trail passes through typical bushveld to fountains high in the mountains, making its way through patches of indigenous yellowwood forest, and to 'forests' of tree ferns. Of special interest is the Waterberg cycad, a species that also grows in the Olifants River Valley near Witbank, as well as in the Wolkberg. Following 4x4 tracks and game paths, trailists hike 15 km on the first day and 9 km on the second day.

47. VASBYT HIKING TRAIL
Mookgophong (Naboomspruit)

Trail: 18 km; 2 days; network from basecamp.
Permits: Anvie Ventures, P O Box 60035,
Pierre van Ryneveld 0045,
tel. and fax: (012) 662 1140.
Facilities/Activities: Basecamp with
bunks, mattresses, braai facilities, pots,
pans, kettle, hot showers and toilets.

Situated in the Waterberg range, near Mookgophong, this trail meanders through bushveld, with russet and large-fruited bushwillows, cabbage trees, Transvaal red milkwood and excellent specimens of the common tree euphorbia.

The first day's hike (12 km; 6 hours) makes its way past a small waterfall and then ascends the mountain slopes to the summit. From here the route continues through two magnificent kloofs and then follows the contour around to another kloof, where a rope assists trailists with the climb into the kloof. The Afrikaans name of the trail, Vasbyt, is variously translated as 'hang on', 'grin and bear it' and 'bite the bullet', and this is just what is required here. The trail then descends back to the basecamp.

Day two's route (6 km; 3 hours) passes through a patch of indigenous forest and winds up the mountain slopes to a kloof. From here you follow the kloof down the mountain to a small waterfall and continue over the hills back to the basecamp.

48. RIETFONTEIN HIKING TRAIL
Mookgophong (Naboomspruit)

Trail: 17 km; 2 days; network from basecamp.
Permits: Anvie Ventures, P O Box 60035,
Pierre van Ryneveld 0045,
tel. and fax: (012) 662 1140.
Maps: Sketch map.
Facilities/Activities: Basecamp:
house with bunks, mattresses, braai
facilities, pots, pan, kettle, scullery,
hot showers and toilets.

Located on the farm Rietfontein, northwest of Mookgophong, the first day's hike (12 km; 6 hours) leads along two wooded kloofs, and past magnificent specimens of common tree euphorbia. A steady climb to a plateau is followed by an easy walk to a kloof, which has inviting pools after rains. From here the path ascends steadily to the highest point on the trail, where hikers are greeted by wonderful views of the Waterberg. Further along the trail passes an exceptionally large marula tree and the remains of the stone-walled settlements of the early indigenous inhabitants, before winding back to the basecamp.

Day two (5 km; 2.5 hours) begins with a steep climb up the mountain and then descends along a wooded kloof, with streams after rains. From here the trail ascends gradually to a plateau and then loops back to the basecamp.

49. SABLE VALLEY AND SERENDIPITY TRAIL
Mookgophong (Naboomspruit)

Trail: 22 km; 2 days; circular.
Permits: Mr J Kloppers,
P O Box 1640, Mookgophong 0560,
tel: (014) 743 3540, fax: 743 1665.
Maps: Sketch map.
Facilities/Activities: Sable Valley and
Tierkloof camps: restored farmhouses
with beds, mattresses, pots, pans, braai
facilities, firewood, showers and toilets.
Serendipity Camp: restored thatched
farmhouse with bunks, mattresses, pots,
pans, braai facilities, firewood, scullery,
showers and toilets. 4x4 trails.

This delightful trail traverses two farms, Naauwpoort and Tierkloof, northwest of Mookgophong. The trail passes through deeply incised gorges, with crystal clear pools, and mountain streams, valleys and bushveld. From viewpoints on the route trailists will be rewarded with panoramic views of the Waterberg to the west. Trees along the trail have been marked with their national tree numbers, and among the species growing in the patches of indigenous forests are real yellowwood, bladdernut, cheesewood and tree fuchsia.

Antelope occurring in this area include mountain reedbuck, common reedbuck, kudu and klipspringer. Among the more than 200 bird species recorded in the area to date, which you may be able to tick during the course of the hike, are black and martial eagles, terrestrial bulbul and Cape batis.

Starting at Sable Valley, the first day's hike (12 km; 6 hours) makes its way to Serendipity, from where the second day's trail (10 km; 5 hours)

winds back to the start. Alternatively, the hike can be done in reverse, commencing at Serendipity.

50. STAMVRUG HIKING TRAIL
Modimolle (Nylstroom)

Trails: Overnight trail; 17.3 km;
2 days; circular. 2 trails; 3 and 8.3 km;
1 and 4 hours; circular.
Permits: Jacana Marketing and Reservations,
P O Box 95212, Waterkloof 0145,
tel: (012) 346 3550, fax: 346 2499,
email: info@jacanacollection.co.za
Maps: Trail pamphlet with map.
Facilities/Activities: Kloof Basecamp:
farmhouse with beds, mattresses,
kitchen with two-plate gas stove, pots,
pans, braai facilities, firewood, hot
showers and toilets. Stamvrug Camp:
same facilities as Kloof Basecamp.

Situated in the foothills of the Waterberg, the Bateleur Nature Reserve covers 2,000 ha of bushveld, rocky hills and kloofs with delightful streams.

Among the wide variety of bushveld trees to be seen is the Transvaal milkplum (*stamvrug* in Afrikaans), the species to which the trail owes its name. One of the largest concentrations of this species in the area can be seen in this reserve. Other typical bushveld species found here include velvet and large-fruited bushwillows, wild seringa, Transvaal beech, Waterberg medlar and the Transvaal cabbage tree.

Antelope you may encounter include kudu, blesbok, bushbuck, reedbuck, klipspringer, steenbok and common duiker. Leopard, aardwolf, brown hyaena, warthog, baboon and vervet monkey also occur here.

Birdlife is prolific, including raptors such as gymnogene, Wahlberg's and black-breasted snake eagles and Cape vulture, as well as wattled plover, black crake and greater double-collared sunbird. Blue crane breed in the reserve.

1. Stamvrug Hiking Trail The first day's hike, the Kloof Route (10.8 km; 5 hours), begins with a steady climb to a koppie, from where there are extensive views of the Waterberg to the north,

Kranskop to the east and the Nyl zijn Oog to the west. From here the trail descends gradually and then follows a ridge, which offers wonderful views of the Waterberg. The remainder of the Stamvrug Trail follows a gently undulating course to a patch of indigenous forest and a magnificent natural rock garden before descending to a farm dam, where you can cool off before hiking the final 1 km to the Stamvrug Hut.

The second day's hike, the Stamvrug Route (6.5 km; 3 hours), gently ascends along a ridge to a koppie and traverses a grassy plateau, before reaching another koppie. The trail then descends to a patch of indigenous forest and, further along, a detour leads to the Krans Dam. An easy climb is followed by a descent into a delightful kloof, which you follow until the final climb to the Kloof Basecamp. **17.3 km; 2 days; circular.**

2. Panorama Route makes its way above the deep gorge carved by a tributary of the Buffels River for a short distance, and then crosses a small plateau. Further along, the trail follows an easy route along a stream and, after traversing the slopes below a koppie, winds downhill, back to the Kloof Hut. Along the way there are fine views over the kloof and the surrounding landscape. The trail can be done either as a short walk or as an extension of the Stamvrug Route. **3 km; 1 hour; circular.**

3. Moepel Route is named after the fine specimens of Transvaal red milkwood (*moepel* in Afrikaans) that can be seen along the trail. It follows the Panorama Route for 500 m, and after an easy climb up the slopes of a koppie traverses its northern slopes before swinging south to descend gently back to the start. Highlights include a section of indigenous forest, splendid views of the Waterberg and interesting rock formations. **8.3 km; 4 hours; circular.**

51. WAG-'N-BIETJIE HIKING TRAILS
Bela-Bela (Warmbaths)

Trails: 3 trails; 4 to 12 km; 2 to 6 hours; network from basecamp.
Permits: Anvie Ventures, P O Box 60035,

Pierre van Ryneveld 0045, tel. and fax: (012) 662 1140.
Maps: Sketch map.
Facilities/Activities: Basecamp: wooden houses with bunks, mattresses, kettles, braai facilities, showers and toilets.

Traversing two farms in the Bela-Bela district, this network of trails has been developed by the land owners to share with trailists the beauty of the area in which they live.

The network wanders along beautiful kloofs, past interesting rock formations and through bushveld vegetation, consisting of wild plum, Transvaal red milkwood, wild medlar and the black monkey orange tree.

Whilst hiking, trailists might chance upon a variety of animals, including baboon, kudu, bushbuck and klipspringer. Brown hyaena are also known to occur in the area.

1. Uitsig Route climbs steeply up the mountain, traverses cliffs with striking rock formations and then comes to the Bosveld viewpoint. From the 1,574-m-high crest trailists are rewarded with wonderful, sweeping views of the surrounding bushveld landscape. The trail then descends past stands of mountain aloe to return to the start. **4 km; 2 hours; circular.**

2. Kloof Route meanders up the mountain slopes and follows a kloof to a second, larger kloof, which makes an ideal reststop, where you can get your breath back before continuing. From here the trail leads over the mountain and further along winds in and out of a kloof, where a small waterfall can be seen after rains. After following an easy route along the contours, the trail then descends steeply back to the basecamp. **6 km; 3 hours; circular.**

3. Kruin Route mainly follows the mountain crests to the south of the basecamps, but there are some steep climbs. Along the way trailists hike through a dense stand of wild seringa trees and pass an enormous Transvaal gardenia. Near the halfway mark hikers can link up with the return leg of the Kloof Route. **12 km; 6 hours; circular.**

52. DIEPDRIFT HIKING TRAILS
Bela-Bela (Warmbaths)

> *Trails:* 2 overnight trails; 24 km; 2 days;
> circular. 2 day-trails; 4 and 8 km;
> 2 and 4 hours; circular.
> *Permits:* Diepdrift Safaris, P O Box 543,
> Bela-Bela 0480, tel: (014) 743 1729,
> cell: 082 874 2644.
> *Maps:* Sketch map.
> *Facilities/Activities:* Basecamp
> with beds, mattresses, braai facilities,
> scullery, hot showers and toilets.
> Sand River Hut: beds, mattresses,
> braai facilities, hot showers and
> toilets. Sable Hut: beds, mattresses
> by arrangement, braai facilities and
> toilet (no shower).

The walks and overnight trails on the 4,000-ha bushveld farm Diepdrift provide an opportunity for hikers to view a rich variety of game on foot. Diepdrift is a nature reserve and hunting farm, and among the 21 species of antelope to be seen here are sable, kudu, blue wildebeest, nyala and waterbuck. Trailists may also chance upon hippo, giraffe, warthog, bushpig and zebra.

Some 121 species of bushveld trees have been identified, including some exceptionally large wild fig trees. With 128 bird species having been recorded in a day here, birding can be rewarding.

1. Hippo Pool Hiking Trail traverses typical bushveld countryside to a pool, where you can see hippo and crocodile. Hikers are, however, warned to be extremely cautious, as these animals can be very dangerous. Other game found here that you may chance upon includes giraffe, sable, eland, kudu, red hartebeest and blue wildebeest. **24 km; 2 days; circular.**

2. Sable Hiking Trail follows an undulating course, with steep ascents and descents over Diepdrift and Elandsfontein farms. Giraffe, kudu, sable, waterbuck and nyala are among the game you might spot. At one point the trail crosses a mountain range and then leads through a wild kloof to a plateau, from where you can enjoy breathtaking panoramic views over the surrounding countryside. **24 km; 2 days; circular.**

3. Bontebok Hiking Trail is especially enjoyable in the late afternoon when the sunset, reflected off the stone koppies, is spectacular. Game that you might see along the trail includes Hartmann's mountain zebra, bontebok, reedbuck, kudu, impala and klipspringer. **4 km; 2 hours; circular.**

4. Klipspringer Hiking Trail passes through a particularly beautiful area of Diepdrift to fascinating rock formations, from where game can be viewed. Along the route trailists may well see most of the game species occurring in the reserve. **8 km; 4 hours; circular.**

53. TSHUKUDU HIKING TRAIL
Vaalwater

> *Trail:* 19 km; 2 days; circular.
> *Permits:* Anvie Ventures, P O Box 60035,
> Pierre van Ryneveld 0045,
> tel. and fax: (012) 662 1140.
> *Maps:* Sketch map.
> *Facilities/Activities:* Oppi-Koppie Basecamp:
> thatched hut with beds, mattresses, kitchen
> with coal stove, pot, pan, kettle, braai
> facilities, hot showers and toilet. Krans Hut:
> beds, mattresses, pot, pan, kettle, braai
> facilities, hot shower and toilet.

Set on a farm in the Waterberg, 38 km from Vaalwater, this trail traverses a variety of landscapes, with a rich diversity of bushveld trees. In addition to the prolific birdlife here, hikers may see kudu, bushbuck and common duiker.

On the first day's hike (12 km; 6 hours) a steep ascent along two kloofs leads to the summit of the mountain, where hikers can have a refreshing swim. Further along you will be rewarded with magnificent views over the Alma Valley, and after passing through stands of sugarbushes you reach Wonderfontein, a perfect lunch spot, with braai facilities and toilets. Still further on, a short detour leads to the ruins of a South African War (1899–1902) site on the slopes of the mountain. The second day's hike (7 km; 3.5 hours) follows the mountain crest to a fountain and then descends gradually to a stream, which you follow back to the basecamp.

54. RHENOSTERPOORT HIKING TRAIL
Alma

Trail: 12 km; 6 hours; circular, with
a shorter option; 8 km; 4 hour; circular.
Permits: Anvie Ventures, P O Box 60035,
Pierre van Ryneveld 0045,
tel. and fax: (012) 662 1140.
Maps: Sketch map.
Facilities/Activities: Two private bush
camps with fully equipped kitchens and
bathrooms; angling; 4x4 trail.

This trail can be started at either Dassie or Bosbok Camp. There are yellow markers on the trail from Dassie Camp and white ones from Bosbok Camp, leading you to the junction of the two routes. From here the trail ascends steeply and follows the contours above Donkerkloof to a vantage point with spectacular views of the Waterberg. The trail then descends, and at the halfway point an optional 4-km loop splits off to the right. Continuing on the direct route you will reach a delightful picnic place alongside a river with natural pools. From here the trail follows the contours above the river to Dassie Camp and onwards, to the highlight of the trail: a waterfall plunging into a magnificent pool. The remainder of the trail winds above the river back to Bosbok Camp. **12 km; 6 hours, or 8 km; 4 hours; circular.**

55. WATERBERGKRUIN HIKING TRAIL
Alma

Trails: 2 trails; 7 and 18 km; 3 hours and
9 hours; network from basecamp.
Permits: Anvie Ventures, P O Box 60035,
Pierre van Ryneveld 0045,

tel. and fax: (012) 662 1140.
Maps: Sketch map.
Facilities/Activities: Basecamp: A-framed
thatched huts with beds, mattresses, kitchen
with hotplates, fridge, pots, pans, kettle,
scullery, braai facilities, firewood, hot showers
and toilets. Angling and canoeing on the dam.

1. Skilpad Summit Route makes its way over easy terrain through a game camp, where 15 species of game can be seen and hikers can enjoy magnificent views of the Waterberg. A dam surrounded by shady trees, reached beyond the halfway point, provides an ideal reststop. The remainder of the route is an easy walk back to the basecamp. **7 km; 3 hours; circular.**

2. Perdekop Route Laid out high up in the Waterberg, the Perdekop Route initially traverses easy terrain before climbing steadily along a kloof and up Perdekop's slopes. The final push to the 1,800-m-high summit of Perdekop, the second highest peak in the area, is a steep climb, but the spectacular views of the Alma Valley are ample reward. The return leg follows a different route. **18 km; 9 hours; circular.**

56. KRANSBERG NATURE TRAILS
Thabazimbi

Trails: 2 trails; 8 to 15 km; 4 to
9 hours; circular and out-and-return.
Permits: Kransberg Nature Trails,
P O Box 2355, Vereeniging 1930,
tel. and fax: (016) 451 1407.
Maps: Trails are indicated on
aerial photographs.
Facilities/Activities: Basecamp:
rooms with beds, mattresses, pots,
pan, kettle, braai facilities, scullery,
hot showers and toilets.

Situated below the 2,085-m-high Kransberg, the highest point in the Waterberg, this trail on Hartebeesfontein Farm passes rugged cliffs and deep gorges.

Among the antelope you might come across are kudu, bushbuck, common duiker and klipspringer. Also keep an eye out for baboon, vervet monkey, bushpig and warthog. Leopard, caracal and serval occur, but are seldom seen, owing to their secretive habits.

Kransberg has the largest breeding colony of Cape vulture in the world and they can usually be seen soaring overhead. Also recorded are white-backed vulture, black eagle, bateleur and a number of other bird species.

1. This hike (which does not have a specific name) offers three different trail options, which are suited to hikers who are very fit, moderately fit and beginners respectively. The advanced route (15 km; 8–9 hours) is difficult and should only be attempted by extremely fit hikers who do not suffer from acrophobia or claustrophobia. The general route (10 km; 6–7 hours) caters for average and experienced hikers, and begins with a steep climb for 2.3 km and then follows a relatively easy route before descending between the cliffs, where caution must be exercised as the descent is rather steep. Further along you pass through a 'forest' of mountain aloe (some are up to 7 m tall) and the trail then eases off. The short trail (8 km; 4 hours) offers an easier alternative to the general route, as it avoids the ascent and descent through the cliffs, and is ideal for those new to hiking or anyone who has a fear of heights. **8, 10 or 15 km; 4, 6–7 or 8–9 hours; circular.**

2. Lo-Hani Swimming Trail winds down into a gorge and then continues to a natural rockslide and the Lo-Hani swimming pool, a perfect lunch stop. From here you backtrack up the gorge to the signposted route out of the kloof. **10 km; 4 hours; out-and-return.**

57. MATEKE HIKING TRAIL
Thabazimbi

Trails: 2 trails; 9 to 19 km; 6 to 9 hours; circular, with shorter options.
Permits: Anvie Ventures, P O Box 60035, Pierre van Ryneveld 0045,

tel. and fax: (012) 662 1140.
Maps: Sketch map.
Facilities/Activities: Tree Camp and Tree House: bunks, mattresses, pot, pan, kettle, braai facilities, firewood, hot showers and toilets. Bush Camp: bunks, mattresses, fridge, two-plate stove, pots, pans, kettle, braai facilities, scullery, hot showers and toilets. Mountain biking; 4x4 trails; horse-riding; game-drives.

Situated on the farm Tweeloopfontein, in the Kransberge, this trail network alternates between mountains, with deep kloofs, and plains. Among the 95 tree species marked along the trails are red ivory, wild seringa, tambotie and wild fig tree.

Antelope that you might encounter include kudu, red hartebeest, waterbuck, gemsbok, nyala, impala and klipspringer. Baboon and warthog also occur here, and the large cats are represented by leopard and cheetah. Birdlife is prolific and birding can be rewarding.

1. Koedoe Route leads through typical bushveld to a magnificent fig tree, and after ascending along a kloof the trail descends another kloof to a fountain, surrounded by lush vegetation. Here trailists have an option of doing a difficult 7-km loop to the Mamba River or descending a kloof and then climbing up to a saddle, from where the route drops down to the basecamp. On the longer route trailists can enjoy splendid views of the Kransberge and a swim in the Mamba River. From the Mamba River the trail loops back to the fountain, where it joins the shorter trail. **9 or 16 km from Tree Camp, 14 or 19 km from Bush Camp; up to 9 hours; circular.**

2. Nyala Route follows the course of the Mamba River and, after ascending a hill covered in aloe, the trail returns to the river and its pleasant pools. Keep an eye out during the hike for waterbuck, kudu, baboon and African fish eagle. Further along, you come to a kloof with a lovely pool, where you can relax and enjoy your lunch. After crossing the river, the trail meanders along its southern bank to take you back to the basecamp. **13 km; 6 hours; circular.**

GAUTENG & NORTH WEST PROVINCE

Despite being South Africa's most densely populated province, Gauteng offers a surprising number of outdoor opportunities for those wanting to escape the hustle and bustle of city life, as does the adjoining North West Province. These two provinces provide everything from short walks in botanical gardens and overnight trails in nature reserves, within easy reach of the Johannesburg and Pretoria metropolitan areas, to guided walks in conservation areas such as Pilanesberg National Park.

Over a large part of southern Gauteng and the Highveld areas of North West Province the altitude ranges between 1,200 and 1,800 m. The vegetation here is characterised by extensive, almost pure grassland, with hardly any trees on the open plains. Woodlands are confined to river valleys, and patches of woodland and shrubland, known as Bankenveld, occur on the quartzite ridges of Gauteng.

To the north of the Magaliesberg, the vegetation of the two provinces is characterised by vast areas of bushveld. Typical trees found here include weeping wattle, marula, large-fruited and red bushwillows, silver cluster leaf, wild seringa and common wild pear.

Birding is especially rewarding in summer and among the species to be seen are greywing and redwing francolins, blue crane, whitebellied korhaan, several lark and pipit species, grass owl and cisticolas. Species of the more arid west include crimson-breasted shrike, Marico flycatcher, Burchell's courser and Kalahari robin.

Among the typical game species of the Highveld plains are blesbok, red hartebeest, black wildebeest, eland and Burchell's zebra. Although the large herds that used to roam the Highveld plains have long since disappeared, game has been reintroduced into several nature reserves, national parks and farms in the two provinces. In small conservation areas such as the Rustenburg and Suikerbosrand nature reserves there are good game-viewing and birding opportunities for outdoor enthusiasts doing self-guided hiking trails and walks.

In Borakalalo National Park visitors have a choice of a self-guided walk and guided walks. Among the big game species that may be seen on foot are white rhino, hippo, buffalo, giraffe, roan and tsessebe.

Pilanesberg National Park is a Big Five (elephant, rhino, buffalo, lion, leopard) park and can, therefore, only be explored by joining a guided walk, for safety reasons. Established in 1979 on severely degraded land, the park was restocked with game in what was one of the biggest game translocation projects ever undertaken. Known as Operation Genesis, the project involved the translocation of over 7,000 animals of 20 different species into the park.

The Pilanesberg itself is of great geological interest, as it is one of three largest alkaline volcanoes (formed by a distinct type of molten matter, known as alkaline magma, as opposed to acid magma) in the world. The volcano was active some 1,200 million years ago, but has since been eroded down to its roots. Measuring about 25 km in diameter, the original volcanic centre is surrounded by concentric hills.

There are several other important geological features in the two provinces that lend themselves to exploration on foot. Best known of the three quartzite ridges that dominate the landscape of Gauteng and the east of North West Province is the Magaliesberg. Rising on average 330 m above the surrounding landscape, the range extends eastwards from Zeerust, past Hartbeespoort Dam, and continues through Pretoria to its eastern suburbs. It forms a natural boundary between the Highveld to the south and the bushveld to the north.

The vegetation of Gauteng's quartzite ridges is dominated by Bankenveld, a term referring to vegetation of the low, bench-like hills and ridges occurring in the area. Almost pure stands of grasslands occur on the crests of the hills and ridges, their cool southern slopes and on low-lying plains, while trees and shrubs grow on northern slopes, rocky outcrops and in sheltered valleys. Typical trees include common sugarbush, oldwood, sagewood, tree fuchsia, white stinkwood, mountain cabbage tree and cheesewood.

The quartzite ridges are the habitat of numerous bird species. Noteworthy birds include Cape vulture, lanner and peregrine falcons, ground woodpecker and short-toed rock thrush. The ridges also form natural wildlife corridors for a variety of mammals such as the brown hyaena, reptiles and smaller creatures like beetles, butterflies and insects.

In the past, Gauteng's quartzite ridges also played an important role in the search for gold. The early mines at Kromdraai and in the Kloofendal Nature Reserve provide an interesting perspective on the frantic search that preceded the discovery of the Main Reef in 1886 and the development of Johannesburg.

Rising like an island above the surrounding urbanised landscape, most of the Magaliesberg was safeguarded against uncontrolled development when it was declared a Natural Area in 1977 and a Protected Natural Environment in 1993. Hiking opportunities in the Magaliesberg range from overnight hikes and day walks in the Rustenburg Nature Reserve to walks and trails on private land.

At Tswaing Crater, about 40 km northwest of Pretoria, trailists can explore one of the best preserved and most accessible meteorite impact craters in the world. The almost circular crater, with a diameter of just over 1 km, was formed when a meteorite crashed into the earth some 200,000 years ago.

In the southwestern corner of North West Province lies another geological curiosity, which extends into the Free State, the Vredefort Dome. Its origin is the subject of two theories, one of which attributes it to an upwelling of granite and subsequent geological processes and pressures, and the other to the impact of a huge meteorite.

Situated a mere 40 km from the Johannesburg city centre, the Cradle of Humankind was declared a World Heritage Site in December 1999. It is a palaeontological treasure-trove, and among the important finds made here are the famous 2.6-million-year-old 'Mrs Ples', the even older 3.3-million-year-old 'Little Foot' and the first specimen of a robust ape-human found at Kromdraai in 1935. Trailists can explore this fascinating area on foot by joining a special interest trail conducted on the Kromdraai Conservancy.

Frost is common on the Highveld in winter, when minimum temperatures can drop to below freezing point. Daytime temperatures are generally mild, but can be low. In the bushveld, winter temperatures are not as extreme and seldom drop to below zero. Summer on the Highveld is warm during the day and pleasant in the evenings. In the western parts of North West Province, however, maximum temperatures are several degrees higher than on the Highveld.

The rainy season is during the summer months and is characterised by heavy mid-afternoon thunderstorms and lightning. Rainfall varies from 350 mm in the west to 750 mm on the eastern margins of the Gauteng Highveld. The highest rainfall is generally recorded between the months of October/November and March, with very little rainfall in the winter months. A major attraction for visitors to the two provinces is that they are free of malaria.

IMPORTANT INFORMATION

- Pack sufficient warm clothing and a good-quality sleeping bag when hiking in the Gauteng Highveld and high mountain areas in North West Province during winter.
- In summer thunderstorms occur frequently and lightning can be extremely dangerous. An early start is recommended to ensure that you reach your destination before a thunderstorm sets in, usually during mid-afternoon.
- In the Highveld grassland the risk of fire is very high during winter. Extreme caution must be exercised when making fires and smokers must refrain from smoking whilst they are walking.
- Ticks can be a problem, so it is advisable to apply a repellent and to wear long trousers. It is also a good idea to inspect yourself thoroughly for ticks at the end of each day's hike.
- The grasslands of the Highveld offer virtually no overhead cover, so you should always wear a wide-rimmed hat and apply sunscreen regularly.
- During the winter months, most streams are likely to be dry. Never set off without at least 2 litres of water and use it sparingly until you can refill your waterbottle. On overnight hikes, consult the trail map, or check with the trail authority whether water is available along the trail.

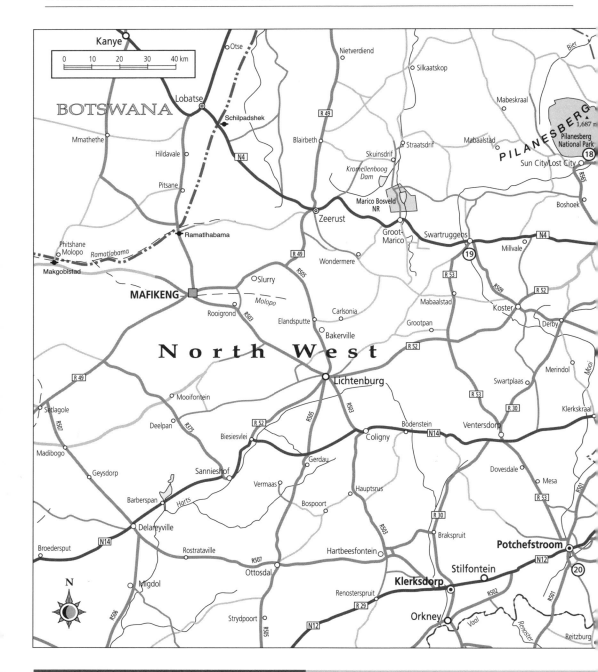

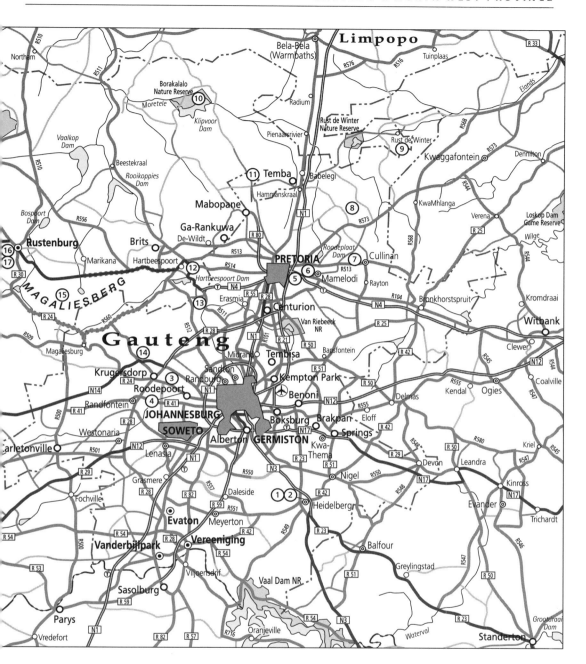

1. SUIKERBOSRAND HIKING TRAIL
Suikerbosrand Nature Reserve,
Heidelberg

See no. 2 (p. 259) for walks.

Trail: 66 km (in total); 2 to 7 days; circular.
Permits: Suikerbosrand Nature Reserve,
Private Bag H 616, Heidelberg,
tel: (011) 904 3930, fax: 904 2966.
Maps: Colour nature reserve and trail map.
Facilities/Activities: Six overnight huts
with bunks, mattresses, outdoor cooking
area, firewood and toilets. Visitors'
Centre; Diepkloof Farm Museum; two
group camps; self-drive game-viewing;
picnic site; guided game-drives; horse
trails; mountain biking.
Pertinent information: Although the route is
well marked care should be taken at intersections because of the large number of
options. A visit to the Visitors' Centre will
enhance your enjoyment of the hike.

Dominated by the Suikerbosrand (meaning 'sugar-bush ridge' in Afrikaans), a quartzite ridge that owes its name to the abundance of common sugarbushes in the area, this reserve covers 11,583 ha of false grassveld (a vegetation type consisting of grass, shrubs and trees, as opposed to pure grassveld), patches of woodland and shrubland. Over 650 plant species have been identified in the reserve, including 61 tree and 115 grass species. Tree species include oldwood, sagewood, karree, tree fuchsia, white stinkwood, cheesewood, wild olive and acacias. Aloes are represented by the mountain aloe and the Transvaal aloe (Aloe greatheadii), while a variety of flowering plants brighten up the grasslands in spring.

Large antelope roaming the reserve include eland, kudu, red hartebeest, black wildebeest, blesbok, mountain reedbuck, reedbuck, grey rhebok and springbok, while common duiker, steenbok and oribi also occur here. Among the other mammals you may see are Burchell's zebra, cheetah, brown hyaena, black-backed jackal and baboon.

With a bird checklist of some 250 species, birding here can be rewarding. Species you might tick include

black, African hawk and martial eagles, grey-wing francolin, ant-eating and mountain chats, orange-throated longclaw, crested barbet and Cape robin.

Situated within easy reach of Johannesburg, the Suikerbosrand Hiking Trail provides the perfect escape for those needing a break from city life. The short distances between trail huts (averaging under 10 km) and the relatively easy terrain make this an ideal trail for beginners and families.

Various trail options are available, allowing you to plan a hike to suit your personal needs. The trail network winds through contrasting flora, from aloe veld in the west to proteaveld in the east, and offers excellent game-viewing and birding opportunities.

A typical four-day trail (particularly suitable for beginners and families with small children) is described here. The route can, however, be covered fairly easily in two days or extended by three days by incorporating the eastern section of the reserve into your hike.

The first day's trail (4.7 km; 2.5 hours), from the Visitors' Centre to Springbok Hut, can easily be hiked after lunch. It ascends gently but steadily along the eastern slopes of Baboon Ridge and, just before crossing the tarred game-viewing road, passes a wall built by one of the early farmers to divert water trapped by a dolerite dyke into a side valley. About 1 km on you will find yourself at the Rantjies Lookout, the highest point of the day's hike. From here the trail skirts Kiepersolkloof as it descends to the hut, which is tucked away in a dense patch of kloof forest.

On day two (12.2 km; 5 hours) the trail follows the densely wooded Koedoekloof for a short distance and then climbs to grassland interspersed with aloes. At Blind Man's Corner the trail swings sharply westwards before descending gently along Doringbos Road, named for the profusion of acacias (*doringbos* in Afrikaans) dominating the valley. After crossing the tarred road to Kareekloof Resort the trail leads through the Aloe Forest, with its tall specimens of mountain aloes. The trail then continues its ascent as it makes its way up to the summit of Perdekop, before winding down to Eland Hut.

Day three's hike offers two options: a short, direct route (6.5 km; 2.5 hours) or a longer option (14.6 km; 6 hours) to Blesbok Hut. From the hut the trail ascends a kloof and heads across Springbokvlakte, where herds of springbok, black wildebeest and Burchell's zebra are likely to be seen. At Swaeltjieshoek the direct route to Blesbok Hut continues straight, while the longer option via Steenbok Hut (described here) branches off to the right. After a short, steep descent the trail levels out below Feeskrans to reach Steenbok Hut 7 km from the start. The hut is a good place to stop for brunch or tea, if it is not occupied by other hikers. About 2 km beyond Steenbok Hut the trail to Hartebees Hut branches off to the right, but you continue straight, and a short way on you will look down onto Hartebeesvlakte. The trail ascends the steep Hyaenakloof before dropping down to Blesbok Hut, which is situated 400 m off the main trail.

On the final day's hike (5 km; 2 hours) you back-track along the last 400 m of the previous day's trail and then ascend the northern slopes of Kwaggakop, before dropping down to Jagluiperdbossie. Further along, the trail passes the remains of an old Iron Age settlement, winds downhill, and then follows the lower slopes of Baboon Ridge back to the start. **28.4 or 36.5 km; 4 days; circular.**

2. SUIKERBOSRAND NATURE RESERVE
Heidelberg

See no. 1 (p 258) for hiking trail.

Trails: 3 trails; 1 to 17 km; 1 to 7 hours; circular.
Permits: Entrance fee. No permit required for walks.
Maps: Trail brochure with sketch map.
Facilities/Activities: Visitors' Centre; Diepkloof Farm Museum; two group camps; self-drive game-viewing; picnic site; guided game-drives; horse trails; mountain biking.

1. Toktokkie Accessible Trail This short interpretative trail provides an ideal introduction to various eco-logical aspects of the reserve. Along the trail there are 14 points of interest, which are explained in the trail booklet. These range from herbs, food chains and climatology to various tree species, the adaptations of succulent plants and the Diepkloof Farm Museum. **1 km; 1 hour; circular.**

2. Cheetah Interpretative Trail focuses on common trees and the ecology of the reserve. Of cultural and historical interest are the stone-walled Iron Age sites along the trail, built by the ancestors of the Tswana people. There are 12 marked points of interest along the trail, explained in the trail brochure. **4 km; 2 hours; circular.**

3. Bokmakierie Nature Trail is named after the bok-makierie, an attractive bird with a conspicuous black collar around a yellow throat. The trail follows a slightly undulating course through the northwestern corner of the reserve and passes six marked points of interest, which are explained in the trail brochure. among these are the importance of surface water in a nature reserve, especially with regard to waterholes for animals, the succession of veld types, indigenous trees, Iron Age sites and food chains. **17 km; 7 hours; circular, or 10 km; 3.5 hours; circular.**

3. WITWATERSRAND NATIONAL BOTANICAL GARDEN
Roodepoort

Trails: Network covering several kilometres.
Permits: Entrance fee. No permit required.
Maps: Available at entrance gate.
Facilities/Activities: Picnic area; cafeteria; book- and gift shop; birdhide; indigenous plant nursery.

Set against the backdrop of the Roodekrans Ridge, the focal point of the 225-ha Witwatersrand National Botanical Garden is the spectacular Witpoortjie Waterfall, where the Crocodile River cascades over a 70-m-high cliff.

The garden provides protection to one of the few remaining patches of Bankenveld vegetation in Gauteng. This vegetation type consists of almost pure grassveld on the crests of Gauteng's characteristic quartzite ridges, their southern slopes and low-lying plains, while the northern slopes support trees and shrubs.

Best known amongst the more than 230 bird species recorded in this botanical garden is a breeding pair of black eagles that has made its nests against the cliffs near the waterfall. Other birds to be seen include arrow-marked babbler, black-headed oriole, Cape rock thrush, fairy fly-catcher and pied barbet.

Parts of the garden have been developed around particular plants and habitats. There are cycad, succulent, wild flower and water-wise gardens, while the remaining area has been left in its natural state.

The garden is criss-crossed by a network of trails, ranging from walks along the quartzite ridges, from where there are fine views over the garden and its surroundings, to walks along the Crocodile River, with its riverine forest.

4. KLOOFENDAL NATURE RESERVE
Roodepoort

> **Trails:** 2 trails; 2 and 6 km; 1 and 2.5 hours; circular.
> **Permits:** Entrance fee. No permit required.
> **Maps:** Available on request at reserve.
> **Facilities/Activities:** Picnic area.

Situated in the centre of Roodepoort, Kloofendal Nature Reserve covers 109 ha of quartzite ridges, characterised by cliffs and unspoilt kloofs, while the Wilgespruit flows through the reserve. The vegetation is typical Bankenveld, with patches of common hook thorn, sagewood, common sugarbush, white stinkwood and tree fuchsia.

Birdlife is prolific and among the species you might tick are black-shouldered kite, rock kestrel, wailing cisticola, grassveld pipit and bokmakierie. Also keep an eye out for Cape robin and black-collared barbet.

Of historical interest is the Confidence Reef, where Fred Strubens discovered the first economically viable occurrence of gold on 18 September 1884. Initial optimism about the discovery prompted Fred and his brother Harry to develop the reef, and the first crushing plant on the Witwatersrand, a five-stamp battery (a machine for crushing ore), came into operation in December of the following year. The Strubens workings can be viewed by making arrangements for a guided tour with Mrs Gilbert, tel: (011) 761 0225 (please call from Tuesday to Friday, between 09:30 and 13:00).

The ridges, hills, kloofs and grasslands of the reserve are traversed by two trails. **2 km and 6 km; 1 hour and 2.5 hours; circular.**

5. RIETVLEI NATURE RESERVE
Pretoria

> **Trails:** Guided hiking trail; 22 km; 2 days; circular. Guided day walk: 10 km; 4 hours; circular.
> **Permits:** Reservations must be made at least two weeks in advance. Rietvlei Nature Reserve, P O Box 1454, Pretoria, 0001, tel: (012) 345 2274, fax: 345 3928.
> **Maps:** Sketch map.
> **Facilities/Activities:** Overnight trail: hut with bunks, mattresses, cast-iron pots, kettle, braai facilities, firewood, hot showers and toilets. Guided bus tours through reserve; guided night-drives; horse-rides (day and overnight); angling; picnic site; birdhide.
> **Pertinent information:** Overnight trails are conducted for groups with a minimum of six and a maximum of eight people. Hikers must supply their own sleeping bags, food, cutlery, plates and mugs. Day walks: minimum 10, maximum 20 people.

Covering 3,800 ha of undulating grassy hills, 20 km to the southeast of Pretoria, the Rietvlei Nature Reserve lies in the catchment area of the Rietvlei Dam. The reserve was established to ensure the supply of clean water to Pretoria; the reserve's dam (built in 1934), six fountains and one borehole supply about 15 per cent of the city's water requirements.

The reserve is home to a variety of Highveld game species. In addition to blesbok, the most abundant of the various antelope species, the reserve has also been stocked with black wildebeest, eland, red hartebeest, waterbuck, springbuck, reedbuck, mountain reedbuck and oribi. Also to be seen are white rhino, hippo, buffalo and Burchell's zebra, as well as a variety of smaller mammals such as vlei rat, spring hare, suricat, slender mongoose and scrub hare.

About 240 bird species have been recorded and among the wetland birds to look out for are black-crowned night heron, greater flamingo, white-faced and knob-billed ducks, African finfoot and wattled plover. Other species you may tick include African fish eagle, blue crane, Burchell's coucal, red-billed woodhoopoe, grassveld pipit and orange-throated longclaw.

1. Overnight Hiking Trail Groups are met at 17:00 on Friday afternoons at the reserve's main gate, from where it is a 2-km walk to the overnight hut. On Saturday a 14-km hike is undertaken to the second overnight hut. Along the way, the guide will give you an insight into the ecology of the area you are hiking through and there will also be stops for game-viewing and birding. Although the reserve is relatively flat, you should be walking fit as you have to carry your backpack. On Sunday morning a 6-km walk takes you back to the start. **22 km; 2 days; circular.**

2. Day Walks start at 08:00 at the reserve's main gate and, in addition to game-viewing and birding, trailists will also gain a better understanding of various aspects of the reserve's ecology. **10 km; 4 hours; circular.**

6. PRETORIA NATIONAL BOTANICAL GARDEN
Pretoria

Trails: Network of footpaths, including the Bankenveld Trail; 2 km; 1 hour; circular.
Permits: Entrance fee. No permit required.
Maps: Available at entrance gate.
Facilities/Activities: Restaurant; guided walks (on request).

Situated on the western outskirts of Pretoria on Silverton Ridge, a mere 8 km from the city centre, this garden was established in 1946 in the grounds of South Africa's National Herbarium, and is one of South Africa's eight national botanical gardens.

Covering 75 ha, the natural vegetation is characterised by Bankenveld trees and over 500 species of flowering plants. In the cultivated section there are gardens with succulents, fynbos and forest, as well as collections of cycads and aloes.

The Desmond Cole Collection of *Lithops* (meaning 'stone-like') and the Hardy Collection of plants from Namaqualand, Namibia and Madagascar contain some of its most important plants.

A network of paved walkways winds through the various plant collections, and the **Bankenveld Trail** makes its way along a quartzite ridge through natural Bankenveld vegetation.

7. WINDY BROW HIKING TRAIL
Cullinan

Trails: 3 trails; 3.2 to 5.9 km; 1.5 to 6 hours; circular. Network from basecamp.
Permits: Jacana Marketing and Reservations, P O Box 95212, Waterkloof 0145, tel: (012) 346 3550, fax: 346 2499, email: info@jacanacollection.co.za
Maps: Trail pamphlet with map.
Facilities/Activities: Basecamp: two dormitories with bunks, mattresses, gas cooker, pots, kettles, braai facilities, hot showers and toilets. Ndaba Camp: beds/bunks with mattresses, kitchen with stove, fridge, pots, pans, kettles, braai facilities, showers and toilets. Farmshed: environmental education centre for groups, with bunks, braai facilities, showers and toilets. Tent sites: you need to supply your own tents and equipment; toilets.

This network of trails traverses the farm Elandsfontein, which once formed part of the farm Elandshoek, where the Premier Mine came into operation in 1902. The world's largest diamond, the famous 3,106-carat Cullinan diamond, was found here in 1905.

The vegetation is characterised by sourish, mixed bushveld and among the 45 common tree species found here are mountain aloe, Transvaal beech, common sugarbush, Transvaal milkplum, Magalies plane, velvet rock alder and mountain silver oak.

Large game species you may encounter include giraffe, kudu, gemsbok, red hartebeest, blesbok and nyala. There is also an abundance of birdlife for birding enthusiasts.

1. Geological Route From the basecamp, the trail ascends through grass savannah to the crest of a koppie with an extensive view over the Cullinan Mine. The route then traverses the northwestern slopes of the koppie, composed of Magaliesberg quartzite, and descends to Gemsbok Corner, where you can link up with the Ecology Route. The Geology Route climbs up a steep koppie, and further along there are great views over the Cullinan Mine. After walking down through a saddle, followed by a steep climb to the crest of a hill, you make a sharp descent to the base-camp. **3.2 km; 1.5 hours; circular.**

2. Archaeological Route wanders past trees and through grass and open plains in the western section of Elandsfontein. After about 1 km the Giraffe Loop, which links up with the Ecological Route, splits off to the left, and the Archaeological Route continues to the right. A short way on are the remains of a stone-walled Iron Age site, probably used mainly as a live-stock post, rather than a large-scale settlement. After a gentle descent on open plains, the trail ascends gradually to the start. **3.5 km; 2 hours; circular.**

3. Ecology Route follows the Archaeological Route for 1 km and then continues along the Giraffe Link, passing through grass savannah interspersed with common sugarbush, cabbage and sour plum trees. A short, steep climb to a rocky outcrop is rewarded with splendid views of the surrounding landscape, and the outcrop provides an excellent vantage point from which to look out for giraffe, nyala and kudu. Continuing further, you soon reach Kudu Link, which links up with the Geology Route, while the Ecology Route continues along Blesbok Ridge, a favourite grazing area of blesbok. The trail then grad-ually descends along Gemsbok Loop until its junction with the Geology Route, which you follow for 1.7 km back to the basecamp. **5.9 km; 6 hours; circular.**

8. MOOIPLASIE HIKING TRAIL
Boekenhoutskloof

Trail: 2 trail routes; 7 and 12 km;
3.5 and 6 hours; circular.
Permits: Anvie Ventures, P O Box 60035,
Pierre van Ryneveld 0045,
tel. and fax: (012) 662 1140.
Maps: Rough sketch map.
Facilities/Activities: Basecamp: three huts with bunks, mattresses, fridge, freezer, kettles, pots, pans, cutlery, crockery, braai facilities, hot showers and toilets; small solar-heated swimming pool.

This trail network near Boekenhoutskloof alternates between rocky ridges, bushveld trees, grasslands and kloofs with indigenous forests. Along the way hikers can enjoy fine views over the surrounding landscape, while an inviting pool in the river on the longer route makes an ideal reststop. **7 and 12 km; 3.5 and 6 hours; circular.**

9. MOBONZ GAME RESERVE
Rust de Winter

Trails: 6 trails; 26 km (in total);
1 to 5 hours; network from basecamp.
Permits: Jacana Marketing and Reservations, P O Box 95212, Waterkloof 0145, tel: (012) 346 3550, fax: 346 2499, email: info@jacanacollection.co.za
Maps: Sketch map.
Facilities/Activities: Thatched rondavel with bunks, mattresses, kitchen with three-plate gas cooker, pots, pans, kettles, braai facil-ities, firewood, hot shower and toilets.

Situated in the hills overlooking the Rust de Winter Dam, Mobonz Game Farm is home to kudu, large herds of eland, red hartebeest, gemsbok and impala, and the diversity of habitats it contains supports numerous bird species. The vegetation is characterised by mixed bushveld consisting of acacia species, Transvaal beech, red bushwillow and wild seringa.

This trail network in the Mobonz Game Reserve has been designed to enable trailists to plan hikes to suit their own interests and fitness levels. The hikes range from short early morning and late afternoon rambles to more demanding half-day morning or afternoon walks.

10. BORAKALALO NATIONAL PARK
Jericho

Trails: *Self-guided walk; 5 km; 2.5 hours; out-and-return. Guided walks; 2 to 4 km; 2 hours; circular.*
Permits: *Entrance fee. No permit required for walk. Guided walks can be arranged at Moretele Camp.*
Maps: *Pamphlet of park with map.*
Facilities/Activities: *Phudufudu: tented safari camp. Moretele: safari tents and campsites with fireplace, hot showers and toilets. Pityane Camp: campsites with fireplaces, communal hot showers and toilets. Self-drive game-viewing from any of the camps. Picnic sites on the banks of Klipvoor Dam and along game-drives; angling on the dam.*
Pertinent information: *Trailists on the self-guided walk must keep an eye out for white rhino, buffalo and hippo, as these animals can be very dangerous.*

Situated 90 km to the northwest of Pretoria, the Borakalalo National Park covers 14,000 ha of bushveld, riverine forest and grasslands around the Klipvoor Dam, which forms the focal point of the park. The name Borakalalo means 'the place where people relax' in Tswana.

The park has been stocked with over 30 large mammal species, including white rhino, hippo, giraffe, Burchell's zebra and a variety of antelope. Among these are buffalo, roan, tsessebe, red hartebeest, kudu, gemsbok, blue wildebeest waterbuck, impala and springbok. Also found here are warthog, black-backed jackal, vervet monkey and a variety of other small mammal species.

Borakalalo offers excellent birding possibilities and to date some 350 species have been recorded. The Klipvoor Dam and a nearby seasonal wetland attract a rich diversity of waterbirds, including the elusive African finfoot, greater and lesser flamingoes, black-crowned night heron, green-backed heron, white-faced duck and several kingfisher species. Also recorded are Wahlberg's eagle, lanner falcon, gymnogene, white-throated and Kalahari robins, Kurrichane thrush, Meyer's parrot and arrow-marked babbler.

1. Self-guided walk This walk wanders through a well-wooded area along the lower reaches of the Moretele River. It offers excellent birding opportunities, especially from the hides overlooking a seasonal wetland, and there is always a possibility that you might chance upon game. **5 km; 2.5 hours; out-and-return.**

2. Guided walks are conducted from Moretele Camp by honorary park officials, either in the early morning or late afternoon. In addition to the excitement of seeing game on foot, trailists will also gain a better understanding of the environment through which they are walking. **2 to 4 km; 2 hours; circular.**

11. TSWAING CRATER TRAIL
Pretoria

Trail: *7.2 km; 3 hours; circular.*
Permits: *Entrance fee. No permit required for walk.*
Maps: *Available at office.*
Facilities/Activities: *Guided tours; kiosk; braai facilities; traditional African meals; accommodation for groups visiting for environmental education purposes.*

Situated some 30 km north of Onderstepoort, the Tswaing Meteorite Crater is one of the best preserved meteorite impact craters in the world. It was formed some 200,000 years ago when a meteorite, estimated to be 60 m in diameter, collided with the earth. The impact created a crater with a diameter of 1.1 km and a depth of 120 m.

The name Tswaing means 'salt pan' in Tswana and refers to the brine lake that lies at the centre of the crater. The salt was mined for centuries by the Tswana, Sotho and Ndebele who occupied the area at various periods, and during the early 1900s a soda factory was established at Tswaing.

The Tswaing Meteorite Crater is one of the nine satellite museums of the National Cultural History Museum and was established in 1992 as the first environmental museum in South Africa.

The vegetation is dominated by bushwillow and acacia species. Among the nearly 300 bird species found here that you may tick are Wahlberg's eagle, crested francolin, cardinal woodpecker, crimson-breasted shrike and ground-scraper thrush.

The 7.2-km self-guided **Crater Trail** is probably the only one of its kind in the world. It starts at the Tswaing Meteorite Crater reception and heads north, to the southern crater rim, and then swings east to run along the crest of the southern and eastern crater rim. From here trailists are rewarded with superb views of the crater. A zigzag route down the wooded crater slopes leads to the crater floor and the peninsula extending into the crater lake. The return leg follows an old wagon route out of the crater and the trail then meanders past the old soda factory back to the reception area. Trees and other points of interest along the route have been marked, among them the site of the borehole that provided conclusive evidence that the crater was formed by a meteorite impact and not as a result of volcanic activity. Rock from the borehole showed a deformation of minerals that could only have been produced by pressures resulting from the impact of a meteorite.

At the time of writing, three more trails were being planned, one of which will pass through dense riverine vegetation with magnificent tree species.

12. UITKYK HIKING TRAIL
Hartbeespoort Dam, Magaliesberg

Trails: 2 trails; 13 km; 6 hours; circular.
Shorter options are available.
Permits: Jacana Marketing and Reservations,
P O Box 95212, Waterkloof 0145,
tel: (012) 346 3550, fax: 346 2499,
email: info@jacanacollection.co.za
Maps: Sketch map.
Facilities/Activities: Fenced car park;
braai facilities; ablution block with
showers and toilets.

Stretching from Zeerust, eastwards, to Pretoria's eastern suburbs and rising on average 330 m above the surrounding landscape, the Magaliesberg forms a natural boundary between the bushveld to the north and the Highveld to the south.

The cliffs at Skeerpoort, to the southwest of the Hartbeespoort Dam, are an important breeding site for the Cape vulture, which can often be seen soaring over the area. Other bird species to look out for include black eagle, short-toed rock thrush, long-billed pipit and black-cheeked waxbill.

Laid out on the northern slopes of the Magaliesberg, this trail network alternates between open woodlands, forested kloofs and grass-covered mountain slopes. The name Uitkyk means 'lookout' in Afrikaans, and along the routes there are spectacular views of the Magaliesberg and its surroundings.

The trail to the Magaliesberg summit descends from the start to a tunnel underneath the R513 and then continues to a kloof carved between two prominent mountain peaks. From here, trailists have the option of either ascending the 1,474-m-high western peak or the 1,517-m-high eastern peak. Along the way there are views of the winding Crocodile River and, once the summit of the Magaliesberg is reached, hikers are rewarded with stunning views. Looking west, you can see the range extending towards Rustenburg, while to the east the Magaliesberg cableway station is clearly visible. To the south the scenery is dominated by the Hartbeespoort Dam, and the Johannesburg skyline further south, while the vistas to the north extend as far as the Waterberg on clear days. The trails to the summit involve altitude gains of 294 and 337 m.

13. HENNOPS HIKING TRAIL
Hartbeespoort Dam, Magaliesberg

Trails: 2 trails; 6.1 and 11.3 km;
3 and 5 hours; network from basecamp.
Permits: Jacana Marketing and Reservations,
P O Box 95212, Waterkloof 0145,
tel: (012) 346 3550, fax: 346 2499,
email: info@jacanacollection.co.za
Maps: Trail pamphlet with map.
Facilities/Activities: Loerie Camp: rondavels
with bunks, mattresses, kitchen with two-plate
stove, fridge, pots, pans, kettle, showers
and toilets. Hadeda Camp: farmhouse
and rondavel with swimming pool and the
same facilities as Loerie Camp; braai
facilities for day hikers.

This trail network traverses the 1,000-ha farm Skurweberg, 16 km southeast of Hartbeespoort Dam. In addition to spectacular views and the possibility of seeing game on foot there are also several interesting historical sites here.

1. Zebra Route traverses the game camp in the north of the farm where hikers may spot blesbok and Burchell's zebra. The outward leg winds steadily up the mountain slopes and passes through several clumps of trees. On reaching the summit of a koppie the trail descends back to the start. **6.1 km; 3 hours; network.**

2. Krokodilberg Route initially meanders along the Hennops River and then leads to an overhang where the Boers set up a field hospital during the South African War (1899–1902) to treat their wounded. A short way on you cross the Hennops River by means of a suspension bridge and then come to Hardekraal, where the remains of a stone-walled settlement can be seen. A steady ascent leads to two viewpoints and, after following the contours, the path descends past an old dolomite mine and a lime oven. From here it is an easy walk to the Hennops River, which you can cross by means of a pulley-operated cable-car to get back to Loerie and Hadeda camps. **11.3 km; 5 hours; network.**

14. KROMDRAAI SPECIAL INTEREST HIKING TRAIL
Kromdraai

Trail: *Guided trail; 20 km; 2 days; circular.*
Permits: *Kromdraai Conservancy,
P O Box 393, Paardekraal 1752,
tel: (011) 957 0241, fax: 957 0344.*
Maps: *General tourist map of area.*
Facilities/Activities: *Overnight hut with bunks, mattresses, fireplace, hot showers and toilets.*
Pertinent information: *Groups must consist of at least eight hikers (small groups can be combined to make up the required number) and are limited to a maximum of 16 people. Persons under the age of 18 years old must be accompanied by an adult.*

The Kromdraai Conservancy lies within the Cradle of Humankind, the collective name for the fossil hominid sites of Sterkfontein, Swartkrans, Kromdraai and their environs, which were declared a World Heritage Site in 1999. It is one of the richest early hominid sites in the world, and to date over 600 hominid fossils, thousands of animal fossils, fragments of fossil wood and stone tools have been uncovered at 12 sites. The earliest known deliberate use of fire took place some 1.3 million years ago on Swartkrans, which lies within the Conservancy.

This special interest hike traverses the Kromdraai Conservancy and has been made possible by the co-operation of nearly 30 landowners who have opened up their properties to hiking groups. The trail is guided by a SATOUR registered field guide and has a strong educational emphasis, covering topics such as flora, fauna, geology and the area's fascinating palaeontology.

About 10 km is covered each day and the hike includes visits to several attractions in the conservancy. Among these is the Wonder Cave, a large underground cavern with stalactites, cave pearls, rimstone pools and formations of up to 15 m high. Also included are visits to the Kromdraai gold mine, which dates back to 1881, an old lime mine and the Rainbow Trout Farm.

The trail starts at the Conserve Booking and Information Office. Overnight accommodation at the end of the first day's hike is provided in an rustic old tobacco kiln.

15. FISH EAGLE COVE HIKING TRAIL
Rustenburg, Magaliesberg

Trails: *3 trails; 5 to 12 km; 2.5 to 6 hours; circular.*
Permits: *Anvie Ventures, P O Box 60035, Pierre van Ryneveld 0045, tel. and fax: (012) 662 1140.*
Maps: *Sketch map.*
Facilities/Activities: *Basecamp: hut with bunks, mattresses, freezer, pots, pans, braai facilities, firewood, hot showers and toilets.*
Pertinent information: *Vehicles must be left at the parking area, 3.2 km from the hut.*

The northern slopes of the Magaliesberg provide the setting for this trail network, situated about 30 km southeast of Rustenburg.

1. Route 1 meanders gently up the slopes of the Magaliesberg, gaining some 100 m in altitude, and then descends along Hamerkop Kloof. **5 km; 2.5 hours; circular.**

2. Route 2 (also known as the Kloof Route) leads past Rotsboom Kloof and, after traversing the slopes above Hamerkop Kloof for a short way, the path comes to a ladder, which takes trailists down into the kloof. From here the trail ascends the kloof and then winds gradually downhill along the outward leg of Route 1. **6 km; 3 hours; circular.**

3. Route 3 follows Route 1 until its split to Hamerkop Kloof. Further along, the path crosses the Hamerkop Stream and then gradually ascends to the crest of the Magaliesberg, where trailists can enjoy stunning views of the mountain range and the surrounding landscape. The trail then descends gently along a stream and loops back to join its outward leg. After retracing your steps for a short way you can either follow the return leg of the Kloof Route or that of Route 1. **12 km; 6 hours; circular, with a shorter 9 km; 4.5 hour; circular option.**

16. RUSTENBURG HIKING TRAIL
Rustenburg Nature Reserve,
Rustenburg, Magaliesberg

See no. 17 (p. 267) for walk.

Trails: 2 trails; 19.5 and 25.3 km;
2 days; circular.
Permits: The Reservations Officer,
Rustenburg Nature Reserve,
P O Box 20382, Protea Park 0305,
tel: (014) 533 2050, fax: 533 0905.
Maps: Colour trail map.
Facilities/Activities: Overnight huts at
Explorers', Avon More, Witkruiskrans and
Naga camps, with bunks, mattresses, braai
facilities, firewood, bucket showers and toilets.

Covering 4,257 ha on the eastern slopes of the Magaliesberg, the vegetation of the Rustenburg Nature Reserve is a mosaic of grasslands, kloof forests, thornveld and woodland with open savannah. Proteaveld is found on the plateau and the middle slopes of the Waterkloofspruit Basin and contains common sugarbush and honey-scented proteas. Conspicuous among the rocky ridges and cliffs is the Transvaal milkplum. The red-hot poker aloe (*Aloe peglerae*) and a small succulent, elephant's feet (*Frithia pulchra* – its common name referring to the appearance of its leaf tips), are two Magaliesberg endemics that occur in the reserve.

The reserve is home to 84 mammal species and among the antelope you might encounter are sable, black wildebeest, blesbok, impala, red hartebeest, springbok, kudu, reedbuck and oribi. Carnivores found in the reserve include leopard, brown hyaena, aardwolf, caracal and black-backed jackal, while the primates are represented by baboon, vervet monkey and lesser bushbaby.

With a bird checklist of over 300 species, birding can be rewarding. Among the species you might tick are Meyer's parrot, lilac-breasted roller, crimson-breasted shrike, paradise flycatcher, arrow-marked babbler and black-headed oriole. Raptors include Cape vulture, black and African hawk eagles, jackal buzzard and lanner falcon. Eleven thrush and chat species have been recorded, among them Cape and short-toed rock thrushes.

1. Baviaanskloof Route can be started at either Explorers' or Avon More Camp. Soon after leaving Explorers' Camp on the first day (10.4 km; 5 hours), you follow the trail as it ascends a steep hill and then follows a gently undulating course to the Zebra Plains. Further along, the trail winds past fascinating rocky outcrops, leads down into the Waterkloofspruit Valley and then climbs Langkloofrug before winding down to the overnight hut.

The second day's hike (9.1 km; 5 hours) begins with an ascent to the Garden of Memory and then continues its upward trend to the Tierkloof Cascades and the spectacular Tierkloof Waterfall, which plunges in several steps into a deep gorge. The pools above the falls are irresistible and a perfect spot for tea or lunch. Further on, the trail winds up Bakenkop and then descends steeply to cross Bobbejaanskloof, shortly before reaching the start.

2. Summit Route can be started at either Witkruis-krans or Naga Camp. From Witkruiskrans Camp the first day's trail (11 km; 5 hours) gradually ascends to Bakenkop and then winds down to Tierkloof Pools. From here the trail climbs steadily, gaining some 200 m in altitude before traversing the slopes below Swartwildebeesrug. After this the trail makes its way past interesting quartzite rock formations to reach Naga Camp a short way beyond Civet Rock Arch.

Day two (14.3 km; 7 hours) crosses Secretary Bird Flats and then climbs gradually to the Mushroom Rocks, weathered quartzite rocks resembling giant mushrooms, before reaching a vantage point on the edge of the vertical western cliffs of the Magalies-berg. The trail now leads to the 1,690-m-high Hoogstepunt and after winding past Zebra Dam begins a long, steady descent along the eastern slopes of the Magaliesberg, back to the start.

17. RUSTENBURG NATURE RESERVE
Rustenburg, Magaliesberg

See no. 16 (p. 266) for hiking trails.

Trail: 5 km; 2 hours; circular.
Permits: Entrance fee. No permit required.
Maps: Trail booklet and sketch map.
Facilities/Activities: Visitors' Centre; picnic facilities; group camp.

Peglerae Interpretative Trail is named after the red-hot poker aloe (*Aloe peglerae*), which is endemic to the Magaliesberg and Witwatersberg. This aloe is particularly striking, with a stunted appearance, and is especially attractive in July and August when its dull red to pale greenish-yellow flowers brighten the grassveld.

Starting at the Visitors' Centre, the trail winds in a northwesterly direction along the slopes above Water-kloof. A trail booklet provides information about marked points of interest along the way. Among these are the eroded quartzite rocks seen along the trail, trees such as the Transvaal milkplum and the wild apricot, the red-hot poker aloe and a Magaliesberg endemic succulent, elephant's feet (*Frithia pulchra*).

18. PILANESBERG NATIONAL PARK
Sun City

Trails: Guided walks; distances variable, 4 to 6 km; 2 to 3 hours; circular.
Permits: Entrance fee. Guided trails can be booked at the Gametrackers's Safari desk at Sun City, tel: (014) 552 1561, and at the Manyane, tel: (014) 555 5469, and Bakgatla, tel: (014) 556 2710, safari desks in the park.
Maps: Tourist map of park.
Facilities/Activities: A variety of accommodation options is available here, ranging from upmarket lodges (Bakabung, Kwa Maritane and Tshukudu) to tented safari camps and campsites; self-drive game-viewing; self-drive Geology Trail; guided game- and night-drives; balloon safaris; Manyane indigenous 'walk-in' bird aviary; bird- and game-viewing hides; picnic sites.
Pertinent information: Guided walks are conducted for groups of a minimum of six people.

Situated 50 km northeast of Rustenburg, the 58,000-ha Pilanesberg National Park is enclosed by four concentric rings of hills, the roots of an ancient volcano that was active some 1,200 million years ago. The Pilanesberg Complex is one of the three largest alkaline volcanoes in the world (the other two are situated in Greenland and Russia), and has the most clearly defined ring structure. Rising some 300 m above the surrounding bushveld plains, the landscape of the Pilanesberg ranges from impressive mountain peaks and rolling plains to deep wooded valleys and ravines. At the centre of the crater floor is a dam, built by the park authorities.

The varied topography and geology of the area have resulted in a rich diversity of vegetation types. Typical tree species found here include Transvaal beech, common wild pear, wild olive, karee and a variety of acacia species. Of special interest is the Transvaal red balloon tree, which is endemic to Pilanesberg.

In addition to being a sanctuary for the Big Five (elephant, black and white rhino, buffalo, lion and leopard) Pilanesberg is home to numerous other species, as it lies in the transitional zone between the dry Kalahari and the wetter Lowveld vegetation. Among the antelope are kudu, gemsbok, red hartebeest, blue wildebeest, mountain reedbuck, impala and springbok. Other species to be seen include giraffe, hippo, Burchell's zebra, warthog and brown hyaena.

With a bird checklist of over 330 species, birding can be rewarding. There are no fewer than 32 bird of prey species here, including Cape and white-backed vultures, black-breasted snake eagle and lanner falcon. Among the other species you may tick are lilac-breasted roller, black-headed oriole, short-toed rock thrush, orange-breasted longclaw, crimson-breasted shrike and plum-coloured starling.

Guided walks enable trailists to explore the park on foot under the guidance of an experienced and knowledgeable guide. In addition to tracking game on foot, trailists also learn more about the trees and the environment through which they walk. The walks are conducted in the morning, when the predators are less active. **4 to 6 km; 2 to 3 hours; circular.**

19. VISAREND HIKING TRAIL
Swartruggens

> **Trail:** 2 trail routes; 6 and 10 km;
> 3 and 5 hours; network from basecamp.
> **Permits:** Anvie Ventures, P O Box 60035,
> Pierre van Ryneveld 0045, tel. and
> fax: (012) 662 1140.
> **Maps:** Sketch map.
> **Facilities/Activities:** Campsite (you need to
> bring your own tents) with braai facilities,
> firewood, pot, kettle, hot showers and toilets.

This trail traverses the farm Klipbankfontein, about 15 km south of the village of Swartruggens.

1. Maselkrans Route follows an undulating course with steep ascents and descents to a number of springs and waterholes. From the basecamp the trail leads to Vaalkoppies, with beautiful views of the surrounding Pilanesberg landscape. The trail then continues to Maselkrans, before returning to the basecamp. **6 km; 3 hours; circular.**

2. Waterfall Route From the basecamp the trail ascends to a plateau and then winds gradually down to the Elands River where you may see African fish eagle. From here the trail leads through valleys and below towering cliffs to a spectacular waterfall in the Elands River, and then winds back to the basecamp. **10 km; 5 hours; circular.**

20. VREDEFORT DOME HIGHLAND TRAILS
Venterskroon

> **Trails:** 3 hiking trails; 13 to 27 km;
> 2 days; circular and open-ended.
> 1 trail combining hiking and canoeing;
> 2 days; open-ended.
> **Permits:** Dome Highlands Trails,
> P O Box 21138, Noordbrug 2522,
> tel: (018) 294 8572,
> email: domeavnt@iafrica.com
> **Maps:** Supplied to hikers on arrival.
> **Facilities/Activities:** Basecamp in the
> historic settlement of Venterskroon: the Mining
> Commissioner's house and office, a small
> hotel, a teacher's house and a pioneer cot-
> tage form the Dorp Street part of the Dome
> Trails Basecamp. Three overnight bush
> camps with bunk beds, mattresses, braai
> facilities, showers and toilets.
> **Pertinent information:** The Rooihaas Trail is
> open-ended, so trailists need either to leave
> a second vehicle at the end of the trail or
> arrange transport back to the start (at an addi-
> tional fee) with the trail authority. The Summit
> Route and the Boot and Paddle Trail are also
> open-ended, but transport back to the start is
> included in the trail fees for these hikes.

This network of trails is named after the Vrede-fort Dome, which is a semi-circular range of hills with a diameter of some 70 km. The origins of the

Vredefort Dome have been the subject of some considerable debate and two main theories have been advanced. Some geologists attribute its origin to the intrusion of granite into the overlying rock, forming a dome. The overlying strata and the top of the dome gradually eroded and were later covered by the rocks of the Waterberg system. A further upwelling of magma then caused the dome to rise again, while uneven pressure from deep inside the earth's crust forced the whole structure northwards and also folded the adjoining rock strata in that direction. This continued for a considerable time, with subsequent erosion removing the overlying rocks.

The second theory suggests that a gigantic meteorite, with an estimated diameter of 10 km, struck the earth's surface over 2 billion years ago. Relieved of the weight of the strata that were smashed in the impact zone, granite moved upwards and turned the edges of the adjacent strata outward. Research has shown that the original impact structure (if this is indeed what it is) had a diameter of between 250 and 300 km. Erosion over countless millennia has left only a semi-circle of hills in the northwest of the original crater, while the southwestern part of the dome was subsequently covered by Karoo sediments.

Vredefort Dome is also noteworthy for the large concentration and variety of stone-walled Iron Age settlements that it contains. Some of the early sites may have been inhabited as long as 1,500 years ago, while occupation of other settlements dates back to between the 1500s and the dispersal of the Tswana people, after the arrival of the Zulu chief Mzilikazi on the Highveld in the 1820s.

Among the typical Bankenveld trees in the Venterskroon area are wild olive, white stinkwood, common sugarbush, sweet thorn, common wild pear, buffalo-thorn and blue guarri. Also to be seen are mountain karree, velvet bushwillow and small knobwood.

1. Rooihaas Trail owes its name to Smith's red rock rabbit (*rooihaas* is Afrikaans for 'red rabbit'), which favours rocky terrain and is found in the large parts of South Africa that provide a suitable habitat for the animal. Starting on the farm Buffelskloof, which lies near the historic mining town of Venterskroon, the first day's hike (12 km; 6 hours) initially winds along the banks of the Vaal River. From here it gradually climbs up the hills and then follows a gently undulating course through small valleys, with several optional detours over the course of the hike. Attractions along the way include far-reaching views of the Vredefort Dome and the Vaal River to the south, as well as the ruins of stone-walled Iron Age settlements and old mine shafts. Hikers can stay overnight in either Bundu or Boplaas Camp.

The second day's trail (7 km; 3 hours) traverses fairly easy terrain, which is dotted with numerous stone-walled Iron Age settlements. The hike ends at Krugerskraal, which is the site of the house where the Bible was first translated into Afrikaans by the writer and poet Totius. The house has been declared a national monument. **19 km; 2 days; open-ended.**

2. Summit Route can be started at either Boplaas or Bundu camps and traverses the summit of the Vredefort Dome hills. The first day's hike covers 12 km (over 6 hours), and the second 7 km (over 3 hours). Venterskroon Basecamp is used as an overnight stop at the end of the first day's hike. **19 km; 2 days; open-ended.**

3. Old Mine Route focuses on the early mining history of Vredefort Dome, which dates back to the late 1880s when gold was first discovered in the area. Venterskroon was established as a mining town in 1889, but since the ore found here was low grade the miners, fortune-seekers and adventurers soon moved off again and the settlement began to stagnate. On arrival, hikers are accommodated at the Venterskroon Basecamp. The first day of the hike (8 or 15 km) makes its way from this basecamp to the Oudewerf Camp. From Oudewerf Camp the second day's hike (5 or 12 km) meanders back to the start of the trail. **13, 20 or 27 km; 2 days; circular.**

4. Boot and Paddle Trail combines 12 km of hiking, which is completed on the first day, with 12 km of canoeing, done on the second day. On arrival, trailists can stay at either Boplaas or Bundu Camp, from where the first day's hike takes them to the Venterskroon Basecamp. On the second day you canoe down the Vaal River for 12 km. **24 km; 2 days; open-ended.**

GREAT KAROO, NAMAQUALAND & KALAHARI

The Great Karoo and Namaqualand are characterised by vast tracts of arid land, wide open spaces and solitude, and the Kalahari is known as a thirstland. Together these regions cover nearly 50 per cent of South Africa's surface and their landscapes range from endless grassy plains and typical Karoo koppies to the imposing granite domes of Namaqualand and the orange dunes and stately camel thorn trees of the Kalahari.

The Great Karoo is bounded in the south by the Great Escarpment and in the north by the Gariep (Orange) River. It extends from the Eastern Cape Midlands, westwards, to the western escarpment, where it gives way to the plains, sandveld and Klipkoppe of Namaqualand. From the Gariep River the Kalahari stretches northwards to the furthest reaches of the Northern Cape and into Botswana.

The apparent bleakness of the landscape belies the rich diversity of flora and fauna that has adapted to survive in these seemingly inhospitable surroundings. Another major attraction of the Karoo is its beautiful scenery: vast open plains that melt into the horizon, conical dolerite koppies and table-top mountains.

Some 280 million years ago much of southern Africa lay in a shallow basin, which was filled during various periods by sand, mud, pebbles and boulders from the surrounding highlands. When temperatures increased after an ice age, around 250 million years ago, ferns, early conifers, horsetails, club mosses and large trees such as *Dadoxylon* began to flourish in the Karoo Basin, while dinosaurs roamed the swamps, shallow lakes and floodplains. The reign of the dinosaurs lasted for 50 million years, from 240 to 190 million years ago, when they became extinct, possibly as a result of drastic climate changes.

The Karoo is world renowned for its fossils, especially those of therapsid (mammal-like) reptiles. These relics from the distant past formed when the body of a dinosaur was entombed in mud and the calcium of its bones replaced by silica from the surrounding sediments to form a perfect replica. The mud then hardened into rock, which was later subjected to millions of years of erosion, exposing the fossils.

The Karoo's characteristic cone-shaped koppies and table-top mountains were created during the middle-Jurassic period when magma was forced along cracks and fissures in the earth's crust, forming dolerite when it cooled down. The less resistant sedimentary rocks under the protective dolerite caps were then eroded to form the typical Karoo koppies and ridges.

Despite its harsh climate the Karoo is home to an estimated 7,000 plant species, including grasses, succulents, a variety of annuals and a wealth of dwarf shrubs, which are dominant over much of the Karoo. Commonly referred to as Karoo bossies (bushes), the shrublands are composed of species with colourful names, such as ankerkaroo (*Pentzia incana*), kapokbos (*Eriocephalus ericoides*), swartganna (*Salsola calluna*), koggelmandervoetkaroo (*Limeum aethiopicum*), perdekaroo (*Rosenia humilis*) and silver Karoo (*Plinthus karooicus*). Other typical trees and shrubs found here include sweet thorn, yellow pomegranate, common spike thorn, cancer bush (*Sutherlandia frutescens*), broom karee and Karoo cross berry (*Grewia robusta*).

Dutch farmers first settled in the Karoo in the 1750s, and soon exterminated the vast herds of game here. Fortunately, game numbers are again increasing in conservation areas and on many farms. Visitors may encounter game while hiking through the Karoo, Doornkloof and Rolfontein nature reserves and the Karoo National Park. Often overlooked, though, is the wide variety of smaller mammals that still occur here naturally. Among these are bat-eared fox, black-backed jackal, caracal, Cape clawless otter, badger, mongoose, hare and a host of nocturnal animals.

These regions, compared with others, have little diversity of bird species. Typical birds found here include Karoo korhaan, Ludwig's and kori bustards, spike-heeled and Karoo larks, tractrac, sickle-winged and Karoo chats, black-eared finchlark, Karoo eremomela and Namaqua warbler.

There are many opportunities to explore on foot, from short day walks to overnight hiking trails. You can enjoy wide open spaces, smell the aromatic Karoo bushes and enjoy extensive views. Early mornings and late afternoons are especially beautiful, as the changing light on the landscape creates a kaleidoscope of colour.

Heading the list of attractions is the Augrabies Falls National Park. The park has as its focal point the Augrabies Falls, said to be one of the world's best examples of a cataract-type waterfall and of the weathering of granite by water.

At Graaff-Reinet titanic forces deep beneath the earth and subsequent erosion combined to create the spectacular Valley of Desolation, with its imposing dolerite pillars. The site falls within the Karoo Nature Reserve, which nearly encircles the town of Graaff-Reinet, and offers day walks, as well as an overnight hike.

The Karoo National Park, on the outskirts of Beaufort West, lies at the heart of the Great Karoo. Dominated by the Nuweveld Mountains, the park's landscape ranges from plains to Karoo koppies and sheer dolerite cliffs. Game species that used to roam the Karoo plains in their hundreds of thousands have been reintroduced here and the vegetation is slowly recovering.

Namaqualand is renowned for its succulents and its spectacular, colourful annual spring flower display, which can usually be seen from early August to mid-September, but depends entirely on good winter rains and well-spaced follow-up rains. The floral carpets are composed of annuals with names such as gansogies (*Cotula barbata*), sambreeltjies (*Felicia merxmuelleri*), gousblomme (*Osteospermum, Arctotis, Ursinia*), beetle daisies (*Gorteria diffusa* spp. *diffusa*) and botterblom (*Gazania*).

Conspicuous amongst the Namaqualand succulents and the broken veld along the Gariep River is the quiver tree, which favours the northern slopes of hills and granite outcrops. It is especially eye-catching in July, with its bright yellow flower spikes.

The prolific herds of game encountered by the early travellers through Namaqualand and the explorers searching for the fabulous wealth of the southern African empire of Monomotapa have sadly long since disappeared. Except in the Goegap Nature Reserve, where large mammals have been reintroduced, mammals throughout the two regions are limited to species that have been able to survive mainly because of their small size.

The climate of the three regions is one of extremes. Summer temperatures are excessively high, often exceeding 35 °C in the middle of the season. In winter temperatures plunge to 5 °C and below, and the high mountain peaks of Sneeuberg north of Graaff-Reinet and the Nuweveld range at Beaufort West are frequently covered by a blanket of snow in the middle of winter.

Namaqualand and the western edge of the Great Karoo fall in the winter-rainfall area and get 50 to 300 mm of rain, increasing from north to south and from the coast eastwards. In the Great Karoo rainfall ranges from 50 mm in the northwest to 500 mm in the east, falling mainly in late summer and early autumn, while the Kalahari's varies from 100 mm in the southwest to 450 mm in the northeast. Rainfall is, however, highly variable and annual evaporation often exceeds average rainfall.

IMPORTANT INFORMATION

• When hiking in summer, it is important to take precautions against the sun: apply sunscreen frequently, wear a wide-brimmed hat and a long-sleeved shirt. In hot weather it is also important to keep your water intake up to counter water loss. Before setting off, enquire about the availability of water along the trail and carry water accordingly.

• An early start is advisable in summer to enable you to cover as much ground as possible during the cool part of the day. If necessary, you should find a comfortable, shady place to rest during the hottest part of the day and resume hiking only once the temperature has dropped.

• Ensure that you pack sufficient warm clothing and a warm sleeping bag for overnight hikes during the winter months.

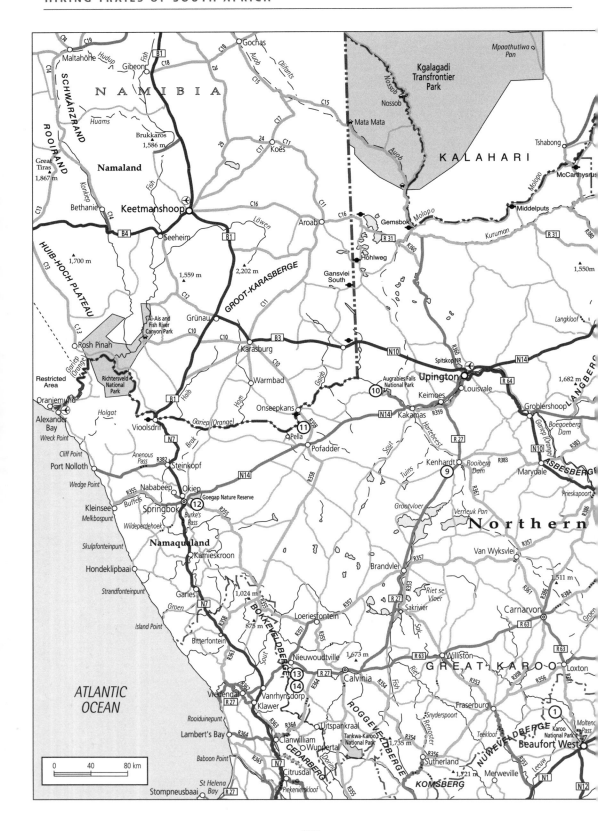

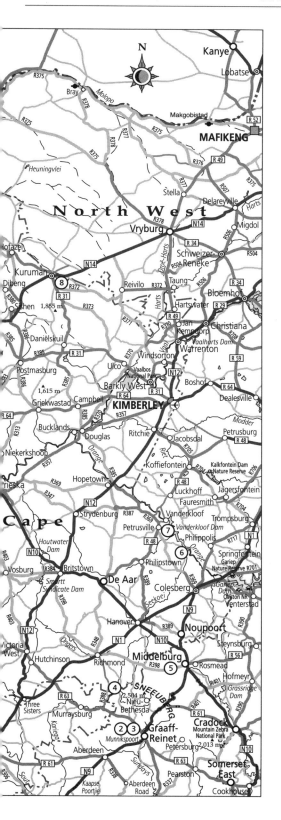

1. KAROO NATIONAL PARK
Beaufort West

> *Trails:* 3 trails; 400 m to 11 km;
> 45 min to 5 hours; circular.
> *Permits:* Entrance fee. No permit required.
> *Maps:* Sketch maps.
> *Facilities/Activities:* Restcamp with
> fully equipped self-catering cottages;
> campsite with hot showers and toilets;
> restaurant; shop; swimming pool;
> self-drive game-viewing; 4x4 trail.

The Karoo National Park, just outside of Beaufort West, was proclaimed in 1979 to conserve a representative part of the Karoo. It covers 86,000 ha of plains, koppies and mountainous terrain, overlooked by the Nuweveld Mountains.

Animals occurring in the park include springbok, Cape mountain zebra, red hartebeest, gemsbok, kudu, mountain reedbuck, grey rhebok, klipspringer, steenbok, common duiker and baboon. A small herd of buffalo was reintroduced from the Addo Elephant National Park and there are plans to reintroduce lion, leopard and wild dog once the park exceeds 100,000 ha (through the acquisition of adjoining land). The park has played an important role in the conservation of the black rhino following the release of three animals in an area specially set aside in 1993. In another significant project to re-establish endangered species, a small group of six riverine rabbits was released in the park in August 1994. Now classified as highly endangered, the riverine rabbit was regarded as extinct until a specimen was found near Victoria West in 1979, 32 years after what was thought to be the last specimen was collected. A breeding programme was subsequently initiated by the De Wildt Breeding Centre, near Hartbeespoort Dam in North West Province.

To date more than 180 bird species have been recorded in the park, including Karoo korhaan, Ludwig's bustard, spike-heeled and long-billed larks, Karoo chat, Layard's titbabbler, Namaqua sandgrouse and ground woodpecker. Some 20 raptors have been recorded, among them booted and martial eagles, peregrine falcon, gymnogene and jackal buzzard. The park's black eagle population is the largest in South Africa and the largest in the world after that in the Matopos area in Zimbabwe.

Other attractions of the park are its typical Karoo landscape of koppies, mountains and wide-open plains, and the treasure-trove of fossilised reptiles, some of them with clear mammal-like features, entombed in the rocks of the Beaufort Group.

1. Fossil Trail provides a fascinating insight into the geological forces that shaped the Karoo, and several fossil specimens are displayed in glass cases along the trail. Some of the fossils have been partially reconstructed, while others are displayed as they were found. Numbered signs indicate points of interest that are explained in a trail pamphlet. Railway-sleeper seats are provided along the trail, which is suitable for wheelchairs. Although this walk is under an hour, it is included here as it is the highlight of the park and the main attraction for most visitors. **400 m; 45 min; circular.**

2. Bossie Trail serves as an ideal introduction to the flora of the Karoo. More than 60 typical Karoo plants along the route have been labelled with their common and scientific names. A short description of each plant is also provided. **800 m; 1 hour; circular.**

3. Fonteintjiekloof Walk leads hikers through an interesting cross-section of Karoo veld. Starting on the plains, the trail alternates between the middle plateau, dense riverine bush and mountain slopes. Part of the trail passes through an area much favoured by kudu and, provided you move quietly, you may see these graceful antelope. **11 km; 5 hours; circular.**

2. KAROO NATURE RESERVE
Graaff-Reinet

See no. 3 (p. 275) for hiking trail.

> *Trails:* 2 trails; 1,5 and 14 km (with
> shorter options); 1 to 7 hours; circular
> and out-and-return.
> *Permits:* Entrance fee. No permits required.
> *Maps:* Colour map of reserve.
> *Facilities/Activities:* Picnic sites; self-drive

game-viewing; angling (permit required) and water sports on Van Ryneveld's Pass Dam; Camdeboo Environmental Education Centre.

Covering 14,500 ha of typical Karoo plains, koppies and mountains, the Karoo Nature Reserve almost entirely surrounds the historic town of Graaff-Reinet. The reserve was established in 1979 to preserve a representative example of the Karoo ecosystem.

The focal point of the reserve is the towering dolerite pillars of the Valley of Desolation, set against a backdrop of Karoo plains. The origin of these rock pillars can be traced back some 180 to 200 million years, when molten magma intruded along cracks and fissures into the overlying sediments of the Karoo Supergroup. As the magma cooled down and contracted it solidified into vertical seams of dolerite rock. Over millions of years the softer surrounding Karoo sediments were eroded, exposing the dolerite columns, which rise to heights of 90 to 120 m. The valley itself was formed by weathering and erosion along a line of weakness in the earth's crust.

Animals occurring in this section of the reserve include mountain reedbuck, Cape mountain zebra, rock dassie and Smith's red rock rabbit.

1. Crag Lizard Trail starts at the Valley of Desolation parking area and is an extension of a short circuit to two viewpoints overlooking the valley. From here the trail meanders westwards along the cliff edge to reveal spectacular views of the rock pillars and the distant plains far below. On reaching a beacon on the 1,400-m-high westernmost point of the mountain, the trail loops back to the start. Keep an eye out for the East Cape crag lizard, to which the trail owes its name. **1.5 km; 1 hour; circular.**

2. Eerstefontein Day Walk starts at the Spandaukop Gate and offers options of 5, 11 and 14 km. The trail makes its way through the southwestern section of the reserve, dominated by the 1,316-m-high Spandaukop, an excellent example of a Karoo koppie. Eerstefontein and Agterstefontein are two inviting picnic spots along the trail, which offer good opportunities to see springbok, black wildebeest, kudu, common duiker and steenbok. **5 km; 2 hours; out-and-return, or 11 km; 5 hours; circular, or 14 km; 7 hours; circular.**

3. DRIEKOPPE HIKING TRAIL
Karoo Nature Reserve, Graaff-Reinet

See no. 2 (p. 274) for walks.

Trail: 26 km (with an optional extra 5 km); 2 days; circular.
Permits: The Officer-in-Charge, Karoo Nature Reserve, P O Box 349, Graaff-Reinet 6280, tel: (049) 892 3453, fax: 892 3862.
Maps: Colour reserve map. Trail sketch map.
Facilities/Activities: Overnight hut with bunks, mattresses, fireplace, firewood, water and toilets; picnic sites; self-drive game-viewing; angling (permit required) and water sports on Van Ryneveld's Pass Dam; Camdeboo Environmental Education Centre.
Pertinent information: The Waaihoek Hut may be booked for two consecutive nights.

This trail is situated in the eastern section of the reserve and is named after the Drie Koppe, three prominent hills dominating the landscape.

The dwarf shrubland vegetation of the plains is characterised by wild pomegranate (*Rhigozum obovatum*), kapok bush (*Eriocephalus ericoides*), perdekaroo (*Rosenia humilis*) and anchor Karoo (*Pentzia incana*). Above 1,300 m the dwarf shrubland is replaced by shrubland composed of species such as wild olive, false olive, Namaqua kuni bush and grasses.

Game found here includes Cape mountain zebra, red hartebeest, mountain reedbuck, kudu, klipspringer, steenbok and common duiker. Buffalo, blesbok, gemsbok and black wildebeest have been reintroduced into the game-viewing area in the north of the reserve.

To date over 225 bird species have been recorded in the reserve. Lookout for ostrich, kori, Ludwig's and Stanley's bustards, secretary bird, black eagle and blue crane. Also recorded are Karoo and blue korhaans, ground woodpecker, sickle-winged and Karoo chats, Cape rock thrush and pale-winged starling.

From the starting point, the first day's hike (10 km; 5 hours) traverses the plains below Hangklip and then joins a jeep track, which you follow to the Waaihoek Hut. About 500 m is gained in altitude to the overnight hut, from where a 5-km circular route can be undertaken via the 1,482-m-high Waaihoek Peak. The second day's hike (16 km; 8 hours) winds between and below the Drie Koppe before joining the outward route of the first day's hike, about 6 km from the start. From here you retrace your steps of the previous day's walk.

4. GROENVLEI FARM
Graaff-Reinet

Trails: 11 trails; 3 to 20 km;
1 to 8 hours; circular.
Permits: Groenvlei Farm,
P O Box 148, Graaff-Reinet 6280,
tel: (049) 845 0305, fax: 845 0302,
email: groenvlei@groenvlei.co.za
Maps: Sketch maps.
Facilities/Activities: Fully equipped
self-catering guesthouse; four-bedroomed
house; two- and one-bedroomed
cottages; cycling; horse-riding; tennis.

Situated in the Sneeuberg Mountains, north of Graaff-Reinet, Groenvlei is a working merino stud farm with a guesthouse. In addition to the scenic beauty of the area, Groenvlei also has added attractions such as fossils dating back 200 million years, Stone Age sites that were inhabited 150,000 years ago and rock paintings.

To date 205 bird species have been identified. Birds you may tick include ostrich, black and booted eagles, peregrine falcon, blue crane, Stanley's and Ludwig's bustards, Namaqua sandgrouse, Cape rock thrush and Karoo robin. Eight lark and three pipit species have been recorded, while a variety of waterbirds are attracted to springs and dams on the farm.

The 11 trails range from the 1-hour-long **Bossie Trail**, which has 50 typical Karoo plant species marked along the route, to the 20-km-long **Grootklip Route**. There are relatively easy hikes across flat plains and up gentle kloofs, as well as more challenging ones, such as an ascent of the 2,000-m-high Aasvoëlberg, but all are on farm tracks. Since all the trails have been graded according to their degree of difficulty, trailists can choose routes to suit their personal level of fitness.

5. TRANSKAROO HIKING TRAIL
Noupoort

Trails: 21 or 40 km; 2 or 3 days; circular.
Day walk; 10 km; 5 hours; circular.
Permits: Transkaroo Hiking Trail,
P O Box 66, Middelburg 5900,
tel. and fax: (049) 843 1506.
Maps: Sketch maps.
Facilities/Activities: Fully equipped
basecamp. Two overnight huts with
stretchers and mattresses, kitchen, braai
facilities, firewood, showers and toilets.

This trail traverses a 10,500-ha farm in the Upper Karoo and affords hikers an opportunity to discover the scenic beauty and rich diversity of Karoo plants. Among the other attractions are imposing rock formations and rock paintings.

Trees you may find along the course of the trail include wild peach and dogwood, as well as a variety of succulents and Karoo shrub vegetation. Typical species include ghombos (*Felicia filifolia*), bloublommetjie (*Felicia muricata*), kriedoring (*Lycium cinereum*), jakkalsbos (*Diospyros austro-africana* var. *austro-africana*), waterharpuis (*Euryops annae*) and basterkaree (*Rhus dregeana*).

Antelope you may see include springbok, mountain reedbuck, grey rhebok and steenbok. The predators are represented by several species, among these are Cape and bat-eared foxes, caracal (depicted on the trail emblem), African wild cat and black-backed jackal. Baboon, vervet monkey, aardwolf, ground squirrel and suricate also occur.

Birds to keep an eye out for include black and martial eagles, blue korhaan, ground woodpecker, pied barbet and clapper lark. Among the other species you might tick are ant-eating and mountain chats, Karoo and Cape robins, Karoo prinia and bokmakierie.

1. Day Walk This is a pleasant walk for visitors who do not have the time or energy to do an overnight trail. From Wilgerfontein the outward leg ascends steadily along a jeep track and then heads in a northeasterly direction to join the Rooivoetpad, which is hiked on the last day of the three-day hike. **10 km; 5 hours; circular.**

2. Two-day Trail The first day's hike (12 km; 6 hours) heads along a jeep track and then gradually ascends Visserskloof, past dolerite pillars, before reaching an inviting rock pool. On leaving the kloof the trail traverses the Stone Desert and then reaches a viewpoint with wonderful views of Kompasberg, 30 km to the south. From here you follow a ridge to Uitsig Camp. On day two (9 km; 4 hours) this hike joins up with the three-day trail route for a short while and then heads in a northeasterly direction to join the Rooivoetpad, which takes you back to the basecamp. **21 km; 2 days; circular.**

3. Three-day Trail This option follows the same route to Uitsig Camp as the two-day trail. On the second day (19 km; 9 hours) the trail leads past oxwagon grooves worn into the sandstone rock and then ascends Beacon Hill, with its 360-degree views. The trail then descends steadily to a windmill and, after passing farm ruins and large pepper trees at Veeplaas, reaches Kanferkloof. The shady poplar grove is an ideal lunch stop, and a swimming hole on the last stretch of the day's hike to Wilgerfontein is especially welcome on a hot day. Day three's hike (9 km; 4 hours) passes rock paintings, estimated to be at least 500 years old, and then follows the Rooivoetpad through the Lichen Paradise, with its rich diversity of lichens. After descending along a beautiful kloof the trail climbs to a ridge overlooking Wilgerfontein, where the trail ends. **40 km; 3 days; circular.**

6. BOKMAKIERIE HIKING TRAIL
Doornkloof Nature Reserve, Colesberg

Trail: 37 km; 3 days, circular.
Permits: Officer-in-Charge, Doornkloof Nature Reserve, P O Box 94, Colesberg 9795, tel. and fax: (051) 753 1315.
Maps: Trail indicated on photocopy of 1:50,000 topographical map.
Facilities/Activities: Trail hut with mattresses, coal stove, fireplace, hot shower and toilet.
Pertinent information: At the time of writing the trail was still being developed and is marked only where there is a change of direction.

Covering 10,000 ha, the Doornkloof Nature Reserve has as its focal points the Seekoei River, which flows for 10 km through the reserve to its confluence with the Gariep (Orange) River and the Vanderkloof Dam.

The landscape is dominated by dolerite outcrops, interspersed with numerous wooded kloofs and grassy plains, sheer cliffs and the twisting shoreline of the Vanderkloof Dam. Situated in the transitional zone between Karoo and grassland vegetation, the reserve's flora contains elements of both.

Game to be seen includes buffalo, gemsbok, kudu, eland, red hartebeest, mountain reedbuck, steenbok and common duiker. Also found here are brown hyaena, black-backed jackal, caracal, warthog, baboon and vervet monkey.

Considering the arid surroundings, the birdlife is rich and includes numerous waterbirds that are attracted to the Vanderkloof Dam, raptors such as black and African fish eagles and a variety of Karoo terrestrial birds. Among these are Karoo, thick-billed and clapper larks, tractrac and Karoo chats, Karoo korhaan, Ludwig's bustard and Karoo prinia.

The trail is still being developed and will appeal to those with a sense of adventure, who want to experience wilderness and a sense of isolation. Fortunately, though, it is difficult to get lost, because of the nature of the terrain – all the kloofs drain into the Vanderkloof Dam, which can be seen from part of the trail. This hike also offers the opportunity to view game on foot; just remember that you may come across potentially dangerous species like buffalo.

This hike meanders along densely wooded kloofs and around and up koppies, with great views of the Vanderkloof Dam. On the first night you sleep in a hut with mattresses, a hot shower and toilets. The second overnight stop is at the ruins of an old stone kraal, with no facilities whatsoever. Fill up your waterbottles before the overnight stop, as the next water point is 2 km along the third day's route.

7. ROLFONTEIN NATURE RESERVE
Petrusville

Trails: 4 km; 2 hours; circular. Guided morning walks for organised groups (these must be arranged in advance). Trailists are

free to blaze their own trails in the reserve.
Permits: *Self-issue entrance permit at reserve gate. No permit required for walk. To arrange a guided walk contact The Assistant Manager, Rolfontein Nature Reserve, P O Box 23, Vanderkloof 8771, tel: (053) 664 0170, fax: 664 0187.*
Maps: *Sketch map of reserve.*
Facilities/Activities: *Two hikers' huts with basic facilities; tent camp for educational groups; picnic sites; night-drives for groups; freshwater angling; watersports.*

Covering 6,250 ha, Rolfontein Nature Reserve lies on the banks of the Vanderkloof Dam in the Gariep (Orange) River. The landscape is characterised by grassy plains, interspersed with many dolerite hills.

The vegetation alternates between False Upper Karoo Veld and Orange River Broken Veld. To date more than 40 grass species have been identified, while a rich diversity of typical Karoo bushes also occurs here. Tree species in the densely wooded kloofs include wild olive, sweet thorn and karee, while cabbage trees, black thorn and wild camphor bush dominate the rocky hills and ridges.

Game roaming the reserve includes white rhino, Burchell's zebra and warthog. Among the many antelope species to be seen are eland, gemsbok, black wildebeest, red hartebeest, mountain reedbuck, springbok and impala.

A wide variety of waterbirds is attracted to the Vanderkloof Dam, among them African fish eagle, yellow-billed duck, Egyptian and spur-winged geese, and South African shelduck. The adjoining dolerite koppies and plains are home to typical Karoo bird species.

Pied Barbet Trail follows an easy route to several marked points of interest that are explained in a trail pamphlet, and some trees along the trail have also been labelled. **4 km; 2 hours; circular.**

In addition to the Pied Barbet Trail, groups can book guided early morning walks with an educational emphasis, while adventurous trailists can blaze their own routes and overnight in two trail huts, one situated in Olienhoutskloof and the other in the western section of the reserve.

8. KURUMAN HIKING TRAIL
Kuruman

Trail: *11 km; 5 hours; open-ended.*
Permits: *Not required for trail.*
Maps: *Sketch map in tourism brochure of Kuruman, obtainable from Kuruman Municipality, P O Box 4, Kuruman 8460, tel: (053) 712 1095.*
Facilities/Activities: *Second Eye Holiday Resort; municipal caravan park; hotels and guesthouses in Kuruman; café and toilets at The Eye Fountain.*
Pertinent information: *At the time of writing the trail was poorly signposted. Since this is an open-ended trail arrangements must be made to leave a vehicle at the end of the trail or for trailists to be collected.*

The trail starts in Kuruman's Main Street at The Eye, one of several fountains that have turned Kuruman into a green oasis in the midst of the Kalahari. Named Gasegonyane by the Tswana people, a word meaning 'the eye', it is said to be the biggest fountain in the southern hemisphere, with a flow of between 20 and 30 million litres of water per day. From here the trail leads to two forts, Denison and Brown, built by the British during the South African War (1899–1902), and continues to a dolomite sink hole and Dikgoiing Fountain, a waterhole used by the Tswana until 1956. Further along you pass the irrigation grounds of Dikgoiing settlement, inhabited between 1880 and 1956, before you reach Dikgoiing Caves and the Wonder Hole, a dolomite cave containing seven streams. The trail ends at the Second Eye Holiday Resort.

9. KOKERBOOM HIKING TRAILS
Kenhardt

Trails: *2 trails; 4 and 15 km; 2 and 7 hours; open-ended and circular.*
Permits: *Bushmanland Crafts and Tours, tel: (054) 651 0022 or 651 0059*

(after hours), email: info@bushmanland.co.za
Maps: *Sketch map.*
Facilities/Activities: *4x4 trail.*

Klipspringer Hiking Trail is only open during the cooler period between April and September.

An unusual concentration of quiver trees, situated about 7 km south of Kenhardt on the farm Driekop, was declared the Kokerboom Forest Reserve in 1993. Here between 4,000 and 5,000 quiver trees grow on a hill amongst black dolerite rocks. The reserve is especially attractive between May and July when sprays of light yellow flowers brighten up the stark landscape.

Birds you may tick include dusky sunbird (during the flowering season), Karoo korhaan, sociable weaver, mountain chat, and long-billed and Sclater's larks. Rock dassies inhabit the rocky terrain.

For those wishing to explore the area on foot there are two trails, alternating between dark dolerite boulders and quartz pebbles. Relics of the South African War (1899–1902) and dinosaur footprints are added attractions. A climb up the highest hill, Driekop, is rewarded with spectacular views of the dramatic landscape. **4 km; 2 hours; open-ended, or 15 km; 7 hours; circular.**

10. KLIPSPRINGER HIKING TRAIL
Augrabies Falls National Park, Kakamas

Trail: *33.5 km; 3 days; circular.*
Permits: *South African National Parks, P O Box 787, Pretoria 0001, tel: (012) 428 9111, fax: 343 0905, email: reservations@parks-sa.co.za*
Maps: *Sketch map.*
Facilities/Activities: *Two overnight huts with bunks, mattresses, chemical toilets. Restcamp with fully equipped self-catering cottages and bungalows; campsites with communal kitchen and ablutions; picnic sites; restaurant; shop; self-drive game-viewing. Black Rhino Adventure (guided drive and walking in northern section of park). Gariep 3-in-1 Adventure (combination of hiking, canoeing and mountain biking).*
Pertinent information: *Owing to the area's extremely high summer temperatures the*

The spectacular Augrabies Falls, the Gariep (Orange) River Gorge and the weathered gneiss rock outcrops of the plains to the south of the river provide the setting for the three-day Klipspringer Hiking Trail.

The focal point of the park, which straddles the Gariep River, is the Main Falls, where the river plunges 56 m into a pool. There are also several secondary falls, among them the Bridal Veil Falls. The noise created by the falls prompted the early Khoikhoi inhabitants of the area to name them Aukoerebis, meaning 'place of the great noise'.

Downstream of the Main Falls, the Gariep River flows through a narrow 18-km-long gorge with an average depth of 240 m. The river's average volume is 45 cubic metres a second, but during the 1974 floods this increased to an incredible 7,000 cubic metres a second.

The vegetation is characterised by Orange River Broken Veld, consisting of common species such as blue neat's foot, Namaqua porkbush, stink bush, honey thorn and jacket plum. Among the other species here are sweet thorn, buffalo thorn, white karree, ebony tree and wild tamarisk. The quiver tree is especially abundant in the vicinity of the Swartrante, which are crossed on the third day's hike.

Animals you may see along the trail include klipspringer, springbok, common duiker, steenbok, rock dassie and baboon. Aardwolf and leopard are also found here, but owing to their retiring and nocturnal habits they are seldom seen. Black rhino were reintroduced in the section of the park north of the Gariep River in 1985.

To date some 195 bird species have been recorded here. Among these are black and African fish eagles, rosy-faced lovebird, Ludwig's bustard, pied barbet, dusky sunbird and black-chested prinia. The broken veld is the habitat of species such as sabota, long-billed and spike-heeled larks, as well as grey-backed cisticola. Also represented are the chats, including tractrac, Karoo and ant-eating chats.

The first day's hike (11 km; 5 hours) initially stays fairly close to the edge of the Gariep River Gorge as it makes its way to Arrow Point, from where there are magnificent views over the gorge and the Twin Falls.

It then meanders through pink gneiss formations, with the dome-shaped Moon Rock dominating the scenery to the south. After passing through four fairly deep river valleys you reach the Ararat Viewpoint and once again are rewarded with awesome views of the Gariep River Gorge. About 30 minutes on you will come to Afdak, a picnic site on the edge of the gorge, and from here it is a short walk to the Fish Eagle Hut situated at the northern edge of the Swartrante.

The second day's hike (10.5 km; 5 hours) descends to the Gariep River, which you follow for about 5 km (2.5 to 3 hours), downstream, past Echo Corner to Witkruiskrans. The initially rocky terrain along the river later gives way to stretches of sand, making the going more difficult. At Witkruiskrans the trail leaves the river to wander down Diepkloof, a dry river course with smooth rock banks. The trail then swings east, following a drainage line for about 30 minutes before heading south along another drainage line, which leads you to the hut, situated amongst a jumble of rocks.

On day three (12 km; 5 hours) the trail steadily ascends the Swartrante's slopes and, after winding down the eastern slopes, crosses a grassy plain dotted with quiver trees. Further along, the trail joins the main tourist road, which takes you to the Moon Rock. This large dome-shaped outcrop is an excellent example of exfoliation (a process of weathering, whereby layers of rock flake off) and from its summit there are 360-degree views of the park surroundings. The last 3 km of the trail passes mainly through sandy veld.

11. POFADDER HIKING TRAIL
Onseepkans/Pella

> **Trail:** 76 km; 4 days; circular.
> **Permits:** Khâu-ma Municipality,
> P O Box 108, Pofadder 8890,
> tel: (054) 933 0066, fax: 933 0252.
> **Maps:** Trail indicated on photocopy
> of topographical map.
> **Facilities/Activities:** Only basic campsites
> at overnight stops.
> **Pertinent information:** For detailed informa-
> tion contact Mr Koos Louw, Rus 'n Bietjie
> Caravan Park and Chalets, P O Box 99,

> Pofadder 8890, tel: (054) 933 0056,
> fax: 933 0366. Owing to very high summer
> temperatures, the trail is open only during the
> cooler period – 1 May to 30 September.

This hike north of Pofadder offers the opportunity to discover the relatively unexplored Bushmanland Dorsland and the historic mission settlement of Pella. The trail, from Onseepkans to Pella, can be hiked in either direction, and there are also two-day options.

The first day's hike (17 km; 8 hours) from Onseepkans is a steady ascent up the Groot Rooiberg before the trail leads down to the overnight stop on the banks of the Gariep (Orange) River.

On the second day (26 km; 12 hours) an early start is advisable, as it is a full day's hike. From the overnight stop the trail follows the course of the Gariep River past the mouth of the ephemeral Cobee River to near Pelladrift. Here the trail swings away from the Gariep River (waterbottles must be filled here as there is no water at the overnight stop), to follow the western foothills of the mountains, in a southeasterly direction, and then heads east to the overnight stop at a usually dry waterfall.

Day three (17 km; 8 hours) heads over the mountains to Swartpad-se-Put where you can quench your thirst with cool water from the well. The trail then traverses Lepellaagte and further along follows the Vier-uur-Rivier to the mouth of the Cobee River and the overnight stop used at the end of day one.

The fourth day's hike (16 km; 8 hours), the shortest leg of the trail, follows the Gariep River upstream, past Onseep, and further on reaches the 30-m-high Ritchy Falls. The falls are also known as the Verkeerd-om-Valle (Back to Front Falls) as the westward-flowing river swings abruptly southeast before plunging over the falls. The remainder of the day's hike continues along the banks of the Gariep River back to the start.

12. GOEGAP NATURE RESERVE
Springbok

> **Trails:** 3 trails; 4 to 7 km; 2 to 3 hours; circular.
> **Permits:** Entrance fee. No permit required.
> **Maps:** Reserve map.

Facilities/Activities: Picnic sites; information centre; mountain biking; horse-riding (you need to bring your own horse); 17-km self-drive route; guided tours during flower season.

Dominated by the 1,342-m-high Carolusberg, the Goegap Nature Reserve covers 15,000 ha of sandy plains and granite hills, which are referred to locally as the Namaqualand Klipkoppe. Centred on the 4,600-ha Hester Malan Wildflower Garden (established in 1960), the reserve was enlarged in 1990 when the adjoining farm, Goegap, was acquired. The Khoikhoi name Goegap means 'waterhole'.

To date some 581 plant species have been recorded in the reserve, which has as its main attraction a spectacular seasonal display of spring flowers. Among these are a profusion of daisies (*Gorteria*), gousblomme (*Arctotis, Osteospermum, Ursinia*), gazanias, and a diversity of vygies of the Mesembryantemaceae that create a blaze of colour, usually from early August to mid-September.

Animals found in the reserve include Hartmann's mountain zebra, springbok, gemsbok, klipspringer, steenbok and baboon. Among the reserve's 94 bird species are ostrich, black eagle, Karoo korhaan, ground woodpecker and pied barbet.

Ian Myers Nature Walks This network of trails in the southwestern corner of the reserve is named after a keen naturalist, Ian Myers, who led groups of visitors in Namaqualand for 30 years. It consists of two loops, with a shorter option, and offers trailists an opportunity to explore the fascinating Namaqualand Klipkoppe on foot. In addition to the flora and birds, there is also a wealth of smaller creatures such as lizards and tortoises to be seen. **4 to 7 km; 2 to 3 hours; circular.**

13. OORLOGSKLOOF NATURE RESERVE
Nieuwoudtville

Trails: 4 trails; 15.5 km to 52.3 km; 8 hours to 7 days; circular.
Permits: The Officer-in-Charge,

Oorlogskloof Nature Reserve, P O Box 142, Nieuwoudtville 8180, tel. and fax: (027) 218 1010 – call between 07:45 and 08:30, weekdays.
Maps: Colour trail map.
Facilities/Activities: Accommodation throughout the reserve ranges from caves, stone kraals and clearings under trees to basic camps with tents and mattresses. Basic camps are available on both overnight routes. Groot Tuin: thatched hut with braai facilities and a toilet available for hikers; picnic sites; parking.
Pertinent information: Distances appear short, but the rugged terrain is very demanding.

The Oorlogskloof Nature Reserve covers 4,776 ha of wilderness in the Bokkeveld Mountains, south of Nieuwoudtville. A focal point of this tract of wild land is the Oorlogskloof River, flowing through a spectacular 500-m-wide and up to 200-m-deep gorge, which forms the reserve's eastern boundary.

The name Oorlogskloof (which means 'war gorge') recalls the violent clashes when the Dutch colonists fought the Khoikhoi and Bushmen here in the 1700s. Reminders of the early inhabitants of the area include rock paintings and ruins of structures built either by the Khoikhoi and Bushmen or farmers who settled in the area during the Great Depression (1929–1934).

Since the reserve lies in the transition zone of fynbos, mountain renosterveld and Karoo flora, an interesting variety of plants occurs here. Among the proteas to be seen are Clanwilliam, laurel, wagon tree and real sugarbushes, as well as other representatives of the protea family. The reserve is home to a rich diversity of geophytes, while the sprawling mitre aloe (*Aloe mitriformis*) and the botterboom (*Tylecodon paniculatus*) are among the conspicuous succulents. Of special interest is a reddish clivia, which was discovered only recently and appropriately named *Clivia mirabilis* (*mirabilis* being Latin for 'wonderful' or 'extraordinary').

Antelope you may see are common duiker, klipspringer, steenbok, grysbok and grey rhebok. Leopard occur in the area, and the smaller predators are represented by caracal, aardwolf, African wild cat and small-spotted cat. Bat-eared and Cape foxes, black-backed jackal, Cape clawless otter, baboon and rock dassie also occur in the reserve.

Among the nearly 100 bird species recorded in the reserve to date are black and booted eagles, Cape robin, southern boubou, bokmakierie, Cape sugarbird and malachite, orange-breasted and lesser double-collared sunbirds. Also to be seen are rock and rameron pigeons, after which the two overnight trails are named. A variety of waterbirds are attracted to the Oorlogskloof River.

Adding to the allure of the reserve is the dramatic scenery of the Oorlogskloof River Gorge, with its sheer cliffs and the spectacular valley carved by the Rietvlei River. There are also fascinating sandstone formations, rock arches, rock tunnels and stunning views to be enjoyed.

1. Leopard Trap Day Hike winds from Groot Tuin

down to Saaikloof and after worming its way through a tunnel and up a chimney, where there is a ladder to assist hikers, it emerges onto the plateau. A short way on, an old stone leopard trap is passed, and the trail then traverses easy terrain above the valley created by the Rietvlei River. Further along it ascends steeply to a viewpoint on the escarpment edge, with extensive views of the Knersvlakte. From here the trail descends steadily to Saaikloof and then climbs back to the plateau, past a cave that has been partly enclosed with a stone wall. After a 15-minute walk along the plateau edge the trail links up with the outward route you took at the start, along which you backtrack for 1.3 km to Groot Tuin. **15.5 km; 8 hours; circular.**

2. Rietvlei Day Hike From Groot Tuin the trail fol-

lows the Oorlogskloof River to Brakwater, where you join a jeep track that leads to the Kareebos turnoff, where you turn right. The trail then follows the magnificent valley through which the Rietvlei River runs, to take the Kleinheideveldvoetpad and climb sharply up a kloof to the escarpment edge and the Knersvlakte viewpoint. From here the trail follows the same route as the Leopard Trap Day Hike back to Groot Tuin. **17.9 km; 9 hours; circular.**

3. Rock Pigeon Route Although the short distances

on the first two days might suggest that they can both be hiked in one day, the demanding terrain makes this inadvisable.

The first day's hike (4 km; 2 hours) descends into Saaikloof and, after climbing out, follows the kloof edge before descending to Brakwater Camp.

On day two (8.5 km; 6 hours) you follow a jeep track across the Oorlogskloof River, and the trail then ascends to the base of the cliffs. Further on you come to a ladder and rope to help you up to the plateau, which you traverse for a short while before descending steeply to the Oorlogskloof River. You follow the river for a few kilometres before once again climbing to the base of the cliffs. After passing through a long tunnel behind the Driefontein Waterfall, you join the outward leg of the third day's hike. A last steep uphill section leads to Driefontein, on the plateau above the Oorlogskloof River Gorge.

The third day's hike (12 km; 7 hours) descends steeply to the Oorlogskloof River, which is easily crossed if it is not in flood, and Kameel se Gat Camp. From here the trail climbs out of the gorge to the base of the cliffs, where two ropes in a rock chimney assist hikers on the ascent to the plateau. Here the Rameron Pigeon Route splits off to the right. Further along, the trail passes through impressive stands of proteas and then skirts the edge of Saaikloof before swinging north to reach the turnoff to Suikerbosfontein Camp. About 1 km on, the trail gently descends and makes its way down a valley to Doltuin Camp.

On day four (17 km; 8 hours) the trail wanders to the head of the Doltuin Valley and, about 3.5 km from the start, passes through the first of the 10 rock arches you will encounter on the day's hike. The trail follows the edge of the plateau, past interesting sandstone sculptures, and, about 6 km after setting off, hikers are forced to crawl through a narrow passage. Still further on a signboard indicates a 2.6-km detour to the highest point of the trail, the 915-m-high Arrie se Punt, from where the Gifberg and Vanrhynsdorp can be seen on a clear day. From the start of the detour, the trail descends to Kouekloof and then returns to the plateau edge, which offers wonderful views of the plains some 600 m below. At Waboombult the trail passes through two caves and, after winding around Pramkoppie, descends steeply to the Rietvlei River and Pramkoppie Camp.

On day five (10.7 km; 6 hours) you initially walk along a jeep track, but after 10 minutes link up with the Kleinheideveldvoetpad and ascend a steep forested kloof to the top of the plateau and the Knersvlakte viewpoint. For the next few kilometres the trail traverses the plateau, with the Rietvlei River Valley constantly in view, before swinging away to Spelonkkop, where an old stone leopard trap is passed. A short way on is a ladder to assist hikers in the climb down a rock chimney, and the trail then winds around and past a jumble of enormous boulders before reaching the junction with the first day's hike. Turn left here and retrace your tracks of the first day for 3.6 km, back to Groot Tuin. **52.2 km; 5 days; circular.**

4. Rameron Pigeon Route This is a circular route, totalling 52.3 km, and can be done as a four-, five-, six- or seven-day hike. The same route is followed irrespective of the number of days over which the trail is hiked, but for the four-, five- or six-day options correspondingly longer distances are covered each day to cover the whole route in time. The seven-day option is described below.

The first day's hike (5.9 km; 3 hours) follows the Rock Pigeon Route to Brakwater Camp, then continues along a jeep track to the Kareebos Camp turnoff. The camp, on the banks of Oorlogskloof River, is named after the karee tree, common to the area.

The second day's hike (7.9 km; 7 hours) follows the western bank of the Oorlogskloof River, then joins up with day two of the Rock Pigeon Route, which you follow to the turnoff for Kameel se Gat (meaning 'Kameel's hollow'), named for a farmer who lived here in the late 1800s and the early 1900s.

On day three (4.6 km; 3 hours) the trail takes the Rock Pigeon Route (day two of the Rock Pigeon Route if you are hiking the four-day option of the Rameron Pigeon Route, or day three if you are hiking the five-, six- or seven-day option) for the first kilometre, making a steep ascent to the base of the cliffs and the turnoff to the Rameron Pigeon Route. You reach a large cave after crawling through narrow cracks in the cliffs of the Oorlogkloof River Gorge, and the route then follows another gorge to a turnoff to rock paintings. Climbing gradually, the trail reaches a crevice, where there is a rope to assist hikers in clambering down, and a short way on you reach Suikerbosfontein.

The fourth day's hike (6.4 km; 3 hours) descends Dwarskloof and then gradually climbs to Draaikraal, from where the route returns to the river. After crossing the river a steady ascent leads to the plateau, where rock paintings and an old stone used for grinding wheat serve as reminders of Oorlogskloof's early inhabitants. Of interest near Swartkliphuis Camp are a caracal trap and another rock painting site.

Day five (8.1 km; 4 hou... plateau to the Donkiestas named after the pack donke during the Great Depression (farmers used them to carry the in the mountains. Further on, above Doltuin Valley and, afte... ...mbing down a ladder, continue to Ghelling se Tenk and two caves with rock paintings. En route to Bo-kloof Camp you will pass another rock painting site.

On day six (7.4 km; 4 hours) the trail ascends gently, passing two rock painting sites, as it climbs to the head of Kouekloof and then descends to a viewsite overlooking the Knersvlakte, Pramkoppie Camp and the De Vondeling Valley. The trail then winds along the cliffs above the gorge carved by the Rietvlei River. Shortly before Olienhoutbos Camp, there is a ladder to help you climb through a hole in a rock.

The final day's hike (12 km; 6 hours) follows a jeep track to the Groot Tuin turnoff, from where you take the return leg of the Rietvlei Day Hike back to the start. **52.3 km; 7 days; circular.**

14. DE HOOP TRAIL
Nieuwoudtville

> **Trail:** 12 km; 6 hours; circular.
> **Permits:** Mr & Mrs W van Wyk,
> P O Box 46, Nieuwoudtville 8180,
> tel. and fax: (027) 218 1246,
> email: papkuilsfontein@cybertrade.co.za
> **Maps:** Sketch map.
> **Facilities/Activities:** De Hoop guest cottage:
> sleeps 12 people (you need to bring own
> sleeping bag and food).

The De Hoop Trail traverses the farm Papkuilsfontein, which borders on the Oorlogskloof Nature Reserve to the northwest.

Starting at the historic De Hoop Cottage, the trail makes its way through interesting sandstone rock formations to a 200-m-high waterfall on the De Hoop River, a tributary of the Oorlogskloof River. From here the trail winds in a northwesterly direction to the boundary with the Oorlogskloof Nature Reserve, and then loops back to the start.

SONAL TRAIL RECORD

This section is for you to record the hikes you have been on and the noteworthy birds, animals and sights you encountered along the way.

NAME OF HIKING TRAIL: _____

_____

BIRDS SEEN: _____

_____

_____

ANIMALS ENCOUNTERED: _____

_____

_____

HIGHLIGHTS OF THE TRAIL: _____

_____

_____

_____

_____

_____

PROBLEMS ALONG THE WAY: _____

_____

_____

_____

_____

ADDITIONAL NOTES: _____

_____

_____

_____

NAME OF HIKING TRAIL: _____

_____

BIRDS SEEN: _____

_____

_____

ANIMALS ENCOUNTERED: _____

_____

_____

HIGHLIGHTS OF THE TRAIL: _____

_____

_____

_____

_____

_____

_____

_____

PROBLEMS ALONG THE WAY: _____

_____

_____

_____

_____

_____

ADDITIONAL NOTES: _____

_____

_____

_____

_____

_____

NAME OF HIKING TRAIL: _____

_____

BIRDS SEEN: _____

_____

_____

ANIMALS ENCOUNTERED: _____

_____

_____

HIGHLIGHTS OF THE TRAIL: _____

_____

_____

_____

_____

_____

_____

_____

PROBLEMS ALONG THE WAY: _____

_____

_____

_____

_____

ADDITIONAL NOTES: _____

_____

_____

_____

_____

_____

NAME OF HIKING TRAIL: _____

BIRDS SEEN: _____

ANIMALS ENCOUNTERED: _____

HIGHLIGHTS OF THE TRAIL: _____

PROBLEMS ALONG THE WAY: _____

ADDITIONAL NOTES: _____

CONTACT DETAILS FOR TRAILS

Ben Lavin Nature Reserve
P O Box 782, Makhado (Louis Trichardt) 0920
Tel & fax: (015) 516 4534
Email: benlavin@mweb.co.za

Borakalalo National Park, Golden Leopard Central Reservations
P O Box 6651, Rustenburg 0030
Tel: (014) 555 6135, Fax: 555 7555
Email: goldres@iafrica.com

Cape Vidal, The Reservations Officer, KwaZulu-Natal Wildlife
P O Box 13069, Cascades 3202
Tel: (033) 845 1000, Fax: 845 1001
Email: bookings@kznwildlife.com

Charter's Creek, The Reservations Officer, KwaZulu-Natal Wildlife
P O Box 13069, Cascades 3202
Tel: (033) 845 1000, Fax: 845 1001
Email: bookings@kznwildlife.com

Commando Drift Nature Reserve
P O Box 459, Cradock 5880
Tel: (048) 881 3925, Fax: 881 3119

De Hoop Nature Reserve
Private Bag X16, Bredasdorp 7280
Tel: (028) 542 1126, Fax: 542 1274

False Bay Park, The Reservations Officer, KwaZulu-Natal Wildlife
P O Box 13069, Cascades 3202
Tel: (033) 845 1000, Fax: 845 1001
Email: bookings@kznwildlife.com

Fanies's Island, The Reservations Officer, KwaZulu-Natal Wildlife
P O Box 13069, Cascades 3202
Tel: (033) 845 1000, Fax: 845 1001
Email: bookings@kznwildlife.com

Giant's Castle, The Reservations Officer, KwaZuluEmailNatal Wildlife
P O Box 13069, Cascades 3202
Tel: (033) 845 1000, Fax: 845 1001
Email: bookings@kznwildlife.com

Golden Gate Highlands National Park (Brandwag/Golden Gate Mountain Resort)
Protea Hotels Central Reservations
P O Box 75, Sea Point 8060
Tel: (021) 430 5000, Fax: 430 5320
Email: reservations@proteahotels.com

Golden Gate Highlands National Park (Glen Reenen), South African National Parks
P O Box 787, Pretoria 0001
Tel: (012) 428 9111, Fax: 343 0905
Email: reservations@parks.co.za

Goukamma Nature and Marine Reserve
P O Box 331, Knysna 6570
Tel & fax: (044) 383 0042

Hans Merensky Nature Reserve (Aventura Eiland Resort), Central Reservations
P O Box 1399, Halfway House 1685
Tel: (011) 207 3600, Fax: 207 3699
Email: info@aventura.co.za

Harold Johnson Nature Reserve, The Reservations Officer, KwaZulu-Natal Wildlife
P O Box 13069, Cascades 3202
Tel: (033) 845 1000, Fax: 845 1001
Email: bookings@kznwildlife.com

Hluhluwe-Umfolozi Park, The Reservations Officer, KwaZulu-Natal Wildlife
P O Box 13069, Cascades 3202
Tel: (033) 845 1000, Fax: 845 1001
Email: bookings@kznwildlife.com

Injisuthi, The Reservations Officer, KwaZulu-Natal Wildlife
P O Box 13069, Cascades 3202
Tel: (033) 845 1000, Fax: 845 1001
Email: bookings@kznwildlife.com

Ithala Game Reserve, The Reservations Officer, KwaZulu-Natal Wildlife
P O Box 13069, Cascades 3202
Tel: (033) 845 1000, Fax: 845 1001
Email: bookings@kznwildlife.com

Kenneth Steinbank Nature Reserve, The Reservations Officer, KwaZulu-Natal Wildlife
P O Box 13069, Cascades 3202
Tel: (033) 845 1000, Fax: 845 1001
Email: bookings@kznwildlife.com

Kruger National Park, South African National Parks
P O Box 787, Pretoria 0001
Tel: (012) 428 9111, Fax: 343 0905
Email: reservations@parks.co.za

Lake Sibaya Nature Reserve, The Reservations Officer, KwaZulu-Natal Wildlife
P O Box 13069, Cascades 3202
Tel: (033) 845 1000, Fax: 845 1001
Email: bookings@kznwildlife.com

Mkuzi Game Reserve, The Reservations Officer, KwaZulu-Natal Wildlife
P O Box 13069, Cascades 3202
Tel: (033) 845 1000, Fax: 845 1001
Email: bookings@kznwildlife.com

Mount Sheba, Three Cities Central Reservations
P O Box 5478, Durban 4000
Tel: (031) 310 3333, Fax: 307 5247

Mpofu Game Reserve, Eastern Cape Tourism Board
P O Box 186, Bisho 5606
Tel: (040) 635 2115, Fax: 636 4019

Ndumo Game Reserve, The Reservations Officer, KwaZulu-Natal Wildlife
P O Box 13069, Cascades 3202
Tel: (033) 845 1000, Fax: 845 1001
Email: bookings@kznwildlife.com

Oribi Gorge Nature Reserve, The Reservations Officer, KwaZulu-Natal Wildlife
P O Box 13069, Cascades 3202
Tel: (033) 845 1000, Fax: 845 1001
Email: bookings@kznwildlife.com

Pilanesberg National Park, Golden Leopard Central Reservations
P O Box 6651, Rustenburg 0030
Tel: (014) 555 6135, Fax: 430 5320
Email: goldres@iafrica.com

Royal Natal National Park, The Reservations Officer, KwaZulu-Natal Wildlife
P O Box 13069, Cascades 3202
Tel: (033) 845 1000, Fax: 845 1001
Email: bookings@kznwildlife.com

Salmonsdam Nature Reserve, The Manager, Walker Bay Nature Reserve
Private Bag X13, Hermanus 7200
Tel: (028) 314 0062, Fax: 314 1814

Sodwana Bay, The Reservations Officer, KwaZulu-Natal Wildlife
P O Box 13069, Cascades 3202
Tel: (033) 845 1000, Fax: 845 1001
Email: bookings@kznwildlife.com

St Lucia, The Reservations Officer, KwaZulu-Natal Wildlife
P O Box 13069, Cascades 3202
Tel: (033) 845 1000, Fax: 845 1001
Email: bookings@kznwildlife.com

Telle Falls Hike, Tiffindel Resort
P O Box 23166, Waterfront, Randburg 2167
Tel: (011) 787 9090, Fax: 787 3667
Email: samsteg@global.co.za

Tembe Elephant Park, Tembe Elephant Park and Lodge
Tel: (031) 202 9090, Fax: 202 8026
Email: tembesafari@mweb.co.za

Tsitsikamma National Park (De Vasselot), South African National Parks
P O Box 787, Pretoria 0001
Tel: (012) 428 9111, Fax: 343 0905
Email: reservations@parks.co.za

Tsitsikamma National Park (Storms River), South African National Parks
P O Box 787, Pretoria 0001
Tel: (012) 428 9111, Fax: 343 0905
Email: reservations@parks.co.za

Tussen-die-Riviere Game Reserve
P O Box 16, Bethulie 9992
Tel & fax: (051) 763 1114

Wilderness National Park, South African National Parks
P O Box 787, Pretoria 0001,
Tel: (012) 428 9111, Fax: 343 0905
Email: reservations@parks.co.za

GLOSSARY

ENVIRONMENTAL AND AND GEOLOGICAL TERMS

Basalt – a fine-grained igneous rock

Bushveld – vegetation typical of the northeast of North West, northern Mpumalanga and Limpopo Province

Carnivore – flesh-eating animals; can be predators or scavengers

Dolerite – a coarse-grained, light-coloured rock of volcanic origin occurring in dykes and sills and containing quartz and feldspar (see below)

Drift – a ford; usually natural, but could be artificial

Dyke – a vertical or steeply inclined wall-like sheet of dolerite that is only exposed during subsequent erosion

Endemic – a plant or animal that is restricted to a particular area

Estuary – a river mouth where fresh and sea water mix

Fault – a fracture along which the rocks on one side have been displaced relative to those opposite

Feldspar – a white or pink crystalline mineral found in rocks

Fynbos – the richly varied fine-leaved bush vegetation of the southwestern Cape which is characterised by ericas, proteas, reeds and rushes

Gneiss – white and black banded rock containing the same minerals as granite, which have undergone a metamorphosis by heat and pressure

Granite – a common, hard and coarse-grained igneous rock, consisting mainly of quartz and feldspar. It is exposed when the overlying rocks are worn away, and its colour ranges from pink to grey, according to the colour of the feldspar.

Highveld – the high-lying area of South Africa, half of which lies above 1,600 m and is largely characterised by treeless grassveld

Igneous rock – formed from molten material, either on the earth's surface from lava becoming volcanic rocks, or underground magma forming plutonic rocks

Indigenous – occurring naturally in a particular area, but not necessarily restricted to that area

Inselberg – A steep ridge or hill left when a mountain has eroded, found in an otherwise flat plain.

Intra-African migrant – birds that migrate seasonally within Africa

Lagoon – an area of water partly or completely separated from the sea by a sand-spit or sand-bar

Lava – molten material forced to the surface by volcanic eruptions and cooling to form basalt

Magma – molten material that does not reach the earth's surface during a volcanic eruption, but is sometimes subsequently exposed through erosion

Metamorphic rocks – igneous or sedimentary rock that have undergone a metamorphosis because of temperature, pressure and chemical reactions

Nocturnal – active mainly by night

Palaearctic migrant – birds that migrate seasonally from the northern to the southern hemispheres

Predator – an animal that kills and feeds on other animals

Quartzite – a sedimentary, metamorphic rock formed from silica and sandstone

Raptor – diurnal bird of prey, i.e. one that hunts and feeds during the day

Sandstone – the second most common, but most familiar sedimentary rock, forming about one-third of the sedimentary rocks exposed on the earth's surface. It consists of rounded grains of sand and usually quartz cemented together; the colour varies according to the mineral make-up

Savannah – grassland containing scattered trees, shrubs and scrub vegetation

Scree – loose fragments of rock covering a slope

Sedimentary rocks – eroded material transported either by wind or water and deposited with the sediments accumulating eventually to form firm rock after a cementation process has taken place

Sill – magma that has been forced between layers of sedimentary rocks subterraneously (underneath the earth). When the magma hardens, it forms near-horizontal sheets of igneous rock, which is then exposed through subsequent erosion

Tarn – small lake surrounded by mountains

Wader – collective name for nine bird families of the sub-order Charadrii, including plovers and sandpipers. However, the term is often used very generally to refer to all wading birds, i.e. birds that wade in search of food.

Woodland – vegetation type characterised by trees with a well-developed, but not completely closed canopy

AFRIKAANS WORDS

Baai – bay

Berg – mountain

Bos – bush

Fontein – fountain or spring

Gat – hole

Klip – stone

Kloof – gorge, ravine, or narrow gully

Koppie – hillock

Kraal – traditional African homestead, or enclosure for farm animals

Krans – cliff

Mond – river mouth

Nek – saddle between two high points

Poort – a narrow passage through a range of hills or a mountain

Rant – ridge

Rug – ridge

Sloot – ditch or furrow

Sneeu – snow; often used to refer to mountains that are often snow capped in winter (e.g. Sneeuberg)

Spoor – tracks of animals, including scent, droppings and urine

Spruit – a stream that is often almost dry, except after rains

Stroom – stream

Tafel – table; used to refer to flat-topped mountains

Veld – open country with natural vegetation

Vlakte – plain

Vlei – a low-lying area into which water drains during the rainy season; usually smaller than a lake

RECOMMENDED READING & BIBLIOGRAPHY

A practical and comprehensive guide – to tracking wildlife, identifying trees, insects, birds, mammals and reptiles, and on what to do in the event of a snake bite – can be very useful when you're out on the trail. The following is a selection of Struik's top titles, and all of these recommended books are small enough for you to take along in your backpack:

- *A Field Guide to Insects of South Africa*, by Mike Picker, Charles Griffiths & Alan Weaving
- *A Field Guide to Tracks & Signs of Southern & Eastern African Wildlife*, by Chris & Tilde Stuart
- *Mammals of Southern Africa*, by Chris & Tilde Stuart
- *Sasol Birds of Southern Africa*, Third Edition (2002), by Ian Sinclair, Phil Hockey & Warwick Tarboton
- *Snakes and Other Reptiles of Southern Africa*, by Bill Branch
- *Snakes and Snake Bite in Southern Africa*, by Johan Marais
- *The Wildlife of Southern Africa – A Field Guide*, by Vincent Carruthers
- *Trees of Southern Africa*, by Braam Van Wyk
- *Wild Flowers of South Africa*, by John Rourke

The following sources have been consulted by the authors in the course of writing this book, and will prove useful if you wish to obtain more detailed information. Titles in bold are especially recommended, and books marked with an asterisk are currently in print:

* Acocks, J.H.P. (1988) *Veld Types of South Africa*. Memoirs of the Botanical Survey of South Africa, 57.
* Barnes, K. (ed) (1998) *The Important Bird Areas of Southern Africa*. Johannesburg: BirdLife South Africa.
Berutti, A. & Sinclair, J.C. (1983) *Where to Watch Birds in Southern Africa*. Cape Town: Struik.
Bristow, D. (1988) *Drakensberg Walks – 120 Graded Hikes and Trails in the 'Berg*. Cape Town: Struik.
Bristow, D. (1992) *Western Cape Walks – A Practical Guide to Hiking along the Coast and in the Mountains*. Cape Town: Struik.
Brooke, R.K. (1984) *South African Red Data Book – Birds*. South African Scientific Programmes Report 97. Pretoria: CSIR.
Cameron, T. & Spies, S.B. (eds) (1986) *An Illustrated History of South Africa*. Johannesburg: Jonathan Ball Publishers.
Chittenden, H. (1992) *Top Birding Spots in Southern Africa*. Johannesburg: Southern Book Publishers.
* Coates Palgrave, K. (1992) *Trees of Southern Africa*. Cape Town: Struik. (New edition available)
Greyling, T. & Huntley, B.J. (eds) (1984) *Directory of Southern African Conservation Areas*. South African National Scientific Programmes Report 98. Pretoria: CSIR.
Irwin, D. and Irwin, P. (1992) *A Field Guide to the Natal Drakensberg*. Grahamstown: Rhodes University.
Levy, J. (1993). *Complete Guide to Walks and Trails in Southern Africa*. Cape Town: Struik.
Low, A.B. & Rebelo, G. (eds) (1998) *Vegetation of South Africa, Lesotho and Swaziland*. Pretoria: Department of Environmental Affairs & Tourism.
* Maclean, G.L. (1993) *Roberts' Birds of Southern Africa*. Cape Town: The Trustees of the John Voelcker Bird Book Fund. (New edition available)
Mountain, E.D. (1968) *Geology of Southern Africa*. Cape Town: Books of Africa.
* Newman, K. (1993) *Newman's Birds of Southern Africa*. Johannesburg: Southern Book Publishers. (New edition available)
Olivier, W. & Olivier, S. (1988) *The Guide to Hiking Trails*. Johannesburg: Southern Book Publishers.
Olivier, W. & Olivier, S. (1989) *The Guide to Backpacking and Wilderness Trails*. Johannesburg: Southern Book Publishers.
Olivier, W. & Olivier, S. (1995) *Hiking Trails of Southern Africa*. Johannesburg: Southern Book Publishers.
Paterson-Jones, C. (1991) *Table Mountain Walks*. Cape Town: Struik.
* Paterson-Jones, C (1999) *Best Walks of the Garden Route*. Cape Town: Struik.
Raper, P.E. (1972) *Streekname in Suid-Afrika en Suidwes*. Kaapstad: Tafelberg.
Raper, P.E. (1978) *Directory of Southern African Place Names*. Johannesburg: Lowry Publishers.
Ryan, B. and Isom, J. (1990) *Go Birding in the Transvaal*. Cape Town: Struik.
* Sinclair, I., Hockey, P. & Tarboton, W. (1993) *Sasol Birds of Southern Africa*. Cape Town: Struik. (New edition available)
Skinner, J.D. & Smithers, R.H.N. (1990) *The Mammals of the Southern African Subregion*. Pretoria: University of Pretoria.
Viljoen, M.J. & Reimold, W.U. (1999) *An Introduction to South Africa's Geological and Mining Heritage*. Randburg: MINTEK.
Von Breitenbach, F. (1974) *Southern Cape Forests and Trees*. Pretoria: Government Printer.
Von Breitenbach, F. (1986) *National List of Indigenous Trees*. Pretoria: Dendrological Foundation.
* Von Breitenbach, F. (1989) *National List of Introduced Trees*. Pretoria: Dendrological Foundation.
Wilcox, A.R. (1976) *Southern Land – The Prehistory and History of Southern Africa*. Cape Town: Purnell & Sons.

The Sabie River, in
Mpumalanga, plunges down
the 68-m-high Lone Creek
Waterfall into a natural rock
pool below.

INDEX

Page numbers in *italic* refer to photographs, and entries in **bold** type indicate main entries.